Hitler IN Vienna 1907-1913

Hitler in Vienna 1907-1913

J. Sydney Jones

STEIN AND DAY/Publishers/New York

First published in the United States of America in 1983
Copyright © 1983 by Limes Verlag Niedermayer und Schlüter
Verlag GmbH, Wiesbaden und München. English language copyright
© 1982 by J. Sydney Jones
All rights reserved
Designed by Judith E. Dalzell
Printed in the United States of America
STEIN AND DAY/ *Publishers*
Scarborough House
Briarcliff Manor, N.Y. 10510

Library of Congress Cataloging in Publication Data

Jones, J. Sydney.
   Hitler in Vienna, 1907-1913.

   Translation of: Hitlers Weg begann in Wien, 1907-1913.
   Bibliography: p.
   Includes index.
   1. Hitler, Adolf, 1889-1945—Homes—Austria—Vienna.
2. Heads of state—Germany—Biography.
3. Vienna (Austria)—History.   I. title.
DD247.H5J5613   1982   943.6'1304   81-48454
ISBN 0-8128-2855-0

For my mother

Contents

Illustrations

Illustrations
(between pages 198 and 199)

Acknowledgments

During my three years of work on this book, many groups and individuals who've helped have earned special thanks. I've one excuse only—that I cannot fit all the names in here, but I appreciate their help nonetheless.

Thanks goes first to the staff of the Carmel Library in California who helped me gather much of the early research material. My appreciation also to the Stanford Library and the Hoover Institution for their help.

In Vienna the staff of the National Bibliothek and their Photo Sammlung are due special thanks. They have always been courteous and more than generous with their time and patience. Dr. Malina from the Institut für Zeitgeschichte in Vienna also gave freely of his time and resources.

I should like to thank also those many individuals who helped shape the book with private interviews: Dr. Wilfried Daim and Dr. Müllern-Schönhausen in Vienna and Dr. August Priesack in Munich. In this category fit also countless people whom I interviewed in person, spoke with by telephone, and communicated with by letter. Thanks to you unmentioned ones also.

Special thanks also go to my good friend and tireless supporter, Mr. George Vance, who not only encouraged the project all along the way, but also greatly helped with the editing.

And finally there is my wife, Linda. She has put up with me and Hitler through all the frustrations and emotional high points of the writing and research. Her critical eye is responsible for much of what is good in this book. Her understanding and care—not only for the project, but also for me—has made it all possible.

Hitler IN Vienna 1907-1913

Prologue

(1)

Late September 1907:

HE sat snugly in the corner of the third-class compartment and watched the tawny landscape race by under a low autumn sky. Sometimes, focusing to a shallower field of vision, he caught his own reflection in the smoky window.

He was a youth of eighteen; a mixture of old, tired virtues and young dreams. He was of medium height and weight at five feet nine inches and one hundred fifty pounds. His peasant's face had a large, protruding nose and gaping black nostrils which he was trying to hide with a sparse growth of hair on his lip. There was little graceful about his face. It was thin and rather bony at the time, but would have a tendency with age to puff out, as if he were a farmer from the Waldviertel who had spent his life drinking wine and eating pork. His dark brown hair was parted on the right side.

The youth had large feet, which added to the general air of his peasant origins, but the finely molded hands, which he held in his lap as if protecting his genitals,[1] countered this impression. They were the delicate hands of a pianist, painter, or surgeon. His clothing and the ivory-tipped cane resting in the overhead rack went with the hands. They were the accouterments of a dandy, not a worker. Peasant origins were battling with artistic aspirations in this young man.

His eyes also, extraordinary in their light blue color with the greenish-grey hint deep within, added to the dichotomy. They stood out of his coarse face unexpectedly as did the hands from the body.

Alone in the compartment, he smiled at the thin, youthful face he saw reflected in the window. He had good reason to smile. The train he was on, the slow five-hour milk run from Linz to Vienna,[2] was carrying him to his future; puffing and winding along the Danube valley to his greatness.

Many other young men, filled with the same hope and nervous excitement, had made this journey before him. Few of those had succeeded.

But he was not reckoning the odds. This young man knew he would succeed where others had failed. On the rack over his head, next to his walking stick, lay his entry card to the world of greatness: his portfolio of drawings. Next to that was the bruised and bulky leather suitcase that contained his worldly belongings.

He continued to look out at the landscape, now dampened in rain, and dreamed of fame and fortune in the capital.

The hours passed, and the train lurched in and out of one station after the other. Darkness fell so discreetly in the gray sky that the change from day to night was one of degree, not of quality. The young man now most probably sat fidgeting in the darkness of his compartment, cursing himself for saving a crown or two by taking this damnably slow train, which was growing colder by the minute.

Reluctantly, he wrapped his heavy winter coat tight around his thin frame against the evening chill, afraid to rumple the well-cut black suit he wore for this momentous journey. He occasionally brushed at the unruly flop of hair that dangled onto his forehead.

As with generations of train passengers, excitement had turned to impatience in young Adolf Hitler . . .

(2)

Hitler was an aspiring artist in his younger years, long before the world had ever heard of him or the Nazis. At fifteen he had left *Realschule* without graduating and had spent the three years since then in sketching and going to the opera in his native Linz. He lived the life of a dandy and young man about town.[3]

By September of 1907 he wanted to try his talents and chances in the big city, just as his father before him had done as a teenager in the 1850s when he had come to Vienna to learn the cobbler's trade before eventually taking work in the Ministry of Finance as a customs official.

Young Hitler was no stranger to Vienna. In May of 1906 he had made his first journey to the city, probably staying with his godparents, Johann and Johanna Prinz.[4] He saw as much opera as possible; Wagner was and remained his idol. He also visited as many museums per day as his senses would allow. He took in all the impressions of Vienna during his four-week visit like a child at Disneyland.

Hitler wrote postcards to a friend of his in Linz documenting the successive stages of his initiation to the hurly-burly world of Vienna. Three of these postcards were written within the first two days of his trip in early May. The fourth was written a month later, on June 6, 1906.[5] This lapse in correspondence testified to the winning power of a city which could make even a seventeen-year-old rustic forget his homesickness.

The first postcards that Hitler wrote his friend, August Kubizek, or Gustl as Hitler preferred to call him, were filled with names of operas and wishes to return to Linz.

"Tomorrow I am going to the opera, *Tristan,* and the day after, *The Flying Dutchman,* etc. Although I find everything very beautiful, I am longing for Linz. Tonight, Stadt-Theater."[6] Hitler wrote this on May 7 on the back of a fold-out tryptich-like postcard of the Karlskirche. His thirst for opera could not yet overcome his longing for home.

The next postcard shows the stage of the Hof Opera house.

"The interior of the edifice is not very stirring," he wrote. "If the exterior is mighty majesty, which gives the building the seriousness of an artistic monument, the inside, though commanding admiration, does not impress one with its dignity. Only when the mighty sound waves flow through the hall and when the whispering of the wind gives way to the terrible roaring of the sound waves, then one feels the grandeur and forgets the gold and velvet with which the interior is overloaded. Adolf H."[7]

Hitler, the budding artist, managed to express some sensitive insights despite his atrocious grammar. He had to find fault with something in Vienna so as to remain loyal to Linz. Why not criticize the very thing that Vienna held over Linz, its grandeur? There was too much gilding in the auditorium of the Hof Opera, not like the gentle simplicity of the Linz opera house.

A postcard from the next day shows the outside of the Hof Opera with a note on the reverse side saying Hitler would be coming home the following Thursday.

He did not return to Linz so soon, however.

No further word came from Hitler for several weeks. Vienna had worked its peculiar charm on him. The last postcard was again of a building, attesting to his early and abiding interest in architecture. It showed the Parliament building on the Ringstrasse. A very courteous message accompanied this: "To you and your esteemed parents, I send herewith best wishes for the holiday [most likely *Pfingsten* or Pentecost] and kind regards. Respectfully, Adolf Hitler."[8]

Hitler in his short stay in Vienna had suddenly become infected with the city. Back in Linz, he was filled with what he had seen in the capital. His friend Gustl later remembered that "he had stayed there long enough to grow enthusiastic about everything that had especially attracted him—the Hof Museum, the Hof Opera, the Burgtheater, the magnificent buildings on the Ring—but not long enough to observe the distress and misery that were concealed by the magnificent façade of the city. This deceptive picture, largely produced by his artistic imagination, held a powerful attraction for him. In his thoughts he was often no longer in Linz but already in Vienna."[9]

Because of lethargy on his part or resistance on his mother Klara's part to his plans of becoming an artist, it took Hitler a year and a half to make his return trip . . .

And Hitler must have felt thankful, sitting in his chilly third-class compartment, that the return trip was finally coming to an end as the train crawled through the outer districts of Vienna. Large, silhouetted houses flashed by the train window. Glimpses of life could be seen in a strobe flicker of warm yellow lamplight thrown out of uncurtained windows.

The station house of the Westbahnhof loomed cavernous ahead, and the hissing of the brakes slowed the engine to a gentle nudge against the wooden rampart.

Only now did the reality of the situation strike Hitler. A slight pang of fear must have mingled with his excitement as he realized he was alone in the big city with no place to sleep. Looking out the window at the flurry of crowds everywhere hustling and bustling, it is probable Hitler even thought of catching the next train back to Linz. He pushed the window down and filled his lungs with chilled and diesel-fouled air.

He felt the chill bite deep down in his lungs, the remains of a lung ailment which he had used as an excuse for leaving school at age fifteen rather than facing the disgrace of dismissal for failing grades.[10]

The momentary fear passed, and Hitler gathered his bag and portfolio and made his way off the train and through the crowds in the train station, past the porters and taxi drivers waiting for fares.

The newly installed arc lights made the scene seem unreal, for now the stealthy encroachment of night had been reversed. It was day for night as bright light glistened off the wet pavement.

Hitler must have made his way with difficulty, assuming he was carrying a goodly sized bag with all his possessions. He was not a large youth, nor was he strong. He had been once. A picture of him exists in a class photograph from 1899. The young children look very serious, wearing short pants and ties. There, top row center, stands young Adolf Hitler, proudly, almost defiantly, staring into the eye of the box camera. The white lightning of the flash exploded, and he was recorded in silver nitrate with his arms crossed, a look of superiority on his face, fairly towering over his classmates.

Yet another picture exists, this one from the following year, 1900, when he was eleven. It is the same serious class picture, but off to one side now, sickly looking, pale and seemingly helpless, is Hitler. Almost frightened, he is smaller than the rest now—hunched.

It is a transformation for which sickness could hardly account. As the arc lights now transformed the Westbahnhof to cheap imitation daylight, so that earlier year had changed Hitler.[11]

The first problem was one of accommodation. During his visit in 1906, Hitler perhaps learned the ropes of apartment hunting in the capital. Perhaps it was blind luck, perhaps just another sign of laziness on his part, as if the whole city was comprised in the quarter in which one arrived. For whatever reason, Hitler began looking for his lodgings near the train station.

All around the Westbahnhof were the raw, new building projects of the previous half century, the *Gründerzeit*. Speculators' blocks of flats went up one after the other to provide housing for a population that quadrupled to two million in fifty years.[12] Huge, gray blocks of forbidding, dark, and airless apartment houses were the price of Vienna's industrial revolution.

Stumbling along under the load of his heavy suitcase, his precious portfolio under one arm, Hitler probably stopped at the first of the buildings he saw with a room-for-rent sign hanging out. It was across the street from the Westbahnhof and down a narrow lane called the Stumpergasse at number 29. Hitler banged his suitcase through the front door and out into the courtyard to the second stairway and then up the steps. The smell of cooked cabbage and kerosene lamps may even have seemed cozy to him that first night.

It was up two flights to Frau Zakreys's at door number 17 where the sign had announced the room for rent. The *Frau* was a "little old withered"[13] Polish lady of a rather "comic appearance,"[14] who was happy enough to rent out her back room at ten crowns per month.[15] The room was small and dark, looking out onto another wall and air shaft. A kerosene lamp burned all day long to fight off the darkness. It was a room of his own, that is the best that can be said of Hitler's first room in Vienna.[16]

It would not be the worst room he would inhabit during his five-and-one-half-year stay in the city.

(3)

The Vienna that Hitler came to in 1907 was a study in deception. Gallant young officers strolled the boulevards in colorful uniforms with pretty young women in white frills on their arms. The magnificent buildings of the Ringstrasse towered over the Viennese and reassured them of the power inherent in the Habsburg state. The strains of waltz-time music filled the air; cafés were crowded with well-to-do customers chatting over afternoon coffee; the new wine was ripening in oak kegs in the damp cellars of vineyards surrounding the city. All seemed well with the world in this best of all possible cities.

One visitor to Vienna in 1900 noticed this sugar-coated world of dreamy old Vienna and voiced the fear that an entire empire was running the risk of diabetic death.[17]

It was a nice turn of phrase, but in reality the sickly sweetness that observer smelled in the fin-de-siècle Viennese air was that of death. He smelled the sugary sweetness of decaying funeral flowers. The empire had already died: sugar was not the death weapon, merely one of the pallbearers.

Nothing was what it seemed in Vienna in 1900.

By the time Hitler came to Vienna, the old Austro-Hungarian Monarchy, or Dual Monarchy, or Habsburg Empire, or just plain

Austria as it was called in everyday parlance, was moribund. Everyone in Europe knew it but the Austrians.

The empire stumbled into the twentieth century under the benign, God-inspired guidance of its *"kaiserlich-koniglich,"* imperial-royal, emperor Franz Joseph, who had been at the helm since the bitter year of the 1848 revolutions.

Franz Joseph attempted to guide a realm of fifty million souls, consisting of twelve ethnic groups, all compressed into a giant mélange between the Alps, the Carpathians, and the Adriatic Sea.

In the modern age of democracy and nationalism, Franz Joseph's tired old imperial rule was failing miserably, as was the emperor himself. Old and white mutton-chopped, his gait slowed somewhat by the tragedies of his life—his brother Maximilian executed in Mexico; his son Rudolf, the crown prince, dead by his own hand at Mayerling; his wandering, enigmatic wife Elisabeth murdered by an anarchist at Geneva—Franz Joseph was part and parcel of the deception that Vienna played on the world.

In spite of his confrontation with life's cruelest realities, the emperor rode stolidly through the streets of Vienna in his gilded carriage drawn by eight white horses mounted by lackeys wearing raven-black and white-trimmed uniforms and white perukes. On each side of the carriage strode two Hungarian guards, yellow-black panther furs thrown over their wide shoulders.

The last refuge of the emperor's reign was pomp. The gilded imperial carriage traveling along the Mariahilferstrasse toward the lovely summer palace of Schönbrunn was a sign of weakness, not strength.

The same is true of that other façade of pomp and show, the Ringstrasse with its awe-inspiring buildings, constructed between 1858 and 1888.

Contests were held in 1858 to create fitting monumental architectural pieces to line the magnificent new boulevard created with the destruction of the old city walls. Museums, theaters, government buildings, a university—all were thrown up within a few decades in one mighty architectural sweep of the hand. The resulting buildings were lovely jewels in the necklace of the Ring.

Taken as a whole they were enough to steal the breath of any visitor from the country. Taken out of their jeweled setting, however, and looked at from a functional standpoint, the Ring buildings constituted a gigantic museum of kitsch.

Like the emperor's gilded carriage, the Ringstrasse was only the elaborate staging with which the dying empire disguised its own emptiness.

The Viennese love their wine and love the vineyards that ring the city in dappled greens. Viennese songs laud the joys of drinking the new, fruity wines beneath the shade trees, bees buzzing in vines heavy-laden with dusty grapes. But between the vines of the Vienna woods and the renowned Ring lay the slums, the not-well-hidden price of most industrial societies of the time.

Behind the myth of the leisure-loving, hedonistic Viennese sitting in his café each night or dancing to a Strauss waltz, there lay the reality of a housing shortage that forced people out of cramped, airless rooms to find breathing space in public places of the city.

Strauss himself was another symbol of Vienna's deceptive façade. Something of a manic-depressive, Johann Strauss wrote lovely, lilting waltzes and operettas that were not the spontaneous creations people would like to believe they were. Strauss, the patriot, wrote the "Blue Danube," that misnomer, as a gay antidote to the Austrian defeat by the Prussians at Sadowa, the battle that ended Habsburg claims to hegemony in the German-speaking world.

Even his most famous operetta, *Die Fledermaus,* was written as much to take the citizens' minds off the stock market crash of 1873 as for any self-expressive motive. More than a symbol of the Viennese joie de vivre, the waltz was a palliative for the woes of the day.

There were many in the decaying Vienna of 1900.

Yet it is said that "swamp fires burn high."[18] Blind people develop incredible powers in their other senses through nature's fair tit-for-tat compensation. Some of the greatest artistic contributions the world has seen grew out of oppressive societies that gave the artist and thinker a cause—something to battle, something that would unlock otherwise hidden powers.

So it was with Vienna in 1900. As politics sank deeper into that morass from which it would not reemerge; as fantasy and façade welded together in Vienna to completely curtain reality from the masses; as the center began to give way very quietly and desperately like a rug being pulled out from under one—at this time one of the greatest intellectual/cultural renaissances of the modern world took place. It was a renaissance in which the overripe façade of the post-Romantic world was stripped bare. It was a renaissance which brought man to the verge "of understanding his own condition and being articulate about it, no longer relying on images and parables for his highest flights into the unknown."[19]

What we now recognize as the modern sensibility was born in the years between the birth of Hitler in 1889 and the outbreak of World War I in 1914.

In the face of societal weakness and stagnation, all of Europe in 1900 was alive with an intellectual and artistic ferment: aglow with a cultural flame until August 1914, when the lamps went out all over Europe.

Einstein in his Zurich café was destroying the center of the Newtonian world with his theory of relativity. Picasso and the Cubists explored new realms of plastic expression in Paris. Stravinsky teamed with Diaghilev to turn music and dance into a pagan joy. Thomas Mann bit into the soft underbelly of the bourgeois with his novel *Buddenbrooks* and exposed the foibles of that newly powerful class. In *The Magic Mountain,* Mann explored the Einsteinian and pre-existential universe with a poet's keen eye.

Yet in this twilight glow, Vienna was still the main star. Gathered in that city were more of the artistic and intellectual luminaries who created the modern sensibility than in any other one metropolis.

How fitting that, in the city of dreams, the interpretation of dreams should be turned into a science. Sigmund Freud's name is synonymous with fin-de-siècle Vienna; his discoveries are unimaginable in any other city.

The sensuous Jugendstil line snaked through the paintings of Klimt, the polyphonies of Mahler, and the architecture of Otto Wagner. Schnitzler and von Hofmannsthal added their eloquence to Impressionist letters.

And this initial stage of the Viennese renaissance was followed close upon by a second, Expressionist phase, which discarded old forms, forgot the business of chiseling away at the Viennese façade which the first movement had started. Rather, the Expressionists threw up new forms altogether. Schoenberg in music, Kokoschka, Schiele, and Gerstl in painting, Loos in architecture, and writers and philosophers such as Kraus and Wittgenstein led this new wave completing the Viennese renaissance.

It was, for too many decades, a forgotten renaissance. It was a renaissance—an overflowing of creativity—that happened in spite and not because of its milieu. Faced with open hostility to their revolutionary art and ideas in Vienna, these caretakers of the Viennese renaissance redoubled their efforts, refused to moderate, pushed themselves into a new and exciting century.

And if the official political life was stagnating in feudal forms in a modern world, there were also seminal political thinkers at work in turn-of-the-century Vienna trying to reshape the world. Bertha von Suttner devoted her life to the cause of peace and was the first female recipient of the Nobel Peace Prize; Theodor Herzl turned a romantic dream of a Jewish homeland into the reality of Zionism; Viktor Adler was shaping a new brand of evolutionary socialism; and men like Schönerer and Lueger were beginning to see the power inherent in winning the masses. They appealed to this newly enfranchised sector with the simplest of arguments: nationalism and anti-Semitism.

As if this list of who's who is not enough for the alchemist, there were also men of action on hand in Vienna to watch the Habsburg circus and learn from its political blunders. Leon Trotsky, exile from Russia, played chess and dreamed of revolution in the Café Central. Stalin came to town for a month in 1913, and Tito worked as a mechanic in nearby Wiener Neustadt that same year.

Adolf Hitler, aspiring young artist, provincial dandy on the make, was also an inmate of fin-de-siècle Vienna. When his train pulled into the Westbahnhof and he stepped out into the chill night air, the course of his life was to change. He would, in the next six-odd years, learn the façade quality of life in that Vienna. But where it inspired others, it would embitter him. Like the members of the Viennese renaissance, Hitler would be rejected by that city. Unlike them, he would give up, search for scapegoats to rationalize his failures. Rejected, he would retreat into himself; down and out, he would learn the refinements of hate.

It was a lesson that would change the course of world history.

A city and an age that could produce both a Hitler and a Freud was a chameleon one.

This is its story.

1

Beginnings

(1)

HITLER'S room may not have been a palace, but he had not come to Vienna to sit there all day. All the city was waiting outside his apartment building. Moreover, Hitler had come to Vienna that fall with a definite plan.

He was determined to sit for the entrance examination of the painting school of the Academy of Fine Arts. Hitler was just in time, as these tests were given only once a year, in late September or early October.

The Fine Arts Academy was one of those products of the Ring project of the last half of the nineteenth century. Built to a design by Theophil von Hansen, who also built the Parliament, the building was one of the lesser jewels of the Ring that Hitler so admired.

Hitler carried his portfolio of drawings—mostly architectural sketches done during his Linz years—confidently to the Schillerplatz that morning in early October. He was sure that the examination would be "child's play"[1] for him and that he would soon be starting out on his career as an academic painter.

The test was an ordeal. The first part of the exam alone covered two three-hour sessions over two days.[2] The first day the one hundred and twelve applicants, including Hitler, chose two subjects from such themes as the Expulsion from Paradise, Spring, Woodcutters, Cain

Killing Abel, Autumn, Carters, Shepherds. These subjects were a mixture of Christian, mythical, and classical themes of which the conservative Academy so heartily approved.

The second day was more of the same, with such possibilities as An Episode from the Flood, Morning, Shipwreck, the Story-teller, End of the Day's Work, the Good Samaritan, and An Excursion.

The theme Hitler chose for the first day is unknown, but recent evidence[3] shows that he chose the theme of an excursion for the second day of drawing. Four test drawings exist from the 1907 entrance exam. The sketches are all of a country landscape with some form of house or shed or bridge in them. The drawing and line are sure and firm, especially for an untrained hand such as Hitler's was. To turn out these four sketches under the pressure of time and out of his imagination was no small achievement, and was enough to get Hitler over the first hurdle of the entrance exam where thirty-three other hopefuls failed.

Things were working out according to schedule for the young Hitler. All he had to do now was present his portfolio to the examiners and he would be accepted. That grand world of academic painting he had so long dreamed of in Linz was slowly opening to him.

Full of confidence now that he had gotten over the most difficult part of the test, he presented his portfolio. A shock as if sent like a "bolt from the blue"[4] awaited Hitler, however, when the examiners rejected him. He had failed the second part of the test. The sample drawings had not been good enough. The official judgment is recorded in the 1905-1911 Classification List of the Academy: "Adolf Hitler, born Braunau/Inn, Upper Austria on 20 April 1889 . . . Catholic, Father: Civil Servant. Sample drawings, inadequate, few heads."[5]

Only twenty-eight of the hundred and twelve applicants were admitted to the Academy that year in the painting faculty. Hitler was not among them.[6]

Hitler could not believe that he had failed. It was the first major setback in his unconventional life since his father had died. He requested an interview with the director of the Academy, Siegmund l'Allemand, to find out why he had been denied admission.[7]

The rector was kind enough to Hitler at first, but finally had to tell him that he had little aptitude for painting. The bitterness of this statement was sweetened somewhat for Hitler by a hint of a promise: from his sample drawings it would appear that Herr Hitler would be better suited to the architectural school of the Academy.

A quick check at the architectural faculty was, however, enough to squelch this chance for Hitler. Having quit school in 1905 at age sixteen, he did not have a *Matura* from the *Realschule,* one of the requirements for admission to the architectural school.[8]

For Hitler, accustomed as he was to his easy life of artistic dreams and future greatness, this lack of a *Matura* must have seemed an impossible obstacle to overcome. To start at the beginning and make up the two or three years needed to graduate from *Realschule* was unthinkable for Hitler—as bad as feeding dried beans to a man who has feasted for decades on oysters. The dream of Hitler the famous painter or architect precluded such a mundane course of action as working from the bottom up.

Hitler left the Academy angry and disappointed. "Downcast, I left von Hansen's magnificent building on the Schillerplatz, for the first time in my life at odds with myself. The fulfillment of my artistic dream seemed physically impossible."[9]

Hitler remained silent to his family and his friend Kubizek in Linz about his failure. He was only in Vienna on a sort of probation, on condition that he enter the Academy. Before he left home, his guardian, Josef Mayrhofer, had found a baker who was willing to take the youth on as an apprentice. Others in the family had felt he should follow in his father's footsteps in the civil service. His mother Klara, seeming to have recovered from a mastectomy the previous January, had backed her young dandy as much as possible. She had even allowed her son to take out his 700-crown patrimony that summer[10] for his Vienna plans. With careful living, Hitler could stretch this sum to cover the expenses of one academic year.

All this, however, had been dependent upon Hitler starting a real career as a student at the Academy. Now that he had failed to gain admission, he knew he could tell no one or else the apprenticeship idea would be thrown in his face again and there would be endless battles with his family about entering a safe profession.

Hitler's friend in Linz, Kubizek, grew worried after a week or so of not hearing from his friend. After the flood of postcards from the 1906 trip, he had expected at least word that Hitler had arrived in Vienna safely. He went to visit Hitler's mother to get word of Adolf and found that she knew no more than he and was growing a bit doubtful herself about Hitler's "crazy trip to Vienna."[11]

"If only he had studied properly at the technical school," Klara Hitler complained to Kubizek that night in Urfahr, near Linz, "he would be about ready to matriculate. But he won't listen to anybody. . . . He's as pigheaded as his father. . . . Nothing will come of his painting. And story writing doesn't earn anything either. . . . He goes his way just as if he were alone in the world. I shall not live to see him make an independent position for himself."[12]

Suddenly Kubizek realized that Klara Hitler spoke the truth about not living to see Adolf get ahead. She was a very sick woman. "Her face was deeply lined. Her eyes were lifeless, her voice sounded tired and resigned. . . . She certainly had concealed her condition from her son to make the parting easier for him."[13]

In Vienna, Hitler was hiding out from all these responsibilities. Denied admission to the Academy, he had done the next best thing and taken a private art teacher associated with the Academy, Professor Panholzer.[14] It appears that Hitler studied in Panholzer's studio during 1907 and 1908. Perhaps he was recommended to this Viennese sculptor and art master through the examiners at the Academy.

Besides these lessons, which could not have taken up Hitler's full time, he continued to explore Vienna. The whole city was at his feet. There were buildings to see, operas to go to, and new discoveries to be made. Hitler learned early in his career that the best way to overcome adverse reality was to ignore it with a "radical withdrawal into himself."[15]

For the next few weeks, Hitler became a tourist in the big city again, devoid of responsibilities and cares. He strolled along the Ring, sketching the public buildings and parks that line it. He probably watched the emperor ride into town each day in his gilded carriage and was awed by the display of horses and guards; or he passed idle hours in the warm coffeehouses of the city, sipping mocha and reading newspapers from around the world.

At night he stood at the Hof Opera for a couple of crowns and heard the best voices in Europe sing his favorite operas: *Tristan and Isolde; Lohengrin; Rienzi.*

Hitler was soothed out of his disappointments by the sweet lyricism of Johann Strauss played at the Volksoper and was swept into forgetfulness by a drink or two of the new wine. He was quickly becoming Viennese.

This idyll could not last forever. If the mother would not tell her son of her worsening condition, there were always neighbors who would take things in their own hands. The local postmaster's widow got the young man's address from a card he finally wrote to the people back home[16] and wrote to him that his mother was deathly ill. The cancer was eating her up. He should return immediately if he wanted to see her alive.[17]

This letter must have been as big a shock as rejection from the academy had been. Hitler was back in Urfahr, just over the river from Linz, by October 22[18] and consulted with the family physician, Dr. Bloch, on the proper treatment for his mother, Klara. The Jewish doctor told young Hitler that the breast surgery had been too late and that "there were already metasteses in the pleura."[19] Radical treatment was necessary if they wanted to try to save the patient's life. There was a little hope with an iodoform treatment—putting large doses of the iodoform into the open wound. The treatment was not only painful but costly. Hitler told the doctor that cost was no problem and agreed to pay in advance for the iodoform. By November 6, Klara was receiving an almost daily treatment, which not only burned the wound, but could also hamper swallowing once it soaked into the tissues.[20]

Kubizek was happy to have his friend back in Linz, but the two spent little time together. Hitler occupied himself most of the day caring for his mother in their three-room flat at 9 Blütengasse in Urfahr. The family had moved into the little furnished apartment the previous June to economize after Klara's first operation had partially depleted their money.

Klara was moved into the kitchen on Blütengasse as that room was heated all day long. Hitler moved a couch in with her there to be in constant attendance on her. Aunt Johanna, Klara's hunchback sister from Spital in the Waldviertel, was also on hand to help out. As November passed into December, there was nothing any of them could do but wait for the end.

(2)

In Vienna at this same time something else was ending. An epoch in art was passing—a golden decade of Viennese productivity.

Gustav Mahler, composer and director of the Hof Opera, was leaving Vienna for an appointment in New York.

Mahler's life story could be the story of the archetypal Viennese intellectual of 1900.[21] Born in Moravia, that German-speaking section of Bohemia that also produced Freud and Kafka, Mahler's early life was decisive in determining his later fascination with death, his darkly brooding introspection.

Mahler's mystical approach to music was not a little affected by the deaths in his own family. Out of fourteen children in the Mahler family, five died in childhood of diphtheria, the same affliction that would later claim his oldest daughter; one sister died of a brain tumor; one brother died of heart trouble; and yet another brother, a promising musician in his own right, killed himself.

Two other early friendships with struggling musicians in the 1870s also ended with insanity and suicide.

During his student days, Mahler roomed for a time with the young musician Hugo Wolf just down the Praterstrasse from where the Freud family lived and around the corner from the Herzls. The Second District, surrounding the northern train line that brought the migrating eastern European and Bohemian Jews to Vienna, had become a ghetto by the time of Hitler's arrival. Just as Hitler had searched for quarters close to the station at which he had arrived, so these Jewish families had limited themselves to their train line.

Studying under the pious Anton Bruckner, Mahler early proved his talent with the composition "Das Klagende Lied," written when he was eighteen. During his impoverished student years, Mahler had been, like hundreds of other nineteenth-century aesthetes, including Hitler, swept up by Richard Wagner's dramatic music and philosophy and his creed of vegetarianism, just shy of sharing the Master of Bayreuth's anti-Semitism. Along with other Jews such as the later socialist leader Viktor Adler, Mahler regularly met at a vegetarian restaurant or at friends' homes to discuss and play Wagner's music. Hitler, too, throughout his life maintained something akin to a vegetarian diet.

Finished with his studies, Mahler soon began the slow process of working his way up in the musical world. Beginning in small German opera houses as a conductor and composing in his spare time, he quickly graduated to more and more elevated positions, in Budapest and then in Hamburg, where he was first conductor from 1891 to 1897.[22]

While in Hamburg, Mahler came under the spell of one of his lead singers, Anna von Mildenburg, to whom he for a time became engaged. Theirs was a stormy affair, made all the more difficult by the professional pressures under which they both lived. Mildenburg quickly was to learn the lesson of Mahler's unfailing devotion to his music over the women he loved. To her, Mahler owed a large debt, for she had used whatever influence she had in Vienna, through her old music teacher, to help Mahler gain the position of director of the Hof Opera at thirty-seven years of age.

Also helpful in Viennese eyes was the fact that Mahler had left the Jewish faith. As he so diplomatically put it to the Hof Theater management: "As things stand at present in Vienna, I should tell you that quite a while ago, in pursuance of a long-standing resolution, I entered the Catholic faith."[23]

By 1898, Mahler was settled in his flat in the Third District at Auenbruggerstrasse 2.[24] This was just off the posh embassy row of the Rennweg and at the foot of the Belvedere Park. Though it was within easy walking distance of the Opera for a hardy walker like Mahler, he was nevertheless provided with one of the few motorcars in Vienna at the time. In it he could speed to and from the Opera at the alarming speed of twenty kilometers per hour. In his flat was also a telephone, which enabled him to get in touch with the Opera at any moment.

Mahler, with all of these modern conveniences, was far ahead of the emperor, who still plodded to work at six every morning in his horse-drawn carriage; who lived by candlelight in the sumptuous Schönbrunn palace until Thomas Alva Edison himself came to town at the turn of the century and personally oversaw the wiring of the palace; who distrusted such modernism as the telephone and forbade the noisy clatter caused by the typewriter.

Success was not instant for Mahler, for he had his critics and enemies from the outset. In a town where only the punctilious emperor came to the Hof Opera on time, no director would be popular who barred the doors to latecomers until intermission. Mahler's insistence on perfection in his performers as well as his audience, his detestation of tradition as an excuse for slovenliness, was bound to anger the Viennese who used the opera as their social outing, a forum for self-display.

Yet this is exactly what Mahler did at the Hof Opera. He created what has since been known as a golden age of opera in Vienna. He was the first to play Wagner uncut;[25] to revitalize Mozart, bringing back the real power and subtlety of that composer's work. He brought in a breath of fresh air with new productions and new standards of excellence.[26]

Between 1899 and 1901, the busy Mahler personally conducted 240 performances at the Hof Opera and 36 of the Philharmonic's performances.

Seldom did Mahler go out socially in these first years in Vienna. His group of friends was limited and very private, consisting of musicians and a few old compatriots picked up along the way in various cities.

By 1902 such a strict regimen had paid off. The Hof Opera played to sold-out houses every night and the usual glaring red of the Opera's ledger pages quickly changed to profitable black.

As a composer, too, Mahler was beginning by 1902 to have some success. After the performance in 1900 of his "Wunderhorn Songs," even the conservative critic Hanslick who had been the great opponent of Wagner and who at first dubbed Mahler's music crazy and falsely naive, had then to admit that: "As we stand at the beginning of a new century, we are well advised to say of each new work produced by the musical 'Secession' (Mahler, Richard Strauss, Hugo Wolf, etc.): 'It may well be that the future lies with them.'"[27]

Mahler, by 1902, also changed the rule of isolation that cut him off from the rest of artistic Vienna. The previous fall he had met a young woman at a dinner party given by Bertha Zuckerkandl, daughter of the editor of the influential *Neue Freie Presse* and wife of an eminent anatomist. It was Mahler's habit to avoid such functions, but this one night he had made an exception and met there the young Alma Schindler, daughter of the deceased landscape painter Emil Schindler and step-daughter to Carl Moll, one of the more prominent of the new artists on the Vienna scene.

Alma was a wide-eyed and sensual woman who was studying music under the same teacher with whom Arnold Schoenberg was studying. She was something of a composer in her own right, with a few promising *lieder* to her credit by 1901.[28]

Young Alma was not so sure at first that she liked the way Mahler commanded the attention of the room upon arrival. The nervous twitching of the composer's right foot upset her sense of ease and calm, and she was sure she had caught him chewing on his fingernails when he thought no one was looking.

But when Mahler turned his full attentions on her, she could not refuse his energy and passion. There was something almost hypnotic in his power as he spoke of things musical and artistic. She quickly discovered that Mahler was no musical pedant, but well versed in subjects from physics to philosophy.

The two sequestered themselves in a corner and talked the night away. Mahler, almost twice the age of the young woman, was beguiled by her charm, good looks and intelligence. Alma, for her part, was overpowered by the man of genius.

The most unlikely of couples, with Alma towering over his five-foot-four-inch height, the two became instantly engaged after that night and were married at the Karlskirche on February 9, 1902. Mahler's sister, Justi, was married to Arnold Rosé, the concertmaster of the Philharmonic, the very next day.

This marriage brought Mahler into closer contact with members of the "Secession" or breakaway art group that turned Vienna into a Jugendstil capital at the turn of the century. That group had been formed in 1897, the year Mahler had come to town, at meetings held at the home of the painter Carl Moll, now Mahler's father-in-law. Uncrowned king of the Jugendstil Secessionists was the painter Gustav Klimt, close colleague of Moll's and one-time aspiring lover to the young Alma.[29]

Klimt was a ruggedly handsome man with a thick beard and broad hands that had more the look of a butcher's hands than an artist's. His love affair with the dress designer Emilie Flöge and the blatant sensuality of his canvases periodically shocked and then later won over the Viennese. Gathered around him were young men such as the architect and designer Josef Hoffmann; the architect Josef Maria Olbrich; the painter and craftsman Kolo Moser; and the older, well-known architect, one of the founders of modern architect, Otto Wagner. These men had rebelled against the staid classicism of the Academy and its exhibition hall, the Künstlerhaus. It was the same conservative prejudice that was so apparent in the test drawings that Hitler had to do for the entrance examination to the Academy.

Now that Mahler was brought into closer contact with this artistic group, a "Sacred Spring" of Viennese art came into being. The climax of this cooperation in the arts came at the 1902 exhibition put on by the Secessionists honoring Beethoven and using a statue by Max Klinger as the centerpiece. There were also friezes by Klimt that went hand in hand with a reinterpretation by Mahler of Beethoven's Ninth Symphony.

It was as if the fresh wind of a renaissance had come to Vienna; a new spring blooming of art after decades of hackneyed and played-out conservatism.

(3)

It was to be a miserable Christmas for Hitler that year of 1907.

He sat at his mother's side in their modest apartment. It was warm and snug in the kitchen. The glow of candles on the lighted Christmas tree cast flickering shadows on the wall and lit up Adolf's and his mother's faces in a warm yellow light.[30] The coal stove hummed in the corner with heat.

It was December 20, but there was no Christmas cheer at the Hitler household. Instead of the cozy smell of Christmas cookies and fir boughs, the sickly hospital odor of iodoform filled the apartment.

Hitler had sat by his mother's side since his homecoming and watched the painful process of soaking her wound in the iodoform. He had watched his mother's face reflect agony as the chemical burned its way into the tissues, slowly seeping into Klara's system to clog up her throat with a burning sensation that made all liquids taste like poison to her, leaving her terrific thirst unquenched.[31]

Hitler had charge of the household and shared the housework with his younger sister Paula and his Aunt Johanna. He became cook, nurse, and part-time father to his little sister, assuming responsibilities for the first time in his life.[32]

By that December 20, Hitler was tired out and despondent. The lighted Christmas tree probably did nothing to lift his spirits. His mother slept fitfully that evening. Kubizek came by, hoping to cheer up his friend. Klara drew Gustl to her and whispered in his ear: "Go on being a good friend to my son when I'm no longer here. He has no one else."[33] She rasped the words out through her parched lips, and Kubizek took them to heart.

After his friend left, Hitler got out his sketch pad and began to draw a likeness of his mother's head. Always much better with inanimate objects like buildings than with people, as the examiners at the Academy had remarked, Hitler had trouble recording the tortured features, the hair damp with the sweat of pain.[34]

Dr. Bloch paid two visits that day and knew the end was near for poor Klara. In the early hours of December 21, Klara Hitler died in her bed. She was just forty-seven.

Dr. Bloch was called the next day to sign the death certificate, and the sight of the grief-stricken Hitler, who had lost the one human being in the world for whom he had ever felt any emotional tie, greatly moved this doctor who had witnessed many deaths in the course of his duties. "In all my career," the doctor later remembered, "I never saw anyone so prostrate with grief as Adolf Hitler."[35]

Klara was buried two days later on a dismal, foggy day in a funeral ceremony that spared no expense. Hitler's mother was put to rest next to her husband Alois, who had died five years earlier in the village of Leonding. The family stood quietly in black around the gravesite. The next day Adolf, accompanied by his older, married half-sister Angela, went to Dr. Bloch to settle the accounts. They paid off the remaining 300 crowns owed the doctor for his work.[36]

It was a joyless Christmas Eve. Hitler did nothing to make the evening more pleasant when he refused an invitation to his sister Angela's home. Hitler's brother-in-law, Leo Raubal, was a twenty-seven-year-old tax inspector and was trying to urge the impetuous Adolf to give up his artistic dreams and take a safer course in the civil service. A wall of resentment grew up between the two because of this, and Hitler had no wish to spend Christmas listening to lectures.

Finally, mercifully, Christmas passed. The estate left by Klara was divided between the siblings, giving Hitler between 500 and 1,000 crowns. Added to this was an orphan's pension for which both Adolf and Paula were eligible until age twenty-four. This pension provided both the siblings with 25 crowns per month each. There was also the approximately 700 crowns Hitler had inherited from his father and which he had already taken with him to Vienna. Hitler's twelve-year-old sister Paula was to be raised by Angela. Young Adolf did not exactly face the coming years destitute.[37]

During the next weeks in Linz, spent taking care of business affairs, Hitler renewed his old friendship with Kubizek. He began to fill the upholsterer's son, who had musical aspirations, full of romantic dreams of a career in Vienna. Hitler told Kubizek he was wasting his talents in provincial Linz and should come to Vienna to the Conservatory. Hitler instinctively knew it was to Gustl's parents that the real power of argument must be brought to bear. This Hitler did with gusto and won over the conservative father into believing in a musical career for his son. Hitler the rhetorician was already coming into being.

Hitler's friend Gustl would be following him to Vienna. He would have someone with whom to share his ambitions. He could not conclude his affairs in Linz fast enough. Hitler was anxious to get back to the big world of anonymity and also to the world of opera, theater, concerts, and the glories of the Ringstrasse.

Though his family and his legal guardian Mayrhofer were set against it, Hitler knew nothing could keep him from returning to Vienna. He had told no one of his failure to enter the Academy and as far as his family was concerned, they all believed him to be a student there. That was one argument in favor of his return.[38]

Hitler soon had another argument in defense against the pleadings of his relations that he find a secure job. Normally Hitler had no use for neighbors. In most cases they were nosy busybodies. But in the case of Frau Hanisch, Hitler had to make an exception to his rule.

Magdalena Hanisch was the owner of the apartment building on Blütengasse where the Hitlers lived. She was not the only Hanisch Hitler was to know in his life, and not the only middle-aged woman to take an interest in the young man. She began now to take an interest in the eighteen-year-old Hitler as he went through all the formalities that follow the death of a close relative. She knew of his desire to enter the Academy . . . and of his failure to do so. Seeing as how Hitler confided this information to no one in Linz so that his plans to return to Vienna would not be spoiled, it would seem that he and Frau Hanisch must have had a very close and trusting relationship. They were conspirators against the bourgeois mentality of Linz.

Frau Hanisch took it upon herself to write to her mother in Vienna, Frau Motlach, to try to use whatever pull or *Protektion* she could to further the career of Hitler.

Frau Motlach knew the brother of Professor Alfred Roller at the Vienna Handicrafts School, member of the Secession and well-known stage designer for Gustav Mahler.

"Dear Mother," Frau Hanisch wrote,

> I am going to ask you a favor and hope you will forgive me if it is too much of an imposition. I should be immensely grateful if you could write a letter of recommendation to Professor Alfred Roller on behalf of the

son of one of my tenants. He wishes to become a painter and has been studying in Vienna since the autumn. He had intended to enter the Academy of Fine Arts but, not having been accepted there, he had recourse instead to a private establishment. . . . He is a serious, ambitious young man of nineteen [sic], mature and sensible beyond his years. He is nice, steadygoing, and comes of a very respectable family. His mother died just before Christmas. . . . The family name is Hitler and the son on whose behalf I am writing to you is called Adolf.

Not long ago we were discussing art and artists and he happened to mention the reputation enjoyed by Professor Roller in the artistic world, a reputation which, he said, was not confined to Vienna alone but could be almost described as worldwide . . . and he went on to speak of his own admiration for the Professor and his work.

Hitler had no idea that Roller's name was familiar to me, and when I told him I had known the great man's brother and asked whether it could help if he was given a letter of recommendation to the stage director of the Hof Opera, the young man flushed deeply and his eyes grew bright. . . . I would very much like to help this boy; there is no one, you see, to put in a good word for him or to advise and encourage him. When he went to Vienna he was a stranger and entirely on his own. He had no guide or mentor and had to conduct all his own negotiations when he was trying to find a place that would accept him. He is firmly determined to undertake a regular course of study. From what I know of him so far he won't fritter away his time, since his aim is a serious one. I feel sure that you won't be putting yourself out in an unworthy cause. Indeed you may be doing something really worthwhile.

If you feel able to do so, mother darling, I do beg you to write a few lines of recommendation to Alfred Roller . . . and hope that you will not be vexed if the favor I ask is burdensome for you. . . . He is now waiting for the Board of Guardians to confirm the pension due to him and his sister.[39]

By February 8, Roller had replied to the request that Frau Motlach must have put to him via his brother. Doubtless these requests from friends of friends must have been a bit tedious for the professor, busy as he was at the Opera. But what could one do when approached by one's own brother? Besides, the young man in question might have a spark of talent that needed to be kindled and blown upon for him to grow into a real artist. He agreed to see the young Hitler when next the youth came to Vienna.

Frau Hanisch wrote back to her mother that same day to thank her for running interference for her and Hitler.

> You would have thought yourself well rewarded for your pains if you could have seen the boy's radiant face when I sent for him and told him that you had recommended him to Professor Roller and that he would now be able to call on him.
>
> I gave him your card and allowed him to read Professor Roller's letter. I wish you could have seen him! He was beaming as he read the letter in silence and almost with awe, lingering over every word as though he wanted to learn it by heart. Then, thanking me sincerely, he returned it to me and asked whether he might write to you to express his gratitude. I told him that he might.
>
> May heaven reward you for your kindness! . . . Although nothing has yet been decided by the Board of Governors, Hitler is determined to wait no longer and will be returning to Vienna in a week's time. His official guardian is a simpleminded innkeeper, a good enough fellow but, I believe, somewhat limited. He doesn't live here but in Leonding. The boy has to attend to all the business that really should be dealt with by his guardian. I return Professor Roller's letter herewith. If you should happen to see him, please tell him how grateful I am for his kindness in agreeing, despite his busy life, to see young Hitler and give him advice. Such good fortune does not befall every young man, a fact I feel sure Hitler fully appreciates.[40]

Hitler must have taken Roller's letter in his hand like a godsend. Looking at the strong signature at the bottom, he probably thought back to the wonderful Wagnerian sets the man had designed and which Hitler had seen that past fall at the Hof Opera. Hitler had read the contents carefully, as Frau Hanisch had mentioned to her mother. He was balancing every word for nuance and looking for hidden meanings that he could put to his account against the arguments of his family for remaining in Linz and starting out in the civil service.

Here finally was Hitler's credential of respectability. No longer could his guardian and family accuse him of having no direction. The stage director at the impressive Hof Opera was now behind him. Armed with this promise from Roller to advise him, Hitler felt he could face whatever the world had to throw up against him.

On February 10, Hitler wrote a letter to Frau Motlach thanking her for her help. It is a perfect example of Hitler's Austrian manners, which he kept with him, especially in letters, all the way through his political career.

> I wish to offer you, dear madam, my most sincere thanks for your intervention in securing an introduction for me to the great master of stage design, Professor Roller. It was, I feel sure, overbold on my part to expect you to put yourself out like this for a complete stranger. So I would beg you to accept my heartfelt thanks for the steps taken by you which have met with such success, and also for the card which your much respected daughter was kind enough to put at my disposal. I will at once take advantage of this most happy opportunity.
>
> Once again, therefore, with my sincerest thanks, I sign myself, very respectfully yours.
>
> Adolf Hitler[41]

Hitler returned to Vienna in mid-February of 1908. His friend Kubizek helped him carry his four heavy bags full of the rest of his possessions from the Urfahr apartment to the train.[42] Hitler spoke to Kubizek quickly of Stephanie, a young girl in Linz for whom he had formed an attachment without having ever spoken to her. He boarded the train, found an empty compartment, pulled down the window, and shook hands with Gustl. As the train pulled out, Hitler called to his friend, "Follow me soon, Gustl."[43]

Little Frau Zakreys was happy to see Hitler back. He had kept the room, confident of his return, but she was no doubt a little worried whether the meager belongings he had left as insurance of his return were worth the ten crowns' rent he owed her.

The room had not improved in his absence. Now the cold was worse than before he left, as if pockets of chill air hung in the corners not to be beaten off even with the hottest of coal fires. Hitler sat down at his paper-littered table the second night back, February 18, and wrote to Kubizek. This postcard was of the armor collection at the Art History Museum.

> Dear Friend! Eagerly awaiting news of your coming. Write soon and definitely so that I can get everything ready to receive you in style. All Vienna is waiting. I will of course come to meet you. Now the weather is improving. I hope you will have better weather, too. Well, as I said before, at first you will stay with me. Later we shall see. One can get a piano here in the so-called "Dorotheum" for as little as 50/60 florins.

Well, many regards to you and your esteemed parents, from your friend, Adolf Hitler.
P.S. Beg you again, come soon.[44]

The writing is tight and cramped on this postcard, and there are many misspelled words. It must have been important to Hitler to have a companion share his life in Vienna, for the tone of the note is jolly yet insistent. Also the fact that it was written so soon upon his arrival in Vienna points to his loneliness.

Hitler was putting his life in order, setting it up so that his friend from the provinces would be there to share experiences with him. He had, however, never told Gustl of his failure to enter the Academy. It was a lie that was sure to catch up with him when Kubizek saw his life in the capital. Hitler did not seem to care. He would cross that bridge when he came to it. No use planning ahead.

(4)

The Roller letter surely was a great aid to Hitler, not only with his family, but because Roller was most definitely a man of importance in the Vienna art scene. Until 1902, Roller had been only a professor at the School of Handicrafts. That year, though, at the Beethoven exhibit put on by the Secession, Carl Moll had introduced Mahler to him and the two had formed a working partnership as a result of the meeting. Roller had played an important part in that "Sacred Spring" of Viennese art that men like Mahler and Klimt had created.

It was a short spring.

The Vienna Opera has always had, and still has, the reputation of intrigue. Politics were played by many, from the lowliest member of the chorus to the director himself. Mahler worked his singers to the peak of their ability, and then moved them even beyond that. He demanded more of a performer than any director before or since. He was not interested in excuses, only in performance.

His productions of such Wagner operas as *Rienzi* and *Tristan and Isolde,* with sets by Roller, were landmarks in their time. Mahler's enthusiasm for Wagner's youthful opera *Rienzi* parallels Hitler's love for it. "*Rienzi* is ultimately Wagner's greatest work,"[45] Mahler said as he was preparing the work for production. The opera was performed twenty-seven times during Mahler's reign in Vienna.[46]

Hitler as a young man in Linz had also seen this opera, and was so moved by the tribune Cola de Rienzi, the solitary, proud, remote, and heroic man of the people who freed the Romans from the oppression of the nobles, that he suddenly saw himself in such a political role. Kubizek remembered Hitler after the performance walking up the Freinberg mountain above Linz, looking at the stars and dreaming new dreams of becoming a tribune of the people just as Rienzi had.[47]

Despite Mahler's innovative productions, his audiences were still piqued at his heavy-handed autocracy, making them come on time and be silent during the performance. That he presented them with some of the best operatic performances ever given was only small compensation as far as they were concerned. Why, the man was even trying to get rid of the claque, every mediocre singer's friend.

That Alfred Roller broke through the old and stale bounds of stage design, utilizing daring colors and enormous, three-dimensional sets, still did not make up for the loss of glamour of seeing and being seen under the full house lights.

As early as 1904, concerted attempts were made to oust Mahler from his position. The only thing that saved him was the sponsorship of the grand chamberlain, director of all Hof Theaters, Prince Montenuovo. The only thing, in turn, that won this sponsorship was Mahler's amazing financial record. The Hof Opera was making money as never before. So long as the balance sheets stayed in the black, Mahler was safe. But his enemies were not deterred. They waited patiently for him to make a slip.

As a composer, too, Mahler was beginning again to upset the Viennese. They finally had come to accept his early works, or at least to tolerate them as they tolerated the Secessionists, and they incorporated the most obvious parts of the artistic movement into their lives.

By 1904, however, three years before Hitler came to Vienna, Mahler had moved out of his old Secessionist style of composing. He ripped apart the old Romantic tradition by leaping into a revolutionary polyphony freed from the tyranny of the piano.

With his first four symphonies, Mahler had worked out the rough score on the piano. From the Fifth Symphony onward, his compositions were geared to the spirit and technique of the orchestra as a whole. He created a new orchestral idiom containing a potpourri of fanfares, marches, rustic dances, and waltzes, all intermeshed with endless melodies.

Mahler burst out of his old definitions to point the way to a new symphonic future. His very use of instruments points up his new idiom. Mahler experimented with such nonmusical instruments as cow bells, whips, and hammers to make these nonmusical sounds representative of some idea in the composition. While the Impressionists such as Debussy were waging war on the classical symphony, Mahler was trying to breathe new life into it with polyphonies completely independent of the piano. More and more he became a builder of sound collages, intended to be heard, literally, on many different levels.[48]

Mahler's Fifth Symphony was played in Vienna in 1905 to lukewarm audiences. It was to be the last of his later pieces to be played in Vienna during his lifetime.

The worst happened in 1905. Cash receipts at the Hof Opera went down, nearing the dangerous red mark. Renewed attacks came from Mahler's enemies declaring that he was spending far too much time abroad directing his compositions. Mahler could not fight back at these criticisms, for they were only too true. The Viennese would not allow his pieces to be premiered in their city.

At the same time there was a bright young star at the Theater an der Wien cutting a silver streak for himself across the grey skies of Vienna. On December 30, 1905, Franz Lehár's mindless operetta *The Merry Widow* premiered amidst cheers from the audience and raves from the press. The melodies were so irrepressible that even Alma and Gustav Mahler played them for each other. The age of the catchy tune was being born in Vienna just as the spurt of Jugendstil creativity was burning out.

Mahler went on for another year amidst growing press criticism and increasing intrigue at the Hof Opera. By April of 1907 even Grand Chamberlain Montenuovo began to criticize Mahler's frequent absences and to account them responsible for the loss of revenue at the Opera.

Finally Mahler began to see which way the wind was blowing. In June of that year he met with the director of the New York Metropolitan Opera, a former actor at Vienna's Burgtheater who in 1903 had signed the singer Enrico Caruso to the Met. Mahler signed with him, cutting off his life in Europe, but also opening up a new life in America.

That summer of 1907 when his family, now grown to include two small girls, packed to go to their summer house on the Wörthersee, there was real hope in the Mahler household for the first time in some years. Mahler would have an uninterrupted summer of composing in his little hut built near the house, rising every day at six and taking a brisk swim before beginning the work. Working until lunch and walking and rowing in the afternoon, he would have a trouble-free summer. No worries about intrigues at the Opera. He would be setting out for New York late that fall.

It was too good to be true. By July 5, Mahler's world had fallen in around him. His older daughter had died of scarlet fever and diphtheria and he had collapsed with a heart attack that would number his days.

The summer turned into an agony. Back in Vienna, he conducted for the last time at the Opera on October 15, one week before Hitler returned to his dying mother in Urfahr. The performance was of Beethoven's *Fidelio*. One wonders if in the front row of the promenade standing room there was a young man with a lock of brown hair hanging onto his forehead, with eyes slightly bulging, and eager for the lights to go down so the performance could begin.

By December, Mahler had wrapped up his affairs in Vienna and was ready to depart for America. A group of Mahler supporters[49] sent out a note to other friends inviting them to see Mahler off: "The admirers of Gustav Mahler will meet for a final farewell on Monday the 9th before 8:30 A.M. on the platform of the Westbahnhof. You are cordially invited to attend and to inform people of your acquaintance."[50] Among the other signatories of the letter was the young Anton von Webern.

Over two hundred people gathered to say farewell to Mahler. Among them was the painter Klimt, who summed up how everyone felt as the frail Mahler boarded the train and steam jetted out onto the platform. "*Vorbei*," he muttered. "All over."[51]

An artistic epoch had passed.

When Mahler left his office in the Hof Opera for the last time, he left behind him in the drawers of his desk all the medals and decorations awarded him over the past ten years. He also tacked a farewell note up on the bulletin board in the Opera thanking his colleagues for the fine work they had done with him and hoping there was no animosity left between them.

The note was torn down the second day after Mahler departed.[52]

Mahler was forty-seven that year, the same age as Hitler's mother. The confidence he had had of new beginnings the previous summer had been drained from him. He felt like an immigrant now.

He once told his wife Alma that he was three times homeless: "A

Bohemian among Austrians; an Austrian among Germans; and a Jew among all peoples of the world."[53]

Now he was four times homeless. One can understand how he felt when later that year in New York he told Alma, "How strange and lonely I sometimes feel. My whole life is one long homesickness."[54]

(5)

Hitler was there to meet Gustl's train in the third week of February when his friend finally came to Vienna. Adolf had decked himself out in his dark hat and overcoat and carried his ivory-tipped walking stick. Kubizek descended from the train into the foggy night looking like a ruffled country bumpkin after the long, slow trip.[55] He was tired and ready to go to sleep after they had reached Stumpergasse, cleared the table of Hitler's architectural sketches done in hard, straight lines with charcoal, and consumed the little food-package Frau Kubizek had sent along with her son.

Hitler would hear nothing of sleep now. How could anyone just arrived in Vienna go to bed without at least first seeing the Hof Opera?[56]

So down the Mariahilferstrasse through the gray fog they strode. Kubizek began to get an entirely different picture of Vienna as they neared the inner city. The buildings were fine and majestical. Gone was the sickly kerosene smell of Stumpergasse. These houses were large and warm-looking.

They walked around the Ring to the Opera, and Kubizek duly admired the entrance hall, the magnificent staircase, the deep, soft carpets, and the gilded decorations of the ceiling. This was like another planet compared to the lowly house on Stumpergasse.[57]

From the Opera the two walked down the Kärtnerstrasse, past the women of the night lurking in recessed doorways, their *"Du, Schatzi"* ignored by the intrepid duo.

St. Stephan's was quickly reached, but the spire was lost in the fog.[58] All that could be seen was the heavy dark mass of the nave stretching up into the mist. It looked huge and unearthly, just as its builders had intended.

Then for a finale Hitler led Gustl north up through the heart of the old town, through the Jewish sector with all the little shops closed up for the night, the corrugated metal shutters covering the doors and windows. They went down winding, cobbled streets, their steps echoing against the buildings on each side. Amidst these narrow lanes they suddenly came upon the lovely, delicate church of Maria am Gestade, like a Gothic chapel compared to the bulk of St. Stephan's. Its silhouette was graceful and filigreed in the deep darkness.

Then there was the journey back out of the First District, leaving the grace and charm behind for their small dark room. It was near midnight when they arrived, and as the doors were locked every night at ten P.M., they had to awaken the concierge and pay the grumpy man a tip, a *Sperrsechserl,* for letting them in.

It had been a long day for Kubizek, but still Hitler kept up his nonstop tour guide patter about the city, the architecture, the great times they would have together, and the great men they would become one day.

Gustl fell asleep on his improvised bed on the floor, to the excited tones of Hitler's voice.

Next day, after long hours spent looking unsuccessfully for a room suitable for Kubizek, and after a conference with Frau Zakreys, it was decided that the two would live together in the *Frau*'s bigger room. She would take the small one that Hitler had been renting alone. Each of the young men would pay ten crowns per month rent.

The larger room had a little better light than the smaller one. Patches of sunlight even dappled their floor in the afternoons when it wasn't too cloudy. The *Frau* also had no objection to piano playing, which Kubizek would surely have to do for his classes. The room was just large enough to accommodate an upright piano, so the move into the larger room seemed the simplest solution for both Hitler and Kubizek.

The day following this move, with Hitler still fast asleep in his bed, Kubizek made his way to the Conservatory and produced references from the music school in Linz, took the appropriate tests, and was forthwith admitted to the school. In addition, he was accepted as a viola player in the Conservatory orchestra. On his second day in Vienna, Kubizek already began to feel a part of the great metropolis.

On his way home, the elated Kubizek passed Feigl's music store in the Liniengasse, just around the corner from their lodgings, and in a moment of euphoria, rented an enormous grand piano for ten crowns per month. Seeing that this was the same rent he paid for his room, one might say that the young musician had been carried away with himself.

When Hitler got home that night he was shocked to find the piano taking up most of the space in the room. Finally, though, he succumbed to Kubizek's enthusiasm and arguments that a future conductor needed a grand piano. But he immediately set about placing the instrument to the best advantage in the little room.

After much ruminating and huffing and puffing, the two maneuvered the piano and table to one side of the room, under the windows, which looked out onto the bare, sooty side of the house in front. Looking sharply upward out of the window one could, on a rare clear day, catch a glimpse of blue sky.

On the other side of the room went the beds, washstand, and wardrobe. Hitler reserved himself a three-stride pacing ground between the door and the curve of the piano. Three steps up, quick turn, and three steps back would be enough for his incessant pacing.

"I had no idea I had such a clever friend,"[59] Hitler told Kubizek. But his voice was filled with irony as he complimented his friend on getting into the Conservatory and orchestra all in one day. The irony would have been easier for Kubizek to understand had he known of Hitler's failure to attain a similar goal for himself.

And so the two settled into a routine in the capital. All day long Kubizek had his classes at the Conservatory, and he believed Hitler to be doing the same at the Academy, although Hitler's hours did seem a little strange to Kubizek, whose classes were scheduled at regular times.

Kubizek figured the Academy must be a strange place, for Hitler would stay up late at night reading, sketching, or talking about the rebuilding of Vienna, and then rise only after Kubizek had already left for the day.[60] Hitler's classes seemed to be scheduled at very irregular times and his curriculum varied enough to include not only architectural sketches, but also watercolors, musical composition, and writing.

Rain trickled down the two windows in little rivulets. Outside the sky was gray and dense. An incessant plinking sound arose from the corrugated roof of the outbuilding in the courtyard below as the rain splattered upon it.

Kubizek had had to light the kerosene lamp that morning against the dullness of the day. There was always something very depressing about having to light the lamp in daytime. It seemed such a futile gesture somehow—a little globe of light that became diffused and eaten up by the somber grayness. The lamp stank too, which did not add to its charm.

Kubizek studied the composition before him. He would have to begin practicing soon. He looked over to his friend's bed, hoping Hitler would awake soon so he could begin playing the piano.

Hitler lay on his back, brown hair ruffled with sleep, his chest rising and falling rhythmically. His mouth twitched as if to speak, and one hand, outside the coverlet, gave an involuntary jerk at the dream running through his somnambulent consciousness.

The lamp burning in the early morning was making Kubizek nauseous. Kerosene smell filled the room, and though already bundled against the cold and the dampness of the plaster walls, Kubizek decided he'd rather risk cold than suffocation. He opened the window over the table—the cold air from the window over the piano would be bad for its tuning. The window he opened was just opposite Hitler's bed. Kubizek took three greedy gulps of the damp air. It tasted charred from the sooty, rain-slickened cobblestones in the courtyard. He heard his friend stirring in back of him and quickly closed the double windows.

The cold air had awakened Hitler. As he had been up late the night before reading and jotting down notes, Hitler woke probably feeling deprived of sleep and a little grouchy.

Once dressed and having taken a meager breakfast of bread and milk, he picked up a book and began reading from where he had left off the night before. Kubizek began his practice on the piano. It was a difficult piece, and this being his first time through, Kubizek made many mistakes.

Hitler, grouchy anyway, could not concentrate on the book of myths he was reading and suddenly exploded.

"This eternal strumming! One's never safe from it!"[61]

But there was nothing for it. Because of the rain, Hitler could not go to the bench he had staked out in Schönbrunn.[62] He would have to stay in all day.

Kubizek very reasonably suggested a possible solution.

"It's quite simple," Gustl said. Rising, he searched out his schedule from his music case and tacked it to the wall.

"And now you can tack your schedule at the Academy under this so that in future we will know when one of us will be in or out."[63]

Hitler railed at this. He did not need any timetable. He kept it in his head.

But the timetable posted on the wall became a constant reminder to Hitler of how he had failed at the Academy while Kubizek had succeeded so well thus far at the Conservatory.

Finally, a few days later, this symbol brought out the confession. It was early evening, and the two were talking after their light supper.

"This Academy ought to be blown up," Hitler suddenly shouted. He instantly flew into a fury about the school. "A lot of old-fashioned, fossilized civil servants, bureaucrats, devoid of understanding. Stupid lumps of officials." Hitler's eyes were glittering, his face was livid.[64]

This sudden outburst took Kubizek by surprise, and he was trying to act the part of moderator, saying that these men were still Hitler's teachers and there must be something of value in them, when Hitler blurted out:

"They rejected me. They threw me out. They turned me down."

Kubizek was shocked and relieved at the same time. Shocked at the lie Hitler had been living these months; and relieved because now he understood better Hitler's actions of the past weeks. Not only the irregular hours, but also the growing bitterness he had noticed in Hitler. Kubizek wanted to turn the conversation away from self-pity to more practical thoughts.

"And what now?" he asked.

"What now, what now?" Hitler mimicked him. "Are you starting too?—what now?" He muttered something to himself and sat down with a book. "What now?" he mimicked again sarcastically.

He began reading, and Kubizek got up to take his timetable down from the wall. Looking up, Hitler saw what he was doing and said, calmly now, "Never mind."[65]

The schedule remained.

2

Portrait of the Artist

(1)

THE short, gray winter days crept along so discreetly that the Viennese barely noticed their passing. As cold February drew into drippy March, the first indication any Viennese had that spring might be approaching was that the gaslights needn't be lit until about five instead of four-thirty.

Now that the secret was out between Hitler and Gustl, some of the darkness went out of their relationship, too. Before, because of the lie between them and Kubizek's success, Hitler had "wallowed in self-criticism" and needed only "the slightest touch for his self-accusation to become an accusation against the time, against the whole world . . . choking with his catalogue of hates . . . against mankind in general who did not understand him, who did not appreciate him and by whom he was persecuted."[1]

Now that the lie was out, however, the old ease of their friendship came back between the two. Their one great bond was music,[2] and the two began to attend the Opera or a theater or concert almost nightly.[3]

At two crowns per performance at the Opera,[4] this was no cheap entertainment. For the two-crown ticket, Hitler and Kubizek secured standing room in the promenade, directly under the imperial box. No women were allowed in the promenade, a fact that pleased Hitler as he felt they would only be there to flirt anyway.[5] The disadvantage of this standing room was that the section was divided in half—one side for the military and the other for civilians. Hitler often railed at the supercilious lieutenants who paid only ten hellers to attend a performance and did not give a damn about the music. They only came to see and be seen.[6]

Once the lights went down, though, such complaints were forgotten. Hitler became "transported to an extraordinary state"[7] by the music, especially by Wagner's music.

"His violence left him" when listening to Wagner, and "he became quiet, yielding and tractable. His gaze lost its restlessness; his own destiny, however heavily it may have weighed upon him, became unimportant. He no longer felt lonely and outlawed and misjudged by society. He was intoxicated and bewitched. Willingly he let himself be carried into the mystical universe which was more real to him than the actual workaday world."[8]

No other composer "could compete with the great mystical world that the Master conjured"[9] for Hitler. The two studied all the Wagner operas together and could quote whole arias by heart.[10] *Lohengrin,* which Hitler saw ten times with Kubizek, was one of his favorite Wagner operas.[11] The two friends forgot the small-time opera productions of Linz after seeing the "perfect Wagner interpretations by Gustav Mahler at the Vienna Hof Opera."[12]

Enthusiastic as anyone after the performance,[13] Hitler still disliked the claque that made its home in the promenade. Though Mahler had tried his best to rid the Opera of these paid adulators, he had not been totally successful. On one occasion when the claque continued its bravos even after the orchestra had resumed, Hitler punched one of the claque in the side to quiet him and supposedly had to explain his actions afterward to a policeman.[14]

All the Wagner and Mozart operas the two young men saw together had been newly produced by Mahler. "Italian opera never attracted Adolf,"[15] however, and one day, hearing "an organ grinder playing '*La donna è mobile,*' Adolf said, 'There's your Verdi!'"[16] For Hitler, music was a German affair, as was all culture. "He rejected the contention that music should appeal to all races and nations. For him nothing counted but German ways, German feeling and German thought. He accepted none but the German masters."[17]

When Hitler was not busy at the Opera or at the concerts to which Kubizek sometimes, as a student at the Conservatory, got him free tickets, he was continuing in a desultory way with other artistic pursuits.

One day, finding Hitler hard at work writing, Kubizek asked him what he was up to.

"A play," Hitler replied.[18]

Kubizek looked at the sheets of paper Hitler had in front of him on the table, and began reading: "Holy Mountain in the background, before it the mighty sacrificial block surrounded by huge oaks; two powerful warriors hold the black bull, which is to be sacrificed, firmly by the horns, and press the beast's head against the hollow sacrificial block. Behind them, erect in light-colored robes, stands the priest. He holds the sword with which he will slaughter the bull. All around, solemn bearded men, leaning on their shields, their lances ready, are watching the ceremony intently."[19]

Hitler went on excited, gesticulating, to explain the action of the play to Kubizek. It was set in "the Bavarian mountains at the time of the bringing of Christianity to those parts."[20] The natives in the mountains were against the new religion and had to take an oath to kill the Christian missionaries. The play revolved around this central conflict.

Hitler poured out a torrent of ideas for other plays during this time also, all based on German mythology, with magnificent Wagner-like staging that even "dwarfed anything devised by the Master."[21] But so pretentious were all these attempts that they ultimately ended in a few ragged jottings on paper.

Of the few books Hitler read during this early time in Vienna, Kubizek later remembered one especially. It was *Legends of the Gods and Heroes: The Treasures of Germanic Mythology,* one of Hitler's favorite books.[22]

From this book and from his love of Wagner, Hitler also started to write an opera. Partly he wanted to show Kubizek that he could even write music with no formal training,[23] partly he had an honest love of music.

The opera he began dealt with the legend of Wieland the Smith, one of those typically brutal German myths filled with rape and murder.

Hitler had taken piano lessons for a time in Linz; but for that, he had no musical training. This would be no hindrance for him. With a music student for a friend, there would be no problem.

"I shall compose the music, "Hitler explained to Kubizek, "and you will write it down."[24]

Hitler set about the work with a vengeance, harking back to the "elemental possibilities of musical expression,"[25] using ancient instruments to achieve a pagan sound.

Hitler played the prelude from memory to Gustl one night. It was an attempt to link isolated sounds to musical notes to build a new musical vocabulary uniting sound and color.[26]

The resulting music was primitive in the extreme, partly because of Hitler's lack of facility on the piano, partly because of the attempt at primitivism.

Kubizek began to comment on the music, first telling Hitler that it was good. Yet he had also to tell his friend of the impossibility of his project without proper theoretical knowledge.

Confronted with such scholastic criticism, Hitler as usual flew into a rage about the inadequacies of formal education. Wagner was self-taught, a dropout from school; why couldn't he also achieve his dream without the absurdity of schooling?

"Do you think I'm mad?" Hitler yelled at Gustl. "What have I got you for? First of all, you will put down exactly what I play on the piano."[27]

Hitler stumbled against the block of his inadequate training time and again with the opera and finally thought he had discovered a way around this deficit. He would compose the opera "in the mode of musical expression corresponding to that period in which the action was set."[28]

Hitler busied himself with the music, libretto, and stage design, in the true Wagner tradition, to the point of physical collapse. He pushed himself and Kubizek to the limits of their endurance with the project. He set the opera in the rugged wastes of Iceland where so many of the Germanic legends are set. There was a Wolf Lake[29] surrounded by flaming volcanoes, icy glaciers, and floating Valkyries in shining helmets. These staging difficulties alone would have been enough to kill the project. Kubizek, writing about the winged Valkyries in the work, recalled that "altogether there was a lot of flying in our opera."[30]

Night after night was spent in discussion of the opera. More than once Frau Zakreys had to knock on the door to make Herr Hitler stop playing the piano so that a person could get some sleep.

Then one day, as suddenly as he had begun the project, Hitler stopped work on the opera. Other things came up. Some other art form interfered. Their hard work was left incomplete.

Kubizek, who had put so much of his valuable time into the project, did not mention the opera to Hitler nor ask why he had stopped the work. He was becoming the perfect roommate for Hitler, whose moods had cowered Kubizek into silence. He knew that one word was all that was needed to set Hitler off on a hate diatribe directed at pedants and scholars.

"Altogether in these early days in Vienna, I had the impression that Adolf had become unbalanced. . . . He was at odds with the world. . . . He was ceaselessly busy . . . one day he would be sitting for hours over books, then again he would sit writing till the small hours, or another day would see the piano, the table, his bed and mine, and even the floor, completely covered with his designs. He would stand, staring tensely down at his work . . . improve something here, correct something there, muttering to himself all the time and underlining his rapid words with violent gestures."[31]

It would seem that Hitler's dreams of painting were left behind for the time. Kubizek never mentions any art lessons, though it is possible that Hitler was continuing with his classes from Professor Panholzer. What happened to his letter of introduction to Professor Roller is even more of a mystery. One report has Hitler meeting with Roller, having his work judged by the man, and actually working on a part-time basis for the stage designer.[32]

More probably, as reported by another source, he tried several times to see Roller, but each time his fear of rejection stopped him. He finally tore up the letter "so he would not be tempted again."[33]

The reality of the letter was probably too much for Hitler. Here was the opportunity—or threat, as Hitler probably viewed it—of having his dreams once again measured against the yardstick of the real world. For a young man who wanted to compose an opera without any formal musical training, who built fantasies out of the myths he read and called them plays, such a course of action was much too mundanely logical to consider.

Hitler had gotten what he most wanted from the Roller letter—a passport out of Linz and his relatives off his back.

Suddenly freed from familial responsibilities and from the burden of keeping up a pretense in front of Kubizek, Hitler felt enabled once again to sink into the *vie bohème* he had enjoyed in his Linz years. His interests were no longer confined to charcoal and paper but were free to roam to other forms of expression with no real purpose.

And underneath it all there was a seething—a vague feeling of having been wronged by the world.

(2)

Hitler's unused letter to Roller would have been much more than just the opportunity of a part-time job painting scenery at the Hof Opera. If he had not torn up the letter out of fright, Hitler would have had an introduction to the world of modern art in Vienna, of which Roller was a foremost member.

Besides being a professor at the Vienna Handicrafts School and an important colleague of Mahler, [34] Roller had been a founding member of the Secession and one of the first editors of that group's magazine, *Ver Sacrum*.

All this was ancient history by the time Hitler arrived in Vienna. As with Mahler's reign, the reign of the Secessionists had been all too short. Hitler was too late to enjoy any but the copied effects of the first great revolution in the arts in Vienna before the First World War.

As intrigue and jealousy had destroyed Mahler, so the same intrigue and Viennese provincialism was partly responsible for the end of the Secessionists as a revolutionary force. Strangely enough, success had been another culprit.

At first the Secessionists, not necessarily all Jugendstil artists but all dedicated to the promotion of modern art, had been ridiculed by the Viennese. Gustav Klimt, the man who had uttered *"Vorbei"* as Mahler's train pulled out of the station, had been elected first president of the breakaway group ten years before Hitler came to Vienna. He had announced the intentions of the group as the bringing of "artistic life in Vienna into more lively contact with the continuing development of art abroad," and to put "exhibitions on a purely artistic footing free from any commercial considerations."[35]

The principal aim of the group was to exhibit, something the more conservative Künstlerhaus had in the past prevented. Exhibit they did, and with a vengeance, in 1898. Their first exhibition was held in rooms rented on the Park Ring virtually out from under the rival Künstlerhaus group who had been about to rent them. The show was a smashing success financially. There were paintings done by members of the group including Klimt and Moll, plus paintings by foreigners such as Whistler that were completely new to the Viennese. Influenced in part by the British arts and crafts movement and the Scottish Charles Rennie Mackintosh and his Glascow School, Hoffmann and Olbrich put together rooms designed in the flowing Jugendstil style.

The Viennese loved it. More than 57,000 visitors saw this first show, and some 218 of the works displayed were sold.[36]

But when the profits earned from the show were put to use to build a permanent exhibition hall on the Friedrichstrasse across the Karlsplatz from the Künstlerhaus and behind the Academy, the Viennese were no longer so sure in their opinion of these self-styled rebels. The austere lines of this cube-shaped building designed by Olbrich earned the place such nicknames as "the Mahdi's Tomb" and "the gilded cabbage," which referred to the cupola adorning the building.

Hermann Bahr, a turn-of-the-century Viennese writer and part of the Jung Wien circle, which included among others Schnitzler and Hofmannsthal, was an early supporter of the Secessionists. He put his money where his pen was and bought Klimt paintings and Hoffmann furniture to place in his Olbrich-designed house. Bahr describes the scene during the construction of the Secession building: "You can see a crowd of people standing around a new building. On their way to work . . . they stare, they interrogate each other, they discuss this 'thing.' They think it strange, they have never seen anything of the kind, they don't like it, it repels them. Filled with serious reflections, they pass on their way, and then turn around yet again, cast another look backwards, don't want to depart, hesitate to hurry off about their business. And this goes on the whole day!"[37]

The Secessionists rapidly became the *enfants terribles* of Vienna. Laughed at in the press for their overelaborate decoration, sometimes excoriated for depravity because of the Jugendstil emphasis on woman's body, the Secessionists nevertheless sold, and sold well. Exhibit after exhibit attracted praise and outrage—but above all attracted the money of the Viennese while still maintaining high artistic standards.

Moved into their strange new building, their exhibits still attracted the Viennese, partly out of curiosity to see what new idiocy the Secessionists had thought up this time.

Success is a fine thing. Sometimes, however, success can be worse than public scorn. Too quickly did the Viennese public swallow the Jugendstil style. The movement became coopted as commercial companies quickly and cheaply copied Jugendstil designs in furniture and textiles. Architecture made Olbrich's pioneering work almost kitsch overnight by mass-producing the Jugendstil/Secessionist style in bits and pieces into new houses.

Kolo Moser, one of the founders of the Secession, wrote about the craze, calling it a "trend, an entire industry. The originals were imitated in a careless and tasteless fashion, and there we had that 'false Secession.'"[38]

Shops could not get enough of the pseudo-Jugendstil and Secession-style articles to keep their customers satisfied.

Partly as a reaction to this heavy copying, Hoffmann and Moser, along with the industrialist Fritz Wärndorfer, founded the Wiener Werkstätte, the workshops where the true styles of the time were to be cultivated and produced individually. In the Werkstätte everything from bookbinding to cutlery design was elevated to an art form to make all of life's functions conform to the *Gesamtkunstwerk* ideal of Richard Wagner.

Though initially intending to reach all social levels with their original productions, the artistic handwork of the Werkstätte put itself out of the price range of all but the most wealthy. But no matter. For the middle classes there were the ready-made reproductions of all the same designs. By the time Hitler reached Vienna, that old Danube fortress was decked out in the new clothes of Secession like an aging widow preparing for a ball.

As usual the Viennese had picked out the easiest to digest of the Secession style. They flocked to a Lehár operetta while avoiding Mahler's more serious symphonies. So it was with the new artists and painters, too. As long as the new art work was *gemütlich* and put them at ease, the Viennese heartily approved. The minute there appeared something a bit out of the ordinary that might put their brains to the test, a storm of protest would break over the impolite offender.

Gustav Klimt was one such offender. With his paintings done on commission for the main hall of the new University on the Ring, just such a storm of abuse poured forth over him.

Klimt, in spite of his popularity and sales, had always had a rough time of it at the hands of the Viennese critics. This prince of eroticism pleased the Viennese with his portraits and landscapes done in a Neo-Impressionist and Jugendstil style, but when he finally came into his own genre and expressed his own inner self, the Viennese fled from him as they would a leper. His life was to be an ever-recurring cycle of going in and out of favor with the Viennese.

If Mahler is the archetype of the Viennese intellectual, Klimt is its archetypal sensualist. Alma Mahler, for whom Klimt had had one of his many passions, describes the man as "tied down a hundredfold, to women, children, sisters, who turned into enemies for love of him."[39]

Klimt was a sensualist with a large appetite for life. Women were, for his life as for his painting, the most important subject. The one self-portrait Klimt left is a caricature of himself as walking genitalia.

Even on neutral Nature, Klimt imposed his own brand of sensuality in the lines he once wrote: "The water lily grows by the lake/It is in bloom/The yearning for a handsome man/Is in her soul."[40]

Worse than any outlandish behavior Klimt could be guilty of (his dress, too, was terribly unconventional)[41] was the turn his painting had taken over the years. As early as 1900, the same year that Freud's *Interpretation of Dreams* first appeared, Klimt began offending good taste with the first of his three-so-called University paintings, *Philosophy*, commissioned by the university to go on the ceiling of the Aula, the Great Hall in the new building. The commission had been awarded nine years before, when Klimt was an adequate but far from innovative painter.

By 1900, when he displayed *Philosophy* at the Secession, Klimt, the man and painter, had undergone many changes. His rendering of an allegory of Philosophy with a swarming mass of naked, tortured humanity cast adrift, powerless in the void, was just not what the Ministry of Education had in mind. They would have been very happy with a trite rendition of a Rubens beauty—if there must be nudity, at least let it be Rubensesque—which would evoke some classic symbol of philosophy. Klimt's pessimistic rendition of man's vain efforts to control his life met with public outcry and professional ostracism. Ninety-eight professors at the university signed a petition against the picture.

The motto of the Secession still stands above its doors: "To Every Age Its Art, to Art Its Freedom." Klimt's picture was exhibited there until March of 1900. Later it went to Paris where it won a *Grand Prix*. This prompted one Klimt supporter to comment: "Gustav Klimt is a Viennese. One can see this clearly from his pictures . . . but one can also tell he is Viennese from the fact that he is honored throughout the world, and attacked only in Vienna."[42]

In 1901 and again in 1903, Klimt continued his affront to the Viennese definition of good taste with two further panels for the University, *Medicine* and *Jurisprudence*. Klimt was compared to a graffiti artist by the press for the full frontal nudity including, horror of horrors, pubic hair, in *Medicine*.

Klimt had found his style, his technique of using the façade to contain the content, much the same as Freud was doing at the same time by examining the symbolism of dreams to get to the unconscious mind. Through the use of erotic, exotic pictures, Klimt described his own personal world view, as every great artist must if he is to escape mediocrity. His flared-nostriled women, openly in the act of orgasm, were branded decadent. His use of nudity was declared an attack on morality. One reviewer commented that he should leave a Klimt exhibition "in a state of acute embarrassment" if he had taken his daughter, wife, or sister to see such trash.[43]

It is not unlikely that Hitler would have agreed with this provincial opinion, as he was ever the guardian of morality, even as a young artist with his own unconventional leanings. But interestingly enough, Hitler later owned several erotic paintings done by Klimt's Munich counterpart, Franz von Stuck.[44]

By 1905, Klimt had had enough. He wanted to escape from all the absurdities of fighting the faculty and trustees of the university. That year he returned the 30,000 crowns advanced to him for the University paintings and quit the commission. Moser bought two of the panels himself, and the industrialist August Lederer, long a sponsor of Klimt, bought *Philosophy* and had Josef Hoffmann build it into one of his rooms.[45]

Klimt retreated more and more into himself and his own idiom after this break. Following Schiller's dictum, which he had once used as an inscription to one of his paintings, Klimt must have often repeated to himself: "You can not please all through your actions and your art. Do it right for the few. To please many is bad."[46]

After 1905, Klimt was no longer the golden boy, that most Austrian of painters, as he had once been described. Joining a mosaic technique that had so excited him on a trip to Ravenna in 1903 to his own love of erotic design and heavy symbolism, Klimt in the following years developed a purely personal idiom in painting. It is only sad that the overtly sexual content of much of Klimt's later work (one pencil sketch shows a woman masturbating, anticipating the *Playboy* centerfold tradition) keeps much of it from display.

In 1905, too, Klimt, Wagner, Hoffmann, Moll, and Moser split off from the Secession, forming their own art group. There had long been a conflict inside the Secession between the pure painters and the arts-and-crafts section. The painters claimed that the architects and designers were getting far too much attention at exhibitions. This was most probably as it should have been, for the arts-and-crafts and architectural group—Klimt aside—were the Secession's most important contributors to twentieth-century art.

The following year Klimt began work with Hoffmann and other Werkstätte artists on that amazing total work of art, the Palais Stoclet in Brussels.

By the time Hitler came on the scene in Vienna, Klimt had formed another art group which was getting ready to stage its first exhibition in Vienna. Though the first thrust of the artistic revolution of turn-of-the-century Vienna in the visual arts had spent itself, Klimt was preparing to inaugurate the second. It was a form of art that would quickly leave the old master, Klimt, behind.

(3)

Ever since his rejection at the Fine Arts Academy, Hitler had begun to have doubts about where exactly his artistic talents truly lay. That the director of the Academy told him his real talents were in architecture rather than painting only confirmed something Hitler himself had felt since Linz.

In those days of easy circumstances, strutting about town in his fancy suit and twirling his ivory-tipped cane, Hitler first began to take note of architecture. As early as 1906, after his first trip to Vienna, Hitler had presented Kubizek with the drawing of a villa in the Italian Renaissance style where the two friends might some day live together.

The sketch shows "an imposing palazzo-like building" with a tower and spiral staircase.[47] Hitler also sketched a villa for his platonic love of the time, Stephanie, among varied other plans for the rebuilding of Linz.[48] One such plan had the two friends living in lively society together like brothers in a home to be built by money won in a lottery. The two young artists would be ministered to by a "refined" but "elderly lady" so as to rule out any "expectations or intentions which might interfere with" their artistic vocation.[49]

As with so many other artistic vocations, Hitler also toyed with the idea of becoming a famous architect. It was never enough for him to be merely competent and happy in his daydreams. He must also be thought a genius by those around him.

Then the rector's encouraging words tipped the scale, Hitler wrote, so that "in a few days I myself knew that I should some day become an architect."[50] Perhaps the desultory studying and dilettantish playing at writing plays and music was only an avoidance technique on Hitler's part. Just as with the Roller letter, Hitler saw that there was a chance for him in something that he must apply himself to, and rather than risk failure, he put it off. Other, more important projects beckoned, he could deceive himself.

"The more tenaciously he repeated his own slogan, 'I want to become an architect,' the more nebulous did this goal become in reality,"[51] Kubizek related.

Finally, however, the call of architecture recaptured Hitler from these other pastimes. His life long he was enamored of the Ringstrasse style of architecture. Often Hitler dragged his unwilling friend Kubizek with him on tours of the Ring, describing at length all the facets of the buildings they were seeing.[52] Hitler knew all the histories of the buildings; their floor plans and even hidden passages that might exist. If Kubizek balked at the monologue Hitler spouted and wanted to move on to another building, Hitler would shout "rudely"[53] that a real friend would share his interests.

The Ringstrasse buildings were a potpourri of building styles, having one thing in common, their "ostentation."[54] Hitler used these buildings as his professional training ground, studying floor plans and other aspects of the construction of each building. "The Ringstrasse became for him an object against which he could measure his architectural knowledge and demonstrate his opinions."[55]

Supposedly when Hitler looked at a piece of architecture, he looked at it from "all sides; he hated nothing more than splendid and ostentatious façades intended to conceal some fault in the layout. Beautiful façades were always suspect. Plaster, he thought, was an inferior material which no architect should use. He was never deceived, and was often able to show" Kubizek that "some construction which aimed at mere visual effect was just a bluff."[56]

Yet Hitler's supposed unerring ability to detect sham in the specific somehow did not come to his aid in detecting sham in the general.

As early as 1898 the Ringstrasse style had been satirized as the product of some sham artist, creating houses "inhabited by nothing but *nobili*. . . . What a deception!"[57]

The Ringstrasse had been created from the old city wall and the buildings built onto the open space, the glacis, surrounding the wall. The ostensible reason for this flurry of building was to glorify the city. Actually, though, the project, begun ten years after the 1848 revolution that unseated the Habsburgs for a time, had more practical considerations. When the Habsburgs had been ousted in 1848, they had had an extremely difficult time getting back into their city because of the very walls they had built over the years to defend it against the Turks. As with Haussmann's renovation of Paris at the same time, which eliminated many of the narrow, cobbled lanes that had proved such strong fortresses for the Parisian mob, so did the Ringstrasse building spree have political and military considerations at its base.

All the buildings that resulted from this project were "Neo" this or "Neo" that—products of unbridled historicism. There was the Neo-Gothic City Hall, the Rathaus; Grecian-columned Parliament; the Renaissance museums; Neo-Baroque imperial palace; Renaissance Opera and Burgtheater. Architects were brought in from all over Europe to transform the Ring into one of the famous boulevards of Europe.

The writer Hermann Bahr was moved by the façade quality of the Ringstrasse to remark that "if you walk across the Ring, you have the impression of being in the midst of a real carnival. Everything masked, everything disguised."[58]

Whether it was in good taste or not was most definitely another question. That the buildings were not functional was made apparent from the start. In their haste to fit symbolism into their designs, the architects of the Ring too often forgot function. The Viennese were moved to joke that "in the Parliament one could hear nothing, in the Rathaus one could see nothing, while in the Burgtheater one could neither see nor hear."[59]

Not long after opening, the auditorium of the new Burgtheater had to be altered. The lyre-shaped room had been a fine symbol and tip of the hat to Greece as the ancestral home of drama, but its acoustics were nonexistent. The Rathaus was lovely Neo-Gothic, but the clerks had to work by candlelight all day long behind its windowless façade.

The twin museums that house the Habsburg art and natural history treasures were mere backdrops for the square around which they were built. The army barracks looked impressively like a medieval fortress, but there were no lavatories for the men who lived there.

All this was Hitler's guideline against which to judge other architectural creations. Influenced by this style at first, Hitler conceived of grandiose building projects only. New palaces, new museums, concert houses were staple products for his sketchbooks. In Linz there had always been some public building that needed a face lift or some quarter of the city that needed beautifying. In Vienna things were different. Even though the Ring was his standard of judgment, he found little opportunity to better it. With all the new architecture around, Hitler needed some area he could claim for his own.

In the workers' suburbs outside of the First District, Hitler easily found what he was looking for.

"Gradually his style of planning changed,"[60] Kubizek wrote. In Linz, Hitler had given full vent to artistic architectural schemes. In Vienna, he suddenly became aware of "social building."[61]

In Linz, Hitler had lived the life of a dandy, cooked for and cared for by his mother. It was easy to be grandiose under such circumstances.

In Vienna, Hitler had suddenly come face to face with some of the harder facts of life. By late March of 1908 he must have seen that his money would not last forever. Nightly visits to the Opera did nothing to bolster a flagging bank account. Though he would have the orphan's pension until age twenty-four, Hitler's inheritance was running out.

Also, the contrast between the splendors of the Ring and the dinginess of his quarters must have created some social conscience in Hitler, no matter how selfish it was. "In the gloomy, sunless back room of the Stumpergasse . . . he felt every morning when he awoke, looking at the bare walls and depressing view, that building was not mostly a matter of show and prestige, but rather a problem of public health."[62]

He began to rail against a new-found enemy, the "professional landlord"[63] who built cramped quarters in the airless center of town for his tenants and himself lived in the green districts of Hietzing or Grinzing on the rents he collected.

Hitler began to visit the "typical working-class district of Meidling . . . . to study personally the housing and living conditions of the workers' families. . . . He was not interested in any individual . . . and therefore did not make any acquaintances in Meidling."[64]

Hitler had no way of knowing that he himself would be a down-and-out inhabitant at a hostel for the homeless in that same district.

He complained more and more to Kubizek. Building had to change in Vienna. The tenements had to be swept away to make room for smaller buildings with more conveniences. Finally one day in late

March, Hitler had enough of merely talking. This youth, who shied away from the masses as if they were so many vermin,[65] decided to go and see what life was really like for the underprivileged in Vienna.

"I shall be away for three days,"[66] he told Kubizek.

True to his word, on the fourth day Hitler came back to the Stumpergasse, dead tired from his walks around Vienna. He had approached the city from the east and walked around much of its perimeter near the Danube. He came back filled with ideas about how to rebuild Vienna with a huge scheme of public architecture that would give green space to all inhabitants and house the masses in small, detached units of four to eight apartments per house. His hastily scrawled sketches lined the walls of the room for several weeks. This work, hectic and unnerving to Kubizek, gave Hitler an "inner equilibrium" that erased the winter gloom and "grave depressions" from his mind and filled him instead full of "hope and courage."[67]

Hitler even tried to devise a new form of mass transit for Vienna utilizing the trains. He tried to cover all aspects of life in this new social project, even to providing the masses with a new "people's drink"[68] to replace wine and beer. When Kubizek argued that perhaps the Viennese might not be too quick to give up their wine, Hitler testily replied, "'You won't be asked!' as much as to say in other words 'Nor will the Viennese, either.'"[69]

Hitler rejected any practical difficulties that might constitute obstacles to his brainstorms. He knew what was best for those concerned and nothing could get in his way. So it was when Kubizek brought up the question of financing for such a huge building project. The "storm of revolution"[70] would take care of all that, he was told.

Slowly the life in the Austrian capital was politicizing the young man from Linz.

(4)

What was happening in architecture in Vienna during Hitler's early years there was far different from the Ringstrasse style. Hitler must have seen the controversial Secession building by Olbrich. That he approved of it is doubtful, especially if he compared it against his standard of excellence, the Ring buildings. Olbrich's building was most likely too utilitarian for Hitler's taste. The building was actually designed and constructed to exhibit pictures, not to exhibit itself.

No one symbolized this new concept of form following function more than did Otto Wagner in turn-of-the-century Vienna. Bahr, the spokesman for the Secessionists, summed up Wagner's importance: "Without Otto Wagner there would be no Secession, no Klimt group, no applied art, no Alfred Roller. . . . For it was Wagner who created the atmosphere in which all this first became possible. And without Wagner's blazing audacity no one would have had the courage to believe once again in Austria's artistic future."[71]

Perhaps Bahr overstates the case a bit, but Wagner certainly influenced an entire generation through his teachings. Both Hoffmann and Olbrich were his students.

Wagner had not always been the innovative giant the world today remembers. Much of his early work was influenced by the very historicism that Hitler so loved. But by 1898, just before joining the Secession, Wagner broke with his old style and moved into a Jugendstil phase. He put the scalpel to the Viennese façade and shocked the Viennese with such buildings as the Majolika Haus just up the street from the Secession. In this building the usual plaster façade of Viennese houses is replaced by majolica tile in a swirling Jugendstil floral pattern. Missing from the front are the heavy stonework and molding of classical buildings. Like Olbrich's Secession, this house, too, comes close to the modern dictum of form following function.

Wagner had been a highly respected professional man in the old Viennese tradition before his break with the Künstlerhaus. He was strictly a middle-class gentleman and family man who would write letters to his dead wife for several years after her death. He most certainly was not the type for rebellion.

Since the early 1890s Wagner, as advisor to the Transport Commission, had designed the immense metropolitan subway system with its distinctive station houses. As university professor and head of the Academy's architectural school, it probably fell to Wagner to reject Hitler's application to that school because of the latter's insufficient education.[72]

When Wagner, like Klimt, tried out his stylistic pen on totally Jugendstil compositions and later when he left Jugendstil behind to develop the initial breakthrough in the clean lines of truly modern architecture, the Viennese howled and hooted. At the ridiculous age of sixty, Otto had to learn how to be an *enfant terrible*. He was vilified in the press, called a sham architect, a destroyer of old Vienna, and a vandal.[73]

Olbrich had been smart enough to leave Vienna in 1899 for the artists' colony of Darmstadt at the invitation of the Grand Duke Ernst Ludwig of Hesse, who was attempting to create a modern Athens there. Olbrich had failed to gain a professorship at the School of Handicrafts, despite the intercession of Wagner at a time when the older architect was still much respected.

Wagner, though, could not leave. For him it was a fight to the end. Klimt had been luckier. When the public reviled him, he could retreat to his studio in the Josefstadt. All he needed was oil and canvas to keep creating. But an architect without a building is a sorry creature.

Wagner did manage to win two large public commissions in the early years of the twentieth century. Both buildings proved to be seminal designs in modern architecture.

The first was the Postsparkasse, built between 1904 and 1906. It is a clear, clean design that does away with much of the needless façade ornamentation of the previous century, employing extensive aluminum and using an ultramodern hot-air blower system to heat the massive building.

The second, and perhaps most famous, Wagner building is the Kirche am Steinhof, built on the grounds of an asylum in the outskirts of Vienna. This is the only sacred building in the world that is Jugendstil in toto, from the dome to the chalice.

Sitting on its hill overlooking the city, the church takes on a surreal appearance with its massive green dome, marble fronting, and huge sculptures. The interior of the church and sculptures outside were the product of a collaboration between many Werkstätte artists, including windows by Kolo Moser. This church, next to the Palais Stoclet in Brussels, is one of the finest examples of Jugendstil *Gesamtkunstwerk* in the world.

Wagner took great care that this church, to be used by the patients of the asylum, would have interiors as practical and hygienic as they were holy. His use of new materials, such as aluminum, glass, and reinforced concrete, and his use of ornament only to draw attention to structural elements are indicative of his genre. Increasingly his motto became "A thing that is not practical cannot be beautiful."[74]

Wagner discarded the notion of symbolic building. No longer should architects be forced to make a building Neo-Gothic because it was a city hall, or Renaissance because it was a museum. Wagner believed that each building is a thing in itself and any symbolism it has should grow out of it as a matter of function, not be imposed on it from without.

To make his church functional for those who would be using it, he built a holy water stoup with running water instead of a stagnant pool where infection could be spread. His pews were benches made purposely short so as to seat only four or five people. In case of disturbance during a service, an attendant could easily reach the patient from one side of the pew or the other.

Such innovations did not please the tradition-minded Viennese. That ultimate arbiter of artistic good taste, Archduke Franz Ferdinand, was heard to say at the inauguration of the church in 1907 that the Maria Theresa style was still the best as far as he was concerned. And as imperial commissioner for the preservation of historic buildings, Franz Ferdinand made his uninformed judgments stick. Wagner went begging for another public commission for the rest of his life. Such plans as the regulation of the Karlsplatz, or the building of a Franz Joseph Museum or a War Ministry, were all turned down.

One of Wagner's biographers echoed the sentiments of so many other native sons of Vienna, as well as of Hitler, when he reported that "this Vienna possesses, in addition to other significant qualities, the extraordinary gift of banishing its most worthwhile talents, or of humiliating them."[75]

(5)

Hitler managed to miss all these movements in modern art. He was still steeped in nineteenth-century classicism and historicism, as in the painting styles of Rudolf von Alt and Hans Makart. The Makart style of life had a real attraction for Hitler. Makart was the handsome womanizer who had to pick and choose between the lovely society women who flocked to his studio to pose in the nude for him. Their faces were disguised, of course, in the final paintings. Makart had even entranced Klimt at first and the young Klimt had stolen into the older man's studio during siesta hour one day to gaze at the huge and flawed canvases that glorified great moments in Austrian history.

Hitler also had his head buried in the historical sand as far as architecture was concerned. The Ring was his ideal then and continued to be, as displayed in the pomp and ostentation of the plans he drew for buildings for his Third Reich. Functionalism was a concept that passed by him unnoticed.

It was as if the initial artistic revolt of Vienna had never existed for Hitler. Mahler, because of his conducting at the Hof Opera and his productions of Wagner, was a name familiar to Hitler, but not Mahler's own music.

Hitler was not alone in his ignorance. The satirist Karl Kraus once quipped that Vienna was an isolation cell where one was allowed to scream. He was not far wrong. Though with the contacts that Klimt and his group had abroad, and Mahler's growing fame outside Vienna, the walls of this isolation cell would soon come tumbling down.

Hitler had his head in the clouds during his first months in the capital. He was living in his own little dream world of created values. In that world he would make his way somehow. His friend Kubizek, much more diligent and earnest than Adolf, was perpetually worried about the frivolous way Hitler approached life. But Hitler had not yet passed his nineteenth birthday. One does not really condemn an eighteen-year-old for dreaming.[76]

Though Hitler played a dilettantish game with the arts in the early months of 1908, it appears that his lasting love was really architecture. That architecture was his last love is probably also true; until the last days in the Berlin bunker in 1945, with the Russians advancing through the streets of the German capital, Hitler continued to study a wooden model of Linz with all the architectural changes he had been dreaming about for the city for several decades.[77]

That Hitler had the basic makeup of an artist is confirmed by no less a witness than Thomas Mann. "Must we not, even against our will," Mann wrote in 1938 before Hitler sank the world into the depths of World War II,

> recognize in this phenomenon an aspect of the artist's character? We are ashamed to admit it, but the whole pattern is there: the recalcitrance, sluggishness and miserable indefiniteness of youth; the dimness of purpose, the what-do-you-really-want-to-be, the vegetating like a semi-idiot in the lowest social and psychological bohemianism, the arrogant rejection of any sensible and honorable occupation because of the basic feeling that he was too good for that sort of thing. On what is this feeling based?

On a vague sense of being reserved for something entirely undefinable. To name it, if it could be named, would make people burst out laughing. Along with that, the uneasy conscience, the sense of guilt, the rage at the world, the revolutionary instinct, the subconscious storing up of explosive cravings for compensation, the churning determination to justify oneself, to prove oneself. . . . It is a thoroughly embarrassing kinship. Still and all, I would not want to close my eyes to it.[78]

The architect Albert Speer, one of Hitler's closest aides in the last several years of the Third Reich, also believed Hitler had a real artist's temperament. Speer thought Hitler was "a frustrated architect and artist whose 'misfortune it was to have to take part in politics and wage war.'" [79]

Hitler himself later confided to colleagues as late as 1942 that "I became a politician against my will. To my mind politics is just a means to an end. Wars come and go. The only lasting things are cultural values. Hence my love of art. Are not music and architecture the forces that will guide the footsteps of future generations?"[80]

Taken in this light, Hitler's later recounting of his rejection by the Academy may have been more than just self-pitying dramatics. He may well have suffered a deep feeling of frustration because of this rejection. It may well have changed the entire course of his life, if not of world history.

In the space of the few months Hitler had spent in Vienna by late March 1908, the city had already begun its work on him. When Hitler came to Vienna he was a spoiled mother's boy from a provincial town. The Linz dandy had been a big fish in a small pond. In Vienna, Hitler received a shock. Here he was just another student. And as his money began to run out, Hitler began to look more and more the role of a down-at-heel student with shiny pants and baggy coat.

By early spring a subtle change already had occurred in Hitler. A process of politicization had begun in him, turning him from his grandiose architectural dreams to social architecture. This process was caused by no obscure humanitarian sympathy for the down-trodden lower classes. Hitler had a personal gripe. Living in his stuffy back room and sketching building plans that nobody besides Frau Zakreys and Kubizek would probably ever see, had given Hitler a new cause.

Having cut himself off from any possibility of joining or working with established society when he destroyed the Roller letter, Hitler now set himself on a course of hate. He had to find the enemies who were keeping him from success. There were the stupid teachers at the Academy; the corrupt bureaucracy; even the Habsburgs themselves. The landlords were out to get him as well as the shallow-minded officers who took his standing room at the Opera.

All too soon Hitler would hit on an even better, all-encompassing scapegoat.

By the spring of 1908 the frustrations were gathering in Hitler as he sat working by smoky lamplight in his back room in Mariahilf or stumped about Vienna passing judgment on buildings and people alike. He was turning himself into a time bomb.

The ticking went on unheard for another five years in Vienna.

3

The Sink of Iniquity

(1)

Vienna, spring 1908:

IT was one of those perfect spring evenings when even the possibility of winter is forgotten. Heavy coats were stored away in naphthalene for another six months. The most pessimistic of Viennese, wary of one last, possibly fatal chill draft, had donned their light summer clothes.

The Ring was lit up in a blaze of new electric lights. The four rows of plane trees that border the boulevard had finally grown into respectable trees instead of the shrubs they had appeared to be for so long.

Smells first: The western mountains were hinted at in crisp, vaguely piney whiffs. Sweet-water smell from the beautiful gray Danube mingled with the faint, acrid smell of horse dung. That acrid odor would become much worse as the hot season approached, especially in the narrow, cobbled streets of the First District. But this spring evening, with the light breeze from the Vienna woods to air out the wide boulevard, the horse dung was merely a pungent spice.

The sounds: Occasional clopping of hansom cabs, the horses a bit bowed and snorting stubbornly at the driver. Then the still surprising and jarring intrusion of one of Ford's infernal, internal combustion machines, of which there were already 300 in Vienna, claiming sixty lives a year.[1] A coupé rattled over the cobbles, honking its squeeze horn at the cab to give way. The horse's eyes rolled white in panic at this noisy monster, and the cab driver had to rein in tight to hold the horse, cursing at the car all the while. This disturbance soon passed, and the quiet gentleness of the evening returned. Subdued, orderly murmur-conversations of passing strollers walking arm in arm; swishing of long dresses; click of a gentleman's walking stick on the sidewalk.

Along that part of the Ring by the Volksgarten, just across the street from the Parliament, spotlighted shiny white on a moonless night, the faint melody of a Strauss waltz, at once gay and melancholy, perhaps drifted out of the park's dance hall.

Just north of this point a new sound filtered into the empty night air, foreign at first, then quickly assimilated into the stillness of night, eaten up by it as were the lights by the darkness. The Burgtheater had just finished its evening performance, and the audience passed out onto the street still talking to one another of the shocking content of the play they had just seen, *Frühlingserwachen* by Frank Wedekind. This exceptionally candid play examining the sexual problems of puberty had first been performed two years before and had kept audiences from Berlin to Vienna talking.

Out of the humming crowd of theatergoers milling around the entrance emerged Hitler and Kubizek.[2] They had made an exception that night and had stayed until the end of the play. They would have to pay their forty hellers to the grumpy concierge to be let in now. Lucky for them at least that there was not bitter wind to freeze their hatless and coatless bodies. The money they saved from the wardrobe fee would partly make up for this extravagance.

The two walked on in silence for a time, following the course of the Ring past the Parliament. From here they turned up and off the main boulevards just before the Natural History Museum, at the corner of Bellariastrasse, past the Royal Stables and the Volkstheater.

The street began the slow ascent out of the bowl of the First District, and they followed the curve of the Breitegasse into the narrow, cobbled Siebensterngasse.

At the third street to the right, Hitler suddenly took hold of Kubizek's arm as if struck with an inspiration.

"Come, Gustl." He motioned down a side street. "We must see the sink of iniquity once."[3]

With that, the two turned down the narrow, ill-lit Spittelberggasse. The street was full of low, one-story houses with windows at street level, allowing the passersby to look directly into the rooms. Many of the curtainless windows framed young and old women who sat doing their nails, or making up their faces.

The women were in various stages of undress, always aware of the men constantly passing by outside. Hitler and Kubizek were not alone on the lane. Soldiers from the barracks up the street provided steady custom to the women, and there were also several middle-class types eyeing the merchandise. All the men were busy window shopping. Occasionally a man would stop in front of the window of a girl he fancied. The woman would lean out the window, leaning forward to give him a good view of her wares. A few hasty, whispered words of price and passion were exchanged, and the man would enter the flat. The light would then be discreetly switched off.

Kubizek tells us in his master-of-understatement manner that it was "the accepted practice not to stand before unlit windows."[4]

Hitler led Kubizek first down one side of this street to the intersection with Burggasse, and then back up the other side, filled all the while with disgust and piety.

For the girls' part, they thought that a couple of country bumpkins had rolled into town and were taking a good long time shopping around before choosing. Sitting in their windows, the whores re-doubled their efforts to score one last trick for the night so that they could go home to their Otto or Franz or whomever out in their dingy little room in Floridsdorf or Meidling or Ottakring—or any such dank and unforgiving workers' suburb.

One of the girls stripped off her chemise just as the two passed, acting as if by accident she had chosen that very moment to change clothes. Another whore rolled black stockings up long white legs as Hitler and Kubizek passed by her window. It was the temptation of Parsifal all over again, and Hitler, the chaste knight, was having none of it.

Back on the Siebensterngasse, a quiet fell between the two like a hush in an adult bookstore.

They followed the Siebensterngasse into the Westbahnstrasse, past the flat where the painter Klimt once lived, and found their way back to the Mariahilferstrasse and finally to the safety and dinginess of their lodgings.

(2)

Vienna 1900 was a schizoid mixture where sexuality was concerned.

It was a bizarre blend of Victorian prudery and subterranean sexuality and decadence. Sex was looked at, by the middle class especially, as something "anarchical"[5] and dirty, to be shunted away to dark, nighttime alleys. "If it were not feasible to do away with sexuality, then at least it must not be visible in the world of morality. A silent pact was therefore reached, by which the entire bothersome affair was not mentioned in school, in the family, or in public, and everything which brought its existence to mind was suppressed."[6]

By the time Hitler came to Vienna there seemed to be a concerted effort abroad with the revolutionary arts and letters to sink this archaic way of thinking. Klimt's orgiastic nudes were as much a reaction to this prudery as were the books and plays of Arthur Schnitzler. Though Schnitzler's women and men were anything but sexually liberated by today's standards, the playwright did at least bring the subject of sex into the light of day. His "*süsses Mädel*," who always loved her fine young men passionately and was always cast aside by them in the end, was far from an emancipated woman. But she was "tarnished without sin, innocent without virginity . . . the good little, bad little daughter"[7] of some lower-middle-class family who was at least honest in her liking of sex.

Schnizler's *süsses Mädel* actually had it lucky. If she was but the momentary plaything of some lieutenant or lawyer, only to be cast aside for a proper young woman of the right class, she still was better off than the proper young woman such men chose.

The girls of good families were kept in a hothouse state of ignorance of their bodies and the world around them, to the point that an accidental glimpse of the sex act was a horrifying experience. It was something other beastly people might engage in, but surely not Mommy and Daddy![8]

These women were supposed to fit into the Viennese mold of the proper *Frau* and to dress in the latest tight-waisted style, using whalebone corsets to accentuate their wasp waists. Women's clothes, moreover, while they accentuated the sexual differences with such stylistic aberrations as the bustle, were designed to hide as much skin as possible, even the wrists and ankles.

"It is neither legendary nor exaggerated to say that old women died, the lines of whose shoulders or knees no one had ever seen, with the exception of the midwife, their husbands, and the undertaker."[9]

Wide-brimmed hats might set off these women's eyes in a fanciful, mysterious, almost seductive manner, but this was no sexual invitation. Above all, the woman was to be the servant of her husband. Even alone with other women, these proper *Fraus* rarely started a sentence without "My husband believes . . ."[10] The proper Viennese woman was supposed to be neither overtly sexual nor intelligent.

Hitler took this operetta view of women with him as excess baggage when he left Vienna for Germany. Later when Hitler would describe the perfect woman to the wife of one of his SA leaders, it would sound very like the good *Frau* of his Vienna years: "A woman must be a cute, cuddly, helpless little thing: soft, sweet and dumb."[11]

It was this good and proper *Frau* who, in the absence of the workaday father, raised the children. Raised in ignorance herself, she could only pass along her ignorance to the children.

Young middle-class men had it little better than their sisters, though it was thought correct for them to sow their wild oats. Some thoughtful parents even brought in a servant girl from the country for this purpose.[12] The unluckier of the boys had to fend for themselves. Normal outlets for sexuality were closed to them as girls of their own conforming middle class could be met only attended by a chaperon. Young boys were told to have their fling, but they did not know how or where to go about it.

This suppressed sexuality had to come out in some way and it often worked itself out in a "childish and helpless fashion. There was scarcely a fence or privy that was not besmeared with obscene words and drawings, hardly a bathing pool in which the wooden walls of the women's quarters were not bored full of peepholes. Entire industries . . . flowered secretly. 'Art' and nude photographs in particular were offered to half-grown boys for sale under the table by peddlers in every café."[13]

One part of the underground industry, which in Vienna was very much above ground, was prostitution. The red-light district Hitler so self-righteously surveyed that spring night was only one of several such areas in Vienna catering to the sexual needs of a repressed population.

"Prostitution was . . . the foundation of the erotic life outside marriage. . . . It constituted a dark underground vault over which rose the gorgeous structure of middle-class society with its faultless, radiant façade."[14]

As a symbol of the schizoid attitude toward sex in turn-of-the-century Vienna, prostitution was legal, unlike the case in many other

European capitals of the time. A statute in 1873 had legalized prostitution and required all prostitutes to register with the police and undergo biweekly medical examinations by police physicians.[15]

Any woman/child over fourteen years of age could practice the oldest profession. The legal age was changed to eighteen by 1900. But because diseased women had to go to a hospital for a cure and thus lose income, the law was unpopular from the beginning. By 1874 it was estimated that only 10 percent of the 15,000 streetwalkers in Vienna were registered.[16]

There were also laws that forbade more than three prostitutes from living and working together. This attempt at outlawing brothels was one more hypocrisy at work: given the legal right to work, the prostitute was at the same time forced to work on the street in the worst conditions.

The laws against brothels were not very effective. Graft and corruption in the police force kept the brothels open. A police surgeon's report in 1907, kept in a separate file just for bordellos, blithely reports six houses operating illegally in the First District alone.[17]

Even if she registered with the police, the legal prostitute still had no legal rights. If cheated out of her fee she could not sue because of counter laws that prohibited immoral behavior.

So, damned if they did and damned if they didn't, it is no wonder that by Hitler's time in Vienna only some 2,000 prostitutes bothered to register with the police.[18]

The legions of unregistered prostitutes were like an army,[19] with rank and division dependent upon where one worked—on the street like the infantry; in love markets such as Hitler's Spittelberggasse like the siege artillery; or the "general staff" kept in the finest bordellos for those with refined tastes and hefty bank accounts. In these elegant establishments the women met their customers in negligees and served champagne.

There was something for every taste in Vienna's underground vault. In the wardrobes of the bordellos were nun and ballerina costumes for the fetishists; peepholes abounded for the voyeuristic. There were hidden doorways and stairs by which members of the highest nobility and perhaps even the court could pay their secretive visits.[20]

The prostitutes even worked the halls of the Hof Opera during intermission, and the sidewalks of the First District "were so sprinkled with women for sale that it was more difficult to avoid than to find them. . . . It cost a man as little time and trouble to purchase a woman for a quarter of an hour, an hour or a night, as it did to buy a package of cigarettes or a newspaper."[21]

All this was representative of that old sacred cow, middle-class morality. The bourgeois classes seem always to be the ones stuck with society's rules and regulations—and the ones to need such underground vaults to express their pent-up sexuality. "This was the same city, the same society, the same morality that was indignant when young girls rode bicycles, and declared it a disgrace to the dignity of science when Freud in his calm, clear, and penetrating manner established truths that they did not wish to be true. The same world that so pathetically defended the purity of womanhood allowed this cruel sale of women, organized it, and even profited thereby."[22]

Bourgeois morality is one thing. Out in the workers' districts like Ottakring and Brigittenau things were a bit different. Living five and six to a crowded two rooms with a *"Bettgeher,"* a roomless tenant who slept nights in the kitchen, did not breed much sexual privacy. Young girls and boys were initiated into sex at a surprisingly early age.

"In my childhood," Josephine Mutzenbacher, the Viennese Fanny Hill, tells us in her memoirs of turn-of-the-century sexual exploits, "boys and girls like my brother and me were all sexually aware and eager to practice that premature knowledge. Boys did it with their sisters and girl friends as a matter of course. They had never heard of the word *incest* or *taboo,* like the rich kids who had the opportunity to listen to the conversation of educated adults."[23]

Sex was one form of amusement to compensate for the poor living conditions of the lower classes and a life of factory work with little hope of betterment. Not surprisingly, it was largely from this class that the legions of Viennese prostitutes were recruited.

The upper classes, too, were fairly free to have their dalliances, as long as they were somehow kept private. Mistresses were a common alternative for the wealthy who could afford a second household. The aristocrats had their ballerinas and actresses to keep them happy. No less a personage than the Emperor Franz Joseph had an open alliance with the actress Katharina Schratt, arranged for by his ever-absent wife Elisabeth. Far from scandalized, his ministers were only relieved that a degree of domesticity could be injected into the old man's life.

Crown Prince Rudolf, before his suicide in 1889, had also had his affairs, remarked on at court only because they were so untidy and so flagrantly public in issuance.

But artists and aristocrats alike were not free from being elementally damaged in their sex and at odds with one of the fundamental facts of life. It is no accident that the Swedish playwright Strindberg, himself married to a Viennese, found nowhere else "so much understanding of his woman-hate as he did in Vienna."[24]

Musicians seemed to be especially burdened with sexual hang-ups. Brahms could not achieve any kind of satisfaction with women other than prostitutes, while Bruckner's penchant for small girls brought him near nervous collapse several times.[25] The same accusations of liking little girls too much were later thrown at the architect Adolf Loos and the painter Egon Schiele. Herzl also fell a victim to this proclivity and at the age of twenty-nine married an eighteen-year-old psychotic who did nothing to make the life of the founder of Zionism run smoothly.[26]

Homosexuality was another outlet for the sexually repressed. Ludwig Viktor, one of the archdukes, was known jokingly to the Viennese as the Archduke of the Bath because of a scandal in a public bath involving young boys.[27] Even the army was not proof against homosexuality, as the Redl affair would later, in 1913, shockingly point out.

And if the men and women of turn-of-the-century Vienna were not caught in a spiritual distortion of sexuality because of the repressive atmosphere, there was always the chance that they might be caught physically. Men such as Hans Makart and Hugo Wolf died of syphilis. It is probable, as court gossip had it, that both Franz Joseph and his son Rudolf passed on venereal diseases to their respective wives. Archduke Franz Ferdinand's brother, Otto, was also a victim of syphilis, having to wear a leather nose to cover the ravages in the later stages of the disease.[28]

Venereal disease was of epidemic proportions in Vienna at the turn of the century. "One or two out of every ten young men had fallen victim" to syphilis, according to one witness.[29]

Partly because of these conditions, Vienna became a world center for dermatology with every "sixth or seventh door"[30] in the streets bearing a plaque for that specialty.

In those days before penicillin, the cures for venereal disease were almost as bad as the infection. For weeks the entire body of the syphilis patient was rubbed with mercury, one ill effect of which was that it made the teeth fall out. Even after this hideous cure the patient could not be sure that the virus would not at any time start up again and work its way into the brain to cause paralysis.[31]

Yet, strangely enough, the young boys made a ghoulish fraternity out of such sexual battle scars, and just as the facial scars sported by saber-wielding boys of fraternity age were a badge of honor, so, too, was the first drip of gonorrhea for boys just out of puberty the initiation rite into manhood.[32]

The fears of venereal disease only heightened the forbidden aspects of sex and served to throw more kinks into the sexual life of the capital.

One of the kinkiest results was embodied in the life of Leopold von Sacher-Masoch, the Austrian who gave his name to define the condition of masochism. Masoch was a writer of some stature in the late nineteenth century who told of his peculiar proclivity in such stories as "Venus im Pelze," the account of his six-month slavedom to a princess in Baden near Vienna.

In another story, "Under the Whip," Masoch writes: "In a holy night of love he lay at her feet and besought her in supreme ecstasy: 'Maltreat me, so that I may endure my happiness, be cruel to me, give me kicks and kisses . . .'"[33]

Masoch was "discovered" by the Viennese psychologist Richard von Krafft-Ebing, an early researcher into the relationship of syphilis to paralysis and the author of *Psychopathia Sexualis,* a catalogue of sexual perversion. It was Krafft-Ebing who coined the word *masochism,* having heard of Masoch's escapades.[34] First published in Stuttgart in 1883, *Psychopathia Sexualis* was in its twelfth printing by 1902 and something of an underground classic. Tradition has it that Franz Joseph, who usually remained blissfully unaware of what was happening in the arts and sciences in his own capital, remarked upon hearing of the book: "It's about time someone wrote a good Latin grammar."[35]

Although most likely apocryphal, the remark does sum up the Viennese treatment of sexuality by sublime sublimation.

(3)

By all accounts, Hitler's only sexual adventure by the time he settled in Vienna had been a furtive visit to the adult section of the Linz wax museum.[36]

His one youthful romance was a puppy love for a blond, blue-eyed

Linz girl a little older than he, named Stephanie. She was his love from afar. Hitler wrote her poems, sketched villas for her, and planned a future with her as his wife while never having once spoken to her.[37]

The "love affair" seems to have begun in the spring of 1906 when Hitler saw the handsome young woman promenading with her mother on Linz's Landstrasse. It was the custom for fashionable young women and men to take the air after five o'clock, and many a romance started with a casual glance, even though the young women were properly escorted by older chaperons.

Hitler sent Kubizek out to learn details about the girl's family, for she had a surname that sounded vaguely Jewish. It was discovered that she came from a good family and despite the name, was not Jewish. Hitler felt he had an unspoken communication going with the girl, even though he never dared speak a word to her.

"Between such exceptional beings as himself and Stephanie," Kubizek later wrote of the affair, "there was absolutely no need for the usual form of spoken communication. He told me that exceptional people come to understand one another through intuition."[38]

When Stephanie did not seem to reciprocate Hitler's unspoken declarations of love and instead saved her smile for the handsome young officers in their braided uniforms on the Landstrasse, Hitler would fly into a rage of jealousy. When he learned that his beloved Stephanie also attended balls with the young officers where she danced in their arms, Hitler threatened to throw himself into the Danube.

Finally, when Hitler left to seek his fortunes in Vienna, he screwed up enough courage to write Stephanie and tell her of his intentions and that he would come back for her in a couple years, a famous academic painter.

Hitler lacked only the courage to sign this letter.

Interviewed years later, Stephanie vaguely remembered receiving such a letter. Busy as she was at the time with her army officers and balls, she had had a good laugh over the letter, thinking it was a joke sent to her by one of her girl friends.[39]

While Vienna seethed in the juices of repressed sexuality, Hitler "lived in his self-imposed asceticism, regarding girls and women with lively and critical sympathy, while completely excluding anything personal, and handled matters which other young men his age turned into their own experiences, as problems for discussion."[40]

That is what Hitler did that spring night returning from the Spittelberggasse red-light district. Once inside the door to their room, Hitler began his ravings about the "monument to the shame of our times,"[41] as he called prostitution. "Now he had learned the customs of the market for commercial love, he declared, and his visit was fulfilled."[42]

Hitler paced the room, shaking his hands and head as he spoke, carrying out a long diatribe on the importance of keeping the "flame of life"[43] pure. This was Hitler's favorite symbol for sacred love between men and women "who have kept themselves pure in body and soul and are worthy of a union which would produce healthy children for the nation."[44]

For Hitler, the whole ugly business of prostitution was a sullying of the "flame" and an abomination of the man-woman bond, the primary purpose of which was to further the state.

As a youth in Vienna, Hitler held a hard line against sexual indulgence. "He had too big an opinion of himself for a superficial flirtation or for a merely physical relation with a girl."[45] Not only did he live in "strict monklike asceticism,"[46] but he also expected his friend Gustl to do the same.[47]

Hitler's prudish approach to sexuality may have been partly due to self-protection. He was shy of all people and had a "constant fear of physical contact with strangers—he shook hands rarely and then only with a few people."[48]

"In the midst of this corrupt city," Kubizek reported, "my friend surrounded himself with a wall of unshakable principles which enabled him to build up an inner freedom, in spite of all the dangers around him. He was afraid of infection, as he often said. Now I understand that he meant not only venereal infection, but a much more general infection, namely the danger of being caught up in the prevailing conditions and finally being dragged down into the vortex of corruption."[49]

Apparently Hitler was not unattractive to women as a young man. In the Hof Opera, despite his modest clothing and youthful appearance, occasionally one of the "passing ladies would turn around to look at him" during intermission in the foyer.[50] One of these women even sent Hitler a message via her liveried attendant, an open invitation to seduction. Hitler read the note with apparent amusement, not at all surprised or shocked by the suggestion of a rendezvous, and handed the message over to Kubizek, offering the lady to his friend.

"Another one,"[51] Hitler is supposed to have muttered with great nonchalance.

For whatever reasons—and the reasons may become more obvious later—Hitler led an asexual life while his friend Kubizek knew him. Kubizek could later say that "with certainty, Adolf never met a girl, either in Linz or in Vienna, who actually gave herself to him."[52]

As far as Kubizek was concerned, the youthful Hitler was "in physical as well as sexual respects, absolutely normal. What was extraordinary in him was not to be found in the erotic or sexual spheres, but in quite other realms of his being."[53] Apparently, the eighteen-year-old Hitler did not even masturbate as did most other youths.[54]

But no matter how hard Hitler tried to avoid the more animal side of life in Vienna, he did run into it on several occasions.

The day after Kubizek arrived in town, the two had set off to find a suitable lodging for him. Walking down the Zollergasse in the nearby Seventh District, they saw a "Room to Let" notice on one of the houses.[55] When they inquired within, a maid answered the door to an elegantly appointed flat and led them into a bed-sitting room, leaving them with the promise that "Madam will be here soon."[56]

"We both thought it a bit too classy for us," Kubizek reports, "but at that moment 'Madam' appeared in the doorway, a real lady, no longer particularly young, but very elegant. She was wearing a silk dressing gown and very dainty slippers trimmed in fur. She smiled as she greeted us, looking us up and down, first Adolf and then me, and offered us a seat. My friend asked which was the room to let. 'This one!' said the lady, indicating the two beds. Adolf shook his head and briefly said: 'One of the beds will have to be taken out to make room for my friend's piano.' The lady was visibly dismayed that it was I and not Adolf who wanted the room, and asked whether he already had accommodations. When he said he had, she suggested that I and my piano should move into that room and he should take this one. While speaking she had become very animated, and a sudden movement loosened the cord of her dressing gown. . . . She at once adjusted the garment but the brief moment had been enough to show us that underneath the silk dressing gown she was wearing nothing but a dimunitive pair of knickers. Adolf went red as a turkey cock, stood up, and took me by the arm saying: 'Come on, Gustl!' I don't really know how we got out of the house. All I remember is that when at last we found ourselves in the street, Adolf blurted out angrily: 'Potiphar's wife!'"[57]

The two decided to go back to the safety of Frau Zakreys's flat and work out some arrangement with her rather than risk another such run-in with a prospective landlady.

On another occasion the two were out for an evening stroll down the Mariahilferstrasse when a respectable-looking businessman approached them on the street, questioning them about their studies.[58] When he learned they were studying art and music, the man invited them to supper at the Hotel Kümmer, allowing them to choose whatever they wanted from the menu. Meanwhile, the man had made it clear that he was not fond of women because they were always interested in his money.

The three ate dinner amid lively conversation and after thanking him for the dinner and returning to the Stumpergasse, Hitler and Kubizek began discussing the man.

"He's a homosexual,"[59] said Adolf baldly.

This startled Kubizek, and Hitler had to explain to his friend just what the word meant. Then Hitler went into a tirade as to how homosexuality would not be allowed in his "ideal state."

"It seemed quite natural to me," Kubizek wrote, "that he should feel horror and disgust at this and other sexual aberrations encountered in the capital."[60]

Despite some wild stories to the contrary,[61] it is most probably true that Hitler led a celibate life during the time Kubizek knew him. It would fit in with his dreamlike state of these years. Hitler's fairy-tale existence had no room for the sweat and musk of sex.

Kubizek was getting tired. Hitler's harangue had lasted into the wee hours again. "It was a typical phenomenon of general moral decadence,"[62] he was telling Kubizek. The prostitutes were a sign of the times they lived in. "The flame of life in these poor creatures was long since extinct."[63] And it was not just on the Spittelberggasse that these ladies were to be found! You could come across them in the "most varied forms, both in the elegant streets of the center, and in the slums of the suburbs."[64] Walking through the streets of the Leopoldstadt across the Danube canal, mostly a Jewish district, "one could witness hideous sexual proceedings that most German people could not even imagine."[65]

Hitler warmed to his topic. He wrung his hands and rolled his eyes and tossed his head. And what was the reason for all of this, he wanted to know?

Kubizek perhaps looked up at his friend now, realizing that the end was near. The conclusion was coming.

The women were forced into it, Hitler concluded. It was pure and simple "white slavery."[66] And who controlled the women? Hitler was on the verge of beginning a new life for himself, had he only known it. A fundamental discovery was building in him, one that formed a coherent universe for him for the rest of his life. He was about to hit on the metaphysic that would sail him through the chaos of a godless universe safely.

Who was responsible for all this shame? It was the *Jew*. He was the "cold-hearted, shameless and calculating director of this revolting vice traffic in the scum of the city."[67]

(4)

Hitler was not the only person looking at sexuality and prostitution in Vienna in 1900. Across town in the Ninth District, just down the street from the Votivkirche, a Jewish doctor was most likely working late into the night at his desk as Hitler was boring Kubizek with his simplistic diatribe against the Jewish white slavers.

Sitting at his massive desk at Berggasse 19, with Roman and Egyptian artifacts surrounding him, Sigmund Freud was settling down to work after his usual evening brisk walk around the Ring.[68] This midnight-hour work was the end of Freud's busy day. Forced to earn the bread for the family with his consultation work during the day, he set aside the night for the important writing he produced in the early years of the twentieth century: *Studies in Hysteria; The Interpretation of Dreams; The Psychopathology of Everyday Life; Three Theories of Sexuality; Beyond the Pleasure Principle; The Ego and the Id.*

Freud, the quintessential product of Viennese intellectualism and repression, also had a theory about prostitution, involved with the schizoid sexual mores of the Victorian world which would not allow a "good" woman to enjoy sex without being called a harlot.[69] Freud saw that "full satisfaction comes only when he (the husband) can give himself up wholeheartedly to enjoyment, which with his well-brought-up wife . . . he does not venture to do. Hence comes his need for a less exalted sexual object, a woman ethically inferior, to whom he need not ascribe aesthetic misgivings, and who does not know the rest of his life and cannot criticize him."[70]

Freud's more reasoned and logical discussion of the causes of Viennese prostitution is as different from Hitler's rantings about the "Jewish white slavers" as night from day. For Hitler, Viennese sexuality was a threat that bombarded the fortress of his Flame. For Freud, the Viennese approach to sexuality lit the path to his discovery of the Unconscious.

It was a long and tortuous path.

It began on May 6, 1856, in Freiburg in northern Moravia. Born Sigismund, Freud later changed his name to the more Germanic Sigmund.

The Freuds were a Jewish wool family who moved to Vienna from northern Moravia during the heavy Jewish migrations of the last half of the nineteenth century. They settled on the Praterstrasse near where the Herzls lived and where young Mahler had his student quarters.

Freud attended the Sperlgymnasium in the Second District from 1865 to 1873 and was first in his class the last six years. In 1873 he entered the Medical Faculty of the University of Vienna, at that time the mecca of medicine in the world.

Freud was as much a product of this famous medical tradition as he was of Viennese morality.[71]

Two of Freud's more direct influences in Viennese medicine were Richard von Krafft-Ebing and Josef Breuer. Krafft-Ebing's pioneering work in sexual research profoundly influenced Freud and the role he gave to sexuality.

Breuer, an unassuming internist with a long paternal beard, was a direct precursor to Freud. The talking cure he developed while trying to cure a young female hysteric, famous to the world as Anna O, was a forerunner of Freud's own psychoanalytic method.

Freud received his degree in 1881; studied further in France under Charcot, and married Martha Bernays in 1886 at the responsible age of thirty. This marriage resulted in six children—a goodly responsibility for a man hoping to do independent research.

Freud's earliest investigations were into the nature and causes of hysteria. He found that hysteria, despite its Greek derivation meaning wandering womb, occurs in men as well as women, and that it often has a psychical rather than purely physiological origin.[72] The psychical causes Freud kept stumbling over time and again with his patients were sexual.[73]

His patients had such horrifying stories of infantile sexual mistreatment to tell him, that at first Freud, who was himself a rather chaste and puritanical sort of man in conformity with the public standards of his time, was appalled at their ramblings.

Then the coincidence of such stories of incest and rape and bestiality from all types of patients led Freud to form the daring, though false, assumption that hysteria is a result of premature sexual experience.

It was not until several years later that the gullible Freud, better judge of intellectual depths than of character, came to the conclusion that he had been mistaken about the reality of all those sexual tales. Yet that such stories were constantly brought up by his patients was still important. It pointed to the prominence of such themes in their neuroses.

Freud then saw that these experiences that had been related as if they were in fact true and had already happened, were really wish fulfillments of suppressed desires. Rather than hysteria and neuroses being caused by too early sexual experience, it now seemed to Freud that repression of sexuality was the guilty party. It was the very suppression of desires that ultimately surfaced in his patients as nervous disorders. And in the city of Vienna, where sublimation and repressed sexuality were the bourgeois order of the day, Freud had no dearth of subjects to help him evolve his theories.

Together with this discovery of unconscious forces at work in people, Freud blended other strains of his research: the cathartic or talking cure as developed by Breuer and himself; the interpretation of dreams to uncover unconscious motives; and a new awareness of infantile sexuality that would help to explain why the suppression of sexual desire was so harmful. Freud postulated that sex, like survival, was an instinct—one of the strongest we have.

From this admixture, a coherent system for the treatment of neuroses was developed. As early as 1896, Freud had dubbed this new system psychoanalysis, and was himself the first person in history to be so analyzed—by himself. Taking to heart the old saying "physician heal thyself," Freud worked through his own neurasthenia, discovering what he called the Oedipal complex of a son's desire for his mother. Only after such rigorous self-examination did Freud feel he was ready to help others to help themselves.

Up to 1905, two years before Hitler's arrival in Vienna, Freud had been considered merely an eccentric by the Viennese. But in 1905, the gentle doctor who looks to us now more like a camp counselor than the sex fiend more caustic critics then claimed him to be, not only shocked his medical colleagues but also outraged the reading public in general. In that year, Freud published his most daring and damning work. Suddenly, Freud was considered truly perverted. He was called a "filthy old man"[74] on the streets of Vienna.

The two publications which caused this furor were *Three Theories of Sexuality,* a book that for the first time formalized Freud's theory of infantile sexuality into the oral, anal, and genital stages of development, and the *Dora Analysis,* a study that let the curtain up to reveal a young woman's sexual desires and repressions.

These subjects were anathema to the Viennese who were willing to laugh over the exploits of one of Lehár's jovial seducers at the Volksoper, but who were shocked by the real facts of life and sex.

It was, after all, unnerving to think that a little baby suckling on his mother's breast was in some kind of sexual ecstasy.

It was also considered foul and evil by the Viennese to discuss the innermost thoughts and fears of a young woman and to interpret these in so "filthy" a manner.

Such recriminations, of course, bothered Freud; he would have had to be inhuman for them not to touch him. But ultimately these objections only reinforced him in his new theories, for if so many people were yelling foul, Freud concluded that he must be getting close to the truth. Like Klimt, he decided that to please the many is bad, and he went on the path he had chosen for himself.

Freud weathered the storms of protest and by 1908, when he and Hitler might have crossed paths, international repute plus a group of disciples had come to roost at Berggasse 19.

The Wednesday Nights, weekly gatherings of his followers at his flat, where psychoanalysis was discussed and debated, became an institution. Papers were read and debated and after all was said and done, the good wife Martha brought in *Gugelhupf*—pound cake—and coffee.

Adherents came and left. Alfred Adler and Karl Jung were perhaps among the best known of the defectors, both ultimately breaking away from the commanding Freud because of his overemphasis on the sexual origin of neuroses. Adler, with his "will to power" and "inferiority complex," and Jung, with his belief in a collective Unconscious, felt too bridled by Freud's sexual monomania, as Freud himself later did when he branched out to look at the death wish and the sources of imagination.

Though there was begrudged renown for him in the city that he both loved and hated,[75] Freud was most definitely a product of Vienna. More intellectually than physically inclined toward sex himself, Freud's sex drive was, according to his friend and biographer Ernest Jones, considerably lower than average. By the age of forty-one, Freud wrote a friend that "sexual excitation is of no more use to a person like me."[76]

A renowned French poetess, Countess Anna de Noailles, anxious to meet the famous sex philosopher, came away from their meeting sorely disappointed. "Surely," she remarked later, "he has never written those sexy books. What a terrible man! I am sure he has never been unfaithful to his wife. It is quite abnormal and scandalous."[77]

One is not quite sure what the countess thought the more scandalous —Freud's marital fidelity or his books. But it is obvious from such reports that Freud did not escape the damaging effects of Viennese morality, even though he tried to cure others of them.

Karl Kraus once summed up Freud's discipline with a pithy and telling remark: "Psychoanalysis is that spiritual disease of which it considers itself to be the cure."[78] Kraus saw that Freud himself was a representative of the repressive society he wished to liberate. Yet this does not negate the ultimate power of his work, nor the fact that his insights transcend mere sexual theory.

"I am not really a man of science at all," Freud once admitted, "not an observer, not an experimenter, not a cogitator. By temperament I am nothing but a conquistador, an 'adventurer' if you want the word translated, with the curiosity, audacity, and the tenacity of such a nature."[79]

We do not blame Magellan for his miscalling that violent body of water the Pacific, but praise him that he had the courage to find it at all.

That Freud made mistakes in generalizing about the human Unconscious from the microcosm of the world that was turn-of-the-century Vienna is to be regretted. That, out of his own temperament and that of the civilization he was a part of, he should see sex as the great determiner of unconscious forces, is the kind of mistake a conquistador might make—the mistake of someone who has no time for experimentation or cogitation, but who is pushing ever forward to new vistas.

Freud the suppressed Jew, the sexual puritan, could only have stumbled upon the Unconscious—that strange, dark region of instincts and forgotten dreams—in turn-of-the-century Vienna, the land of forgotten dreams. And the discovery of the Unconscious, more than any other handy tag words like "Oedipal complex" and "Freudian slip," was Freud's great accomplishment. It opened the doors of twentieth-century thought. Modern ideas, art, and culture are all unimaginable without the power of the Unconscious that Freud revealed.

(5)

Hitler, like Freud, was a product of Vienna's sexual atmosphere. But while Freud was led to the discovery of the Unconscious and of the primacy of the instincts because of that strange permissive-repressive mixture, it is less clear how Hitler was affected. An indication of this influence can be seen in a description of Nazism by a Freudian psychologist: "Every form of organized mysticism, including fascism, relies on the unsatisfied orgastic longing of the masses. . . . Race ideology is a pure biopathic expression of the character structure of the orgastically impotent man. . . . Fascist mentality is the mentality of the 'little man,' who is enslaved and craves authority."[80]

The sadistic nature of the Nazi state has often been commented upon—the extreme sadism of the concentration camps is so obvious it needs no comment. Suddenly in the late thirties and forties of this century it was as if the lid had been taken off the Id and full, unrestrained expression of perversion and sadism was given vent.

How much of the nature of Nazism can be directly traced to Hitler is also unclear. In many cases he merely opened the door to a full warehouse of human cruelties; in others, he himself was the model.

Hitler's own sexuality surely came to play on the atmosphere of the Third Reich.[81] There is little evidence of Hitler's sexual nature from the first few months in Vienna and the Linz years. The one notable fact is his noninvolvement. Kubizek tells us his friend led a chaste life and that all in all he found him normal sexually. One might question how "normal" such enforced celibacy is in an eighteen-year-old man who should be in the bloom of his sexuality. This could however be dismissed as one more romantic notion on the part of young Hitler to play the part of ascetic artist to the hilt.

By the time Hitler's career had taken a political turn, he was able to use his patriotic mission as an excuse for not taking a wife and settling into a normal sexual life. There was always something that Hitler could use as an excuse to avoid normal sexuality. The fact was that he was not a normal sexual animal.[82]

One look at the pages of *Mein Kampf* is enough to determine that. The book is filled with sexual imagery and "every chapter bespeaks a mind that is inordinately excited by rape, prostitution, syphilis, and the 'most disgusting' practices."[83] The man who could write of the "nightmare vision of the seduction of hundreds of thousands of girls by repulsive, crooked-legged Jew bastards"[84] was not just playing to the masses, but had a definite sexual problem.

One indication is Hitler's library of pornography and the blue movies made especially for his viewing. He also drew pictures which, according to a later associate, "only a perverted voyeur could have committed to paper."[85]

Hitler, the product of turn-of-the-century Vienna, could have made it into a later edition of Krafft-Ebing. Stories have abounded about his supposed homosexuality. There was the fact of his knowing immediately that the man who invited Kubizek and him to dinner one night in the spring of 1908 was a homosexual. This points, at the very least, to a knowledge of such practices by this monkish youth who was supposedly keeping away from worldly infection.[86] Early political associates such as SA leader Ernst Roehm and Rudolf Hess were both homosexuals. These were among the few people with whom Hitler ever used the familiar *du*. His very persecution of homosexuals in the Third Reich has been used by other biographers to suggest negative proof for his own latent homosexuality; a case of proving he is not really one of them by persecuting them.[87]

Evidence of Hitler's homosexuality is far from conclusive. Reports such as those of a German doctor, himself a homosexual, who X-rayed Hitler before the war, tend to discount the homosexual theories: "As a homosexual I was fascinated by Hitler's eyes, speech, and gait, but I could tell at once he was not one of us."[88]

Stories about Hitler's perversions are even more numerous.[89] The predominant belief is that Hitler suffered from "an extreme form of masochism in which the individual derives sexual gratification from the act of having a woman urinate or defecate on him."[90]

According to one account of Hitler's sex life with his niece Geli Raubal, the daughter of his half-sister Angela and her husband Leo, the masochism is clear: "Hitler made her undress. . . . He would lie down on the floor. Then she would have to squat over his face where he could examine her at close range and this made him very excited. When the excitement reached its peak, he demanded that she urinate on him and that gave him his sexual pleasure. Geli said the whole performance was extremely disgusting to her and . . . it gave her no gratification."[91]

Geli Raubal shot herself in Hitler's Munich apartment in 1931. Significantly also, six of the seven women whom it is fairly sure Hitler had intimate relations with either committed or seriously attempted suicide. Although at least one of these attempted suicides, that of Unity Mitford, was a political act, the statistics help to substantiate the idea that "Hitler had a sexual perversion particularly abhorrent to women."[92]

There is also the story of the German film star Renate Mueller, later related by her director, that she was invited to the Chancellery by Hitler to spend the night. After he first amused her with stories of Gestapo torture methods, they undressed and Hitler "lay on the floor . . . condemned himself as unworthy, heaped all kinds of accusations on his own head, and just groveled around in an agonizing manner. The scene became intolerable to her, and she finally had to accede to his wishes to kick him. This excited him greatly; he became more and more excited."[93]

Mueller committed suicide not long afterward.

Other indirect evidence of Hitler's perversions abounds: his continual use of the whip, a classic sadomasochistic symbol; his glee in telling scatological stories to his secretaries; and his obvious fecal interest in *Mein Kampf*.[94]

The fact that Hitler was also missing his left testicle may have added to his twisted sexual life.[95] Though monorchism does not in any way rule out a normal sexual life, it is highly possible that this was the reason for his sexual shyness as a youth and lack of normal sexual development later.

The deeper one looks into Hitler's private life, the murkier do things appear: his attraction to very young women—most were twenty years his junior;[96] his attraction for older women who could mother him.[97] Whether the victim of the severe form of masochism mentioned above or not, it is clear that Hitler was wounded in his sex like most of the rest of the Vienna of his youth.[98]

Hitler was supposedly listed in Vienna police records as a "sexual pervert."[99] If this were true, it could perhaps be as a result of his long stay at a men's hostel, some of which were known to be homosexual haunts.

Hitler's walk down the Spittelberggasse is, in this respect, more the act of a voyeur than one of outraged morality. The voyeuristic aspect of his blue movies and later pornographic library and Stuck paintings attests to this thesis.

If, as Kubizek states, Hitler had been a quite normal youth as regards his sexuality, he had certainly developed several aberrations by the time he came to power as the Führer. In this context it would appear that the pressure of wielding power, of maintaining authority, might have been too much of a strain on an already tightly wound psyche. Or it might be possible that the authoritarian personality has a predilection for such aberrations a priori, which is an avenue worthy of exploration in light of the underlying sexual menace of the Nazi state.

Hitler continued to live a chaste existence with Kubizek on Stumpergasse. Outwardly he eschewed the "sultry eroticism which held sway in Arthur Schnitzler's plays,"[100] while inwardly he was burning with unspoken passions.

At night, Hitler would often lecture "by the hour of depraved (sexual) customs."[101] Like Freud and much of the rest of Vienna then, Hitler was caught in a strange warp of sexuality.

Hitler's youthful behavior, outward saint and inward sinner, is a dramatic foreshadowing of the Nazi state itself: like Hitler and turn-of-the-century Vienna, the pristine, almost puritanical ethos the Nazis preached was in stark contrast to the sadistic, sexual overtones of its reality.

4

Political Awakening

(1)

HITLER swung his thin white legs out of bed.[1] He perhaps saw the rays of sun on the walls in front of their windows. It was half-past eight on a fine spring day.[2]

He lifted his mattress and pulled out his dark blue trousers. They were becoming shiny at the seat and baggy at the knees, but at least the crease was maintained by this nightly custom.

Hitler hopped on one thin leg as he put the other through one trouser leg, drew it up, and then repeated the clumsy process with the other leg.

Kubizek watched his friend's acrobatics, noticing for the first time how Hitler was becoming transformed in the big city. His hair was getting longer and bushier, and the wispy moustache was slowly growing into a downy beard at cheeks and chin. There was also a new quality of intensity in his eyes, as if he knew something no one else did, even when stumbling into his trousers in the morning. There was a certain eerie strength in those eyes, a hypnotic power, almost, that made Kubizek turn away from his friend at times, not wanting to establish eye contact.

The two shared the bottle of milk from the window ledge for breakfast. It was warm and half curdled. Their outdoor refrigerator was losing its chill as the year fell in a swoon toward the warmth of summer.

Today was to be a special day for the two—an outing. Hitler had talked his friend into forgoing his studies for one day. He had a surprise for Kubizek and had already procured tickets for it.

They strode down the Mariahilferstrasse like dandies once again now that winter had passed. Hitler gave a jaunty twirl to his ivory-tipped cane occasionally as they walked along. The day was glorious and warm; they had to squint their eyes to adjust them to the outdoor brightness after the dark of their little room.

Traffic was bustling down the main thoroughfare, horses clopping stolidly along, snorting and wheezing. The first sun parasols were out, shading delicate white faces. Shopgirls stood outside store windows, washing off endless flecks of dirt, sweeping down the sidewalk. The whole world seemed to be whistling a happy melody, glad to be alive, warm and cheery in the May sun.

Finally reaching the Ring, they crossed it, dodging the carriages and trams, and proceeded to the Heldenplatz. That square never ceased to impress Hitler. The broad sweep of it with the huge curve of the National Library on one side, the green of the Volksgarten on the other, excited his imagination that day as on other days. Across the broad Ring the square was crowned by two museums, the Art and Natural History Museums. Tough old Maria Theresa sat between the buildings, cold and determined, her ministers at her feet where they belonged. And past her, behind the museums, was yet another monumental building, the Royal Stables, which housed the emperor's 400 steeds, jet black or snow white.

Hitler dreamed of completing that magnificent square, just as had its architect Gottfried Semper, by throwing up another elegant, awesome curve of heavy stone buildings opposite the National Library. From there he would erect arches across the Ring to connect the museums and stables with the main buildings of the Hofburg, making it the most imperial of squares in all of Europe. But even in its unfinished state, the Heldenplatz presented one of the most magnificent urban landmarks in the world. Hitler often told Kubizek that it was the perfect place for mass demonstrations.[3]

Later that day, and every day at noon, the square would be transformed by the military pageantry of the changing of the guard. Crowds would gather along both sides of the roadway cutting through the square. Trumpets would blow and drums thump as the Hungarian bodyguard, established by Maria Theresa, rode by. They would sit tall and rigid on white horses, dressed in scarlet uniforms trimmed in silver, with sable capes thrown over their broad shoulders.

Little children along the route would clap their hands in delight at the spectacle. Old soldiers would tip their bowlers to this elite guard.

Above, from the window of his office in the Hofburg, the grand old man himself, Emperor Franz Joseph, looked down on the changing of the guard every day. Sixty years at the helm, his eyes rheumy with age, he would breathe deeply and go back to his bureaucratic work reinvigorated. That visible symbol of his realm gave him new energy, new hope.

From the Heldenplatz, Hitler led Kubizek through the budding and flowering Volksgarten; past strutting, cooing pigeons, by nannies strolling behind ornate perambulators and an old drunk spitting out a screechy melody on a harmonica, to the white, Neoclassic columns of the Parliament.

Kubizek was surprised. He had imagined their destination to be the National Library where Hitler would resume his attempts to explain the cataloguing system; or the Art History Museum where he would continue his lectures on Breughel or Rubens.

Instead they queued at the visitors' entrance to the Parliament and used the tickets Hitler had bought to go into the visitors' gallery. Kubizek had no idea his friend's interests had taken a political turn and was shushed as he began to ask questions of the impatient Hitler.

Once inside the semicircular assembly rooms, more suitable for a concert than for political discussion, Hitler began to explain the lay of the land.

"The man who sits up there"— Hitler pointed to a white-haired man sitting above the others—"looking rather helpless and who rings his bell every now and then, is the president. The worthies on the raised seats are the ministers; in front of them are the shorthand writers, the only people who do any work in this house.... On the opposite benches there should be seated all the deputies of the realm and provinces represented in the Austrian Parliament. But most of them are strolling around the lobbies."[4]

With that cynical introduction to the working of the Reichsrat, Kubizek and Hitler sat back and watched the performance of that curious body of men. Every once in a while, Hitler would fill in Kubizek on what was happening and what would be happening soon. Kubizek was again surprised at his friend's familiarity with the proceedings of the Reichsrat. Hitler had obviously spent a lot of time there already.

They had watched one deputy talking for quite a while, most of the other ministers buzzing around in the corridors. Suddenly the president rang his bell for debate. The other deputies and ministers flocked back into the chamber and began shouting the most terrible abuse at one another. If the members of the Reichsrat disagreed with someone speaking, they would slam the lids of their desks, whistle, or swear in Italian, Czech, Polish, and even sometimes German.

A Czech member finally got the floor and began filibustering in his native language. Few in the hall understood him and when Kubizek tried to take his departure, Hitler grabbed him.

"What? You're going in the middle of the sitting?"

"But I don't understand a word the man is saying," Kubizek complained.

"You don't have to understand it. This is filibustering! I've already explained it to you."

"So I can go then?"

"No!" Hitler cried furiously and pulled Kubizek back to the seat by his coattails.[5]

Years later Hitler would remember these visits to the Vienna Parliament in *Mein Kampf*:

> The intellectual content of what these men said was on a really depressing level, insofar as you could understand their babbling at all; for several of the gentlemen did not speak German, but their native Slavic languages or rather dialects. I know I had occasion to hear with my own ears what I had previously known only from reading the newspapers. A wild, gesticulating mass screaming all at once in every different key, presided over by a good-natured old uncle who was striving by the sweat of his brow to revive the dignity of the House by violently ringing his bell and alternating gentle reproofs with grave admonitions.
> I couldn't help laughing.[6]

Finally Hitler came out of his absorption in the parliamentary process enough to notice Kubizek's discomfort. They left. Outside the day was still warm but the sun was already deep in the west, sending long shadows of the trees across the Ring. Crowds of workers were bustling home from work.

Suddenly they noticed a workers' demonstration marching up the Ring past Parliament. The men in the demonstration were silent, dressed in rags, and with that look of hunger about the eyes that Hitler himself would all too soon wear. In the front, some carried a large banner with one word struck across it in blood-red letters: "HUNGER!"[7]

Hitler watched the scene in eager silence, taking it all in: the power of that one-word slogan; the dignity of the silent men; the terrible contrast between their need and the artificial pomp of the changing of the guard and the stupid, ineffectual waste of the Reichsrat.

The two walked home after the demonstration passed by. Hitler was suddenly fired with a new purpose, summed up by a slogan he would often repeat in the coming days: "the storm of revolution."[8]

Hitler began to speak of the little man and the "poor, betrayed masses"[9] as they walked up the Mariahilferstrasse to their own poor meal of stale bread and warm milk. The sight of those men had excited the young artist's imagination to thoughts of power, thoughts of the masses.

Hitler never knew that the workers' demonstration he had seen and which did so much to shape his later life had been merely a protest against the increase in the price of beer.[10]

(2)

"We often saw the old emperor when he rode in his carriage from Schönbrunn through the Mariahilferstrasse to the Hofburg," Kubizek tells us about Hitler and himself. "On such occasions Adolf did not make much ado about it, neither did he refer to it later, for he was not interested in the emperor . . . but only in the state which he represented, the Austro-Hungarian monarchy."[11]

The feeling was mutual on the emperor's part, certainly.

In his frugal office in the Hofburg, the next to the last Habsburg emperor was just finishing his work for the day as Hitler and Kubizek made their way home from the Parliament. He was probably putting his signature to yet one more insignificant act that should have been handled by a minor official. He sat at his big, flat-topped desk, kept as neat and empty as his mind, and periodically reached in back of the large, stand-up calendar for the feather whisk to brush off any ash or sand remaining after the ink had dried on his signature.

Franz Joseph, as the highest-ranking bureaucrat in Europe, had never learned the secret of delegating responsibility to his subordinates.

Distrustful of ministers and Hungarians alike, the emperor had built a mission for himself, just as the young and disgruntled Hitler who stood outside his window that morning was doing for himself. The emperor's mission was to uphold the status quo.

Franz Joseph was a tiger of conservatism, and his strongest weapon in that battle was the massive bureaucracy that Maria Theresa and her son Joseph II had built to administer their far-reaching realms. As king of the civil servants, a legend had grown up around Franz Joseph by 1908. Up by five in the morning, he was hard at work by six. He worked tirelessly all day long, eating simply, seeing all supplicants personally, signing paper after paper like some minor official in the Justice Ministry. Entertainments were few for the old man: he ate with the speed of a peasant so that many guests at Schönbrunn or the Hofburg went home hungry as the courses were taken unfinished from in front of them as soon as the wolfish emperor had finished his course.

Legends also abounded around the simple metal military bed on which the emperor slept (though with the best mattresses to be had in the empire) and of the numerous valets he went through like candles, literally burning them out all too quickly with his early mornings. Lamplighters along the Mariahilferstrasse putting out the gas lamps could set their watches with his early-morning trip into the Hofburg, so punctual was he.

He was in no way an intellectual, yet his dogged persistence kept the empire together for almost seventy years. Conservative down to his toes, it was not until 1908 that Franz Joseph took his first ride in one of the new horseless carriages, and then only at the instigation of Edward VII of England who was visiting at Bad Ischl. Edward talked the old man into a forty-minute excursion that reached speeds of thirty kilometers per hour.

One can imagine the thoughts going through the emperor's mind as he climbed into the machine, most likely for reasons of state, putting service to the realm before his own fear of death. Pictures of the time show his pale face and frightened eyes staring dumbly out of his ramrod-stiff body belying his standard *"Es war sehr schön. Es hat mir sehr gefreut"* that he probably muttered to the king of England.

Franz Joseph was an anachronism in the twentieth century: a king in the age of democracy; an imperialist in the era of nationalism.

Vienna had been the seat of the remarkable Habsburg family for more than 600 years by 1908. The Habsburgs had built the city from a tiny principality to the seat of an empire of 50 million people, including twelve nationalities: Germans, Ruthenes, Italians, Slovaks, Rumanians, Czechs, Poles, Magyars, Slovenes, Croats, Transylvanian Saxons, and Serbs. Vienna, despite what the Germans in the empire claimed, was no more German than Constantinople. More Croats lived in Vienna than in Zagreb; more Czechs than in Prague; and several times more Jews than in Jerusalem.[12]

From the earliest times, the Habsburgs had assumed the role of protector of the status quo. As a small outpost of the Holy Roman Empire in the east, Habsburg Vienna was charged with the duty of defending that empire from the persistent Ottoman Empire of the Turks. Twice Vienna turned the Turks away from the door to western Europe: once in the seventeenth century and again in the eighteenth.

With the Reformation, the Habsburg role was modified to the defense of Catholicism against the radical voices of religious change. Vienna was transformed in the Baroque Age into a Jesuit capital with Habsburg importations from Italy of that hard-headed branch of Catholicism.

By the nineteenth century, Austria's mission got another redefinition at the hands of Metternich, that grossly overrated statesman more adept at theorizing than at application.[13] He turned Vienna's fortress role to the use of conservative politics, making the city the bastion of European conservatism, protector of the royal status quo against the "dangerous" ideas spawned by the French Revolution.

By the time Franz Joseph came on the scene, the die had been cast and he did nothing to alter the antiliberal attitude adopted by his predecessors, the Habsburgs, and their ministers. Schooled in the violent uprisings of 1848, Franz Joseph held to his death a basic mistrust of liberal sentiments and of the masses. He was so busy trying to keep his realm the way it had been when he assumed the throne that he never found the time, will, or imagination to develop policies to enlarge life. He could only safeguard life further and further from "dangerous" tendencies such as democracy until the subject peoples, weary of their German overlords, began to turn inward and foment their own brand of revolutionary nationalism.

When the Hungarian magnates and nobility pressed the Ausgleich on Franz Joseph in 1867, creating a virtually independent Hungary, this only stiffened the emperor's resolve not to bow to any more demands from the rest of the diverse nationalities under his rule.

Perhaps the single most basic internal problem for Austria-Hungary from the mid-nineteenth century on was the transformation of a dynastic kingdom made up of little principalities into a modern political organization that could function in an industrial age demanding universal suffrage. Germany under Bismarck had done it, but Austria with its melting pot of nationalities most definitely was not another Germany.

The Hungarians were not the only ones with demands. The Czechs of Bohemia, too, had demands that were increasingly played out around the language issue. Language concessions were given to the Czechs in 1897 and that infuriated the Germans of the realm. All over Austria there were protests by the German population. Students in Vienna carried German flags and pictures of Bismarck, hailing Germany as their ancestral home and denying the right of a mere "dialect" like Czech to be elevated to the language of the civil service in Bohemia.

The Reichsrat, a concession that had been won from the Habsburgs in the 1848 revolution, met to discuss the Badeni Language Ordinance, as this 1897 bill was called. The Germans decided to filibuster so that the ordinance could not be voted on. The subsequent scene in Parliament, recorded by the American humorist Mark Twain who was visiting Vienna at the time, is not unlike Hitler's own description of the Parliament he watched ten years later.

The German deputies, armed with horns, cymbals, and drums, drowned out any Czech member who attempted to speak for the ordinance making Czech and German official languages of the Bohemian civil service.

Twain reported that there were "yells from the Left, counter yells from the Right, explosions of yells from all sides at once, and all the air sawed and pawed and clawed and cloven by a writhing confusion of gesturing arms and hands. . . . On high sat the president imploring order. . . . At intervals he grasped his bell and swung it up and down with vigor, adding its keen clamor to the storm weltering there below."[14]

Soon a riot broke out in Parliament itself between the deputies. Georg von Schönerer, leader of the German nationalist Pan-German party, from whom Hitler was to learn many lessons, took a pair of shears to the upholstery and had to be dragged bodily from the house by policemen. Riots broke out in front of Parliament, dispelled for the time by saber-wielding soldiers.

Not only did this language reform fail, but also Franz Joseph lost what little cynical faith he had in Parliament, and from that time on continued to fall back on Article 14 of the constitution which allowed for rule by decree in times of emergency. Parliament met sporadically and ineffectively from that time on.

Paradoxically enough, the emperor was a supporter of universal manhood suffrage which was finally instituted in 1907. Cynical to the last over the possibilities of a democratic government, Franz Joseph was shrewd enough to see that the middle and lower classes, once enfranchised, could be coopted to the cause of conservatism. Once they had something to lose, they could be used to hold in check the rebellious aristocracies of Hungary and Prague. The bloody revolt in Russia in 1905 was a chilling reminder to all kings of the power of the masses and only served to convince Franz Joseph that suffrage reform was long overdue.

Why not, thought Franz Joseph. Let them vote for a Parliament that can be disbanded at will, if it keeps them all in line.

Austria was by 1908 politically, as well as sexually, a schizoid mixture of liberalism and repression. Censorship was a way of life. There was little surprise when the morning papers appeared with a gaping white space where some story had been deleted for official reasons.

The closest the Habsburgs came to dealing with consolidation of the diverse nationalities in the realm was the bureaucracy which stretched the official German language throughout the empire. But this very bond of German language was being called into question with the minorities, as instanced in the Badeni ordinances in Bohemia. Resentment was growing against the arrogance of the German population in the empire. People were tired of the absurdities inherent in a system where, for example, Magyar army officers had to give commands to their Magyar troops in their 100-word German vocabulary.

The bureaucracy itself had, by the twentieth century, become a force of repression, taking on bizarre, Kafkaesque proportions. Kafka himself was a civil servant in Habsburg Prague at the time. This octopuslike bureaucracy was a grim reminder of a plan gone awry.

Hitler was no stranger to this bureaucracy. His father, the obedient customs official, had been the typical Austrian bureaucrat: dogged; not overly burdened with intelligence; eager for the day he would go into retirement and be able to gossip with his cronies all morning at the local inn. Adolf and his father had many go-rounds about the boy going into the customs service when he came of age. That young Adolf wanted to be an artist was the grossest form of insult to his father, Alois. Hitler was once taken to see the customs house, and bureaucrats "cooped up in cages"[15] only reinforced young Adolf's determination not to get caught in that life. He often "cursed the old-fashioned, fossilized bureaucracy"[16] to his friend Kubizek.

Another crucial problem facing Franz Joseph in his old age was that of a successor. Since his son Rudolf's suicide in 1889, only a few months before the birth of Hitler, this problem had been a thorn in his side.

Rudolf had been Franz Joseph's only son. There were two brothers of Franz Joseph who could have stepped into the heir-apparent role, but both had liabilities. Karl Ludwig was something of a religious fanatic and ultimately died from drinking contaminated water out of the River Jordan. Another younger brother, Ludwig Viktor, was the one who had problems with young boys and who inspired very little confidence in the Viennese.

Next in line was Franz Joseph's nephew, Franz Ferdinand. From a sickly youth for whom shooting constituted his only sport, Franz Ferdinand had turned into a tall and somewhat corpulent man who distressed liberal opinion by slaughtering game on his frequent hunts.

He could be incredibly petty. Much of his time in 1908, for example, was taken up with trying to evict tenants from a piece of land he wanted as a new hunting box, while he already had huge estates for just that purpose. He even engaged the prime minister in this battle.[17]

His comments about the art of the time, as witnessed by his criticism of Otto Wagner's Steinhof church, did not win him any friends in the artistic community. He also earned a reputation as a warmonger, having set up a second military chancellery in the Belvedere in 1906 and sponsoring and befriending the new and very bellicose chief of staff, Conrad von Hötzendorf. Von Hötzendorf was never accused of being a pacifist. He hounded Franz Joseph to let him declare a "defensive" war against Serbia and Italy.

As usual, the Vienna masquerade also obfuscated the real truth about Franz Ferdinand. In spite of his friendship with the chief of staff, he opposed war, especially one in the Balkans that might pit Russia against Austria. A royalist at heart, Franz Ferdinand wanted the royalty of Europe to pull together. He prided himself on the friendly relations he had tried to establish between Russia and Austria.

Though not politically astute—he suffered from the usual Habsburg provincialism and frankly distrusted England, France, Italy, and the Magyars in Hungary on principle—he did have his political opinions and strengths. Even as a young man he refused to take as gospel what his tutors fed him and was forever looking for the information they did not provide. He had his own solution for the nationalities problem in the empire. Along with other contemporary thinkers, he was in favor of creating a federal union of states on the United States or Swiss model that would stress economic dependency among the member states while at the same time affording some degree of political autonomy.

But again, this side of Franz Ferdinand was not seen by the Viennese. They saw only his pettiness; they saw only his arrogance, jumping out of the way of his fast car as he sped along the Ring.

As the historian Edward Crankshaw summed up the man: "He was essentially a torrent overflowing its too-constricted banks."[18] His uncle's inability to delegate authority extended unfortunately to this heir apparent. Just as with Rudolf, Franz Ferdinand, too, was denied any real participation in the running of the country. Franz Joseph, the "grand old man" as he saw himself, was still firmly in control, and no one else was going to put his hands on the reins until he was dead. This *"après moi le déluge"* philosophy of Franz Joseph could render any successor rather anxious and high-strung.

Franz Ferdinand had done nothing for his reputation, either, when he insisted on taking for a wife a member of the minor nobility who was not *"hoffähig"* and therefore most definitely not high enough in court standing for an archduke and heir apparent.

Sophie Chotek and Franz Ferdinand had carried on a secret relationship for years when in 1898 it became known that the two intended to marry.[19] Franz Ferdinand had not only his uncle to battle for this marriage, but also the entire structure of the court and aristocracy.

The court chamberlain, Prince Montenuovo, the man who had finally ended Mahler's reign at the Hof Opera when the profits decreased, was dead set against the marriage. Himself the result of a morganatic marriage, he was all ready to search out any sign of aristocratic infraction. This proposed marriage was grist for his snobbish mill. Enforcement of protocol was his one great passion. He was a small man with hawklike eyes and gray moustaches that one could imagine twitching like a hunting dog's nose at the first whiff of unaristocratic behavior.

The court at Vienna was heavily laden with holdovers from the days of the Spanish Habsburgs. Courtiers had to bow out backward from the presence of his Most Serene High Majesty so as not to present a repugnant rear end to his Most High's visage. At formal dinners, silver was laid in a maze to the right of the plate in the Spanish style.[20]

The Viennese loved their aristocracy. The members of the royal family were actually cheered in the streets as they drove by in their carriages. Martin Freud, son of Sigmund, wrote how his family were all "stout Royalists. . . . [At the Hofburg] we could tell with precision the extent of the passenger's importance by the color of the high wheels and the angle at which the magnificent coachman held his whip."[21] The number of horses a carriage had was another sign of rank in the aristocracy.

The aristocracy's home away from home was the Sacher Hotel, with Anna Sacher, widow of the founder, in attendance, smoking her cigar and greeting each guest personally. The Sacher was the scene of more than one scandal, as when Franz Ferdinand's brother, Archduke Otto, appeared in his cap and sword—and nothing else—in the lobby and greeted astonished women.

The aristocracy was the traditional upholder of the status quo, the most reactionary element in society. They largely controlled what went on at the Hof theaters, even to the point of having plays and operas banned when they displeased one of the more sensitive princesses.

As early as 1878, Rudolf, in an anonymous pamphlet, had criticized this do-nothing aristocracy, but his was a voice in the wilderness. It was this layered class system that Franz Ferdinand's proposed marriage threatened to upset, and Prince Montenuovo and the rest of the court were having none of it.

Franz Ferdinand's stubbornness had prevailed and he won his Sophie in the end, but at the loss of passing the throne on to his child. Theirs was to be a morganatic marriage in which Sophie would not be raised to the future emperor's level. On June 28, 1900, Franz Ferdinand signed the document that would bar his descendant from the throne. Fourteen years later to the very hour, he and his wife would take a fateful ride through the streets of Sarajevo.

(3)

Hitler would often sit at his favorite bench in front of Schönbrunn. It was a stone bench with a stone table in front of it just down from the Gloriette; it would be covered with his papers, drawings, and books like the little table in the Stumpergasse room.[22] Shade trees swayed above in a light breeze, shifting the areas of sun and shade on the ground in front of him like a kaleidoscope. Two little sparrows would hop tentatively toward his worn shoes, looking for bread crumbs.

They had the wrong person.

Hitler would read the papers under this bower of trees, flipping through the pages to find stories that interested him. He would often come across the court news in the *Neue Freie Presse* and such reports never failed to anger him. All this artificial pomp and circumstance. It bothered him enough so that he remembered it years later in *Mein Kampf*:

> What repelled me was the way the press curried favor with the court. There was scarcely any event at the Hofburg which was not imparted to the readers either with raptures of enthusiasm or plaintive emotion, and all this to-do, particularly when it dealt with the "wisest monarch" of all time, almost reminded me of the mating cry of the mountain cock.[23]

Hitler turned back to the front page, scanned the articles for any good news, "good" in this case being bad news for the Habsburgs, whom Hitler hated as degraders of the Germanic element in the empire.

Hitler "welcomed every development which . . . would inevitably lead to the collapse of this impossible state which" he said, "condemned ten million Germans to death. The more the linguistic Babel corroded and disorganized Parliament, the closer drew the inevitable hour of the disintegration of the Babylonian Empire . . ."[24]

Hitler, the little man caught in the urban trap and fearing and loathing any uncomfortable variety which that urban scene provided, "was repelled by the conglomeration of races which the capital showed." For him, Vienna was "the embodiment of racial desecration."[25]

Hitler found many things to complain about with the Viennese, too. He "hated the subservience and dumb indifference of the Viennese, their eternal muddling through, their reckless improvidence. . . . How sarcastic he was about the Viennese partiality to wine, and how he despised them for it,"[26] Kubizek wrote.

Once Kubizek had managed to drag his overly serious young friend out to the Prater amusement park. But Hitler would not join in any of the fun and refused to try any of the rides, even the new giant ferris wheel which would spin him high above the city. Hitler could only look in disbelief at people "laughing uproariously"[27] at some sideshow, unable to understand their gaiety or humor. Hitler, the humorless critic of Babylon, was barred by his own arrogance from such easy human delights.

The Prater for him was like a "Viennese Babel,"[28] accentuating that mixture of tongues for which he despised Vienna.

For the xenophobic Hitler, the amalgam of accents and languages he heard on the streets of Vienna was a sign of an "incestuous"[29] realm. The sooner it died, the better for the Germans in the empire who then could join their cousins in Germany. Any internal or external crisis that might hasten the collapse of the Habsburg Empire was for Hitler a joyous thing.

Slowly, very slowly at first, Hitler began to put together the rudiments of a political philosophy that might see him through the hard times of rejection in Vienna. "Adolf, homeless, rejected by the Academy, without any chance of changing his miserable position, developed during this period an ever-growing sense of rebellion,"[30] Kubizek noted.

More and more now at night, instead of tinkering with various artistic notions, Hitler lectured Kubizek on the ways of power and the "Reich of all the Germans"[31] that must come into existence to save the Germans of Austria. Hitler would "stride up and down, holding forth"[32] as Kubizek lay in bed trying to get some sleep. He would rant and rave at the dozing Kubizek as though Gustl were some sort of political personality who could decide the existence or nonexistence of the German people, instead of a poor music student with tests approaching. "Hysterically he described the sufferings of this people (Germans in the empire), that fate that threatened it, and its future full of danger. He was near tears."[33]

Just as Hitler's ideas about architecture had begun to take a social turn in these early months of 1908, so did his love of music become funneled into political spheres. "Even purely artistic experience," Kubizek remembered, "like listening to a concert . . . became problems of universal concern . . . in the Ideal State."[34] Art must go to the people, not just to those lucky enough to live in a capital. The "Mobile Reich's Orchestra"[35] would bring music to the people. Friend Kubizek, if he played his cards right, Hitler hinted, might be entrusted with conducting the traveling orchestra.

Soon listed in a little notebook Hitler carried in his pocket for that purpose were the names of composers, mostly German, who would fit into the orchestra's program. "It was the highest praise a work could earn if he [Hitler] said 'This will be included in our program.'"[36]

With all these plans abrewing and all his abstract hate for the Habsburgs, there is one concrete piece of evidence of Hitler's real intentions toward the Austrian state (or perhaps of his own irresponsibility). The previous April, when Kubizek had received his papers to report for a physical examination for conscription, Hitler had gone into a fury and advised his friend to cross the border into Germany to avoid the draft if the doctors found him fit for military service. Hitler complained that the moribund Habsburg Empire did not deserve one soldier to fight for it.[37]

Hitler himself, all during his years in Vienna, failed to register for the draft, and was liable anytime after April 1909 for a stiff fine if found out.

Kubizek asked others for advice and managed to get into the reserves. In a letter to the "reservist" when Kubizek was away for his military examination in Linz, Hitler reverted to a humorous mood—forced humor at that—to patch things up again. In reply to a letter from Kubizek, which said he was bringing his viola back with him and that he was having trouble with his eyes, Hitler joked in his usual scrawl that "I shall buy two crowns' worth of paste, for my ears naturally. That—on top of this—you are going blind affects me very deeply; you will play the wrong notes more than ever. Then you will become blind and I gradually deaf. Oh dear!"[38]

This letter was written on April 20, 1908. It was Hitler's nineteenth birthday. He made no mention of it in the letter.

Hitler's visits to the little bench tucked away in the trees at Schönbrunn became a permanent part of his routine that spring and summer. But once Kubizek was back from Linz and Hitler introduced him to the wonders of the Parliament, he talked Hitler into going farther afield into nature. They were becoming too citified, almost forgetting what fresh air smelled like and what earth felt like underfoot.

The first Sunday outing Kubizek dragged Hitler on was the typical Viennese pilgrimage to the top of the Hermannskogel, a hill overlooking the city.[39] Like the other good bourgeois trudging up the hill, Hitler and Kubizek wore their city clothes and shoes as if they were strolling along a city street.

Other excursions took them farther afield: through the Vienna Woods to the west of the city; on a glorious steamer trip down the Wachau with all of May bursting out in glorious colors and fragrances from the banks of the Danube. On one excursion they took the train south to Semmering, royal and middle-class resort for generations, where Alma Mahler would later build a house. There the two decided to climb a mountain. They had never climbed one before, but Hitler suddenly thought this would be the perfect time to conquer the Rax, a high mountain in the Semmering range—with inadequate shoes, no rain gear, and no food or knowledge of mountaineering.

The two set off in the sunshine, but as is common in the high mountains, a thunderstorm came upon them before they could find shelter, drenching them on their way back down.

As they ran down the mountainside, their thin trousers fluttered around their legs. They finally stumbled onto a small hay barn where they could dry out and spend the night. They wrapped hay and canvas bags they found there around themselves and shivered to sleep.

The next morning dawned bright and clear, the air spanking clean after the rain.

"I still remember," Kubizek wrote about the incident, "what a job it was to get Adolf to wake up. When he was finally roused, he worked his feet free of their wrappings and, with the canvas wrapped around him, walked to the door and looked at the weather. His slim, straight figure, with the white cloth thrown toga-wise across the shoulders, looked like that of an Indian ascetic."[40]

For all his political rantings and ravings, his artistic experimenting, his excursions, Hitler forgot one thing. He was living in Vienna on a dwindling income. The only fixed part he had was the 25 crown monthly orphan's pension. He would receive that only until age twenty-four. His inheritance from his mother and father was being eaten up by these country excursions and regular visits to the Opera. The inheritance was dwindling at a rate of about sixty crowns per month.[41]

For some people, the prospect of one or two years' grace from earning a living can be a wonderful thing—a liberating, expanding experience. But for someone like Hitler, who had never earned a living before, the surprise he must have felt when he finally discovered the money slipping away must have been ultimately frightening.

Kubizek, who himself had been bringing in extra money tutoring other students in music harmony, tried several times to get Hitler to take some kind of part-time work. Perhaps illustrations for the newspapers. That was "best left for the photographers," Hitler argued in turn.[42] Then how about work as a music critic? Why should Kubizek be the "only inhabitant of Vienna to hear his opinions?"[43] But with this suggestion, too, Hitler found fault: he could not be objective with Italian and French operas. Wagner was for him the beginning and end of opera, and he would not hide his bias for any newspaper.

Finally Kubizek did get Hitler to try by submitting a short story, entitled "The Next Morning," to the *Wiener Tagblatt*. Kubizek knew a fellow music student who worked there and would try to pull strings for Hitler's story. But once at the office of the paper, Hitler took one look at the friend and then raced down the stairs cursing at Kubizek: "You idiot! Didn't you see he was a Jew?"[44]

Kubizek reports that Hitler lived a spartan existence in 1908, aside from going to the Opera. A day in Hitler's culinary life at this time is not to be envied. A bottle of milk, a loaf of bread, and a chunk of butter was the day's fare. At lunch this menu might be absurdly enhanced by a poppyseed cake or nut cake to satisfy Hitler's sweet tooth.[45] Thus Hitler, though not enrolled at any university, fell into the same easy, rotten nutritional program that almost every university student, away from mother's cooking for the first time, does.

Every two weeks the friends feasted when Kubizek's mother sent one of her wonderful packages. Sometimes Kubizek could convince Hitler, the outraged bourgeois, to join him at the student canteen where students of all nationalities and religions would gather to take their meals. The temptation of nut cake often got the better of his prejudices, and he turned his back on the Jews and Galicians as he greedily wolfed down a sweet or two. Then afterward, stricken by shame or laziness or perhaps poverty, he would revert for days to a diet of milk, bread, and butter.[46]

Hitler during these months developed all the stratagems of economic corner-cutting common to the poor student or artist. As we have already seen, he folded his slacks neatly at night and tucked them under his mattress to give them a good crease. At this period Hitler still tried to keep up his appearance. He "was almost pathologically sensitive about anything concerning the body. At all costs he would keep his linen and clothing clean."[47] He also frequently went to the warming rooms throughout the city where a hot bowl of soup could be had for next to nothing. Walking instead of riding public transport was another way to save money. He often complained to Kubizek of the "dog's life"[48] he was leading, yet Hitler had enough money in this early phase to live adequately had he attended fewer operas.

May gave way to June, a bright and clear month. Hitler continued his hit-and-miss life-style. Undoubtedly Hitler and Kubizek were on hand that month to see the pompous *Festzug*[49]—the parade around the Ring celebrating the Diamond Jubilee of Franz Joseph's rule. In a tradition started by Makart, one of Hitler's artistic idols, scenes from Habsburg history were depicted in floral floats.[50] There were dozens of floral and dramatic scenes involving more than 12,000 men with hundreds of horses passing in a gaudy, three-hour parade in front of the seventy-eight-year-old emperor. Franz Joseph stood tall and erect as all these scenes passed by his reviewing stand.

Most probably also Hitler paid no attention to the opening of the *Kunstschau* of 1908 held in temporary quarters on a piece of land near the Stadtpark, later to be the site of the Konzerthaus. In this show Klimt and his followers were making a comeback to the Viennese art scene. Klimt's famous painting *The Kiss* was first exhibited then.[51]

Hitler's life changed significantly that July when his friend Kubizek left Vienna for the summer to return to his parents in Linz. The two made plans to keep the room on Stumpergasse over the summer. Kubizek agreed to pay his half of the rent while absent. He had passed his tests for the year with flying colors and was confident of success the following year. Perhaps he could even get a job as violinist and help pay more than half the rent to help out Hitler. The parting between the friends was short and emotional. Hitler saw Kubizek off at the Westbahnhof and grasped both of Kubizek's hands, pressed them, and turned quickly and walked out of the station without looking back.

Hitler was now alone in the big city. Even Frau Zakreys was missing to pester him in the mornings, off for her vacation to some relatives in Bohemia. Hitler wrote Kubizek that he "caught an army of bugs which were soon swimming in my blood, and now my teeth are chattering with the 'heat.'"[52] Again there is the feeble attempt at humor. Kubizek reported that Hitler used to gather the bugs he killed in their infested room and place them on the end of a straight pin to prove his night's hunt.[53]

July and August were wet, miserable months. Hitler caught a "sharp attack of bronchial catarrh"[54] from the cold spell. He kept up with his desultory studies through the summer, for he wrote Kubizek later in July to request a guide booklet to Linz[55] to help with his project of rebuilding for that city. Obviously his hot and cold spells for art versus politics were taking an artistic turn, for this old project had again assumed prominence in Hitler's thoughts. Other postcards with pictures of the Graben and the airship *Zeppelin*[56] contained pleasantries and ironies about the rain and his coming trip to the Waldviertel to join his family for a couple of weeks. Hitler complained that his sister Angela would be there, a prospect that he did not relish. "Shan't want to go at all if my sister is coming,"[57] he wrote Kubizek.

One bright spot in the near future was a planned visit to *Lohengrin* in the middle of July. Hitler's beloved Wagner would cheer him up.[58]

Vienna is a lonely place in the summer. Shops are closed, streets empty—the whole town, it seems, removes to the mountains or the coast for the *"Sommerfrische."* Such solitude makes one reflective. Hitler must have succumbed to this desolate feeling, for by late August, sister Angela or no, he had traveled out to Spital to enjoy the fresh air.

(4)

While the rest of Europe, including the heads of government, were hiking in the mountains and taking the waters at some exclusive spa, men were at work in Vienna trying to reestablish some of Austria's lost prestige and stop the decline of the Habsburg state that Hitler was waiting for.

Two years before, in 1906, at the same time the warmongering Conrad von Hötzendorf had taken over as chief of staff, Count Aehrenthal had taken over at the Ballhausplatz as foreign minister. He was a career diplomat fresh from a successful administration of the Petersburg Embassy. Like Franz Ferdinand, Aehrenthal was devoted to a lasting understanding between Austria and Russia and a revival of the old Three Emperors' League of Habsburgs, Romanovs, and Hohenzollerns.

As a member of an old aristocratic family, he had definite diplomatic gifts. But he was no Bismarck.

The diplomat-historian Sir Harold Nicolson describes the man as "unwieldy . . . with heavy, hapless jaws, a stubble head of hair, and sad turbot eyes."[59] He was a clever man, though his cleverness was most definitely not under control as was Bismarck's. Aehrenthal was a vain man who wanted his achievements to shine. He was also convinced that Austria's destiny lay in the southeast of Europe, even at the expense of good relations with Russia.

It was to prove a fatal combination.

Internal relations were only half of the wasplike problems besetting Franz Joseph in his old age. There was also Austria's position, or more properly nonposition, in the world to be considered.

Austria had been so busy in the nineteenth century making the world safe for imperial rule that it had missed the feast of colonialism in which the rest of Europe had been partaking. Its worldwide reputation suffered for it.

Mutual imperial aspirations were sure to cause conflict between the Great Powers. Austria, struggling with its own internal problems, had watched crises come and go. Racing against time and each other for trade concessions, the Great Powers stepped on each others' feet more than once. France and England clashed in Africa, in the Sudan; later, Germany and France had two confrontations at Algeciras and Agadir, with Germany demanding concessions in Morocco.

Europe in the generation before World War I was a continent bristling with crises. Politically it was a powder keg looking for a fuse. Perhaps the biggest powder keg of all lay in lands that a visitor from outer space would never believe anyone could argue over, let alone go to war about.

Rugged and rocky, its major exports being corn, pigs, and plums, the Balkans were the most dangerous political area of them all at the turn of the century. All the Great Powers collided there. There was Russia, which wanted to win the Turkish Straits for an entrance to the eastern Mediterranean, as well as having the messianic mission of uniting all its fellow Slav states in one huge Pan-Slav union. France wanted to preserve its long-standing cultural and economic investments, while England was mainly concerned with keeping other countries away from the eastern Mediterranean, the chief link to Britain's colonies in India.

For Austria, any developments in the Balkans were felt as if they were happening next door, which in fact they were. An empire that contained all races including Slavs, Austria could not tolerate such divisive forces as Pan-Slavism operating so near. Besides, it had expansionist dreams of its own for the southeast.

The Balkans had been in a shambles since 1878 when various Balkan groups had won independence from the dying Ottoman Empire. Serbia, Rumania, and Bulgaria had broken with Turkey through hard-won battles. The Great Powers stepped in at the last minute, however, afraid that Russia might gain too much by these rebellions. At the Congress of Berlin, they had highhandedly given Austria the provinces of Bosnia-Herzegovina to "administer." This interference by the European powers had further disintegrated cordial relations with the Balkans. The Turks were anxious to win back their lost territories; Austria wanted desperately to hold on to any foothold in the Balkan peninsula; and Russia wanted to increase its power there under the guise of sponsorship of Pan-Slavism. Tensions grew and animosities spread.

Austria had held an admirable stewardship over Bosnia-Herzegovina for thirty years. Roads had been built, schools started, railways stretched across the country. The Austrian bureaucracy ruled the country well and as fairly as an unwieldy bureaucracy could rule. The crime rate in these provinces was the lowest in the Balkans.

But the population, primarily Serb with some Croats and Turks, had no use for Austrian rule. They were tired of paying taxes to Vienna; of having their sons taken away for a foreign army. They were close to the land, traditional peoples with their own customs. Pan-Slavism, an import from neighboring Serbia, was a hot issue in the capital of Sarajevo. Students there fanned the flames of a Pan-Slavic union with Serbia. If any outside country was looked on as a protector, it was Russia, the Slavic homeland. Austria could take its roads and schools; Bosnia-Herzegovina could get along quite well without them.

Into this complicated web of emotions and conflicting interests stepped Aehrenthal as Austria's new foreign minister. What von Hötzendorf had wanted to do with his defensive war against the Serbs, Aehrenthal was convinced he could do with high-power diplomacy, à la Bismarck. Aehrenthal's bold plan was simply to annex Bosnia-Herzegovina, Austria's protectorate.

There were many reasons for such a forward action. First was Aehrenthal's own ambition. Then came the situation in the Balkans by 1908. An annexation would give Austria a permanent foothold in the

Balkans and enable Vienna to wipe out the cancer of Pan-Slavism before it spread to the empire. The Young Turks had just staged a revolt and had thrown out the corrupt old Ottoman Pasha and were instituting parliamentary reforms. Aehrenthal was afraid that this new Turkish government would ask for its former possessions back.

In an age of militarism and international crises, Austria was considered a weakling. Bismarck, in his memoirs published after his death, had warned Germany of its Austrian alliance: "It is vain to ally oneself with a corpse,"[60] he had written. What Austria needed for its own sense of worth, and to impress the rest of the world of its renewed stature and firmness of purpose, was just such a reckless show of strength as annexation.

But Aehrenthal could not just take the provinces: war was sure to follow such a move. The foreign minister looked at the international situation and figured that Russia would be the one power to give Austria trouble over such a move. He sought out his counterpart in St. Petersburg, Alexander Izvolsky, who had delusions of grandeur equal to Aehrenthal's. The Russians wanted access to the Turkish Straits. They had desired that for decades. In private meetings held in Moravia in September of 1908, the two foreign ministers concluded an unwritten agreement that was a terrible example of the sort of cynical statesmanship that would lead directly to World War I. In return for Russia's noninvolvement in the forthcoming annexation, Austria would support Russia's "freedom of movement" in the Straits. Though no record was kept of the agreement, this was the crux of the bargain.

Franz Joseph signed the annexation edict on October 6, 1908. The official reason given for this betrayal of the provinces was that in order to raise the population to a higher level of political life, it was necessary for Austria to have a clear and unambiguous juridical position. It was all for the good of the common folk. But public opinion saw it differently. It looked like war. Turkey closed off its borders to Austrian imports and mobilized its army. Serbia cried for war. England, France, and Russia called for a European conference.

At home in St. Petersburg it was felt that Izvolsky had greatly overstepped his authority and had been tricked at that. When the explanations started coming from both foreign ministers, it appeared that Aehrenthal and Izvolsky had agreed to two different things. For Aehrenthal, freedom of the Straits meant freedom both ways. Russian warships could move out of the Black Sea and foreign ships would be free to enter. He had duped Izvolsky, and the Russian minister denied everything when he saw the way the cards were laid. Yet Russia did not mobilize.

In Vienna, Conrad von Hötzendorf beleaguered the emperor for war. Franz Ferdinand, that so-called warmonger, wrote the emperor on October 7 to "put the leash on Conrad . . . he should give up this warmongering."[61] For Franz Ferdinand, a war on two fronts—and that is what it would have been with Russia forced to take up arms for the Balkans in case of Austrian military involvement there—would be suicidal.

For a time it looked as though war could not be avoided. But the crisis passed. Turkey was appeased with a few million crowns. Even Serbia, backed up in its criticism but alone in its desire for war, recognized the annexation the following spring.

The whole affair was a disaster from start to finish. The only good Austria achieved by Aehrenthal's power play was the foothold in the Balkans. But at what a cost: England grew more suspicious of Germany, which had unwillingly backed up its ally Austria in the matter. France, England, and Russia were pushed closer together by this unabashed aggression. Rather than gaining in international esteem, Austria earned the reputation from this annexation as the old bully of Europe. The mutton-chopped emperor became the saber rattler. With the advent of further Balkan crises, this international prejudice would work against Austria more than all the Pan-Slavism of Serbia.

(5)

During all these political machinations, Hitler had been trying to enjoy the countryside around the village of Spital. He undoubtedly had fine memories of the previous summers he had spent out there in the countryside, playing with his cousins in the fields and woods.

This year, however, things were different. Even his hunchback Aunt Johanna, whose favorite he was, had sided with the voices of reason aligned against him. Angela and her husband, Leo, were adamant that he give up his nonsensical life in Vienna and take up something practical. After all, he needed to earn a living like all the rest of them, didn't he?

Another new defector to the enemy camp was Hitler's little sister Paula, who, under the influence of her half-sister Angela, had also taken up the banner of respectability. She now thought he should find some lucrative position, too, and thus the whole family was in league to settle him down. The twelve-year-old sister was beginning to think for herself more and more and refusing to take as gospel everything older brother Adolf said, as she had formerly. He had sent her a copy of *Don Quixote* from Vienna and had devised a reading list for her, but she was having none of it.[62]

The family argued days on end over the matter of Adolf's future and ended by spoiling "each other's pleasure of living together."[63]

Hitler left the bosom of the family that September, at about the same time Aehrenthal and Izvolsky were holding their secret talks. The "last attempt to persuade him to take up the career of an official was in vain."[64]

This time, when Hitler set off for Vienna, for the fourth time, he was definitely setting off for a new life. He was firm in his intent to cut off relations with his burdensome family.

The coming of autumn meant another attempt at entering the Academy. For all of Hitler's political awakening of the spring and summer, he still harbored dreams of an artistic future. He carried his portfolio to the Schillerplatz again, this year more confident than before of success because of the added help of his supposed lessons from Panholzer.[65]

This year, however, Hitler did not get even as far as he had in 1907. Two sketches exist from his test drawings in 1908.[66] The sketches are rather uninspired renditions of villas, not unlike the one he drew for his friend Kubizek back in his Linz days. Again, it is made apparent, through line and attention to detail, that Hitler had a good architectural hand, but these drawings have none of the inspired quality of the four from the year before. The sketches are static and lifeless; the style of architecture, with peaked roofs and turrets, is in the trite manner of the day.

Perhaps Hitler was overconfident for this first part of the test. He most likely felt that because he had passed the first part of the test the previous year, it would be easy to pass it again in 1908. He was relying on the portfolio of work he had prepared during the year to see him through.

The shock must have been as great or greater than the year before when Hitler read on the lists:

> The following gentlemen performed their test drawings with insufficient success or were not permitted to the test . . . No. 24, Adolf Hitler, Braunau am Inn, 20 April, 1889, German, Catholic, father senior official. 4 classes Realschule . . ."[67]

Hitler was not even allowed to show his precious portfolio this year. This must have been a blow he could not shrug off. Twice in a row the Academy had looked at him and found him wanting for their purposes.

It is doubtful that Hitler had much time to sit alone in his lonely room on the Stumpergasse and brood, though. At about the same time as he sat for the Academy entrance exam, Austria annexed Bosnia-Herzegovina and war clamor filled the pages of the newspapers. Surely Hitler was caught up in the war fervor. The Viennese were "torn between loyalty to the old emperor and anxiety about the threatening war."[68] With his old friend Kubizek not yet back from Linz, Hitler must have had a hard time controlling his rage against the Habsburgs. At that time Hitler was supposedly a "pronounced pacifist."[69] "Who wants war?" he had once queried Gustl. "Certainly not the little man—far from it. Wars are arranged by crowned and uncrowned rulers, who in turn are guided and driven by their armament industry."[70]

Hitler must have had to measure such idealistic wishes against his hopes for the collapse of the Habsburg state in that crisis. One wonders whether idealism—if Kubizek's account of his pacifism can be believed—or hatred of the Habsburgs won out and whether Hitler did not join those demanding war with Serbia. For Hitler, such a war would have been for the destruction of the Austrian Empire and not for Austria's glorification.

The crisis did soon pass without war, and Hitler must have learned a singular lesson through it all. That such a cynically blatant act of aggression as annexation could go unpunished by the Great Powers certainly impressed the young Hitler. Thirty years later as Führer he would do the same thing to Austria, annexing it in a swoop into the German Reich. It was the most ironic lesson Hitler learned from Vienna.

The time was drawing near for Kubizek's return. His friend did not know of Hitler's plans to try for admission to the Academy again; Hitler was most likely afraid that the same old story of jealousy would be repeated that year. The more successful Kubizek would become at the Conservatory, the more Hitler would hate him for it. There would be evil words; his friend would not say anything of his failure, but his looks would be worse than words.

Hitler knew he must make some changes in his life. The setbacks had shocked him out of his inertia. The second rejection had hit him hard. The break with his family, even his loyal aunt and younger sister, must have smarted. The money was running out. He needed cheaper lodgings if he were to economize.

This collection of forces was building up in Hitler to induce him to make a radical break with his present life in Vienna. In addition, politics was entering his life and thoughts, even more after the second rejection. Perhaps a change of address could aid a change of life direction.

For whatever reason or constellation of reasons, in the middle of November 1908, Hitler told Frau Zakreys that he was moving. He paid up his share of the rent and left the flat with no forwarding address by which Kubizek could find him. He found another room in the nearby Felberstrasse—still hanging onto his association with the only district he knew. The flat was number 16 of Felberstrasse 22. The room was brighter than that he had shared with Kubizek and having no grand piano, there were no obstructions to his incessant pacing.

He was starting a new life.

On November 18 he registered with the police. At the Stumpergasse address Hitler had registered as an "artist." Now at Felberstrasse he listed his occupation as "student."[71] The artist was suddenly dead. Hitler was looking for answers now. The isolated, misunderstood-genius self-image that had kept Hitler going through the first bruises in Vienna was losing ground. Now he needed a more obvious enemy—some definable societal ill to combat to forget his own dismal failure.

5

The Student

(1)

OUTSIDE the sky was dark in the early afternoon. It looked like a snow sky, but with the temperature hovering at freezing it was not quite cold enough in the city for snow. So the sky sat low and forbidding all day, doing nothing but making the world gloomy. The lights were on over the tables in the café, making it seem from the outside to any passerby quite cozy for all its lack of pretension.

Hitler, his lock of brown hair dangling onto his forehead, sat in the corner reading the newspapers in this "inexpensive people's cafe."[1] The décor was uninspired and the service left something to be desired—there were no "cloudbursts" of water glasses brought to the customers here to make them feel welcome as in the big cafés in town. But it was warm and snug and the *Milchrahmstrudel* was tasty enough for Hitler's sweet tooth.

Winter had set in for good now, and the cafés not only provided comfortable atmosphere, they provided reading material and allowed one to save on the expense of heating one's room. Hitler, by the winter of 1908, probably was finally coming to the realization that he must make some economies if he wanted to keep living in Vienna without working.

The adjustment from living with Kubizek to living alone must have been difficult at first. Friend Gustl provided Hitler with a sounding board for his ideas and a conspirator in his plans to change the world. It was different now. Things had a tendency to get bottled up inside. And he had so much to tell someone.

Though only living a few blocks apart, it seems strange that the two old friends never ran into one another. Hitler must have avoided the Auge Gottes Café[2] which the two used to frequent in the Stumpergasse days. But still, in the small quarter in which they lived, one would expect some accidental meeting.[3]

Life on the Felberstrasse must have been a strange period of limbo for Hitler. It is perhaps his most mysterious period in Vienna, for there are only two direct witnesses from this time. Hitler "made no friends in Vienna"[4] during the time he had lived with Kubizek. There is little reason to assume that the shy youth who was physically afraid of "contact with strangers"[5] had changed overnight with his move to the Felberstrasse. He was beginning to act and look more and more the role of an "eccentric"[6] by this time, with his hair growing longer and the beginnings of a beard to go with his filmy moustache.

Doubtless his clothes were showing the wear and tear of his spare life by this time, also. No amount of mattress-pressing could hide the telltale shiny seat that marked the beginnings of real poverty.

Hitler, once he left the Stumpergasse for Felberstrasse, had embarked on a new life as indicated by his registration form with the police. The student who Hitler now was spent the next year in far-flung studies and sifting around for facts to fit his new cosmology.

For years Hitler's reading habits had been haphazard. Kubizek mentioned that he read everything from Goethe to Ibsen.[7] He was, however, supposedly not much impressed by Ibsen.

As with his taste in art and music, so was Hitler's taste in literature and philosophy solidly nineteenth-century with a heavy bias for things German. The German classics were reportedly his favorites: Schiller, Stifter, and Lessing. He also was willing to go back farther in time to Homer and Dante, by whom he was "profoundly impressed."[8]

Hitler was also entranced, as late as his early Vienna period, by the Wild West works of that excellent faker, Karl May. May's books entertained and still entertain whole generations of German and Austrian schoolchildren with tales of cowboys and Indians. He wrote all his books without ever having visited the American West. In fact, he wrote several of these books while serving two prison terms for fraud between 1865 and 1874.[9]

Kubizek had once asked Hitler if he "intended to read the whole (National) Library through,"[10] so prodigious was his reading supposed to have been that first year in Vienna.

This legend of Hitler's copious reading was spread not only by Kubizek, but also by Hitler in his memoirs. There is, though, a legitimate question about how much Hitler really did read. Admittedly, he was a great fan of the "pamphlet"[11] literature available at the time. He also read the newspapers avidly. It strains credibility to believe that he really read through the number of books Kubizek mentions just in the four-month period they were together. It is also questionable that Hitler ever set foot inside the National Library.[12]

Whatever early reading Hitler did had been very diverse and without any real purpose. By the time he moved to the Felberstrasse he did have a focus for his reading: he would try to discover why the world had handed him his early defeats. Hitler was looking for real enemies to blame. His reading became purposeful and deliberate, both in brochures and in books.

In *Mein Kampf,* some sixteen years later, he was to tell about his art of reading. "I know people," Hitler wrote, "who 'read' enormously, book for book, letter for letter, yet whom I would not describe as 'well-read.' . . . They lack the art of sifting what is valuable for them in a book, from that which is without value. . . . For reading is no end in itself, but a means to an end."[13] For Hitler, a person who has really cultivated the art of reading will instantly discern, in a book, journal or pamphlet, what ought to be remembered because it fits one's own personal opinions.

Kubizek had noticed this trait in Hitler in the months they had spent on Stumpergasse. Hitler "absorbed with great fervor everything he could lay his hands on, but he took great care to keep at a safe distance anything that might put him to the test. . . . He was not interested in 'another opinion,' nor in any discussion of the book. . . . He was a seeker, certainly, but even in his books he found only what suited him."[14]

Increasingly Hitler, in his self-serving search, was focusing on one cause that suited him more than any other.

(2)

Decked out in slouch hat, flowing robes, and sandals, sometimes even in the middle of winter, he was the epitome of the bohemian artist.

His drooping moustaches lent a sad, ironic cast to his face. A contemporary visitor to Vienna reported that he was "one of the 'characters' in Vienna that are pointed out to the foreign visitor, even by unliterary residents, like the Stephansdom or the Burgtheater."[15]

Peter Altenberg was the literary *clochard* of Vienna, roaming from café to café all day long, seldom drawing a sober breath. He would turn up at cabarets as well as bordellos, forever recording the scene, forever preaching like an anachronistic prophet in horn-rimmed glasses that the only perversion was the loss of life's vital energies. This semibum, with his *carpe diem* philosophy, was tolerated by the police and loved by the whores. The tramps of Vienna were his collaborators; the parks and side streets of the capital his stage. He captured the smallest scenes of love and sweet sentiments in fragmentary, miniature sketches that come down to us like faded photographs of his city. Written in a light, aphoristic, impressionistic style, his vignettes defy translation, and Altenberg's name is all but lost beyond the German-speaking world and none too popular in even that world beyond Vienna.

But the importance of Altenberg to our story is as a bridge. It is all too possible that Altenberg, in his ceaseless roamings, might have stumbled across Adolf Hitler in his little workers' café in the Mariahilf. If he did, it would have been the only connection Hitler had to the literary world of Vienna in those years. Hitler never read the people who were entertaining the capital. "Rilke, Hofmannsthal . . . were names that never reached"[16] Hitler. "The mood which prompted the work of these poets was foreign"[17] to him.

That mood was a blend of *fin-de-siècle* symbolism mixed with Viennese "the-situation-is-desperate-but-not-serious" frivolity. This mood was brewed in the pleasant atmosphere of the Vienna coffeehouse along with the coffee.[18]

The literary group that met first at the Café Griensteidl on the Michaelerplatz, and later at the Café Central on the Herrengasse, was known as Jung Wien. It was a group formed around the patriarchal figure of Hermann Bahr, who was so vocal in defense of the Secessionists. Also in the group, besides Bahr and Altenberg, were Arthur Schnitzler, Richard Beer-Hofmann, and Hugo von Hofmannsthal, the boy wonder who had taken Vienna by storm with his tender, melancholy poetry while still a schoolboy of sixteen. By the time of Hitler's stay in Vienna, Rainer Maria Rilke, though not properly a part of Jung Wien, was afloat in the literary world with the 1905 publication of *Das Stundenbuch*. Franz Kafka in Prague was recording that part of the

Habsburg realm in writings that would unnerve the world for generations.

What had started as a literary group espousing art for art's sake had, by the turn of the century, moved away from its purely Impressionistic, sweet, and frail roots to something larger. Jung Wien left behind that aestheticism that had at first characterized their writings. Bahr forgot about plays that dealt with men who were pursued by the color of salmon they ate, and became the promoter of Secession style. Schnitzler as early as 1900 had explored the use of interior dialogue with his story "Leutnant Gustl," and with his 1908 novel *Der Weg ins Freie* explored the possibilities of Zionism. Critical of a movement he felt was too utopian, he declared that "the roads to freedom do not run through the lands out yonder, but rather through our inner selves." The man whom Freud called his double was becoming a different kind of depth psychologist, but one just as powerful as Freud. Hofmannsthal faced a drying-up of his early easy poetry and rejected his own art-for-art's-sake aestheticism to collaborate with Richard Strauss on such operas as *Rosenkavalier, Elektra, Arabella, Die Frau ohne Schatten,* and a revised *Everyman* that the Viennese director Max Reinhardt produced at the Salzburg Festival.

All this made no difference, however, to the young Hitler. No matter what new paths these men were paving by 1908, for Hitler the books and plays written after 1900 were, per se, decadent and unread, dirty, obscene, unclean—mere "symptoms of debility."[19] "This was a pestilence," Hitler thought, "a spiritual pestilence worse than the Black Death."[20] A good Aryan had no need to read these books to know how corrupt they were.

One need only look at the names of the so-called creators to see how horrible the words must be. Hitler was forming his great rationale for failure. He had begun to affix the blame for his lack of success. These poets and authors of Jung Wien all had to share that blame. The one thing most had in common was that they were Jews—even Hofmannsthal, who had come from an old family but one that had a Jewish grandparent hidden in the past.

Hitler, the conscious anti-Semite, was coming into being.

(3)

An American journalist in Vienna in 1900 observed: "After the Dreyfus case and the endless brawling of the French thereover, one does not expect to find a country in which anti-Semitism has reached a lower level than in France. Yet Austria is such a country."[21]

The writer cites examples from the restaurant keeper who gives the customer an anti-Semitic sheet along with the menu, to the politician who hangs a sign over his country estate: "Dogs and Jews Forbidden to Enter."[22]

City and national politics and politicians were not free from this observer's eye: "Keep quiet, you pig Jew! *(Ruhig, sau-Jude!)* is one of the mildest methods used to silence the liberal majority"[23] in the Vienna City Council meetings. And on May 8, 1900, the Reichsrat actually entertained the question of whether or not sexual intercourse between Christians and Jews should be punished under bestiality laws and if at Eastertime the Jews shouldn't be placed under some special surveillance so that they would not murder little children to use their blood in some black rites.[24]

As a reason for this particularly sick and rabid anti-Semitism in the Austrian capital, this same journalist had to admit that "in sober truth, the number of men of Jewish blood occupying positions in which intelligence is the chief requisite, is astounding, and has . . . wakened in the breast of the easygoing Viennese a fear that soon he will not only be outstripped, but pushed to the wall."[25]

The real question for centuries actually had been who was pushing whom to the wall. Long forbidden any other profession but trading and moneylending, the central European Jews by the nineteenth century had developed definitely urban skills. By the time that legal restraints were removed from Jewish migration in 1867, the educated and industrious Jews naturally flocked to the big cities. The Industrial Revolution was a boom time for these Jews. While the small farmer was facing slow death in the mechanized world, the urban Jews, for so long also forbidden the ownership of land, were making their way in the world. The name Rothschild was a symbol for all Jewish enterprise.[26]

Their influx was however creating problems in Vienna. A scant 2 percent of the population in 1857, the Jews in Vienna had grown to 8.6 percent by 1910.[27] Surely not all these Jews were the classic successful entrepreneur of the anti-Semitic imagination. In the sprawling Leopoldstadt, for example, a third of the generally poverty-stricken residents were Jewish. Out in the rough district of Brigittenau, 17 percent of the population was Jewish.[28]

Yet in general the Jews were perceived as a force in Vienna, inconsistent with their percentage of the population. More than a quarter of the enrollment of the university was Jewish in 1909.[29] They were strongest in the faculties of law and medicine, and though often despised by the German Viennese, the Jewish doctor was the first one called in for a serious sickness.

Jews were also strong in big business. The Stock Exchange was looked on by the average Viennese as being a Jewish Monte Carlo that played with the lives and savings of the little man. Most of the investors who had wanted to develop the Wienerwald in the latter half of the nineteenth century had been Jewish. The newspapers were often accused of "Jewish control." Many of the journalists in Vienna were Jewish.

The very renaissance that we are looking at in turn-of-the-century Vienna was largely Jewish. Freud, Mahler, Schoenberg, Kraus, Wittgenstein, Loos, Buber, Schnitzler, Hofmannsthal, Kafka, Herzl, Adler, Weininger, even the merry Lehár—they were all of Jewish origin or had once been of the Jewish faith and had renounced it to advance their careers, as Mahler had done.

Jewish assimilation had become a way of life by 1900. Converts and dropouts from the religion tried to become more German, but revived anti-Semitic attacks in these years brought such men as Freud, Martin Buber, and Kafka back to a stronger avowal of their Jewishness in the end.

Vienna was fertile ground for anti-Semitism. The city had the largest and most successful Jewish population of any German-speaking city. While all the old values were being broken down in the industrial age, the Jews, whose cultural values were fixed by generations of repression, were busy creating culture, amassing wealth. Sentiment for old Vienna made the Viennese feel threatened by the new century and the new world ahead. The Jews were a handy scapegoat for all the ills that beset the Viennese, from failure of the stock market to prostitution.

The mayor of Vienna until his death in 1910 was Karl Lueger, a modern demagogue who used anti-Semitism as a campaign weapon. The leader of the German nationalist Pan-German party was a rabid anti-Semite whose followers wore the effigy of a hanged Jew on their watch chains.

If the *Neue Freie Presse* was considered a Jewish-controlled newspaper, the anti-Semites had their spokesman in the barbaric *Deutsches Volksblatt,* banned at first from public sale. By the turn of the century the ban had been lifted on the paper and the daily circulation was up to 55,000.[30] It printed such "informed" articles as stories of Jewish lechers who were slapped by assaulted Christian girls; of Jewish madames who used their own daughters in their bordellos.[31] The heavy sexual emphasis was staple fare for Viennese anti-Semites.

The *Deutsches Volksblatt* was not alone in its anti-Semitic messages. To a lesser degree, mitigated only by its anti-Catholic stand, the Pan-German *Alldeutsches Tagblatt* and the Catholic paper *Das Vaterland* also "stimulated active anti-Semitism."[32] "That three newspapers, however varying the emphasis, could face the public as representatives of avowed prejudice, if not hatred, was but another symptom of a sick society."[33]

Out of this atmosphere of hate and oppression was created the seed of the idea of the Jewish state. Theodore Herzl, the leader who gave the Zionist movement its political force and goal, came to Vienna from Budapest when he was eighteen, the same age as Hitler at his arrival in the capital.

The Herzl family arrived in 1878. They were reform Jews—culturally they were Germans, and young Herzl was more Viennese than the Viennese, whoever they really were. For the Jews of Herzl's generation, the only escape from trade was into culture. This second generation of successful trading families was barred from the army, bureaucracy, and aristocracy, and thus their one alternative was aesthetic. Like many other Jews, Herzl was an ardent devotee of Wagner and something of an anti-Semite himself, as only a Jew wanting to leave behind his past for assimilation can be.[34]

Forever a dandy, the young Herzl became a fashionable writer for a season. In the year of Hitler's birth, he had a play at the Burgtheater. He became a journalist for the *Neue Freie Presse,* and as an indication of frivolous dandyism at that time, became a master at the art of writing the *Feuilleton,* or subjective essay, that occupied the bottom of the front page. Such an essay could range over all topics, from Parliament to opera news. By 1891 he had become the Paris correspondent for that Vienna newspaper. In Paris he came into contact with earlier Zionist tracts that confirmed for him that the Jew had no roots in Europe and did not belong there. During this period he covered the Dreyfus trial and became radicalized by the blatant prejudice at work in the so-called cradle of liberty.

Herzl toyed with various romantic notions to save the Jews: he would have all the Jews of the empire come to St. Stephans for a mass conversion; or he would fight a duel and become a martyr by pleading the case of Zionism (the very word was coined by another Viennese journalist) at his trial.

But in 1895 Herzl hit on a better idea. While watching a performance of Wagner's *Tannhäuser* he was suddenly struck with the white light of intuition. Wagner's nationalistic ideas had inspired him to dream of a Jewish state where Jews would not be mere guests, but where they would have roots. His *Der Judenstaat* is Herzl's dream set into words that changed the world. He set out simply that Europe should grant a Jewish stock company rule over a portion of some colonial territory at their disposal. He hoped that the Ottoman sultan would allow Jews to settle in Palestine, as a colony of Russian Jews had already been started there five years before.

From that time on until his untimely death of pneumonia in 1904, Herzl became the champion of Zionism. He continued working for the *Neue Freie Presse*[35] but also advanced the cause of Jews. He organized six world conferences of Jewry—to which members were advised to wear frock coats. Dandyism dies hard.

Though ridiculed by Jew and Gentile alike, who scoffed at the idea of urbanized Jews tilling the deserts of Palestine, by the time of his death he had influenced a whole generation of Jews. More than 10,000 Jews flocked from all over Europe to the funeral of the man whom they looked on as their fallen leader.

(4)

Perhaps it was the same day with which this chapter opened. Perhaps it was a few months later. In a Viennese winter the gray days flow together without distinction other than those man imposes. Christmas of 1908 gave way to New Year of 1909 and in its turn to *Fasching,* the Viennese carnival season of balls.

But for Hitler, in his room overlooking the train tracks and in his little coffeehouse, these divisions were lost.

He put down the *Deutsches Volksblatt* and looked out the window at the leaden sky.[36] Then he nodded to the *Fräulein* that he wanted to pay, counted out his money carefully, bundled into his baggy coat, and left. The streets had a greasy, wet feel underfoot, and the air was filled with coal fumes from heating stoves.

As Hitler walked along toward his room, he perhaps saw Fräulein

Rinke approaching from the other direction.[37] As they came closer to one another, Hitler most likely tipped his hat with his best Austrian manners, and went through the elaborate *"Küss die Hand"* courtesy with a flair that impressed the girl even years later. She lived not far away in the same district, in the Flachgasse, and passed Hitler's rooming house quite often and had "spoken with him a few times"[38] already. She felt Hitler had a "quiet and serious character"[39], very different from most of the young men she ran into.

Their relationship was most probably one merely of polite talk, as people who often pass in the street will take to nodding to one another after a time.

It is interesting that Hitler, the shy, retiring youth who stayed away from women, would strike up a conversation with a virtual stranger passing in the street, no matter how often they passed one another. Perhaps the young woman was some small link with humanity that Hitler needed now that there was no Kubizek to talk to. Maybe she was even another Stephanie for Hitler, only this time he was somewhat braver than he had been in Linz.

Whatever the relationship, it would be strong enough to carry over until the very end of Hitler's sojourn in Vienna in 1913.

The two parted company in the cold evening air, blowing vapor clouds of farewell. Hitler continued walking to his lonely room, a bit picked up now after sharing a few words with someone besides himself.

As he walked, the words from the third scene of the second act of Wagner's *Die Meistersinger* ran through his head:

> And still I don't succeed.
> I feel it and yet I cannot understand it;
> I can't retain it, nor forget it,
> And if I grasp it, I cannot measure it.[40]

These words had been a companion and a solace to Hitler now for several years. He had been fond of repeating them to Kubizek, to impress his friend with his own struggling-artist role. But now there was no Kubizek to impress or berate.

But there was still Wagner. The German composer was more than just a musician to Hitler—he was a way of life; a model; a prophet.[41]

Wagner influenced a whole generation of Germans and Jews alike. He had been Mahler's model as a young man; Herzl's inspiration.

Wagner's life had been repeated over and over by romantic youths in the late nineteenth century who rejected the middle-class ideal of safety and domestic security for artistic passion and risk.

Hitler was one of the legion of others who had followed Wagner's example: who had repudiated bourgeois values such as duty and order for the bohemian life. Hitler, the son of a customs clerk, was more than ready for some model that would help him express his rejection of the bureaucratic, bourgeois values of his stern father.

For Hitler, Wagner's life story eased the pain of his own failure. Was not Wagner, too, rejected at first? He had been a failure at school, just as Hitler had been. Paris had been Wagner's Vienna where the public had not understood or appreciated his creations. Wagner had held stubbornly on to his belief in himself, just as Hitler would. Hitler could excuse all his present loneliness, poverty, asocial behavior, by remembering that he was, deep down, an artist just like Wagner. The artist had to perform on the fringes of society, far from the sordid marketplace of ideas. To please the many is bad.

Hitler spoke of the debt he owed Wagner as his "forerunner"[42] and of Wagner's being the "greatest prophetic figure the German people has had."[43] He admired the political influence that the great composer had had "without really wishing to be political."[44]

Thomas Mann, too, noticed begrudgingly the similarities between Hitler and Wagner. Whether or not these are coincidental parallels or whether it was a matter of imitation on Hitler's part can never be known for sure, though it is certain that the artistic pose was an easy one to caricature. There is ultimate safety in that disguise—safety from outside sneers and from one's own nagging voice of doubt.

Hitler was helped along with his "philosophical" growth by Wagner also. Wagner, the rabid anti-Semite, had infected that same generation of German youth with a distrust of the Jew as the despoiler of what is fine and noble in the world. Even in an allegorical sense, once knowing Wagner's personal opinion on the subject of Jews, it was not difficult to see who were the noble, blond Siegfrieds and who were the lowly, sneaky, dark Hagens of the world.

Despite Kubizek's claim that Hitler was already an anti-Semite before coming to Vienna,[45] Hitler maintained in *Mein Kampf* that he learned his anti-Semitism in Vienna. "There were few Jews in Linz. . . . The fact that they had been persecuted on this account sometimes turned my distaste at unfavorable remarks about them into horror. . . .

Consequently the tone, particularly that of the Viennese anti-Semitic press, seemed to me unworthy of the cultural tradition of a great nation. I was oppressed by the memory of certain occurrences in the Middle Ages, which I should not have liked to see repeated."[46]

If Hitler did hold such humanitarian beliefs, they were soon lost in Vienna. Kubizek relates several incidents of the 1908 period that already show a deep-seated prejudice against Jews.[47] There was the incident of the writing job on the *Wiener Tagblatt,* where Hitler had only to see that Kubizek's connection on the paper was Jewish for him to storm out of the office. Another incident took place on the Mariahilferstrasse just outside the new department store, Gerngross. A Jewish beggar, called a *Handele* by the Viennese to designate this type of eastern European Jew who dressed in the traditional caftan and boots and sold small articles on the street, was arrested for begging. Hitler supposedly proudly stepped forward as a witness to the man's unlawful begging and reconfirmed his worst ideas about the Jews when a leather purse filled with 3,000 crowns was found under the man's caftan. This was "concluding evidence, according to Adolf, of the exploitation of Vienna by immigrant eastern Jews."[48]

Hitler even dragged his friend Kubizek to Brigittenau, where there was a preponderance of Jews in the poor population, to visit a wedding at a synagogue. Later, after Kubizek thought his friend was giving anti-Semitism a more considered judgment, Adolf burst into their room and announced that "today I joined the Anti-Semite Union and have put down your name as well!"[49]

The future Führer seems to have wasted no time either in hunting out the smuttiest of those papers he felt to be so unworthy of German culture. Not only was he, by his own admission,[50] a regular reader of the anti-Semitic *Deutsches Volksblatt,* but he also sank to purchasing the salacious pseudo-journal called *Ostara.*

On his way home from the coffeehouse, he often passed a local tobacco store two houses from his own. In the window he noticed the publication with headlines on its title page that caught his attention. "Are You Blond?" the headline demanded to know. "Then you are a culture creator and preserver of civilization. Are you blond? Then you are threatened by perils."[51]

This was just the sort of stuff that Hitler needed in his moments of despair to remind him why, though far from blond and of uncertain parentage and blood,[52] he was having such troubles getting a start in life. For a mere forty hellers he bought the brochure and took it home to read over his evening milk.[53]

Ostara, named after the Germanic goddess of spring, was the bizarre invention of one Adolf Josef Lanz, a man fifteen years Hitler's senior. He is perhaps as good an example as any of the dictum that a little education in the wrong hands is dangerous. What little education he received was gained when he was a monk for six years in Heiligenkreuz, near the hunting box of Mayerling where the Rudolf tragedy was played out.

By the time Hitler picked up the little magazine, Lanz was long defrocked and had upgraded his name to Lanz von Liebenfels, in an attempt to hide his humble origins in the suburb of Penzing, where Gustav Klimt had also been born.

Lanz had put together a flimsy anthropological knowledge with a taste for the occult and the erotic and had come up with his magic philosophy of the conflict of the blond, blue-eyed *Asings* or *Heldings* with the dwarfish and apelike creatures he called the *Aefflings* or *Schrättlings.*[54] Lanz later called Hitler one of his disciples. Others whom he named as semidisciples ranged from Lenin to Kitchener— who was, among other things, the inventor of the concentration camp. Lanz's mytho-historic system declared that man had degenerated from the heroic being he once was, literally made in God's image. Through interbreeding, that race had lost its magic organs, "electromagnetic-radiological" organs and powers that could, however, be recaptured by a strict regime of pure breeding of blond and blue-eyed with their like. Lanz promised to follow through with such a breeding program "to the hilt of the castration knife."[55]

He called for "the extirpation of the animal-man and the propagation of the higher man."[56] Genetic selection, sterilization, deportation to the "ape jungle,"[57] liquidations by forced labor—these were only some of his finer techniques for creating a master race.

The magazine was a calculated mixture, playing on the fears and anxieties of the lower middle class. Not only were these ape-men, clearly to be understood as Jews, in competition with the poor little man for jobs, but they were also destroying the entire race by sexual interbreeding. Lurid drawings of blond women caught in the embraces of dark, hairy men filled the quotient of morbid erotica that appealed to the Viennese. This superpotent ape-man drew the Aryan woman to him and despoiled her.

So heady was the Viennese air with this sexual anti-Semitism that Freud would draw the conclusion that the roots of anti-Semitism were to be found in castration fears on the part of Gentiles because of the Jewish practice of circumcision.

Lanz made his guidelines of racial purity lenient enough so that even if, like Hitler, you were not a perfect specimen of "Aryan" purity, there was a category of the "mixed type" on his scale that allowed membership into the great race war on the side of the strong, beautiful, and heroic.

This was just the sort of pap that Hitler and those at his level on the social scale would devour to make them feel better by knowing there was someone beneath them. The publishers and advertisers in Lanz's pamphlet also knew what kind of audience they were attracting. In one issue was a full-page ad for a new book that promised to help young people find their profession. "What Shall I Become?"[58] the ad questioned the eager reader. The rootless, the undecided, the unformed, the dregs of society, who were always looking for a hand up and fearing the inevitable drop down into the proletariat, were the sort of people to read Lanz's journal.

It is a fine index of Hitler's intellectual powers that he read this magazine faithfully, collected all the issues he could, and carried them with him for the next years from address to address just as a child might carry his comic book collection.[59]

One day in 1909, Lanz von Liebenfels answered a knock to find at his door an apparently poor youth, with a pale, modest-looking face. The young man had come, with great difficulty, to purchase the back issues of *Ostara* that he had missed at his local tobacco store. The young man looked so earnest and impoverished, Lanz later remembered,[60] that he gave him the missing copies and an extra crown to get home. Lanz later remembered that his magazine sold particularly well at this tobacco shop near the Westbahnhof.

It is one of the few personal accounts we have of Hitler's life in this period. After visiting Lanz, Hitler sank back into the world of obscurity for several months.

Lanz was not alone in his bizarre pseudophilosophy. He was merely more extreme than most. The intellectual atmosphere of Europe was alive with such race ideology by 1900, spawned by an oversimplification and extrapolation of Darwin's "survival of the fittest" to the social scale. Social Darwinism, as this new science became known, using the struggle for existence as its starting point, was taken up by the conservatives as a defense for the aristocracy.[61]

An outgrowth of this intellectual and social atmosphere were the race theories of Houston Stewart Chamberlain, the black-sheep son of an English admiral. Chamberlain had come to Vienna in 1889, the year of Hitler's birth, and lived there until the year we are dealing with now, 1909. Originally a student of plant physiology, he soon turned to a love of Richard Wagner's music and philosophy, writing two books on the composer.

Chamberlain was one of the first to turn the Social Darwinian approach to a rationale for Aryan, German supremacy. His most important work, *The Foundations of the Twentieth Century,* was basically an attempt to show history as the result of racial struggle.[62] He used the same old tired scapegoat arguments clothed in respectable-sounding intellectual argument.[63]

This rebellious Englishman ignored all information that would not fit into his cosmology—a device Hitler, too, had learned. He brought with him the English love of dog breeding and the love of *Gestalt,* borrowing the word from the Austrian philosopher Ehrenfels. He stressed the importance of breeding and race and became the intellectual champion of the Teutons and simultaneously a favorite of Kaiser Wilhelm of Germany and the darling of Cosima Wagner, Richard's widow.

It is doubtful that Hitler ever read Chamberlain in his Vienna days.[64] It is likely, though, that Hitler heard the Englishman's name, for in 1908 the fifty-three-year-old Chamberlain divorced his half-Jewish wife of three decades to marry Eva Wagner, the daughter of Richard Wagner. He moved to Bayreuth the following year. It is unlikely that, being the fanatical Wagnerian that he was, Hitler would have let such information slip by him. The two were not destined to meet until the autumn of 1923 in Bayreuth, not long before the Munich putsch. By this time Chamberlain was paralyzed and speechless as a result of accidental quicksilver poisoning and it could not have been much of an interview.[65]

In *Mein Kampf,* Hitler attempts to chronicle his growing anti-Semitism. He states that one day in the inner city he finally took his eyes off the fine buildings and saw "an apparition in a black caftan and black hair locks. Is this a Jew? was my first thought. . . . Is this a German? Wherever I went I began to see Jews."[66]

Hitler's hate supposedly grew quickly, within the space of a few paragraphs. His humanitarian feelings he first recorded are quickly left behind when he notices the Jews he saw "were no lovers of water, and, to your distress, you often knew it with your eyes closed. Later I often grew sick to my stomach from the smell of these caftan-wearers."[67]

From this initial physical repulsion, Hitler says that he soon learned of all the terrible occupations these people had—white-slavers and pimps. "If you cut even cautiously into such an abscess, you found, like a maggot in a rotting body, often dazzled by the sudden light—a kike!"[68] Suddenly Hitler's language turns to the gutter variety. There is the echo of Lanz about this line, and the foul, seething sickness at heart that attaches to the writer.

Hitler said that he started to realize that all the filth written in his Vienna days—none of which he deigned to read—was perpetrated by the Jews. They were the destroyers of culture. At the end of the section, like some old-time revivalist preacher, Hitler winds up his arguments by putting it all on the Lord: "By defending myself against the Jew, I am fighting for the work of the Lord."[69]

There is a pitifully righteous tone about that closing. A good job of salesmanship, Hitler seems to think. Toward the end of *Mein Kampf,* just in case the reader did not get the point, Hitler throws in a little erotica for good measure:

> These black parasites of nations systematically violate our inexperienced young blond girls and thereby destroy something that in this world cannot be replaced. The black-haired Jewish youth lies in wait for hours on end, satanically glaring at and spying on the unsuspicious girl whom he plans to seduce, adulterating her blood and removing her from the blood of her own people . . .[70]

And elsewhere he writes of the "nightmare vision of the seduction of hundreds of thousands of girls by repulsive, crooked-leg, Jew bastards."[71]

These quotes could have come from the illustrations of *Ostara* and show that the young Hitler had learned his lessons well from Lanz.[72]

We are right to feel a nagging doubt about this instant radicalization of the young "student" Hitler. It matters little now whether or not Hitler was, in his heart of hearts, truly anti-Semitic. The results are the same: European Jews were all but exterminated because of him. Yet Hitler's anti-Semitism seems so pat; so calculated in its sensationalism; so calculated to sell to the lower-middle class.

Hitler was aware of the necessity of giving the people one enemy—one clearly defined fiend to be fought for emotional reasons.[73] The socialists had the capitalist class for their enemy. Hitler's object of hate was the Jew. His respect for the anti-Semitic Lueger points to this exploitative use of anti-Semitism. Lueger declared that he would decide who was a Jew; after winning votes on an anti-Semitic ticket, he went ahead to have Jewish advisers. Lueger had seen the power of anti-Semitism for political purposes.

It was a good object lesson for Hitler.

Recent evidence concerning Hitler's responsibility for the "final solution," that horrible euphemism for the liquidation of the Jews, also points to the possibility that Hitler may have been a paper anti-Semite. It is possible that Hitler never gave a direct order for the extermination of the Jews and might even have been unaware, up to 1943, that his orders to the contrary had been ignored.[74]

Somehow the notion of Hitler only using anti-Semitism as a political trick is more monstrous than that of the hate-crazed Hitler trying to kill the Jews to prove to the world that his grandmother had not really had his father by a Jewish grandfather. It is a chilling thought that one man, without feeling it himself, could package hate and sell it to the masses like so many bars of soap. That this product, this false emotion, this sales gimmick could be responsible for the extermination of 6 million Jews (and millions more Gypsies, Slavs, and Communists) is almost too surreal to consider.[75]

Hitler only increases the mystery surrounding his true degree of personal anti-Semitism—or makes it finally crystal clear—by statements given in his political testament of April 29, 1945, one day before he and Eva Braun Hitler committed suicide in the Berlin bunker. His last public words at the end of this testament are: "Above all, I charge the leadership of the nation and their followers with the strict observance of the racial laws and with merciless resistance against the universal poisoners of all peoples, international Jewry."[76]

Imminent death usually destroys all attempts at dissimulation.

(5)

It had been a long, cold, lonely winter for Hitler. His painting had been neglected for a budding interest in things political. Pamphlets such as *Ostara* made up his theoretical reading list. "I studied," he reported in *Mein Kampf,* "and for the rest immersed myself in my own thoughts."[77] There were long afternoons at the local coffeehouse and long nights poring over his collection of Lanz's writings and also over his collection of the monthly installments of Karl May.

Hitler sank into the anonymity that was to create his "granite foundation,"[78] as he called the Vienna education.

Out of this anonymity has grown much speculative history. Some of this speculation takes an occult turn.

Turn-of-the-century Vienna, like all of Europe, was undergoing a rejuvenation of the mysterious. When Nietzsche declared that God was dead, he was like a coroner arriving decades late at the death bed. The Industrial Revolution had killed religion; Darwin buried it.[79]

The philosophers, as usual in the forefront of thought, were the first to react to the material age. Among the new philosophers were Schopenhauer with his "will," Nietzsche with his aristocratic creed of the "superman" who would express the will to power and raise the rest of humanity out of its doldrums; Bergson with his mysterious *"élan vital."*

The Viennese philosopher Ludwig Wittgenstein, though his first important work came out later, during World War I, was a product of this antimaterial milieu. His *Tractatus logico-philosophicus* is usually interpreted as the ultimate in Positivist tracts. His dictum of *"Worüber mann nicht sprechen kann, darüber muss mann schweigen"* (About that which one cannot speak, one must remain silent) is taken as proof positive of a material philosophy which examines things in the world and leaves metaphysics out as unexplainable. But in fact this book can be interpreted as a profoundly metaphysical treatise in itself, outlining what can be fruitfully expressed with words and for the rest . . . the leap of faith is needed. You must in the end take away Wittgenstein's ladder and climb onto a new plateau by yourself. All that is needed is the initial leap.[80]

The philosophers were not the only ones rejecting the nineteenth-century world. The reaction in the arts such as Symbolism, Impressionism, and Expressionism all were a direct result of this rejection of bourgeois values and middle-class life. Richard Wagner was the product of just such a reaction.

Even the new sciences of depth psychology and particle physics expressed this relativity of values—this constant shifting of values which was a step beyond the blind, optimistic faith in science that preceded it. Einstein tearing apart the Newtonian world with his theory of relativity, no less than Freud with his exploration of the human unconscious, was an expression of the same antimaterial trend.

Mystery was alive and well in the world once again. There really were unknown forces at work in the universe—even the scientists admitted as much, though they still insisted on giving these forces names such as X rays and the Unconscious.

The flowering of occult groups was yet another expression of the rebirth of mystery. Madame Blavatsky and her Theosophy codified occult knowledge from around the world and attracted followers from all walks of life.

Rudolf Steiner, a Viennese, borrowed from an earlier philosopher the term Anthroposophy to describe his new mystical philosophy, one more attempt to look at the world as a whole rather than to cut it up into little faculties of knowledge. Steiner's *eurhythmia,* a style of extemporaneous dance, and his schools are still quite popular on the Continent.

These were the years also of Gurdjieff and the formulation of disciplines of self-awareness that preceded transcendental meditation as the pop religion of the twenties.

There were other, more bizarre groups as well. Aleister Crowley, whom Hemingway once called the most evil man in the world, was a product of this same turn-of-the-century rejection of materialism. A member of the occult "Golden Dawn" in England, which had among other members the poet Yeats, Crowley soon left England to practice more diabolical forms of spiritualism, playing with black magic and little boys. His initiation rites took on the sexual turn of devil worship, and his lodge in Sicily became a sort of western Tantric Yoga center of sexual magic.

Vienna was not left behind in this occult respect, either. Guido von List, accused of being the Aleister Crowley of Vienna, developed his own brand of mysticism. List's magic was a pan-Germanic mélange of Aryan supremacy and of the "Old Ones" who were supposed to be the progenitors of the Aryo-Germanic race. This ancient race of German wise men, or *Armanen* as List called them, were literally supermen with psychic powers and gigantic proportions. List claimed he was one of these *Armanen,* and it is certain that he believed it. One need only look at his photograph as he stares blatantly out at the camera like a very conceited self-portrait of Rembrandt, resembling that painter even down to the rumpled cap on his head. A long white beard, longer than Bahr's fatherly whiskers, flows down to his navel. He saw himself as a German "magician."[81]

List's books on mythology and folklore started out in a somewhat factual vein, but by the turn of the century he was writing completely from the unconscious, as he claimed to have psychic connections with the "Old Ones."[82]

By 1898 the Guido von List Society[83] was formed to promote the works of List and to help support the man. Influential men in all walks of life were members of the society, including the mayor of Vienna, Karl Lueger.

According to one report, List was accused of running a "blood lodge." This blood brotherhood had supposedly substituted the swastika for the cross in rituals involving sexual perversion and the practice of medieval black magic. By this account, List fled from Vienna in fear of being lynched by an incensed populace with strong Roman Catholic sentiments.[84]

However true such reports are, it is a fact that Lanz von Liebenfels was a member of the List Society and knew List personally. List, in turn, was a reader of Liebenfels's *Ostara* and a member of Liebenfels's "Order of the Templars." Since Hitler met with Liebenfels the one time to get some back copies of the journal, there was, according to various writers, most likely a connection between Hitler and the self-styled magician List.

Hitler did carry a letter of introduction with him from a Viennese member of the List Society to an important Munich industrialist when he fled to Germany in 1913. This letter was rather like the Roller letter in that nothing came of it. The industrialist had died the year before.[85]

Whether Hitler actually knew List or not, he was familiar with the works of the man. Hitler owned a first edition of at least one of List's works,[86] and on the flyleaf of one of Hitler's books from his personal library was found the following inscription: "To Adolf Hitler, my dear brother in *Armanen*."[87]

List's influence on a whole generation of German nationalists was as strong underground as Wagner's had been aboveground in the previous generation. Secret societies abounded around List. One, the *Armanenschaft,* boasted, among other members, Heinrich Himmler's father. List was taken with ancient symbols, as were Liebenfels and

Hitler. Decades before the Third Reich, List was fascinated by the ancient runic letters ⚡⚡ that Hitler would later use for his elite corps. As early as 1875, List had struggled up a hill near Vienna with a knapsack full of empty wine bottles. It was sunrise of the summer solstice and List buried his bottles on the hill in the shape of a swastika to celebrate the longest day of the year.[88]

Before List died, he prophesied that by 1932 a racially pure Reich would be established in Germany.[89]

Hitler took over in January 1933.

Further occult connections also spring up around Hitler in this missing year. One account[90] has Hitler moving from the Stumpergasse because of a mystical revelation that he experienced in front of the Spear of Longinus in the Schatzkammer (Treasure Chamber) at the Hofburg. Supposedly the spear of the Roman centurion who pierced the side of Christ on the Cross, this spear bears the legend that whoever claims it holds the destiny of the world in his hands.

After one transcendental moment in front of the spear, Hitler supposedly spent the next several years in esoteric study to understand the nature of his revelation. This study incorporated the Parsifal legend with a German version of the search for the Grail. Along the way Hitler, the proto-hippy with beard and long hair, experienced a mescaline trip, practiced yoga, and read Houston Stewart Chamberlain who was also supposedly a devotee of the spear mythology.

Bringing in everybody from Wagner to Himmler, this account presents a unified occult cosmology for the missing Hitler year that could go far toward explaining the bizarre, magical nature of the Third Reich. There is, however, that nasty problem of concrete evidence.[91]

Partial corroboration for this occult interlude of Hitler's life is given by a later friend of Hitler's in Vienna.[92] This witness claims that Hitler's readings took him into such regions of the occult as yoga, astrology, phrenology, graphology, numerology, and hypnotism. His readings stretched from *Parsifal* to telekinesis, and by this account Hitler personally experimented with water witches, trying to find water in the Wienerwald.

Hitler supposedly truly believed in his magical powers. "In my life," he told his friend, "I have often been a prophet, but people have always laughed at me."[93] Already at this time the swastika was an important mystical symbol for Hitler, found in the books on archeology through which he liked to browse.

The occult list could go on and on: from Hitler's supposedly hypnotic eyes to his precognition; from sexual magic to the black-magic rituals of the SS. Charges and countercharges abound as to the magic spell that Hitler was able to cast on people. In many ways this was merely a quick and painless rationale that was especially popular just after the unreal, horrific happenings of World War II.

If by magic we mean those unexplained forces in our lives that make one person's life distinct from every other that has come before or after, then Hitler was a magician. So are we all potentially, but too seldom is each individual's uniqueness realized.

Hitler probably did delve into every esoteric school he could find in these years. He was grabbing at straws to explain his crushing failure in the world. Whether he really was the black magician that some biographers make him out to be, has yet to be proven. Such easy explanations are often a disservice to history, obfuscating the material, day-to-day considerations that build character. After all, magic is much more dramatic than simple frustration and disappointment. Yet disappointment and frustration make for radical solutions; hate is truly a powerful magic.

(6)

Hitler stood with a group of ragged-looking men outside the main door of the convent on Gumpendorferstrasse. It was nine in the morning, and the spring sun shone down heartily into the narrow street. The broad buildings threw triangles of cold shade into the street, and Hitler, standing on the shady side with the other men so as not to lose his place, shivered in his light, blue-checked suit. His hair had grown long now and hung over the collar of his coat. His beard had also grown long and scraggly. More and more he was assuming the appearance of the Jewish *Handele* he despised.

An older female relative of Frau Zakreys, Hitler's former landlady in the Stumpergasse just around the corner from the Gumpendorferstrasse, who knew Hitler in 1908, saw him "queuing up for soup at the Sisters of Mercy . . . and his clothing looked very much the worse for wear."[94] She felt sorry for the young man who just a short year before had been such a dandy. Gone now in the spring of 1909 were the ivory-tipped walking stick and his good suit. They were pawned to the Jewish pawnbrokers along the road to poverty.

Obviously, the nightly visits to the Opera were out now. Such a luxury as a two-crown ticket was no longer in the budget. Besides, he might run into Kubizek there, and he did not know what he would say to his old friend in the condition he was now in. It had taken all the courage Hitler could muster to finally venture into their old neighborhood again to "visit Kathy," as the bums called this daily handout of soup from the convent whose mother superior's name was Katharine.

All of Hitler's studying could not stop his slow descent into poverty. He must have seen it coming for a long time. His orphan's pension of 25 crowns came every month, but his inheritance from his mother and father was quickly depleting, even with the new economies of the Felberstrasse.

The money continued to seep out until later that summer Hitler finally was forced to do the unthinkable. He got a job as a construction worker.[95]

"From the very beginning it was none too pleasant,"[96] he remembered later. He still had not reached the bottom of the social ladder, and his clothes were not those of a worker but of a student, faded and shiny with wear as they were. His speech and his manner also set him apart from the other men—or at least he hoped they did, for that was all that separated him from the lower class at the time. Like most bourgeois, Hitler had a horror of slipping into the lower depths[97]; of being one of the 'fellows' in the working group. He shunned contact with the men, doing his work quietly, taking his lunch of milk and bread apart from the other men on the scaffolding.

Despite his standoffishness, the men soon told him he had to join their labor union.

"I refused. The reason I gave was that I did not understand the matter, but that I would not let myself be forced into anything. Perhaps my first reason accounts for my not being thrown out at once."[98]

For two weeks Hitler worked as an unwelcome nonunion man with the others. He listened to their political discussions and grew to hate these men—both for their social class, as a frightening foreshadowing of what he might become, and for their ideas. Ironically enough, Hitler the bohemian, the rejector of middle-class values, the struggling artist, suddenly in this case made an about-face and became the protector of the status quo, grumbling to himself over the iconoclastic remarks of these workers.

"These men rejected everything," he later complained in *Mein Kampf,*

> the nation as an invention of the "capitalistic" classes; the fatherland as an instrument of the bourgeoisie for the exploitation of the working class; the authority of the law as a means for oppressing the proletariat; the school as an institution for breeding slaves and slaveholders; religion as a means for stultifying the people and making them easier to exploit; morality as a symptom of stupid, sheeplike patience, etc. There was absolutely nothing which was not dragged through the mire of horrible depths.[99]

For the young man who had railed at the stupidity of professors who had refused him entrance to the architecture school because he did not have a *Matura*; who despised the Habsburg state for a Babylonian realm; who equated capitalism with the Jew; for such a young man as Hitler was at the time, to reject the same sentiments when mouthed by socialist workers was absurd.

Hitler, the frightened little middle-class boy shows his true colors in these lines from *Mein Kampf.* Scared of slipping lower in the social hierarchy, and frightened to death of doing anything really revolutionary, Hitler could only act the prig with these men and sit apart feeling superior. Soon his sense of superiority gave way to argument, and he matched wits with these working men, bringing all his massive learning from the gutter press to bear on his arguments.

After a couple weeks of such behavior, the other workers did the only sensible thing. They ordered him to leave the building site at once or else be thrown off the scaffolding.

"Since I was alone and resistance seemed hopeless, I preferred, richer by experience, to follow the former counsel,"[100] Hitler wrote, recalling his sensible behavior in the incident.

Hitler had now found another enemy. Not only were there Jews in the world, but there were also socialists. The two would make a deadly combination of hate for him.

Getting poor is a long, slow, unbearable process. It saps the strength and will of the victim as much as starvation does. There are endless complications and subterfuges involved. One must keep up appearances for the landlady, so she does not become suspicious about next month's rent. The money must be made to stretch with a glass of milk here, a slice of bread there, deciding what to pawn and what to keep. There is a certain artistry involved in the whole affair—a certain frightening and at the same time liberating quality of watching the money go and counting the days left until hunger begins.

George Orwell in his *Down and Out in Paris and London* gives a fascinating account of this process:

> You discover boredom and mean complications and the beginnings of hunger, but you also discover the great redeeming feature of poverty: the fact that it annihilates the future. Within certain limits, it is actually true that the less money you have, the less you worry. When you have a hundred francs left in the world you are liable to the most craven panics. When you have only three francs you are quite indifferent, for three francs will feed you tomorrow and you cannot think further than that. You are bored, but you are not afraid.[101]

To some extent, this quality of being a hypnotized victim waiting for the cobra of poverty to strike must have controlled Hitler's actions. He reports that he tried another time to get work, but the same thing happened over union membership, and he was supposedly forced to quit.

Whether or not these working stories are true, the fact is that by August 22, 1909, Hitler was forced to make another move, this time a few blocks farther afield from his Westbahnhof haunts. He moved into a cheap room at Sechshauserstrasse 58, room 21. This was most definitely a step downhill for Hitler. Today the building is used mostly to provide mass lodging for foreign "guest" workers in Vienna; the rooms are cramped and airless. At the time Hitler lived there the building might have been in better condition, but not much.

He was not yet so dumb-struck by poverty as to go illegal. Hitler filed a moving slip with the police in the Felberstrasse, and the rent was paid up.

This time Hitler registered himself as a "writer"[102] on his *Meldezettl,* police registration. Orwell gives us an idea of the thinking behind these "occupations" that are asked for from jobless vagrants: "An official entered in a ledger our names and trades and ages. . . . I gave my trade as 'painter'; I had painted watercolors—who has not?"[103] And later in the same book Orwell recounts: "When we registered I gave my trade as 'journalist.' It was truer than 'painter,' for I had sometimes earned money from newspaper articles."[104]

This listing of professions, especially in title-conscious Vienna where people are listed by profession in the telephone book and every second man is "Herr Doktor" to his underling, is a matter of prestige. Even if Hitler had never put pen to paper he would want to put down something to impress the anonymous policemen who were filing his registration.

Whether this self-appellation of "writer" should be taken seriously is thus doubtful. Perhaps Hitler really was making new dreams for himself. Now that he had spent his period as a student, perhaps he felt competent enough to make his fame as a writer, rather than as a painter or architect. These were new dreams built on the power of the word, while outside the winter was fast approaching again, and along with it sure poverty.

Hitler spent the next three and a half weeks in something of a euphoric daze, waiting for his dreams to materialize. No writing, if there was any, exists from this time. Hitler made the mistake sometime that fall of pawning his winter coat, as if because it was still warm at the time, it would never get cold again. Such an action only shows how totally unprepared and unfit he was for his soon-to-be profession of vagabond.

Hitler's dreams did not last long. They were interrupted by harsh reality. His money finally ran out altogether but for the 25-crown monthly orphan's pension. By September 16, 1909, he had had to slip out of his lodgings on the Sechshauserstrasse without paying rent. On the registration form next to the question of "When moved out," is written "Unknown."[105]

Hitler was on his own on the streets of the city he had come to conquer. He was swallowed into the underworld of Viennese poverty and the homeless for the next three months.

When Hitler sat down to write his memoirs in Landsberg prison fifteen years later, he must still have been smarting from this ultimate failure, this horrid slip into the lowest depths of society. Perhaps he remembered his last stated occupation before going under, for he uses the medium of the pen to berate writing. With his own pen he scorned the "fops and knights of the pen,"[106] and advised these writers to "remain by the inkwell"[107] where they belong with their theoretical activity. They were fit for nothing else in Hitler's eyes. Hitler still believed in the power of the word, but with a new twist.

The power which has always started the greatest religious and political avalanches in history rolling has from time immemorial been the magic power of the spoken word and that alone.[108]

The student had graduated from the solitary reading of words to a direct experience of life. As much as his frustrations at his failure to gain admittance to the Academy shaped the future Hitler, so the experience of poverty was to play its role in forming the future Führer.

6

Down and Out

(1)

IT was a cold night just before Christmas in 1909. The crowd of destitute men, women, and children lined up outside the locked doors of the Asylum for the Shelterless in the Meidling district behind the Sudbahnhof. Women held crying youngsters to their breasts trying to comfort them. Men stood quietly, shifting from foot to foot, clasping their arms around their chests for warmth, blowing puffs of vapor into the chill. The raw smell of the train yards filled the air. A train whistle cut through the other city noises.[1]

When the doors finally opened, the people streamed in eagerly to get out of the cold. The men pushed ahead, anxious to get a place in the main building and not be shunted out to the annex building that in the winter housed the overflow of bodies.[2]

The Meidling Asylum was run by the Association for the Shelter of the Homeless, a private philanthropic society recognized and sponsored by Franz Joseph. The wealthy, Jewish Epstein family were the main sponsors of this asylum, which housed a quarter of a million destitutes in 1909.[3]

Once inside, the poor were separated by sex, the children going with their mothers. For a nominal fee they all received cards entitling them to five nights' lodging. The people sat down in a big hall on wooden benches waiting their turn to shower. They went in twos to the showers, and those who were full of vermin had their clothes wrapped in bundles to be disinfected, a process of "burning out" which bleached out the clothes.[4]

Once out of the showers, the people filtered back into the hall where rows of tables were set up and bread and soup served. The meal was not the best of fare, but the soup was hot and the bread thick and nourishing. After slurping the soup down greedily, they all retired to the sleeping areas—huge, open dormitories with cots orderly lined, the number of each cot marked above a metal clothes rack. The wire springs of the cots creaked as the men lay back on them, rubbing sore feet, exchanging stories with other down-and-outers. The experienced tramps gathered their clothes together as a pillow, carefully folding them so that in the morning there would still be a crease in their ragged trousers, as Hitler had already learned to do. There was a strange degree of social pretension in these men who had slipped into the lowest rank of poverty.

Shoes were kept shined and placed neatly under one's bed. Tailors and shoemakers were in high demand among these men to give a semblance of gentility to their poverty. They bartered their skills for cigarettes, pennies, and lodging tickets.

One group of tramps, their evening toilet performed, their pillows rolled, and their shoes tucked away out of harm and temptation's way, swapped stories of their travels. They were mostly young men on the road, looking for work or a lark. Jokes were exchanged and new traveling friendships formed. This one group was made up mostly of Germans from the Rhine, Saxony, and Bavaria.[5]

Hitler sat on his cot near the laughing men, his eyes downcast, staring at the brown sheets. His blue checked suit had faded into lilac with the delousing treatment and all the rain it had seen in the previous months.[6] His stomach was still growling with hunger even after the evening meal. He felt alone and embarrassed by his poverty. For a young man as private as Hitler, the experience of the public shower was the ultimate humiliation, much worse even than sleeping on park benches in the Prater had been.

His hands hung limply from his wrists like the tail of a dog that has been thoroughly beaten by the world.

One of the joking tramps, a man about the same age as Hitler who spoke with a heavy Berlin accent, took notice of the dejected fellow sitting alone on his cot. He asked Hitler about himself and soon found that this twenty-year-old was a babe in the woods. He had no idea of how things went in the asylum. The other men joined in and tried to cheer up the young man. With that strange camaraderie forged of poverty when there is nothing left to lose, the men took Hitler under their protective arms. The Berliner, Reinhold Hanisch, became fast friends with Hitler, the first Hitler had had since Kubizek.[7]

Hitler slept better that night than he had for several months, disliking the snoring men around him, yet feeling safe with them at the same time.

In the morning there was a new difficulty. How to pass the day? The asylum closed during the day and some sort of shelter against the winter weather had to be found. Hitler and Hanisch began to make the rounds of other charitable institutions. As they walked, they talked, and Hanisch soon found that they shared a youthful artistic dream, which gave their unlikely friendship more basis.

First was the "call on Kathy," with which Hitler had already become familiar from his Felberstrasse days. By the time they arrived at Gumpendorferstrasse, Hitler "was blue and frostbitten"[8] because he had only his light suit to protect him from the cold since his overcoat had gone to the pawnbrokers that fall.

From the Gumpendorferstrasse the tramps, with Hitler tagging along as apprentice, strolled over to the Westbahnhof to try to earn a few hellers carrying luggage. Hitler, with his emaciated appearance, must not have been very convincing as a redcap, for he seldom earned any money and his companions had to share their bread with him during the day.

From the Westbahnhof, Hitler and the others trekked across the city again to Erdberg where there was another shelter for the homeless, this one run by Baron Königswater, another Jewish philanthropist. Here they could warm their hands and feet and get another portion of soup and bread before trudging on back to Meidling for the opening of the asylum.

It was a full-time job, this poverty. Such a circuit took two and a half hours in each direction. But it was one of the few alternatives a tramp had in the heart of winter. The men had to keep moving to avoid frostbite. Back at the asylum at night, Hitler was cold through and through and happy for the oily smell of soup which he had at first found repugnant.

He began to come out of his shell with the other men. With Hanisch, especially, he opened up. Hanisch told Hitler tales of Germany, the magic land, the land of the pure race, unlike Vienna with its melting pot of peoples and languages. Hitler slowly unrolled his story for Hanisch also. He told of his Linz days and his father, the customs inspector. Their shared dreams of painting made for long conversations. Hitler told Hanisch, too, of his rejections from the Academy and of his studies on the Felberstrasse. Turning into a real German nationalist by this time, Hitler was overjoyed when Hanisch taught him the words to the Bismarck song, *"Die Wacht am Rhein": Wir Deutschen fürchten Gott da droben/ Sonst aber nichts auf dieser Welt.* (We Germans fear only God above/ And no one else in this world).[9]

In a few days Hitler had learned a good deal about survival in his new status. It was a miserable life but better than the one he had been leading for the previous few months. He was still in rather a state of shock from those bitter weeks. Once when Hanisch tried to convince Hitler to do something better with himself and asked what he was waiting for. Hitler could only reply in a dejected tone of voice: "I don't know myself."[10] Hanisch had never before seen such hopelessness among tramps.

Hitler's hopelessness can be better understood if we know what happened to him before he arrived at the asylum in Meidling.

(2)

From the middle of September the previous fall, to the middle of December when he lined up in front of the Meidling Asylum with the other outcasts of society, Hitler had been on the run. For three months there are no police records of where Hitler lived. No account of anyone who knew Hitler in this period exists. There are only his stories that he told later comrades in the flophouses of Vienna.

There are indications he spent some evenings in a cheap coffeehouse on the Kaiserstrasse in his old neighborhood near the Westbahnhof.[11] When the weather was still fine he slept in doorways and on park benches in the Prater. If there was rain he would take refuge at night under the arched gateway of the rotunda in the Prater where he could sleep on the floor with his overcoat—not yet pawned—rolled under his head for a pillow.[12]

Winter came early that year. There were snow flurries already by late October. The thermometer was low and the rain fairly constant.[13]

Inside shelter had to be found. One researcher reportedly tracked down sixteen different addresses that Hitler used in this time of need.[14] Addresses as far afield as the Simon Denk Gasse in the Ninth District by the Nordwestbahnhof have been mentioned as places where Hitler rented a bed for a short time and then perhaps ran out on his rent.[15] It is most probable that Hitler, with his monthly twenty-five crowns from the orphan's pension, could still afford cheap flophouses or *Bettgeher* situations in private homes even in his worst times. In one of these places his meager bag of belongings was stolen from him and he was forced back out on the street again, penniless until his next month's pension came.[16]

Hitler tried sleeping out in the cold for a few nights before he finally buried what was left of his pride and walked out to the Meidling Asylum to accept charity.

Hitler was not alone in his poverty.

Turn-of-the-century Vienna, like other industrial cities of the West, had rot at its center. Besieged by a 259 percent increase in population in the forty years from 1860 to 1900,[17] the city was bursting at the seams with its 2 million population. There was neither room nor work for that many people in Vienna. The age of urban poverty en masse was born. The flight from the farm to the city, especially in Vienna which had never really passed through the Industrial Revolution, was a disaster.

Electric light was fast becoming the norm in Europe, but Franz Joseph used candlelight and kerosene lamps in the Hofburg. The typewriter did not come to the aid of weary bureaucrats until 1918. Water was still hauled in barrels from the high mountains to the suburbs. Telephones and elevators were rare and refrigeration, modern plumbing, and central heating were virtually unheard of at the time in Vienna. Business practices were just as backward. The use of the check was unknown. Department stores were allowed only in 1900 after a long prohibition that all but subsidized small shopkeepers.[18]

The age of technology had not yet dawned upon the city by the Danube, though the waste products of that advance were transforming the old Vienna Hitler now called home.

The huge influx of bodies to Vienna from the country played havoc with the city's perpetually insufficient housing. By 1910, the average Viennese dwelling housed 4.4 people—about 1.24 rooms per person including kitchen and the occasional bathroom.[19] Almost half of the population lived in one- and two-room flats. Many of these flats in the new workers' districts such as Brigittenau and Favoriten were primitive one-room affairs with no water. The rooms were small and airless and despite already being crowded by the members of the family, there was inevitably an extra bed rented out by the night to a *Bettgeher* to help meet the rent. These bed renters, who did not even have a room of their own or cooking privileges, constituted about 5 percent of Vienna's population,[20] and it is probable that Hitler was a *Bettgeher* more than once during his three months on the run from ultimate poverty.

These were not the worst conditions to be found in Vienna. We can follow in the footsteps of a young Viennese journalist, Emil Klaeger, to discover the real down-and-outers of Vienna. It was this aspect of the city that Hitler was to experience firsthand.

The frontispiece of Klaeger's book *Durch die Wiener Quartier des Elends und Verbrechens* (Through the Viennese Quarters of Poverty and Crime), which caused such a sensation upon its publication in 1908, shows the young journalist with fashionably rumpled hair, shirt unbuttoned, jacket slung over one shoulder, boots knee-high. Klaeger appears much more the poet than the patient sociologist. But when the journalist went to the Soup and Tea Institute in the Tiefer Graben, he looked anything but a poet. Donning the old and battered clothes of a tramp, Klaeger was a bit nervous about his first encounter with the substratum of poverty, but was surprised to see that this charitable institution was filled with comparatively well-dressed customers. These people, many of them lowly clerks or porters, had a cheap and somewhat nourishing meal at this tearoom. Bread and tea were served to the needy at cost in hopes of preventing the consumption of spirits. Hitler had visited such rooms during his first months on the Stumpergasse with Kubizek. The one Klaeger visited dispensed almost a quarter of a million portions of bread and tea each year[21] and was one of the more reputable of its kind in the city.

There were also asylums for the poor. The city ran one such asylum which gave shelter to thousands of homeless, and other asylums, such as the one in Meidling, were sponsored by private philanthropists, many of them Jewish.

One step below these first two institutions for the poor were the series of warming rooms across the city. Hitler told Kubizek he had used one of these the months before that friend joined him in Vienna; he did so in order to conserve his own fuel supply. Hitler was not totally unfamiliar with the choices of the destitute when he himself faced destitution. The warming rooms were free and fairly reputable places run by private charities. These were the years before the welfare state. Jewish funds were again predominant in supporting these institutions. It is difficult to calculate the real number of different people served and saved at such warming rooms, for many men, women, and children came back night after night. More than a million servings of soup and shelter were provided by these rooms yearly, and even ignoring repeaters in this figure, the numbers of poor would seem to have been epidemic. The warming room on the Erdberg where Hitler went during the days was one of the best-known rooms in Vienna.

When Klaeger first visited one of these warming rooms he was horrified to see the bodies packed onto benches and the floor like sardines. The men and boys sat at tables all night and went to sleep sitting up, heads nodding back and jerking automatically forward in frustrated sleep. Smoking and talking were forbidden. When a newcomer came in he had to jab his way into the mass of bodies around the table with his elbows. A space around the heater in the back of the rooms was reserved for women, and the children were allowed to sleep on the floor around the heater.

The watery soup and paper-thin slice of bread the needy received at these rooms was fine fare compared to what other destitutes received elsewhere. Many men and women, because of police records, did not frequent these legitimate institutions in fear that the police might find them there. As long as they had a few hellers in their tattered pockets, they roamed the streets by day and searched out some flophouse by night. These flophouses abounded in Vienna by 1909. Most of them were privately run and all of them were illegal. Sometimes the police closed them down, but like prostitution, they obviously filled a need and were usually left to take their own course. Mostly these flophouses were mass quarters with forty or more people, regardless of sex, jammed into a two-room flat where they slept on chairs, beds, couches, and the floor. Often chance had a man and woman, strangers up to that time, sharing the same bed.

Klaeger was something of an old hand by the time he visited these mass quarters, yet he was still frightened enough not to shut his eyes all night.[22] The girl who lay under his couch sold her favors all night for the price of the night's lodging. One young man came into the room in the middle of the night and reported to his friends the progress of a robbery then going on. The stench in these crowded quarters was unbearable; the filth unbelievable; the degradation of the spirit enough to make any sensitive person want to commit either a robbery or suicide.

Pictures from Klaeger's book show the bodies in such quarters all askew, a leg sticking up here, an arm there, crooked over chairs and beds and on the floor; bits of blanket used as covering, faces hollow and anonymous as if no one lived inside anymore.

Surprisingly enough, a bum could sink lower than these flophouses. For the really enterprising and independent among the tramps, there were always the sewers which ran parallel to the Danube Canal and the River Wien. Favorite spots for the tramps to go were near the Stephanie and Ferdinand Bridges. The iron gates to the sewers there were not difficult to open and dens had been arranged near the canals with straw for sleeping and wood for fires. The best locations were near the corridors that led to the actual sewage canals, for the moist warm vapor, although hideous to smell, at least cut through the winter chill. One of the most heavily populated sewage canals Klaeger found was under the Karlsplatz where the tramps, dropouts from conventional society, were ironically forced to form a more rigid social structure than the one they had rejected. One man was elected as overseer of the rest to pick out cooking spots and to limit the number of inhabitants of this underground city. Watches had to be manned to warn of a police raid. Internal control of this society was terribly strict. If the man on watch was caught sleeping, punishment was dealt out quickly and violently.

Life underground was a simple affair, Klaeger reported. "Their love is bread; their ambition is a bed for the night; their hate is complacent society."[23]

The portraits of the men living underground are the most poignant in Klaeger's moving book. The hollow-cheeked men stare out of their cavelike shelters along the stinking sewage canal, their hungry eyes wide and bright in the artificial light made with the flash. There is a quiet desperation to their look; sometimes almost a playful joking and posing for the camera, but always in back of it all the hungry, lost expression.

It is doubtful Hitler ever sank so low as to resort to Vienna's sewers. That was an insiders' tip and Hitler was a most incompetent tramp, all but paralyzed by his rapid descent into destitution. He probably stumbled from one warming room to another and one private room to the next as long as his little money held out. He may have spent some nights in the mass quarters Klaeger describes, kept awake all night by the fetid air and the sounds of some drunk who was beating his wife.[24]

By the time Hitler arrived at the Asylum for the Shelterless in December, he was a beaten man. His world of illusion had crumbled around him. He learned in the tough school of life that even if you do not make a decision, the world makes it for you.

Hitler needed rest and recuperation before setting out on any further dreamy plans. In December of 1909 the only dream Hitler could muster was of a warm bed and hot soup.

Long forgotten, probably, were his exploratory trips to Meidling while living with Kubizek in 1908. At the time Hitler, playing the young sociologist, was examining the fringes of poverty for his own building projects. Hitler had "made no acquaintances in Meidling (in 1908), his aim being to study a cross-section of the community quite impersonally."[25]

Hitler had not studied the life in Meidling with any sympathy, but rather with the cool objectivity of a scientist looking through a microscope. Now he was on the other end of the lens.

(3)

Hitler stayed for two months in the Meidling asylum. He soon learned some of the ins and outs, such as purchasing the partly used lodging tickets of others who were hitting the road again—there was a time limit to occupancy in the asylum—so as to prolong his own stay. When the weather broke somewhat and the men were freed from their endless rounds of warming room to warming room, Hitler would again try his luck as a porter at the Westbahnhof. If there was snow, he and Hanisch got up early and tried for work as snow shovelers. Hanisch had often to explain to the foremen that, in spite of his puny appearance, Hitler was a good shoveler.[26]

One time Hanisch had to advise Hitler against taking work on road construction, knowing that the work would be too hard for him. Hanisch, the psychologist, sweetened this bitter pill by appealing to Hitler's snobbishness. He did not need to convince Hitler overmuch, for the young man from Linz, despite his impoverished condition, still detested any form of manual work. Hitler was eager to accept Hanisch's argument: one shouldn't stoop too far for work, otherwise one could never pull oneself up again.[27]

Money-making schemes abounded in the asylum. At first Hitler also tried his luck at panhandling, but he had no talent for it. Shopkeepers would ignore him, telling him "Nothing today. Come again Friday."[28]

A good day of begging would net him only fifty hellers.[29] This was a sad come-down for the dandy who only a year before had spent four times that amount to go to the Opera.

Soon Hitler was taken under the wing of another tramp at the asylum who made his living selling addresses of soft touches and of good one-liners to use with them when begging. Hitler had to split any profits he got from these addresses fifty-fifty with the tramp who supplied them. There was the old lady on Schottenring who, once approached with a "Praise be to Jesus" and a hard-luck story about being an unemployed church painter, would open her purse to the tune of two crowns. But Hitler botched this sure thing and got religious platitudes instead of money.[30] There was also the lame Dane who worked at the Consulate who was usually good for a couple of crowns if flattered about all the strings he could pull to get the unemployed tramp a job. But the Dane didn't care for Hitler's line. Hitler apparently had a black thumb for begging.[31]

His one great success at begging came at a cloister on Landstrasse-Hauptstrasse, where he could usually get some meat patties and one crown for a "Praise be to Jesus" directed at the mother superior.[32]

Even though Hitler was learning the tramping routine, his situation was still a precarious one. Walking around Vienna in his light suit he had developed a cough. The energy he expended on all these schemes and dodges more than negated any money he earned. The more he worked, the hungrier he got. He was treading water and was not very far from going under.

Finally Hanisch, with a tramp's cunning, figured out a new scheme. Hitler had told him he was a painter—he even had some little postcard-sized paintings with him at the asylum.[33] Why not go into business together—Hitler painting postcards and Hanisch selling them for him? They would get around the necessity of a license by Hanisch acting the role of a consumptive or disguising himself as a blind man and appealing to the pity of tavern customers.

The one big hitch in this plan was that Hitler had sold his paints along with his clothes. How could he paint without paints and brushes? Hanisch perked up, however, when he learned that Hitler still had family in the country who might be enticed to lend him some money.

Once Hitler had blurted out that he had family, Hanisch and a salesman from Silesia who was listening in on the conversation had heard enough. They immediately dragged Hitler across the Meidling cemetery to the Café Arthaber where, for the price of a small cup of coffee, they could use pen and paper.[34] Hitler wrote a letter to some relative—most probably his Aunt Johanna. He probably asked for help in continuing his studies, for surely he could not tell his family of his real plight.

Help came a few days later via Poste Restante. Hitler showed up in line for the asylum brandishing a fifty-crown note. Hanisch quickly stuffed the money back in Hitler's pocket, warning him not to go showing it around or he would be approached for a loan or else robbed in his sleep.[35]

Hitler was a changed man. With this instant wealth he began to feel a little cocky again. He had not realized how easy it was to play on his aunt's emotions. He sat back and relaxed for a couple of days until Hanisch built a fire under him before his fifty crowns was squandered on pastries.

First, Hitler needed a warm coat. He refused to go to the Jewish quarter to buy one, afraid of being cheated.[36] Finally he bought a dark winter coat from the government pawn shop, the Dorotheum, for twelve crowns.[37]

The next problem was finding Hitler a place where he could work during the days. The Meidling Asylum couldn't be used; they had to find some other hostel to live in.

Word travels fast along the tramp grapevine. All through Klaeger's wanderings through the Viennese underworld of poverty and crime, he heard one word over and over—a kind of mantra of paradise imagined but never achieved, like the word California used to be for those living in winter snow. The word was the Männerheim, a home for men on the Meldemannstrasse in Brigittenau. This new home for men built by the city was supposed to be the Ritz of the downtrodden. Klaeger had made his way there to see for himself.

Asking directions of a shabbily dressed workingman, Klaeger soon learned how the lower-middle-class Viennese felt about the luxurious home. Klaeger had gotten no directions, only abuse. The petit bourgeois looked on the home as an exorbitant expenditure for undeserving people.

Exorbitant it was, as compared with other places Klaeger had spent a night. The building's new façade stood out incongruously in its neighborhood of rundown houses and shabby factory fronts.

As was his practice, Klaeger had given the name of the hero or the author of the last book he had read when registering. The director of the Männerheim, Johann Kanya, was not a little surprised to read the name Conan Doyle on the registration blank, but only thought it a very pretentious name for a bum to have. Kanya should have been beyond surprise. His home housed more than one down-and-out baron. The clientele at the Männerheim was distinctly a step above those Klaeger had been dealing with up to then. There were, besides the black-sheep barons, a full complement of society. There were traveling salesmen, day laborers, half-baked artists. Vienna's Fifth Estate was gathered here trying to pull themselves up by their bootstraps, or at least not slip any lower down the scale.[38]

The inside of the home was immaculate, and if the rules posted all over the walls were a bit annoying, there was at least some positive result from them. Order was kept and the place was spotless. The men each had their own cubicle to sleep in, on an iron cot with a three-sectioned mattress and a horsehair pillow. There were ample sanitary facilities—baths, showers, footbaths. There was also a kitchen for those who wanted to cook for themselves and a cafeteria with inexpensive, wholesome meals. A workroom gave the men somewhere to gather in the days when the sleeping quarters were closed, and a library supplied them with food for thought. Chess, checkers, and dominoes were the only games allowed. Undue noise was forbidden and Director Kanya was empowered to evict any man for infraction of the rules. All of this luxury came fairly cheaply—a half crown per day or three crowns per week. No one was allowed in the home who had more than a 1,500-crown salary per year.[39]

The word on the Männerheim had also reached Hanisch at the Meidling Asylum. Here was the perfect setup, Hanisch figured, almost as good as living on one's own. Hitler would even have a workroom for his painting.

On February 9, 1910, after spending his first two years in Vienna in the southwest part of the city, mostly near the train station that had brought him to town, Hitler packed his few belongings and walked to the northeast corner of the city, to the Twentieth District, to take up residence at 25-27 Meldemannstrasse.[40] He would live there for the next three years.

To raise some money, Hanisch took a job as a servant—he had worked as one for a time in Berlin before coming to Vienna. After four days, Hanisch put together enough money to follow Hitler to the Männerheim. It was the beginning of a successful partnership.

(4)

Sunday was the sacred day in Vienna. Everybody but the cooks and waiters put their feet up on Sunday, propped their hands over full bellies, and sighed with relief at some rest from the work routine. The pubs and taverns of Vienna bristled with customers. Those out at the huge amusement park of the Prater were busier than most. While the children were kept busy at the penny rides and the shooting galleries and on the giant ferris wheel, the parents sat in the taverns sipping tart white wine or guzzling foaming mugs of beer.

Hanisch made his way through the crowds in the taverns filled with blue smoke. He coughed and hunched over tables, giving the cheery drinkers a hard-luck story about the poor consumptive artist sitting in his garret turning out those priceless little postcard scenes of Vienna. The customers' watery eyes turned from Hanisch's impassioned face to the card he held out in front of them. It was a hastily sketched scene of Vienna—a church, a well-known square—done in watercolors, completely devoid of any human form or warmth but not without a certain architectural accuracy.

Hellers were fished out of oily pockets, thrown on stained tables along with ancient lint balls and other pocket scrapings. Hanisch smiled and placed the card down in front of the new owner to be sent to that aunt in Bohemia or the brother in America.

In the lower left-hand corner was the barely legible scrawl: "A. Hitler."[41]

The two had set up their small-time business, and it was doing well. Hitler sat at the corner he had staked out in the writing room at the Männerheim. He sat at a long oak table near a window with his paints spread out around him and the photograph of the building or scene he would copy in front of him.

Around him were the other occupants of the home: One old man copied addresses of betrothed couples from the newspapers and sold them to furniture stores and other firms interested in the trade of newlyweds. One Hungarian cut out postcards from cardboard, which he also hawked at Prater taverns. Others made little signboards and price bills.[42] The Männerheim was alive with more money-making schemes than the asylum in Meidling. It had to be for the inhabitants to pay their half crown per day rent and have money left over for food.

Hitler's painting technique was rusty after such a long layoff. He started out slowly, reluctant to put brush to paper at first, but with Hanisch's coaxing he was soon turning out a good supply of postcards. He used existing photographed postcards as a template, tracing the lines and then filling in the colors. He painted as many as Hanisch could sell. The two split the profits fifty-fifty. Hanisch walked his feet off and went hoarse selling the cards. Hitler kept busy, with constant prodding from Hanisch. He painted two or three postcards a day and then held some of them near the flame in the kitchen to give an Old World, sepia effect to the colors.[43]

"We were doing better," Hanisch recalled some thirty years later. "Misery was at an end . . . and new hopes sprang up."[44]

At first there must have been a terrific exultation at beating the game and coming back up from the underworld of despair. As long as Hitler stuck to his worktable during the day, the two did all right. There must have been a fine luxuriousness to sleeping on clean, white sheets again, in the privacy of one's own little cubicle room. Hitler lodged on the third floor[45] in a little space five feet by seven. There was enough room for a small table, clothes rack, chamber pot, mirror, and a small iron cot. The bed was a real one with the standard three-part mattress and pillow,[46] and the sheets were changed once a week.

There were plenty of showers, too, with sparkling tiles, and every floor had a few toilets and footbaths. In the basement, just as there had existed unofficially at the Meidling Asylum, there were a tailor, shoemaker, and barber.[47]

Hitler even began eating well again—or as well as Hitler ever ate. For nineteen hellers, a tenth of what he used to pay to go to the Opera, Hitler could enjoy a meal of roast pork and vegetables. Most of the time, however, he did his own cooking in the kitchen provided for that purpose.

"In the home," Hanisch wrote, "Hitler and I both did our own cooking, one day corn pudding with margarine, the next day margarine with corn pudding. One day Hitler was showing off his culinary art; he was going to make a milk soup, but it turned into pot cheese because it curdled. The next day I made some, and though he said he didn't want to eat it, I served it to him nevertheless. He asked me how I made it and I told him that I had just done it the opposite of his way and it had turned out all right."[48]

Hitler's sweet tooth had not deserted him. When he was well off from the postcard selling, he would fix rice in milk and sprinkle the concoction with chocolate.[49]

Soon, though, both Hitler and Hanisch realized there were better ways of making money than by painting postcards. At the turn of the century there was a brisk business done among the frame manufacturers of the city for cheap pictures to be sold along with their frames. This is not unlike the practice today of selling small frames with movie stars' photographs already in them to show what the frame looks like with a photo in it. The frame manufacturers were not selling art, merely frames.

The upholsterers were also a ready market for cheap paintings. In those days it was the custom to make divans with pictures inserted in their backs so that they could be stood in the middle of the room if need be.

Soon Hanisch was out beating the streets for larger painting commissions while Hitler set to work on larger paintings, two to three times the size of the postcards. Some of the paintings were in oil, some in watercolors. Still Hitler painted only scenes of Vienna, rarely from real life. One time Hanisch had an order for a picture of the church on the Gumpendorferstrasse where they "called on Kathy," but there was no postcard available for the church from which Hitler could copy. Hanisch dragged Hitler down to the church to do it from nature, but Hitler botched the painting.

"He used all sorts of excuses: it was too cold, his fingers were too stiff."[50] The truth of it was, Hitler could not draw from nature.

When Hitler found a successful motif, he would copy it over and over until he had glutted the market. The pictures usually ran about twelve by eighteen inches,[51] though occasionally he did some twice that size.

Hanisch tracked down the frame dealers. There was Jakob Altenberg, an immigrant Polish Jew who had come to Vienna with nothing and built up a business with four shops and a sizable trade.[52] There was also a Morgenstern in the Liechtensteinstrasse and Joseph I. Landsberger at Favoritenstrasse 68.[53] Morgenstern and Landsberger were "keen competitors with shops in the same vicinity."[54]

Mostly these frame manufacturers were Jewish, but Hanisch tracked down some Christian dealers also, though they did not "pay any better than the Jews."[55] All in all the pair began to prefer selling to the Jewish dealers because the Christian dealers "only bought again when they had disposed of the first lot, while the Jewish dealers continued to buy whether they had sold any or not."[56]

"Hitler often said," Hanisch wrote, "that it was only with the Jews that one could do business, because only they were willing to take chances."[57]

Hanisch put Hitler on a strict regime for the first month in the Männerheim. He had him working diligently every day and turning out a picture a day of medium quality that could earn about five crowns at the dealers. Sometimes one of these Hitler originals brought in as much as ten crowns, which the two always split evenly.[58]

Life was no longer a day-to-day struggle for survival. They had some measure of security by early March of 1910. They no longer suffered from the cold, and they had enough to eat. They had made it through a Viennese winter, which was enough to make anyone feel proud and self-satisfied.

Outwardly Hitler had not changed much from his down-and-out days at the Meidling Asylum. He still wore the streaked and tattered blue checked suit. His appearance was not helped any by the baggy winter coat he had purchased at the Dorotheum. He wore an "incredibly greasy derby on the back of his head"[59] to give him some flare, apparently. His hair had grown long now so that it flooded over the back of his collar and hung in long, tangled clumps. "He grew a beard on his chin such as we Christians seldom have, though it is not uncommon in Leopoldstadt or the Jewish Ghetto."[60]

The men in the home began to call him Paul Kruger because he resembled that bearded South African statesman.[61] The characteristic lock of hair still hung down onto his forehead.

Hitler had only one shirt. He washed it when he took a shower and thus became the home's meteorologist, for, as one of the inhabitants joked, it would have to be fine weather the next day for Hitler to go shirtless waiting for his to dry.[62]

These were still hard times for the youth whom Kubizek had described as almost "pathological"[63] in his personal cleanliness.

(5)

Hitler's knowledge of survival skills accumulated. He was slowly learning all the dodges, all the soft touches. He continued to visit the convents and cloisters around town for charity, besides bringing in his 25-crown monthly orphan's pension. His medical needs were taken care of for him by the Barmherzige Brüder.[64] Life was settling into a fine and simple routine once again.

Soon there was enough money for an occasional visit to a coffeehouse for a little cake. On a very rare occasion, Hitler scraped together two crowns and indulged in his old delight, the Opera.

Hitler had also acquired a new friend in the first month at the Männerheim, a Jewish part-time art dealer named Neumann. Later on, Neumann would be important to Hitler as a broker of his paintings and an agent for advertising orders. But at this time, when Neumann was still living in the Männerheim, he had another method of making a living. He worked with another Jew buying old clothes and peddling them on the streets of Vienna.[65]

Hitler and Neumann fell into an unexplainable friendship, partly because Neumann, though a Jew, was an ardent German nationalist and talked incessantly of emigrating to the fatherland. Neumann often gave Hitler old clothes and the future Führer became the proud owner of an oversized frock coat in this manner.[66] Hitler felt very elegant in his tails and greasy derby hat as he strolled to the Opera.

Hitler also began indulging his old love of the art galleries. He and Hanisch would go down to the Ring and look at the buildings, and Hitler would rave over the work of Gottfried Semper, the architect responsible for the twin museums. The two had to spend a crown each to enter the museums,[67] so this was truly an indulgence. Hanisch would try to point out paintings like Rudolf von Alt's that Hitler should try to copy, but Hitler was usually too busy at these times picking out artists he considered inferior to him, to listen to Hanisch's words of advice.[68]

The old interests began coming back one by one, just like a stroke patient's recovery of his motor faculties. First came the music, painting, and architecture. Then all too soon, as far as Hanisch was concerned, came the political interest.

Marx had his reading room in London's British Museum; Hitler had his writing room at the Männerheim. Between these two rooms, the course of world history was changed.

The Männerheim could hold 500 occupants, most of whom were transients in the true meaning of the word. They came and they went and never stayed in one place for very long. Many of the inhabitants only stayed in the home as one would stay at the YMCA today, while looking for work and lodgings in a strange city.

Other lodgers were men like Hitler—essentially outsiders, men who did not fit into society for one reason or another. There were the street prophets who sold their esoteric tracts on the corner, the failed aristocrats, even a retired major.[69] There were also semiskilled workers and craftsmen who used the writing room, and one old man, who was a failed academician, was called the Professor[70] by the others.

Here was a fine, captive audience before whom Hitler could exercise his rages, just as he previously had used Kubizek as his sounding board. There was a bond between these permanent fixtures of the Männerheim: they were the old guard, the "intellectuals,"[71] as they called themselves.

These men—and Hitler slowly became one of them—maintained a strong sense of community, shutting themselves off from the vagabonds who passed through, and thus feeling superior to them. They refused to use the rough street argot of the tramp and developed traditions such as saving certain places at table and the like for the old-timers.[72]

At first Hitler walked on tiptoes in this inner sanctum. He sat at his reserved spot near the window and painted. The others accorded him a degree of respect for his initial businesslike manner and because he was an artist of sorts. His appearance did nothing to enhance his image with these men, but it did increase his reputation of being an eccentric.

After Hitler and Hanisch had achieved their initial success, Hitler, no longer motivated by the pressing need to avoid starvation, fell into his old desultory ways. He would wait for Hanisch to go out in the mornings to canvass the frame dealers, then he would put away his paints for the time and read the newspapers. As soon as some new member of the writing room group came in, he would trade papers with him, until he had read most of the news.[73]

Then Hitler would think over the news for a time, dab a few strokes onto his paper, and perk up his ears at the conversations going on in the room. If someone dared to venture an opinion counter to his unspoken one, Hitler would leap to his feet, swinging his T-square in the air, and begin a long harangue on the socialists or the state of the Habsburg Empire.[74]

At first Hitler could not hold himself back from these discussions. These men who had formerly looked on him as an eccentric but respectful young man began to change their minds about him. They began to see they might just have a troublemaker in their midst.

All clubs have their initiation rites. The writing-room gang was no different. These rites began one day when Hitler began to vent his opinion of Schopenhauer and the "professor asked Hitler if he had ever read Schopenhauer. Hitler turned crimson, and said that he had read some. The old gentleman said that he should speak about things he understood. After that Hitler was careful not to talk where he might suffer a fresh rebuke."[75]

Hanisch also tells the story of how the group tried to cure Hitler of his habit of leaping to his feet and orating in the middle of their discussions. "A joker would often tie Hitler's coattails to the bench and then someone else would discuss politics with him. All of them used to contradict him, a thing he could never stand. He'd leap to his feet, drag the bench after him with a great rumble, and then the supervisor would send his servant up to this turmoil and order everyone to be quiet."[76]

According to Greiner, things got so bad at one early point in Hitler's stay at the Männerheim that Director Kanya, an ex-military man and a strict disciplinarian, was ready to evict Hitler from the home for causing so much disruption. Ostensibly Kanya was using Hitler's disreputable attire as an excuse for getting rid of him. In fact, the other inhabitants had complained about him.[77] At the last minute, he was saved from expulsion by another new friend who supplied a change of clothes for him and who had a talk with the director, promising that Hitler would improve in the future.

That Hitler was nearly evicted is not known for sure; we have only Greiner's testimony. But he did undergo a mild hazing by the other men and apparently took some of the lessons to heart.

This did not make him change any of his ideas, rather it convinced him more thoroughly to pick up where he had left off with his studies the previous August when he had left the Felberstrasse. He would no longer be caught unprepared to defend his views. Next time he would have some facts and figures to back up his arguments. Hitler was back on the road from which destitution had, for a time, detoured him.

As far as Hanisch was concerned, such a road could only lead back to the poorhouse.

7

The Granite Foundation

(1)

HANISCH threw his hands up in despair. Here it was a perfectly good work day. There were orders to be filled, deadlines to be met, and Hitler's place by the window in the writing room was empty. The rest of the writing-room cronies had told Hanisch that Hitler had gone off to some public funeral!

Hanisch's scrape with poverty had done nothing to increase his civic spirit. He was beginning to have his doubts about Hitler. His partner was a little too erratic in his working habits to suit Hanisch.[1]

The date was March 10, 1910, and outside it was one of those indeterminate days between the February thaw and the beginning of spring. Hitler was not the only Viennese to leave his work to attend this funeral. A Viennese legend had died.

Mayor Karl Lueger was dead at sixty-six, a victim of the diabetes that had left him all but blind in the last year of his life. Hundreds of thousands of Viennese lined the Ring that day to watch the funeral cortège as it left the Rathaus.

"When the mighty funeral procession bore the dead mayor from the Rathaus toward the Ring, I was among the many hundred thousands looking on at the tragic spectacle," Hitler later wrote. "I was profoundly moved and my feelings told me that the work, even of this man, was bound to be in vain, owing to the fatal destiny which would inevitably lead this state to destruction."[2]

Full of his passion for the life and death of this mayor who had transformed Vienna into an internationally renowned capital, Hitler strode back to the Männerheim to eulogize the man to his comrades.

"Hitler told us a lot about Dr. Lueger," Hanisch remembered, "who had been forced to fight hard for his position as mayor."[3]

There was a lot to tell, for Lueger was part of Hitler's granite foundation of political beliefs.

(2)

Karl Lueger was born in 1844 to a lower-middle-class family. His father was one of the janitors at the Technische Hochschule and later was promoted to the position of one of the caretakers. Young Karl did not speak during his first four years of childhood, and later in his life when he had become a successful politician and orator he liked to joke that he had made up for those first four speechless years.[4]

Lueger was a hard-working youngster and attended the prestigious Theresianum Gymnasium, a school usually reserved for the monied.[5] From here Lueger went to the law faculty of the University of Vienna and finished his studies in 1866.

During his struggle for an education, Lueger's father had died, and his mother had managed to scrape together enough money to open a small tobacco shop to make ends meet.

Lueger began his active public life as a reforming lawyer to whom as much money in fees was owed as was received from his poor clients. Lueger's roots were among the working class and petit bourgeois. He could move among these people as one of them. His manner of speech was inflected with the heavy Viennese accent and dialect. Lueger could rattle on with the best of the *Fiaker* drivers. But at the same time, he had received at the Theresianum the polished manners that allowed him to move among the higher classes. He was equally at home in the suburban beer houses and *Heurige* of the people and in the salons of the wealthy.

By 1870 Lueger was moving into politics. By 1875 he was a member of the city council. He started out his political life as a devoted liberal, but within a decade he had won a seat in the Reichsrat and had broken with liberalism, dismayed by the wasteland of poverty that laissez-faire liberalism created for the little man. Lueger also needed a stronger lever to catapult himself into the political power he dreamed of. An extremely ambitious and exploitative man, Lueger found that lever in the perennial Viennese anti-Semitism. Lueger was such a complex personality that it would be unfair to judge him on one ground alone, but for the next twelve years until he became mayor of Vienna in 1897, Lueger became the complete demagogue. He used economic anti-Semitism as a political platform to rally the distressed and disenfranchised little man, the class of artisans and shopkeepers whom the Industrial Revolution had hurt most. Lueger's anti-Semitism was a political tool, which in its cynicism was terrifyingly effective for him.[6]

By 1893 Lueger had befriended Catholic aristocrats wary of what laissez-faire liberalism might eventually incite in the masses. There were men such as Baron Liechtenstein[7] who had moved away from nineteenth-century liberalism which had created the horrors and the disruptions of the Industrial Revolution. They were developing their own brand of socialism, which would involve a cooperation between state control and private initiative. In this mixed system, insurance would be provided for the workers, the accumulation of huge amounts of private property by the individual would be stopped, as would child labor, and provision would be made for the old.

These men tied such social reforms to the Catholic banner, ultimate symbol of order and the foe of Marxism. It was an effective combination. When Lueger joined the ranks he brought with him a third selling point—anti-Semitism.

As far as Lueger was politically concerned, the Jews were single-handedly responsible for laissez-faire liberalism. Only "fat Jews" could survive the murderous competition of economic freedom.[8] He declared that Christians had to be protected from such capitalism and that "anti-Semitism is not an explosion of brutality, but the cry of oppressed Christian people for help from church and state."[9]

Lueger did not stop with that. His greed for power goaded him on to test the limits of humanity, limits that were ultimately breached in 1939. Ending one speech in the Reichsrat in 1890, he had quoted a friend's suggestions for the solution of the Jewish problem: the Jews should all be put on a large ship, sent to sea, and the ship should be sunk with no survivors.[10]

Lueger never shied, in his early political years at any rate, at rallying his constituency of "little men" by scourging the Jews. He blamed the

Jews for everything: from having a monopoly in international capitalism, to Hungarian unrest, to control of the press.

In 1893 Lueger and his political friends formed the Christian Social
party, which with its blend of municipal socialism, Catholicism, and
anti-Semitism, took Vienna by storm. Even the Pope was averse to
censuring Lueger for his anti-Semitic attacks because he was such a fine
spokesman for the Church.

Lueger's party gained enough strength in two years so that by 1895 a
Christian Social majority on the city council could elect Lueger as
mayor. But not everyone loved the "*schöne Karl*" as his admirers called
the handsome, bearded mayor.

Franz Joseph for one disliked and distrusted the man. It was not so
much Lueger's ugly use of anti-Semitism as his popularity with the
people that scared the old emperor.

A police report on Lueger gathered for Franz Joseph sheds some
light on the power of this demagogue and how such a disruptive force
as Lueger represented was thought harmful for the state:

> Medallions with his portrait, photographs and busts of Lueger are being
> sold en masse. At concerts people call for the "Lueger March" and it is
> stormily applauded. The women are being caught by dangerous excite-
> ment.... Anti-Semitism therefore is carried into the bosom of the family;
> the result is a coarsening of sentiment and a poisoning of family life.[11]

Franz Joseph had to do something about this young scoundrel. He
would not let him lead his imperial, capital, and residential city. He
dissolved the Municipal Council and for the next two years, ruled the
city himself. Lueger was denied the mayorality four more times by
Franz Joseph until April 1897 when, alarmed by Lueger's increased
popularity as a martyr, he finally gave in and confirmed the man as
mayor.

For the next thirteen years, Lueger ruled Vienna like a king, and with
great and consummate care. His one love was the city—he gave up all
women for it and lived out his days cared for by his two sisters. Like
Freud, Lueger's one great pastime was the card game Tarok. He
worked long hours in the cause of Vienna and was responsible for much
of the charm of the present-day city.[12]

In these thirteen years Lueger, thrust into the position of power he
had always longed for, suddenly did an about-face. He gave up his old

demagoguery and assumed the dignified air of one who is mayor of a capital city. He still kissed babies and by 1904 had attended about 1,400 golden wedding anniversaries[13] and could argue down the best of his opponents in his Viennese dialect. But Lueger had given up the ugly anti-Semitism of his early years. He no longer needed it, but he did need the support of the Jewish community. *"Wer a Jud is bestimm i"* (Viennese dialect for: "I'll decide who's a Jew.")[14] was his slogan from then on.

By the time of his death in 1910 he was universally loved. Lueger, along with Franz Joseph, was the elder statesman of Vienna. It was apparent that he was to be Archduke Franz Ferdinand's choice as minister-president when the latter came to power. Neither would live that long.

This and more Hitler told his friends that night and in the coming days. He bent their ears till they begged him for quiet or until one of the men tied his coattails to the bench again.

(3)

Hitler sat alone in the darkened theater as the changing images on the screen reflected on his face, changing it like a mask at Carnival.[15] But Carnival time had already come and gone in Vienna, as well as Easter, and Hitler and Hanisch were money ahead. Hitler could indulge his new pastime—the cinema. It was cheaper and quicker than the opera. Hitler sat watching the action like one entranced.

The new art form of cinema had a slow birth in Vienna. But once started, it skyrocketed. Deprecated initially by the artists and intellectuals such as Franz Kafka who argued that "cinema disrupts looking,"[16] movies had nonetheless taken root as a popular art form by the time Hitler lived in Vienna. And by the time Hitler sat in Landsberg prison writing *Mein Kampf,* Vienna had 200 movie houses serving audiences of 300,000 daily.[17]

Hanisch and Hitler had decided to celebrate their work and success. Hanisch had gone off to have some wine with his hard-earned profits, but Hitler had never developed a taste for alcohol and had distrusted its effects on him ever since he was a young boy.[18]

Watching the moving pictures was much better than drinking. Besides, this movie, *The Tunnel,* adapted from a novel by Bernhard

Kellermann, had something to teach Hitler. The flickering images danced by Hitler's watchful eyes, and as the story unfolded, he was more and more taken with a new passion. The scene in the movie where the orator makes the speech in the tunnel and turns into "a great popular tribune"[19] set Hitler's brain on fire with new thoughts. When the lights came up, Hitler crowded his way through the other people walking to the exit. He had to get back to the home and tell someone about what he had seen. As he walked along in the cool spring night, the images of the movie played through his head again. There was a feeling coalescing in his body. By the time he reached Brigittenau, those feelings had become transformed into the beginnings of a personal philosophy.

Hanisch was in the writing room joking with some other men before going to bed. Hitler grabbed him by the arm, "aflame"[20] with his new idea. He described the movie to the slightly intoxicated Hanisch and then concluded that "this was the way to found a new party."[21] The popular orator, a man with great speaking skills, could mold the people together in a great new and powerful mass movement.

Hanisch hiccoughed once, laughed at his overzealous friend, and went off to bed.

Hitler was getting used to not being taken seriously. All his life, friends had laughed at his great schemes. But he would prove them wrong someday.

Hitler walked the flights of stairs up to his bedroom cubicle and sat on the wire-springed cot. Over the cot hung the mottoes that he had known since his Linz school days. He had had these mottoes framed recently, perhaps at one of the Jewish frame shops where Hanisch sold his paintings. This was one of his first extravagances after beginning his partnership with Hanisch.

The top motto read: *"Ohne Juda, ohne Rom/Wird gebaut Germaniens Dom. Heil!"* ("Without Jews, without Rome/We will build Germany's Cathedral. Heil!") The one below, in the same type of cheap frame, read: *"Wir schauen frei und offen, wir schauen unverwandt/Wir schauen froh hinüber ins deutsche Vaterland. Heil!"* ("We gaze freely and openly, we gaze unflinchingly/We gaze happily over there into the German fatherland. Heil!")[22]

These mottoes, which also became part of Hitler's "granite foundation," were the touchstones of the Pan-German party and its erratic founder and motive force, Georg von Schönerer. By 1910, this party had been eclipsed by Lueger's strong Christian Social party, but for Hitler, the movement was not dead.

"When I came to Vienna," Hitler wrote, "my sympathies were fully and wholly [Hitler was ever the master of redundancy] on the side of the Pan-German movement."[23]

The "Knight of Rosenau," as Schönerer became known after the feudal estate he maintained in the Waldviertel very near the Hitlers' ancestral home, was sixty-eight the year Lueger died. He had long withdrawn from active political life and was in no condition to fill the void left by the mayor's death. He was an arrogant old man—as arrogant in his age and girth as he had been in youth.

The absence of hair on Schönerer's head was more than compensated for by his long, flowing beard that gave the old politician a Tolstoy-like appearance. The similarity between the two men ended there, however. Schönerer had none of the humanity of the great Russian writer. His only public duties by 1910 were leading pilgrimages to Bayreuth and to Bismarck's grave. He was an old war-horse who had, because of his stubbornness and irascible temper, always managed to offend his followers and had failed to form a mass party. The Pan-Germans were a mere sprinkling in the Reichsrat. In 1911 only four Pan-Germans were returned to that legislative body.[24]

Schönerer had undoubtedly been a boyhood hero of Hitler's as he was for many another German-Austrian youth. The self-styled aristocrat began political life, like Lueger, as a liberal.[25] And though labeled a liberal, he was initially a zealous reformer, anxious to correct the urban wrongs and poverty with his fresh country outlook. He joined the left democrats in their fight against economic corruption and the tyranny of unrestrained laissez-faire capitalism. Like Lueger, his fight was for the little man, cut off from the political process by the powers of big money.

By 1882, Schönerer had completely split with the old liberals and helped to draw up what is known as the Linz Program with, of all people, the future leader of the Austrian Socialists, a Jew, Viktor Adler.[26]

The Linz Program was an attempt on the part of young and frustrated politicians to save the Germanism of Austria by tying it ever more closely to Germany and by uniting the unwieldy lands of the Habsburg Empire under Hungarian rule so as to protect the original

German core of the realm from being overrun by the minorities should universal suffrage ever come about. Progressive income tax was also part of this plan to remedy tax inequalities; the railways were to be nationalized and social insurance broadened. It was not a thoroughly new plan to save the dying empire—there had been others—but it was a concerted effort on the part of young, disenchanted liberals at positive solutions to the ills of the day.

At forty, Schönerer was still the perfect portrait of the thoughtful, creative politician. A year later, six years before Hitler was born, we have quite another picture of him, this one rendered by Hermann Bahr.[27] Schönerer had long been a favorite of the radical German nationalist student groups at the University. In 1883, at a fraternity gathering to mourn the recently deceased man-god Richard Wagner, Schönerer was among the honored guests. Bahr gave a speech at this meeting pleading for Germany to save the German part of Austria from being engulfed by the minorities knocking at the door of Vienna. The students broke into a fervent rendition of "The Watch on the Rhine," the song that Hanisch had taught Hitler when they first became friends.

At this point the police, fearful of further demonstrations, ordered the meeting to disperse. Bahr remembered a saber-wielding Schönerer, his eyes filled with rabid fury, screaming to the students for total resistance to the police.

In the same year, Schönerer's new journal, the *Unverfälschte Deutsche Worte,* was declaring that no Jew, even if he could speak German, could be a true German. Full of the fear of inundation of the German culture by the hordes of immigrating Jews from the east fleeing the tsar's latest pogrom, Schönerer began to bring his German nationalistic paranoia to bear on the "Jewish problem." He asked for a limitation of Jewish immigration into the empire.

The next year he and Lueger both battled the Rothschild interests in the renegotiation of the Nordbahn railroad line which was privately owned by that family. He fought for the nationalization of the railways and in this fight began to focus more and more on the "system of exploitation pursued by the Jewish nation."[28]

More and more Schönerer sank easily into anti-Semitism, which won him even more followers among the students and lower middle class. Unlike Lueger's anti-Semitism, which was every bit as exploitative, Schönerer based his on "racial" arguments rather than economic.

In 1885 he changed the Linz Program by adding another point: "To carry out the reforms aspired to, the removal of Jewish influence from all spheres of public life is essential."[29]

Schönerer had found his enemy. Fueled with the popularity of his antiliberal stand joined to his anti-Semitism, he was launched on new extremes of hate. Schönerer was never interested in a large mass following, but in a loyal core of true believers. At one point his followers wore watch fobs of silver worked into the effigy of a hanged Jew and carried canes with models of "Polish-Jewish-type"[30] heads on top. The death's-head of the Nazi SS was foreshadowed by decades in Austria.

Schönerer also turned to more acts of pure hooliganism, like a frustrated little boy who does not get his way. The government watched his actions closely, anxious to catch him in a seditious act that would allow them to end his power. Schönerer was more than accommodating to that end.

In March of 1888, Wilhelm I of Germany was dying in Berlin. One night as Schönerer and some of his associates were gathered for their weekly meeting at a local beer hall, the news came that the German emperor had died. The friends fell into silent reverie at first for their fallen leader. This was followed by the inevitable German recourse to patriotic songs in times of great sadness or happiness.

By midnight this raucous wake was interrupted by a special edition of the *Neues Wiener Tagblatt.*[31] This late edition announced that the earlier news had been wrong—Wilhelm lived on.

Schönerer and his friends were at first relieved and then, after a congratulatory beer or two, they began to get angry at what they considered to be exploitation by the Jewish press. It was all a cheap, money-making scheme to sell more papers, they concluded. They had had enough of the Jewish press and its lies. This time they would not be allowed to get away with their underhandedness. Schönerer called for vengeance, and twenty-seven other hoodlums rallied to the cause.

Armed with brass knuckles and heavy canes, the men stormed the editorial offices of the *Neues Wiener Tagblatt* and rounded up the predominantly Gentile staff of the paper. "This is the day of vengeance," the enraged Schönerer shouted at the frightened newspaper workers. "No mercy for the Jewish devils. On your knees, you Jews, and beg pardon!"[32]

Printers at the paper soon came to the aid of the beleaguered editorial staff and a real brawl followed, causing considerable damage to the offices of the paper and to bodies on both sides of the foray.

This was just what the government was waiting for. The paper appealed to the courts, and Schönerer stood trial. The verdict was severe. He was sentenced to a four-month prison term, a permanent loss of his noble title, a five-year suspension of active and passive political rights, and immediate expulsion from the Reichsrat.

The "Knight of Rosenau" had overplayed his hand. Even though a loyalty parade of 200 carriages visited his country home when the verdict was handed down—Lueger was in one of the carriages—Schönerer's political power was at an end. By debasing himself with violence, he had also debased his movement. The civilized world was not ready yet for the politics of thugs. That came thirty years and a world war later.

After this time, though Schönerer's fame lived on and was recounted by schoolboys like Hitler, real political power of an anti-Semitic cast fell to Lueger and his Christian Social party.

Schönerer did make one comeback, winning a Reichsrat seat from the Sudetenland, that German-speaking area of Bohemia, in 1897.[33]

But to all it was clear that Schönerer was a laughable creature. He chased away potential adherents by his gruff methods, and even began to enlarge his sphere of hate to include the Catholic Church. The *Los von Rom* movement was one of the strongest-selling cries of the Pan-Germans at the turn of the century.

For Hitler, who used to bait his religion teacher in school unmercifully and who had a deep and abiding disgust for religion, this new plank in the Schönerer movement was almost as appealing as anti-Semitism.[34]

As the years passed, so too did Schönerer. He simply faded away from the political scene. His last speech to the Reichsrat was given in January 1907, several months before Hitler came to take up residence in the capital. It was a speech full of gloating about German supremacy, calling again for union of the German nations. He ended it with a hearty finale: *"Heil dem Deutschen Kaiser! Heil dem Deutschen Reiche!"*[35]

(4)

Hitler sat in his corner of the writing room dressed in the dirty old frock coat Neumann had given him. In front of him were photographs of buildings in Vienna scattered amidst paints and brushes. The hollows of his cheeks were beginning to fill in again with a better diet. It had been almost three months since he had come to the Männerheim.

There was not much work going on this morning. Some days it was like that. There was just too much to talk about. Work could wait. There was always work.

Robinsohn, the little one-eyed Jewish locksmith, sat next to Hitler.[36] Hitler had just put the touch on Robinsohn for a few hellers to go out to a café later that day. The locksmith was a friendly sort of fellow, the beneficiary of an accident insurance annuity when he lost the eye. He was always good for a loan.[37]

Neumann had just come in, and he took a bench across from Hitler. He looked over at some of Hitler's work. Neumann was between jobs and looking for some new way to make a living. The old-clothes trade was not the most rewarding for a salesman of his caliber. He liked best dealing with the art world—even securing advertising poster commissions or selling watercolors to the frame dealers. He was hoping to increase his stable of painters, but the Hitler-Hanisch partnership looked a little too steady for him to intervene.[38]

Soon the men started talking of the topic of the day. The conversation soon got around to Herzl and the idea of Zionism. Hitler joked with Neumann that it might not be a bad idea to send all the Jews to Palestine—he'd even pay Neumann's way. Then Hitler suddenly went into a compounded Lueger-Schönerer tirade, blaming the economic situation on the Jews.[39]

"But if the Jews should leave Austria, Herr Hitler," Neumann politely said, "it should be a great misfortune indeed for the country for they would take all their money with them."

"No," Hitler quickly pointed out, "they would not be allowed to. It would be confiscated."

"But still, Herr Hitler, it should be a great misfortune for Austria. For when the Jews cross the Red Sea all the coffeehouses in the Leopoldstadt will fail for want of customers."[40]

It was an old joke between the two, but it never failed to bring a slight chuckle from Hitler and to cool him down when he became too heated in a discussion.

Soon quiet consumed the room again, and the men got back to their work. The scratching of quills and daubing of paint and the quick click of scissors cutting out profiles were the only sounds to be heard. The morning dragged on to afternoon and Hitler was about to call it a day and go to a coffeehouse with the money Robinson had loaned him, when in walked one of the lodgers all aglow with something to say. In his buttonhole he wore a red carnation.

It was the first of May, and this Socialist worker began telling of the fabulous parade held that day out in the Prater where normally all the fancy carriages of the rich cruised in the afternoons. It had been a glorious parade, according to this worker.

But he had very little opportunity to describe it, for Hitler jumped to his feet and began screaming at the worker. "You should be thrown out; you should get a lesson!"[41] The man looked at Hitler in disbelief. How could he react so violently and so quickly? The Socialist's natural reaction was to laugh, and the rest of the men in the room joined in, having a good laugh at the expense of this eccentric painter Hitler. One could not take him seriously.

Hitler was first and foremost, deep beneath his bohemian veneer, a frightened bourgeois. The son of the civil servant had enough of the bureaucrat in him to fear the proletariat once it was armed with an ideology like Marxism.

Yet even in his hatred there were lessons to be learned for his "granite foundation."

There were other men learning lessons from the Austrian Socialists in these years, too. One of them, a full decade older than Hitler, sat in the back room of the Café Central[42] on the Saturday evening following the May Day march of 1910 in the Prater Hauptallee. He was concentrating over a chess move and waiting for his friends to come for their weekly meeting.[43]

The man looked younger than his thirty years. His hair was curly and brushed back from his forehead. He wore a well-clipped moustache and clothes that had seen better years. His frameless oval glasses marked him off as an intellectual. By 1910 he was already a veteran of one revolution and two terms in Siberia—from both of which he had escaped.

Lev Bronstein, alias Leon Trotsky,[44] had lived in Vienna since 1907, as had Hitler. He and his second, common-law wife and their two small boys had just finished their yearly move from their winter villa in the fashionable suburb of Hütteldorf, to the suburb of Sievering to the north.[45]

Trotsky, during his years of exile in Vienna, was almost as poor as Hitler. The villa was rented cheap in the winter when no one used it. The flat in Sievering "was a poor man's house, poorer than that of an ordinary working man. . . . His three rooms . . . contained less furniture than was necessary for comfort. His clothes were too cheap to make him appear decent in the eyes of middle-class Vienna. . . . The only thing that cheered the house were the loads of books in every corner."[46]

Trotsky made a tenuous living writing for Russian journals such as *Kievan Thought* and other European radical-liberal newspapers. Trotsky himself reported that in this Vienna period his wife was no stranger to the Dorotheum, where Hitler had often visited, too. In times of dire need, Trotsky even pawned his books.[47]

Trotsky wrote articles for *Kievan Tought* on the annual Viennese art exhibitions—his wife had taken his artistic education as her responsibility and often dragged him to the Viennese galleries that Hitler loved to haunt. Most probably names like Klimt and Otto Wagner were quite familiar to this Jewish-born Russian revolutionary.

His one great project during the Vienna years was his newspaper, *Pravda*.[48] Begun in 1908 in Austrian Galicia, by November of 1909 the paper had shifted its publication to Vienna. While Hitler was living through the bitterest month of his life, shivering under newspapers on park benches or huddled in doorways, Trotsky took over full management of the paper.[49]

But Trotsky's was obviously not a one-directional life in Vienna. Besides his education in the arts, he apparently had a strong family life and even helped his children with their homework just like any other bourgeois papa.[50] Through a co-worker at *Pravda*, A. A. Joffe, who was undergoing psychoanalysis by Alfred Adler, Trotsky came into contact with this unique Viennese development also.[51]

For his part, Trotsky found the new depth psychology "tempting" but ultimately too "shaky and unsteady."[52] It opened too many doors to "fantasy and arbitrariness"[53] for the pragmatic Trotsky. But he did concede that there was more to the Freud-Marx relationship than most Marxists liked to admit.

Trotsky's thoughts and chess game were interrupted by the arrival of three other men. One of them was slightly built, with a walrus moustache and heavy-lidded eyes behind rimless spectacles. His hair was parted on the left with a flopping wave that fell low over his forehead. As he greeted Trotsky, he spoke with a stutter.[54] His name was Viktor

Adler—no relation to the psychologist Alfred Adler. He was leader of the Social Democratic Worker's Party, the only party to compete with the Christian Social party.

The other two men with Adler were Austro-Marxist theorists: Otto Bauer, who would, after World War I, serve as foreign minister in the republic; and Karl Renner, later to be chancellor from 1918 to 1920 and president of the Second Republic from 1945 to 1950. An amateur poet of some skill, Renner wrote the words to the national anthem of the First Republic.

Trotsky tried to meet with these men regularly to keep his thumb on the pulse of European socialism during his exile. But he quickly learned that the Austrian brand of socialism was a far cry from his own revolutionary Russian product.[55]

During his stay in Vienna beginning in 1907, Trotsky came into contact with all the major leaders and theorists of the Austrian Socialists. They were all educated men "who knew more about various subjects" than Trotsky did and he "listened with intense and, one might say, reverent interest to their conversation" when he first saw them at the Café Central.[56]

Like Hitler, Trotsky was at first taken with the fine façade of culture and Ringstrasse elegance that Vienna threw up around its urban rot: the slums of Brigittenau, Favoriten, and Ottakring. Trotsky, at first, went so far as to contrast the "sunlit zone of European ideology . . . the vaulting arches . . . gothic spires and lacework" of Western European civilization with the barbarous "log cabin" of Russian history.[57] He was being drawn by the ideal of *Kultur* during his first months in Vienna, impressed by witty coffeehouse chatter and bedazzled by the city of Vienna itself and its new public buildings lining the Ring.

Like Hitler, Trotsky soon came to his own interpretation of the realities of life in Vienna. He began to see the comfortable coffeehouse chatter as so much oversophisticated cynicism. He saw the Austrian Socialists largely as academic skeptics, lacking the firmness of purpose that a revolution would require. He soon saw behind this group of thinkers and leaders a "phalanx of young politicians, who have joined the party in the firm conviction that an approximate familiarity with Roman law gives a man the inalienable right to direct the fate of the working class."[58]

Though Trotsky admired Bauer and Renner, he discovered they were far from revolutionaries. Renner, the poet-politician-theorist, was as far from being a revolutionary, Trotsky felt, as was the most conservative pharaoh.[59] The whole Viennese scene of strained courtesy, of Herr Doktor this and Herr Professor that, became anathema to Trotsky. Everything had to be just so and all in order for these men. For example, even though Trostsky was a member of the Austrian Socialists, he was never allowed to take part in their May Day parades, because the organizers feared that the police might cite the presence of an "outside agitator" in order to interfere. The Socialists were even so bourgeois, in Trotsky's eyes, as to hold their own ball during *Fasching,* the "Workers' Ball."

For Adler, alone, did Trotsky feel a warm affection and deep admiration. He was taken into that man's home and even became close friends with Adler's son, Friedrich.[60]

Viktor Adler was a good choice for Trotsky's admiration. Born in 1852 to wealthy Jewish parents—he was later baptized a Protestant—Adler grew up with all the benefits that accompanied wealth. He attended the "Eton" of Austria, the Schotten Gymnasium, and studied medicine at the university, working in Meynert's clinic where Freud and Schnitzler also studied. He debated Freud at one point during his university career, and in this city of coincidences, lived during the 1880s in the same building at Berggasse 19 where Freud would later set up his practice.[61]

After finishing his studies, Adler came increasingly to feel that his role was to serve the poor. To this end he worked for several years as a physician among the destitute, but this knowledge of poverty and downtrodden lives soon moved him to larger spheres of activity. By 1882 we see Adler putting his name to the Linz Program along with Schönerer. This liberal attempt to put an end to the ills that beset Austria was but a half-hearted swat at an unruly fly.

Within three years of the Linz Program, Adler had joined the Socialist groups operating in Austria at the time. It was only in the 1880s that labor organizations became legal. Until that time the more moderate Socialist groups that preached gradual change through political activity had suffered because of their more radical cousins. The anarchists, who gloried in the deed, and the reputed excesses of the Paris Commune had chased the frightened bourgeois to the wall and they were lashing back at the proletariat with laws that branded socialist activity as treason. Senseless assassinations such as that of Elisabeth in 1898 did nothing for the reputation of legitimate Socialists who had nothing to do with such anarchical gestures.

Adler set out to reverse the middle-class distrust of socialism, though at first other Socialists distrusted him even more than the middle class did because of his moderate, well-reasoned stands. A few jail terms and several confiscations of his newspaper, *Gleichheit,* brought these skeptics around. By 1888 he had rallied the divergent Socialist clubs and organizations to form a political party, the Social Democratic Workers, and they started their own newspaper, still in operation today, the *Arbeiter Zeitung.*

In the year of Hitler's birth, Adler took his group to the Second International in Paris. It was there he spoke the cogent lines, often repeated, describing the political situation in Austria as a "despotism tempered by slovenliness."[62] It was this slovenliness that allowed the Socialists to operate within a politically repressive state.

In 1890 Adler staged the first of the great May Day parades, a spectacle that Wagner would have appreciated. For weeks before the march, the Viennese were all atwitter with fear that the mob would ransack Vienna. Iron shutters were closed on shop fronts the day of the parade; mothers kept their children in; the rich left town for a bit of fresh air. The *Neue Freie Presse,* in an article of April 30 of that year, while condemning such fears, still described the atmosphere of besieged Vienna: "The soldiers are in readiness, the gates of the houses are being locked, victuals are being prepared in the houses as before a siege, businesses are deserted, women and children do not venture upon the streets, on all minds weighs the impression of heavy anxiety."[63]

Adler, the consummate mass psychologist, had however planned things differently from what the Viennese expected. There was no violence, no rowdiness—just thousands and thousands of workers walking through the Hauptallee of the Prater, taking the place of the fancy carriages that usually trotted along that chestnut-tree-lined boulevard. It was a moving spectacle—a solemn occasion. It changed the Viennese opinion of the working class overnight and won new respect and consideration for the demands for an eight-hour day and universal suffrage.[64]

Adler's Socialist party had found legitimacy at long last. From this time on it campaigned for the worker with political demonstrations and in the pages of its newspaper. Never a lover of the party line, no matter whose line it was, Adler had his own interpretation of Marx. In an exchange of letters with Engels on the subject, he showed his position not as a revolutionary but firmly as an evolutionary Marxist: "The critics of tactics always believe that it is and can be a straight line (the Marxian dialectic), while it must be an undulating line, just like world history"[65]—or just like the fecund line of Jugendstil art, in love with itself.

By the time Hitler was in the Volkschule, Adler's party was continuing agitation for election reform, but did everything short of organizing the ultimate weapon, the general strike.

The Socialists did support strikes such as that of the tramway drivers for shorter hours. The men worked sixteen hours per day while the horses that pulled the trams worked only four. Such discrepancies did seem a trifle unfair. Through strikes of this sort, there was a moderate improvement in the life of the worker.

The main battle of the party, however, was for universal manhood suffrage. The Socialists believed that once the masses had the vote, they could change their conditions through their own elected representatives. Adler was finally elected to the Reichsrat in 1905, and in November of that year he organized the largest demonstration Vienna had ever seen—a quarter of a million workers trod silently along the Ring. The bright red banner at the front, demanding universal suffrage, was the loudest thing about the march. The stillness was much more psychologically effective than all the shouting in the world.

Such a sublime spectacle was not without results. By 1907, Franz Joseph had reformed the election laws, granting universal manhood suffrage. In the elections of 1907 the Socialists captured eighty-seven seats, the largest bloc of any party in the Reichsrat.

As Trotsky sat and talked with these men in May 1910, the tactics had once again changed and the party was now concentrating on improving the life of the workers through direct legislation. With political power in hand, they now tried to pass social legislation through the Reichsrat.

For Adler, the battling physician, things were beginning to look up.

For Hitler, painting his postcards out in the men's hostel, socialism was no more than a "pestilential whore."[66] Despite, or perhaps because of, its success, socialism was the one mass movement Hitler could not tolerate in his Vienna days.

(5)

Ranting and raging at his fellow occupants of the Männerheim in the spring of 1910, Hitler certainly had no codified philosophy. He had a smattering of likes and dislikes, blind prejudices and equally blind loyalties. It would take another fourteen years and the rest and solitude of a prolonged stay at Landsberg prison for him to finally develop his political manifesto. In *Mein Kampf,* Hitler gives a vivid outline of the lessons he learned in Vienna.

The political world of that time was inspired by the failure of liberalism. The stock market crash of 1873, the grim workers' suburbs, the cutthroat tactics of unrestrained capitalism—these were the political and economic facts of life that young men and women grew up with in Vienna at the turn of the century. Lueger, Schönerer, Adler—all these men had turned away from liberalism. They were frustrated by its lack of responsiveness to political change, disillusioned by its grand promises. All but Schönerer turned to mass political parties, enlisting the support of the forgotten masses. They all incorporated social reform in their party platforms. The Pan-Germans, the Christian Socialists and the Social Democrats all spoke of reform: reform of the election processes; of the workers' lot; of the social injustices of laissez-faire capitalism.

Hitler took all this in. He recorded the machinations and progress of each party in turn. Though it was all but dead during his sojourn in Vienna, the Pan-German party did provide the slogans Hitler admired.

The party he most respected was the Christian Social. With Lueger at its head, that party was the most successful of its day. As he wrote in *Mein Kampf,* "By aiming at essentially winning the small and lower-middle-classes and artisans, it obtained a following as enduring as it was self-sacrificing. It avoided any struggle against a religious institution and thus secured the support of that mighty organization which the church represents."[67]

More important, as far as Hitler was concerned, was the fact that Lueger recognized the importance of the foe in mobilizing support. "In general, the art of all truly great national leaders at all times consists . . . in not dividing the attention of a people, but in concentrating it upon a single foe. . . . It belongs to the genius of a great leader to make even adversaries far removed from one another seem to belong to a single category. . . . Once the wavering masses see themselves in a struggle against too many enemies, objectivity will put in an appearance."[68]

In Hitler's mind, Lueger was a genius. Others, too, saw Lueger's manipulations for what they were. Arthur Schnitzler was one who realized this: "As unscrupulously as he used mass instincts . . . for his own purposes, so little was he a convinced anti-Semite, even at the height of his power."[69] Schnitzler despised Lueger all the more for this hypocrisy while Hitler admired the same trait for its political acumen.

Another strength of Lueger and his party was its understanding of "the value of large-scale propaganda . . . in influencing the psychological instincts of the broad masses of its adherents."[70]

Hitler learned from Lueger the importance of running a tight social ship—of providing social benefits to the masses and offering them ladles full of security. Once the masses were made happy, then any leader would become a near-god in the eyes of his people.

By 1924 Hitler had tempered his early blind respect for the Christian Social party and could see its faults. Ultimately it failed to save Austria because of its one great weakness: it failed to accept racism as a raison d'être of the new state. Both in their attempt to unite the diverse nationalities of the realm instead of concentrating on the German Reich and in their insistence on an anti-Semitism based merely on religious and economic grounds rather than racial, the Christian Socialists diffused their power, Hitler felt. As he wrote,

> It is obvious that combating Jewry on such a basis could provide the Jews with small concern. If the worst came to the worst, a splash of baptismal water could always save the business and the Jew at the same time. . . . Through this halfheartedness the anti-Semitic line of the Christian Social party lost its value. . . . It was a sham anti-Semitism which was almost worse than none at all . . ."[71]

Schönerer's party, on the other hand, was not afraid to be blatant German nationalists and "racially" anti-Semitic, but it was "unfortunate in its choice of methods."[72] For example, "its struggle against a definite denomination (the Catholic Church) was actually tactically wrong . . . unhappily not socialistic enough to win the masses."[73]

Hitler felt that Schönerer was not an accurate judge of human character and that his failure to create a mass party, or to want to do so, condemned his movement from the start. What Hitler was striving for in the pages of *Mein Kampf* was a combination of the two movements:

> If in addition to its enlightened knowledge of the broad masses, the Christian Social party had had a correct idea of the importance of the racial question, such as the Pan-German movement had achieved; and if, finally, it had itself been nationalistic, or if the Pan-German movement had, in addition to its correct knowledge of the aim of the Jewish question, adopted the practical shrewdness of the Christian Social party,

especially in its attitude toward socialism, there would have resulted a movement which even then in my opinion might have successfully intervened in German destiny.[74]

Through his analysis of the faults and virtues of the two parties, Hitler would have us believe that it was left for him, the humble postcard painter in the Männerheim, to devise the inevitable synthesis. But in this claim he is again cheating his audience. As early as 1904 there was an early version of the National Socialism Hitler would sell to the German public in the late twenties. The German Workers Party was formed in Bohemia and Moravia as an early synthesis of nationalism and socialism. Made up largely of former Marxists disenchanted with Marxism's failure to solve the nationality problem, the movement was essentially aimed at defending German workers' interests against the incursions of cheaper Czech labor. This forerunner of Hitler's National Socialist German Workers' party even had as part of its ideology the term *Volksgemeinschaft,* that mystical communal ideal that Hitler later propagated.[75]

Hitler was eager to hide any intellectual debt he might have to these organizations, so as to appear the only theorist of National Socialism.

For the Socialists, Hitler reserved a special vindictiveness in the pages of *Mein Kampf.* It seems he had learned Lueger's lesson well—he was focusing on one enemy and making even far-removed adversaries seem like the same thing. Thus, while he could on the one hand blame the Jews for monopoly capitalism, he could also on the other excoriate them for being behind the Marxist conspiracy: "The Jewish doctrine of Marxism rejects the aristocratic principle of nature and replaces it with the eternal privilege of the power and strength of the masses and of their dead weight."[76]

Wasn't Marx himself a Jew? And the Austrian Socialists: Hitler could uncover still more Jews there. The baptized Jewish Adler, the Jewish Bauer. If Hitler had met Trotsky then it is sure he would have had something to say about the ancestry of Herr Bronstein. As soon as Hitler connected the Jews with his archenemy, Marxism, he had invented a powerful enemy that he could hold before the masses. It was the subversive Jewish Communists who wanted to destroy all the traditions of old Austria, from the family to the Church. This was a magical combination for Hitler.

But he did thank the Socialists for one of the building blocks of his political "granite foundation." As we have already seen, once as he was watching a Socialist parade, Hitler was filled with awe: "[I stared] at the endless rows of Viennese workers marching four abreast in this mass demonstration. I stood almost two hours with bated breath observing this immense human snake as it rolled slowly by. In fearful depression I finally left the place and wandered homeward."[77]

It was exactly this "fearful depression" which Adler hoped to instill in Vienna's self-satisfied and sated bourgeois. Adler's direction of such mass demonstrations was highly dramatic—Wagnerian in fact. Not even Hitler could discount the power of such silent demonstrations. His own party rallies a quarter of a century later in Nuremberg obviously owed much to the mass demonstrations he had seen in Vienna.

Hitler also recognized another Marxist imperative—the importance of the strong leader:

> The masses love a commander more than a petitioner and feel inwardly more satisfied by a doctrine tolerating none other beside itself. . . . They are unaware of their shameless spiritual terrorization and the hideous abuse of the human freedom, for they absolutely fail to suspect the inner insanity of the whole doctrine. All they see is the ruthless force and brutality of its calculated manifestations, to which they always submit in the end.[78]

Though commenting here on what he perceived to be the tactics of the Social Democrats, Hitler could equally well have been laying down guidelines for his own Nazis.

In italics after this, Hitler adds:

> *If Social Democracy is opposed by a doctrine of greater truth, but equal brutality of methods, the latter will conquer.*[79]

And just to leave no doubt in the reader's mind that he has learned the lesson of terror very well, Hitler later adds:

> The terror in the workshop, in the factory, in the assembly hall, and on occasion of mass demonstrations will always be accompanied by success as long as it is not met by an equally great force of terror.[80]

Above all, Hitler learned from the Socialists to found his own tactics "on precise calculation of all human weaknesses."[81] He praised the

Socialists for their correct use of not only terror but also propaganda; the intelligent use of unions; and the mobilization of the little man.

Out of the hodgepodge of contrary beliefs and movements, and even out of the lack of political involvement on the part of the artistic citizens of turn-of-the-century Vienna, Hitler brewed a cynical political *Weltanschauung.* "At that time [1907-13]," Hitler later remembered, "I formed a view of life which became the granite foundation of my actions."[82]

Hanisch and Hitler worked hard during May and the first part of June. Productive members of society, they turned out and sold pictures and postcards. Hanisch quickly sold off the more expensive paintings that Hitler produced. Hanisch wanted them to get some money ahead so that they could abandon the small-time postcard business and specialize in the more lucrative line of painting for the frame and upholstery shops. He wanted to play the part of a small-time capitalist and to reinvest their profits and expand operations.[83]

As the summer solstice approached and the days lengthened out long, warm, and lazily, Hitler's thoughts turned to things other than working like a slave, stuck inside the writing room every day.

A showdown was sure to come between the two men over their respective views of their partnership.

8

Super Egos

(1)

HITLER completely lacked the facility to see causalities. This amorality would later be both his strength and his weakness.

It was warm outside in the early summer of 1910. The birds began to chirp at five A.M., with the first light of the sun.

As Hitler sat in the writing room trying to convince himself to do some work, his mind probably wandered to summer days in Leonding, the little village near Linz where he had spent much of his boyhood. He fondly remembered the cowboys-and-Indians and war games he and his gang had then played.[1]

Those warm summer days of boyhood were most likely much more real to him now than was the past winter of near-starvation. The frostbitten toes were a thing of the past, buried in his memory until their recall would serve some purpose.

The sun spilled across the table in a great golden shaft, lighting up floating dust particles like tiny birds suspended in a head wind. Hitler was twenty crowns ahead after working on a big commission with Hanisch,[2] so why not live a little?

For Hitler, when it was summer, it would always be summer. The winter would never come again. He would never be poor and cold again—even if he did nothing to prevent it. One thing did not necessarily lead to another for Hitler.[3]

Josef Neumann came into the writing room to collect some commissions from the other men working there. There was a new man in the home, a sign painter named Josef Greiner who had started to work for Neumann.[4] Greiner had previously worked as a lamplighter in a cabaret, a new entertainment form in Vienna. The cabaret was called Hoelle in the Theater an der Wien.[5]

Hitler and Greiner had hit it off pretty well, mainly because of Greiner's fine ability to build "castles in the air"[6]—castles which Hitler was also not unaccustomed to inhabit.

But today it was not Greiner who tempted Hitler from his work, but Neumann. The weather must have affected him, too. Or perhaps it was the date, the twenty-first of June, the summer solstice. Hitler, with his love of Nordic myth and ancient rites, would surely remember such a day.[7] It was also his father Alois's name day. There must have been many reasons in Hitler's mind why he should celebrate that day. Neumann was merely the excuse.

The two went off together to enjoy themselves on the town. Hitler even rented a hotel room[8] to sleep in privacy again. Hitler and Neumann took in the museums and had a fine time. Hanisch soon got wind of the desertion, tracked Hitler down, and implored him to come back to work.

But Hitler was having none of it. His money was still holding out. He pleaded that the arduous work schedule he had been keeping had worn him out. He needed rest and relaxation. He was no coolie to be ordered about.[9]

There was nothing Hanisch could do but wait. Hitler was his bread and butter. He had no faith in his own meager artistic talents.

Within the week Hitler trudged back to the home, penniless and a little plumper for his orgy of pastry eating which had accompanied his museum visits. Hitler was known to eat "four or five pieces of pastry with whipped cream in a cheap coffeehouse"[10] at one sitting. Now he had to earn his daily bread again, and pastries had to be left behind until he had saved more money.

The taste of freedom had, however, tainted Hitler for work. If political debate had been the only thing that hindered Hitler from working, perhaps the Hanisch-Hitler partnership could have survived. But now back home, Hitler started to form more of a comradeship with the schemer, Greiner.

Between bouts of haranguing the other occupants in the writing room with his views on everything from the Church to socialism, and planning great money-making schemes with Greiner, Hitler managed to scratch out a few pictures in June and early July for Hanisch to sell.

Hitler's new friendship stood an early test of loyalty when Greiner got a commission through Neumann to sketch some corsets for a shop on the Landstrasse.[11] Busy with his work, Greiner had Hitler, who was ever eager for an excuse to leave his own work, deliver some of the sketches to the shop. Hitler took the sketches and made his way into the First District and down the Wollzeile to the other end of the inner city to the Landstrasse and past the School of Arts and Crafts where Klimt had studied. Once at the corset shop, Hitler's nerve failed him. The shop was full of female customers and Hitler, like a young man purchasing his first prophylactic, was too embarrassed to go in with the sketches of women in corsets. He waited outside for the crowd to thin out, but as soon as one lady left, another brushed past the very grubby-looking young man to take her place.

Finally giving up, his mission unaccomplished, Hitler crawled back to the Männerheim. He told Greiner that the firm had rejected the sketches, but Greiner could not believe it and rushed to the shop, arriving just before closing. He had almost lost the commission because of Hitler's prudery.

Strangely, this episode did not deter Greiner from becoming closer friends with Hitler. Perhaps he needed a friend and partner badly enough to overlook it. Soon the two—though Hitler was still officially painting for Hanisch—were working on an advertising commission that Neumann got them. Hitler at first saw little use in such foolishness, but a poster was, after all, easier to produce than a painting.

Neumann's new commission was for a shoe store bearing the illustrious name of Ha-Ha. Hitler and Greiner's job was to draw twenty shoe styles for use as ads. It was a fat contract: they stood to make thirty crowns for the drawings from which Neumann would take only 20 percent. Compared to the 50 percent that Hanisch was getting, this seemed more than fair and started Hitler thinking about his existing partnership. The only problem with the drawings was that they had to be made from the shoes Neumann had brought with him from the shop, and they were all left shoes.[12]

That evening Greiner, Hitler, and Neumann went out to celebrate the commission at the Gasthaus Marhold on the Fleischmarkt in the Greek quarter of the First District. Hitler ate well, consuming a double portion of the sweet little dumplings, *Kaiserschmarm*. His tastes were getting expensive again.

After dinner, the trio wandered out to the canal at the Franz Joseph Kai and went into the Café Siller, where Hitler started his usual rampage about Schönerer and how the Jews were ruining the economic health of the empire. That it was Neumann, the Jew, sitting across from him, who had secured them the commission that they were celebrating, Hitler never mentioned.[13] He could somehow separate his convictions from real life. It was part of his "gift" of amorality.

The next day Hitler and Greiner were to start work on the shoe sketches, but Hitler had an "accident" in the kitchen that morning that prevented him from working for a few days. While cooking his rice and milk dish, he had made the mistake of spouting his antisocialist ideas in front of two "herculean moving men"[14] staying at the home. After they heard enough, the two men calmly boxed Hitler's ears and threw him bodily out of the kitchen. Hitler ended up with a sizable knot on his head, a red and swollen face, and a bruise on his right arm that kept him from sketching for a few days.

Finally, though, the shoe sketches were finished. Hitler was ready for some more of the good money from advertising posters. Meanwhile, Hanisch would have to look after himself.

Neumann brought Hitler another commission from a drugstore advertising a deodorant foot powder.[15] The brand was Teddy Schweisspuder." Hitler struck on the idea of the most logical people to advertise such a product: the mailmen who walked more kilometers per day than any other Viennese. His sketch slowly developed.

Two postmen sat on house steps, one with his shoes off, looking disgustedly at his sweaty socks. The other mailman, looking on in amusement, still had his shoes on his feet. He laughed and told his friend that he should learn the secret of Teddy Powder. At the bottom of the sketch was the jingle:

Zehntausend Stufen, Tag für Tag,
Ist eine riesengrosse Plag!
Zehntausend Stufen, liebe Bruder,
Ist eine Lust mit Teddy Puder!

(Ten thousand steps day in day out,
Is an enormous pain!
Ten thousand steps, dear brother,
Is a joy with Teddy Powder!)[16]

The idea was not bad—whether it was Hitler's or the firm's is not known. The sketch, however, was not quite up to par. Instead of smiling, the postmen seemed to sneer. The painting was so full of grimaces that Neumann was all but thrown out of the shop when he brought his poster around to the customer.

Hitler had tried his wings alone and failed. After this, he went back to work for Hanisch. To make up for his long vacation, Hitler began a large painting of the Rathaus. He figured he could get 50 crowns for this painting from the art dealers, and this became his major project for the rest of July.

Hitler had been bitten, though. The art of advertising was beginning to excite him, just as had the movie about the orator. There were possibilities in this new field.

One morning before beginning work, Hitler was going through the morning papers and came across an ad that especially appealed to him.[17] There was a sketch of a woman with floor-length hair and a testimonial that started "I, Anna Csillag with the Lorelei hair . . ."[18] and recommended an amazing hair pomade that would make hair grow "even on a billiard ball."[19]

Hitler was amazed by the number of people who wrote in testimonials for the hair pomade, but after checking into the names he reportedly discovered that these people had long been dead.

"Now that's called advertising," he laughed. "Propaganda, propaganda, until the people believe this trash will help them."[20] He waved his T-square at the other men in the writing room as if conducting an orchestra. Some noses lifted out of newspapers; rheumy, sleepy eyes met his.

> . . . Until they no longer know what is fantasy and what reality. Anna Csillag has hit the nail on the head with propaganda. She sells her hair pomade under the promise of testimonials . . . the only thing she forgets to tell you is that the hair only begins to grow underground . . . [21]

For days Hitler was filled with new schemes for separating the unwitting public from their money. One scheme was the development of a paste to keep windows from freezing, which Hitler would only sell in the summer so that it could not be tested.

Hanisch, coming back from his rounds of the galleries and frame manufacturers, took the flailing T-square out of Hitler's hands, sat him down at the table again, and laid this scheme to rest by saying that merchants would never buy such a paste in the summer.

Hitler looked up at Hanisch through his lock of hair, and replied that the essential ingredients were oratory and propaganda.[22] "Propaganda is the essence of every religion, whether it be for heaven or hair pomade."[23] With propaganda Hitler believed he could sell even an antifreeze paste in the summer.

During all this time, Hitler held true to his old love of music and Wagner. They were synonymous for Hitler. He always held the image of Wagner before him: Wagner the revolutionary; Wagner the struggling, misunderstood artist; Wagner the acclaimed master of his day, winning against all obstacles. This image still sustained Hitler, though his own path seemed daily to be diverging from that of the artist.

Most probably he bought some two-crown tickets during his week off with Neumann. And when he was short of cash he could still get his fill of Wagner by walking over into the Second District to the Prater. There he would stand outside the scenic railway[24] and listen to the organ grind out tunes from Wagner operas such as *Tannhäuser* and *Fliegende Holländer*. Sometimes Hitler dragged along his cronies and would stand listening quietly until his favorite passage came up, and then would grab an arm and excitedly declaim "That's the passage! Do you hear? That's the passage!"[25]

All the way back to the Männerheim he would relate the action of the opera and twitch his arms about as if conducting. When the organist decided to play some Mozart, Hitler would fidget and get his friends to leave. For him Mozart was a thing of the past, suited for the sentimental centuries gone by, but long outmoded in the twentieth century.

One wonders if Hitler ever realized that his precious Wagner, already dead for more than a generation by that time, was also a phenomenon of the past and that new composers had come to take his place.

(2)

Gustav, Alma, and their daughter Gucki had come back to Austria for the summer of 1910. The hectic schedule of musical New York had depleted Mahler's energy, and he longed for the peace of the Alps to begin writing his Tenth Symphony.

He was a different Mahler from the active outdoorsman of three years before. The terrible summer of 1907—his other daughter's death and the discovery of his heart condition—had ended the excessive bicycling, hiking, and swimming that Mahler was so fond of doing in the summer. He had aged. He celebrated his fiftieth birthday on July 7, and he felt his age and more. He now carried a stopwatch to count his steps and measure his pulse. He stopped at intervals, even on the easiest of walks, to have Alma listen to his heart.[26]

Mahler grew superstitious about his work, too, and felt that he had cheated God by not calling his *Das Lied von der Erde* a symphony. It would have been his Ninth, and nine had been an unlucky number for composers. Neither Bruckner nor Beethoven had lived past their Ninths. Mahler had already written a symphony after *Das Lied von der Erde*—his Ninth. He felt that he had gotten past the danger zone now that he had started work on his Tenth.[27]

In less than a year he would be dead, his Tenth left unfinished.

Taking care of Mahler had taken a toll on Alma, too. Once settled in their house at Toblach in the South Tyrolean Alps, Alma discovered she needed a change of scenery and a complete rest herself. Her doctor prescribed a cure at a small spa in Styria.

Alma got more than she bargained for, though, in the form of a handsome young man from Germany who soon fell in love with her and expected her to return the love.[28] The young man's name was Walter Gropius, later to be a world-famous architect and driving force in the Bauhaus in Germany.

Alma left the spa pursued by Gropius. Back in Toblach, a letter came one day addressed to "Herr Direktor Mahler"—it was an impassioned plea for Alma from Gropius, asking Mahler for her hand.[29]

It was a shock for both Mahler and Alma. Mahler's secure domestic world was suddenly torn apart. For Alma, the shock of someone else truly being interested in her had a catalytic effect and she poured out her heart to Mahler. She told him of her lost composing ambition; her feeling of isolation from him when he was so absorbed continually in his work. Mahler saw Alma suddenly for the first time as his wife and someone deserving of inner obligations from him—the inner obligations he had until then reserved only for his music.[30]

This crisis brought the two together for a time. They clung to each other like lost children—their world of safe illusions that they had folded around their life which hid the hollowness at the center of their so-called domestic happiness, was now forever shattered. All those little subterfuges that man and woman use to escape absolute honesty with one another now disappeared from between them and they were faced with some startling discoveries.

Mahler became almost desperate in his love for Alma now that he knew someone else wanted her and that she had been so personally unfulfilled for so many years. He wrote her little notes that he would leave on her bedside table in the morning:

> My breath of life! I've kissed the little slippers a thousand times and stood by your door with longing. You took pity on me, glorious one, but the demons have punished me again, for thinking of myself and of you, dearest. I cannot move from your door; I would like to stand there until I have heard the sweet sound of your living and breathing. But I must leave! My queen has sent me into exile below. I bless you, my beloved— whatever fate awaits me at your hands. Every beat of my heart is for you![31]

Mahler had gone through a complete reversal in his emotions—from pouring his love into his music and using his wife as chief cook and bottle washer, he had turned into a fawning, jealous husband.[32] Sleeping in adjacent rooms, Mahler suddenly ordered that the doors must stay open between them so he could hear her breathe. Alma would wake in the night to see her husband standing over her in the dark, staring down at her, looking to her like a "departed spirit." [33]

One day, riding through the village of Toblach, Alma saw Gropius hiding under a bridge. When she told Mahler, he decided to have it out with the young man. He walked into the village and brought Gropius back with him. The three met in the study, two candles burning on Mahler's desk and Mahler pacing back and forth with the Bible in his hand, reading from the Scriptures.

He looked at Alma and beckoned her to choose between them. "Whatever you do," he said, "will be well done. Choose!"[34]

There was no choice. However much Gropius's wooing might have opened up the wellsprings of Alma's passion, she could not leave Mahler. While Hitler sat in the writing room at the Männerheim working on his masterpiece of the Rathaus, Alma drove Gropius to the train and saw him off. But that was not the end of it. Something had happened to Alma.

"My infinite love had lost its vigor and warmth,"[35] she wrote. Passion, long missing from her life, had suddenly been awakened and all "of a sudden I knew that my marriage was no marriage, that my own life was utterly unfulfilled."[36]

Though she did not confess it to him in so many words, Mahler knew it. The torment he suffered on account of this knowledge was written into his Tenth Symphony. This time, however, musical expression was not enough to slay the ghost of wounded emotions. The old therapy of pouring out his soul onto the musical staff no longer worked.

Many things came together at one time for Mahler: his age; his jealousy over a younger, more handsome suitor; his doubts about his music. Today, we might call such an experience the classic example of a midlife crisis.

For such people today, there are many avenues of escape from such a crisis: there are counselors and books to lead them out of the forest. But for Mahler, in the summer of 1910, there was only one man who could help him—Dr. Sigmund Freud.

(3)

Hanisch was tired of waiting for Hitler. The Rathaus painting was taking altogether too long. He had to do something. One day on his rounds he found an antique dealer in the Jewish section of the city, the Leopoldstadt, on Grosse Schiffgasse, who needed some quick work done. Tausky, the dealer, [37] showed Hanisch a silhouette on gilt glass and asked him if he could do anything like that.

Hanisch painted the silhouette of a lady on the glass himself, as Hitler was preoccupied with other things, and Tausky was pleased enough with the job to give Hanisch a larger commission. This time, the dealer wanted a silhouette of a Schubert evening concert, a favorite theme with the Viennese, who had scorned that composer during his lifetime.

Hanisch, aware of his lack of education, had to turn this one over to Hitler, as he "didn't know at that time who Schubert was."[38]

Hitler was happy enough to put aside the Rathaus painting and have a go at this new art form. He pulled out the ever-present postcard reproduction of the scene from the stack of cards he used for reference and began copying.

Hanisch, too, began to work on another silhouette for Tausky, and worked nonstop for two days until he had completed his work. Hitler was, however, still working sporadically on the Schubert silhouette. Hanisch sat and dogged him all day long, nipping any political discussions in the bud, until Hitler had finished his silhouette.

As Hanisch was leaving to deliver the glass, Hitler yelled after him: "Demand a hundred crowns for that one!"[39]

Hanisch had to take time to convince Hitler that a hundred crowns was a ridiculous demand, and finally Hitler sheepishly gave in and told Hanisch to get as much as he could.

Upon delivery, Tausky was a bit disappointed in one of the silhouettes. To Hanisch's surprise, it was Hitler's work that caused the discontent. The dealer actually liked Hanisch's work better than Hitler's, even though Hitler had supposedly had art lessons.

As with Hitler and the discovery of Neumann's reasonable 20 percent commission, this discovery by Hanisch worked in the same way. A great hole of doubt was formed in the midst of the Hitler-Hanisch partnership, now on Hanisch's side. Why bother to split anything with that worthless Hitler, if he could do the painting himself? Hanisch must have figured.

Hitler resumed work on the Rathaus painting, but at the same time kept devising new schemes. Painting on the glass had inspired Hitler with the idea that etching on gilded glass for the printing plates of banknotes might be a good way to make counterfeiting harder.[40]

Finally the big painting was finished. Hitler was sure he could get at least fifty crowns for it. He even accompanied Hanisch for a few days in search of a customer. Normally the better-dressed Hanisch acted as front man for the two, but now Hitler was beginning to distrust him. He wanted a complete list of the customers whom Hanisch visited to sell the paintings. It looked to both of the men as though their partnership were soon to go on the rocks. The Rathaus painting made it a sure thing.

After a few days of going the rounds and having the painting refused to his face, Hitler decided to save himself the disgrace. As with the Schubert silhouette, his first grandiose expectations had to be reduced just to sell the painting for anything they could get for it. After all, the rent had to be paid at the Männerheim; food had to be purchased.

Greiner, who never had any delusions about Hitler's artistic talent, did not think much of the painting. As he looked at the canvas before Hanisch wrapped it up to take it off to the markets, he noticed the "muddied color tones . . . and the poor construction . . . worth less than a poor print."⁴¹ In his opinion, it was worth far less than fifty crowns, but it was not up to him to tell the unreasonable Hitler. He had lately gotten another commission for some advertising posters for a clothing firm on the Mariahilferstrasse, and he had no time for Hitler and his furies.

Along with the Rathaus painting, Hanisch took another watercolor Hitler had painted, probably worth around ten crowns. Hitler still had high hopes of making a killing on both pictures.

It was hot in the last week of July. Locked in at the foot of the Wienerwald, Vienna sweltered in its usual summertime humidity. The horse dung and urine in the streets brewed under the high sun into an evil-smelling concoction that attacked the nose and sensibilities. The sun glared off the sidewalks as ladies scurried along under white parasols, a light rustle of skirts in the still heat.

Hanisch was nearly ready to give up. The "no's" were no longer even polite. He was wet clear through his jacket and the two paintings under his arms were gaining weight with each step.

He thought for a moment of the Pichlers' upholstery shop out on the Hernalser Hauptstrasse. The *Frau* there seemed to have taken a liking to Hitler's work. They might even buy one of these pictures. Then it suddenly struck him that he had already sold the Pichlers an earlier version of the Rathaus along with a watercolor of the Gloriette in Schönbrunn.⁴²

Hanisch finally headed up into the Ninth District, past the building where Freud lived. (Freud was not there at the time. He was on his way to Holland for a vacation. Vienna was no place to be in the height of summer.)

There was a frame shop in the Ninth District on Porzellangasse that Hanisch sometimes tried when his Jewish frame dealers had turned him down. Wenzel Reiner, the owner, was not overjoyed with the Rathaus picture, but he decided to take it for twelve crowns, six now and six more in a few days. Hanisch decided to accept the offer and he got rid of the other watercolor, of the *Dominikanerkloster*.⁴³

Hanisch gave Hitler the six crowns he had received, reserving the other six to be collected later as his share. Hitler was silent about the money, but obviously not pleased. The next day when Hanisch asked him for another picture that he had ordered two weeks before, Hitler told him that he had not finished it. There had been a political debate, and Hitler had had to add his bit to it. Hanisch could handle the frame dealers. He was a hustler who had a thousand different pitches to sell a painting and an equal number of dodges to explain why he could not deliver on time. But faced with the little old lady who had commissioned the painting based on a photograph of her birthplace in Bohemia—a painting to be taken home as a gift—Hanisch was putty. He had promised her the painting and now he would have to disappoint her. This put the cap on all his repressed anger at Hitler's laziness.

Hitler, for his part, was fed up with Hanisch's constant proddings to work; the terrible price he had gotten him for the Rathaus piece was one more straw on their overstrained relationship. Hitler didn't trust Hanisch anymore, and he would not be bullied into painting. One had to be in the mood for artistic work.

"Mood!" Hanisch shouted at him. "You're nothing but a hunger artist. Don't talk to me of mood."

"And you're nothing but a house servant!" Hitler retorted.[44]

The two had a fine argument then, Hanisch yelling that he was not ashamed to work. He had done all kinds of labor and was never too lazy to earn his living.

Hanisch stormed upstairs to his cubicle, packed his few things, and left the home that very day to find private lodgings somewhere in the city.

Hanisch had good luck, for when he went to Reiner's to collect his six crowns, there was a bank director there by the name of Sigmund Reich. Reich had just purchased the Rathaus painting for thirty-five crowns and believed Hanisch to have painted it. Hanisch did nothing to dissuade Reich of this idea, and the director commissioned Hanisch to do seventy watercolors of Austrian folk costumes.[45]

Hitler was not faring as well as Hanisch. Greiner was too busy with his own work to come up with any new schemes, and Neumann had not dropped around to the Männerhein lately. Hitler was stuck with some paintings and didn't know how to go about getting rid of them. He did know some of the customers now, after going the rounds with Hanisch in an attempt to sell the Rathaus painting. But he was too shy to go out and hawk his own wares. He had not stooped to being such a petty businessman as that yet.

Besides, Hitler suddenly realized that his partners had been shielding him from rebuffs of his art. It was a difficult thing to stand in front of a dealer and hear criticism of his own work.

Hitler had other reasons for lying low. He did not want to run afoul of the police in any way, and dressed as he was and looking like the tramp that he did, he did not want to risk arrest for peddling.

Hitler sat brooding in the Männerheim until the first week of August. His money was running out. In a few months it would be cold again and how would he survive then? No food. No shelter. He suddenly remembered the chilblains from the previous winter. A hot flash of fear must have twisted his stomach at the memory and the prospect.

And whose fault was it? That damn Hanisch! He'd left Hitler high and dry with a few miserable crowns for all his trouble. He had probably been cheating all along. How could Hanisch afford to go out and live in private lodgings, anyway?[46]

Hitler's thinking must have gone along lines such as these, for at any rate, by early August he was so distraught that he overcame his fear of the police and of the possible consequences of his draft evasion, to go to the Brigittenau police station and sign a complaint against Hanisch.

In the complaint, Hitler stated that his former friend Hanisch had embezzled fifty crowns from him in the form of a painting he was to have sold. Hitler claimed he had never received any money from Hanisch for the painting.[47]

Meanwhile, Hanisch was in high spirits. He was walking along the Favoritenplatz one fine afternoon calculating how much he would make from seventy watercolors, when he met one of the new men from the Männerheim. Siegfried Löffner. Löffner was a Jew who sold postcards for a living and was perhaps hawking some of Hitler's work now that Hanisch was gone.[48]

Löffner came up to Hanisch and accused him of being a thief. Hanisch could not quite figure out what Löffner was getting at, but the postcard salesman went on to reproach him for making off with the Rathaus painting without paying the poor painter. Hanisch tried to explain about that poor painter, Hitler, but Löffner was more and more insistent and a violent argument ensued. In the middle of their shouting, a policeman walked up to find out what the trouble was, and Löffner told the policeman about the "theft." Both of them were taken off to the Commissariat of Police in Weiden, where it was discovered that Hanisch was living under an assumed name, Walter Fritz. He was taken into custody and Löffner signed an affidavit:

4 August 1910: Reinhold Hanisch—embezzlement, false registration: Siegfried Löffner, local agent, XX, Meldemannstrasse 27, declares: I have learned from the painter in the Männerheim that the accused sold

this picture *(Rathaus)* and embezzled the money. I don't know the painter by name, only from the Männerheim where he always sat next to the accused . . ."[49]

Hanisch obviously tried to get out of this double charge of embezzlement and the use of an assumed name by blaming the latter on Hitler, for in Hitler's deposition from the next day, he states that the name was not his idea:

Adolf Hitler, artist, born 20/4/1889 in Braunau, domiciled in Linz. Catholic, single, now living at 27 Meldemannstrasse, XX District, declares: It is not correct to say that I advised Hanisch to take the name of Walter Fritz. I have never known him by any other name except Walter Fritz. As he was without means, I gave him the pictures I painted so that he could sell them. He regularly received from me 50 percent of the sums realized. For roughly two weeks Hanisch has not returned to the Männerheim and he has defrauded me of the painting *Rathaus,* worth fifty crowns, and a watercolor to the value of nine crowns. The only document that I have seen is the said employment book in the name of Walter Fritz. I have known Hanisch from the time I lived at the Asylum in Meidling. 5 August, 1910   *Adolf Hitler*[50]

Hitler blatantly lied to the police to get back at Hanisch for deserting him. Hanisch had paid Hitler and had not defrauded him of the fifty crowns which Hitler claimed in his statement. In Hitler's mind, however, Hanisch's treachery of "leaving" him had to be avenged somehow and he was prepared to use any means—even a perversion of the legal system—to get back at Hanisch.

The trial was held six days later. Hitler had decided, meanwhile, to change his story and admit to receiving some money for the second painting of the Dominican Cloister. To everyone's surprise but Hitler's—for such was his scheme to begin with, as witness his slip of the name in the transcript—the court did not even deal with the question of fraud, but only with the fact that Hanisch was living under an assumed name. Hanisch held back the name of the dealer to whom he had sold the Rathaus picture, knowing that he was certain to be sentenced anyway for living under a false name, and not wanting it to get back to the bank director that he had not painted the picture that had won him the further commission.[51]

The judge sentenced Hanisch to a few days in jail and as the witnesses were filing out, Hanisch called to Hitler in his threadbare coat and long hair: "When and where will we see each other again to make a settlement?"[52]

Most likely Hitler had started the whole action just to turn Hanisch in for using an assumed name as punishment for leaving him. It was a petty victory for Hitler and one that did nothing for his status at the home. The rest of the men blamed Hitler for what he had done to Hanisch[53] and would have little to do with him for months afterward.

Still, it was a victory for the little would-be artist. It was a telling foreshadowing of the ruthlessness he would later employ to seek revenge on anyone who had crossed him—a fine mixture of truth and lies that could pervert justice to his ends.

(4)

It had been a busy year for Freud. There was the publication of his work on Leonardo, illuminating the inner nature of artists in general, and tracing two motive forces in Leonardo's life back to early childhood events. That May, also, the prestigious *Neue Freie Presse* had asked him to contribute an article on his work—an offer he refused, saying that he was already "conspicuous enough in Vienna."[54]

These were positive signs, though. After the kudos received at the American conference the year before, even his hometown could no longer ignore his existence and work.

He sat by the seashore and watched his two young sons as they jumped in the water, splashing one another. He felt a sharp gas pain in his belly and thought that fame was not, however, without its price. It was the abominable American cooking that had given him his bad stomach. You had to take the good with the bad in this world, Freud believed.[55]

It was too bad about Karlsbad, though. The Freuds had planned a summer vacation there for 1910. A few weeks at Karlsbad would have taken care of his ailing stomach, and then on to Switzerland to visit Jung in Zurich. But Martha's mother had become very ill with the cancer that would claim her life the next fall, and they had to change their plans to be close to her in Hamburg.

So now, with his wife, Martha, staying with her mother, Freud was away in The Hague with his two boys. He had already spent the previous few days visiting every art collection in the area. He had visited Haarlem and Delft and was enchanted with that small town. But he was getting restless as he often did on vacations after exhausting all the cultural possibilities in the area. And here it was the twenty-sixth of July and it was Martha's birthday, the first one in over twenty years on which they had not been together.

He rubbed his stomach again, settled back on his elbows in the sand, and drew doodles as his sons had a fine time in the surf.

Three days later the entire family met in Leyden and then went out to the cozy little pension they had booked, Pension Nordsee, on the coast at Noordwiyk to spend a carefree month.[56]

For Freud the prospect of a month at the seaside, now that he was reunited with his wife and other children, was pleasant indeed—especially when he knew there was some good traveling ahead of him in September, to Italy and Sicily.

In the second week of August, Freud's friend Ernest Jones from the United States came to visit him and the two spent long hours walking together on the beach talking about psychoanalysis.

"On our long walks on the edge of the sea," Jones later wrote, "he would stride along swiftly, and I noticed he had to poke every bit of seaweed with his stick, his quick eyes darting here and there all the time. I asked him what he expected to find, but got the noncommittal answer, 'Something interesting; you never know.'"[57]

Even at ease, Freud's curious mind was at work.

This was only the third time in his life that Freud had seen the open sea—the first time for his sons. Though the turbulence of the water at first excited him, he soon tired of the flat Dutch landscape and longed for his beloved mountains in Austria.

Just as Freud was languishing in the initial stages of boredom, he was saved. An urgent telegram came from the South Tyrol from a man whose name was familiar to Freud.

Gustav Mahler was a man of worth in Freud's eyes, though all in all Freud was a bit suspicious of music "because its effect upon his senses could not be as clearly analyzed as the plastic arts or literature. A doctor specializing in the mind must be wary of abandoning himself to such dubious influences."[58] In this fear, Freud rather echoed Trotsky's doubts about psychoanalysis.

From the sound of Mahler's telegram and the letter from the psychoanalyst in Vienna who had recommended him to Freud, the composer was "greatly distressed about his relationship to his wife."[59]

Freud immediately acknowledged the appointment and Mahler just as quickly cancelled it. He had thought better of seeing Freud—perhaps he did not really need analysis after all.

Freud well understood such apprehension. He persisted and two more appointments and cancellations ensued before Freud gave Mahler a deadline: he was leaving for Italy by the end of the month. Mahler had one more chance to meet with Freud, and that was on August 26 in Leyden. Mahler agreed.

On his way to meet with Freud, Mahler sent a telegram to Alma from Innsbruck: "All good and evil powers accompany me; you sit enthroned above them all. Good night, my lyre. I feel only joy and longing."[60]

Meanwhile, Freud arrived in Leyden from his seaside resort, took a hotel room for the day, and awaited Mahler's arrival. Mahler was hesitant at first, filled with the sort of nervous premonitions that usually accompany a visit to the dentist. Both men were known to be great walkers, and Freud decided to conduct the analysis on foot, lacking his famous couch as he was. For the next four hours, the two strolled the streets of Leyden, Freud asking questions to open up the famous composer and Mahler responding with alacrity, his complex mind taking well to the new discipline.[61]

It seems Mahler had developed an impotency with his wife as a result of their crisis—most likely the impotency was also expressed in his music of the time, for Freud's approach concerned Mahler's creative as well as his domestic life.

After listening to Mahler ramble for several hours, Freud suddenly stopped and turned to him.

"I take it that your mother was called Marie," he said. "How comes it that you married someone with another name, Alma, since your mother evidently played a dominating part in your life?"[62]

Mahler was shocked. It was as if Freud had seen into his soul. He stammered that Alma's name was Alma Maria, but that he called her Marie, and he'd never understood until now the significance of it.

Freud obviously thought Mahler had a mother fixation and that this played a dominant part in Mahler's emotional life. From Freud's notes, it comes out that Mahler's mother was lame and that she had determined his feminine ideal. Her careworn face from a hard life of bearing twelve children was what Mahler wanted to see in his own mate. He often complained to Alma that he wished her face were "more marked by suffering."[63]

Names played another significant unconscious part in his and

Alma's relationship. He was not the only one transferring a mate into a parent, for Alma was perhaps seeking out her dead father, the famous painter, when she chose a man older than herself, a man in the arts who bore a name very much like the German word for painter.

Freud dispelled Mahler's fears that his age separated him from his wife. "I know your wife," Freud told him. "She loved her father and can seek and love only his type. Your age, which you are afraid of, is just what attracts your wife. Don't worry about it."[64]

From his domestic life, Mahler was suddenly able to jump to a self-analysis of his creative potential and understand why his work was at times ruined by the most banal of melodies at the most crucial dramatic moment.

Mahler spoke to Freud of the ugly scenes he had witnessed as a boy between his mother and father. During one of their particularly brutal arguments, he ran out of the house. There on the street in front of the Mahler house was an organ grinder churning out *"O du lieber Augustin, alles ist hin."* Somehow the dissonance of the commonplace with the tragic struck the young Mahler and stayed with him all through his life, creeping into his music as silly tunes that kept him from achieving the pure dramatic intent he aimed for. It was this, Mahler thought, that kept him from creating music of the highest order.[65]

It was only a band-aid cure. Freud could not hope to get to the base of any neurosis in so short a time. He offered suggestions to give some immediate relief to the situation, and seemingly they helped. Mahler wrote to his wife on the train back to her of his treatment in poetical terms:

> *Nachtschatten sind verweht an einem mächt'gen Wort,*
> *Verstummt der Qualen nie ermattet Wüheln.*
> *Zusammen floss zu einem einzigen Akkord,*
> *Mein zagend Denken und mein brausend Fünlen.*
>
> (Night shades were dispelled by one powerful word,
> The tireless throb of torment ended.
> At last united in one single chord,
> My timid thoughts and my tempestuous feelings blended.)[66]

Back in Toblach, Mahler and Alma found new peace. He got out her early compositions, played them, and promised to have them published. Their marriage resumed some order for the next year of Mahler's life.

Freud later wrote of the meeting: "I analyzed Mahler for an afternoon in Leyden. If I may believe reports, I achieved much with him at that time. . . . In highly interesting expeditions through his life history, we discovered his personal conditions for love, especially his Holy Mary complex (Oedipal fixation). I had plenty of opportunity to admire the capability for psychological understanding of this man of genius."[67]

But Freud was not fooled by quick results: "No light fell at the time on the symptomatic façade of his obsessional neurosis. It was as if you would dig a single shaft of light through a mysterious building."[68]

(5)

There have been many attempts at sending a psychoanalytic shaft of light into Hitler's life.[69] Freud would have had a marvelous exercise with Hitler's life story. Hitler's was in many ways the typical Austrian family, with the autocratic, nonverbal father and the put-upon little *Frau,* enduring his abuse and steamroller sexuality while keeping an immaculate house.

Klara Hitler was the niece of papa Alois—his third wife under somewhat strained circumstances. She was a helper in the home during the death of Alois's second wife and became pregnant long before the second wife died. Being a good Catholic, Klara could not have failed to feel guilt from this episode.

By the time Adolf was born, several years after her marriage to Alois, Klara had already lost three children from sickness. Adolf was born on Easter eve and was, from all accounts, a sickly child. Undoubtedly Klara poured out all her motherly love and guilt upon her fourth baby. She must have been terrified of losing this one, too.

Though there were other children after Adolf, and two older ones from Alois's second marriage, it is clear that Klara and Adolf formed a special bond with one another, apparent enough for the family physician, Dr. Bloch, to have mentioned it.[70] Neighbors noticed the strange attraction between mother and son. From his Munich days onward, Hitler would be sure to hang a picture of his mother over his bed no matter where he went.

The stern father who regularly beat his children[71] and the quiet housewife who kept a spotless home and harbored a secret guilt is a formula that Freud often came across in his cases. Had Freud analyzed

Hitler, he might well have come to the conclusion that later psychoanalysts were to reach: that Hitler had a strong Oedipal complex.

There was the classic love-hate for his father; he wanted to please him, yet received little more than a whipping as a show of affection from that undemonstrative man. Thrown into the devoted care of a mother frantic to redeem her sin and anxious not to lose another little baby, Hitler was almost bound to form the classic mother attachment.

There were also two more variables in Hitler's case. As was mentioned earlier, when the Russians examined Hitler's corpse in 1945,[72] it was discovered that he was missing the left testicle. Klara could not have failed to notice such an absence. Her undoubted subsequent searches of little Adolf's scrotal sac most likely served to cement a sexual bond between the baby and its mother.

Other psychologists[73] have found evidence in Hitler's own writings that he witnessed some primal scene between father and mother that caused the youngster a sexual trauma, increasing the competition for his mother's love between son and father.

In *Mein Kampf,* Hitler usually plods along with mixed metaphors to build a case for his beliefs and the rightness of his purpose. In a rare bit of very personal writing, he describes a typical life of an average poor Viennese working family.

> Let us imagine the following. In a basement apartment of two stuffy rooms lives a worker's family. Among the five children there is a boy, let us say, of three. This is the age at which a child becomes conscious of his first impressions. In gifted people, the traces of these early memories are found even in old age. The smallness and overcrowding of the rooms do not create favorable conditions. Quarreling and nagging often arise because of this. In such circumstances people do not live with one another, but push down on top of one another. Every argument . . . leads to a never-ending, disgusting quarrel. . . . But when the parents fight almost daily, their brutality leaves nothing to the imagination; the results of such visual education must slowly but inevitably become apparent in the little ones . . . especially when the mutual differences express themselves in the form of brutal attacks on the part of the father toward the mother or to assaults due to drunkenness. The poor little boy at the age of six, senses things which would make even a grownup shudder. Morally infected . . . the young "citizen" wanders off to elementary school.
>
> The three-year-old has now become a youth of fifteen who [has been dismissed from school and] despises all authority. . . . Now he loiters about and God only knows when he comes home . . .[74]

This is perhaps the strongest piece of autobiographical writing we have from Hitler, and he could only have done it through unconscious projection and displacement. Too many facts tally to make the story merely an accident. First of all, where would Hitler have gotten the information of such a family except from his own? We have no evidence of his having lived with this kind of family, though it was possible that he lived as an unregistered *Bettgeher* in the autumn of 1909. The crowded room with five children also describes the Hitler family in the early years of Adolf's life. The father, Alois, though no common laborer, did like his wine and was known as a rough sort of lout. One wonders what scenes the young Hitler saw that would make "even a grownup shudder." And there is little doubt to whom Hitler is referring when he mentions that traces of these early memories are to be found later in life with "gifted people." Hitler surely considered himself one.

If such an early scene had been sexual, which it could easily have been in such close quarters, it might well have remained fixed in Hitler's mind. Even if no such scene of brutal sexuality[75] occurred, the option is that Hitler's fantasy was at work. Perhaps he even imagined himself making love to his mother and felt guilty about it.

Freud was to hear many far more bizarre stories than that and he believed them until he finally realized these stories were the results of sexual fantasies of sexually repressed men and women.

Hitler's parents—like Mahler's, it would seem—quarreled often and as a result of these quarrels and a resulting physical assault, some traumatic scene likely was imprinted on both Hitler's and Mahler's minds.

As Mahler searched for a surrogate Marie with a careworn face in his wife, Alma, Hitler found grace with older women. The budding Nazi party in Munich was funded to a large extent by the elderly wives of industrialists.

And just as his father married very young women, so did Hitler form attachments with women much younger than he. One of the first loves of his life was a sixteen-year-old girl, Mini Reiter. He was thirty-seven at the time. Just as father Alois had married his niece, so, too, did Hitler have an affair with his own niece, Geli Raubal, who later committed suicide. The woman Hitler finally married, because she had agreed to die with him, Eva Braun, was twenty-three years younger than he.

Hitler's mother-love and father-competition became a way of life for him. He transferred his love of mother to love of the Motherland. The female principle took on for Hitler the Goddess of Fate aspect.[76]

But the female element also took on a dark, chaotic aspect for Hitler—his own mother had fooled him and given her love to his father. There must have been an element of betrayal in his vision of this brutal scene between mother and father. There is, too, a high degree of sadism in his later appraisals of women: "Like a woman whose psychic feeling is influenced less by abstract reasoning than by indefinable sentimental longing for the complementary strength, who will submit to the strong man rather than dominate the weakling, thus the masses love the ruler rather than the supplant . . ."[77]

In a society such as turn-of-the-century Vienna, where the outside world was ruled by the patriarchy and the home ruled by a matriarchy, such a dualistic approach to the female as Hitler's was not without ground. In a society where the men thought that they had the power, and the women knew that *they* did, the price of male supremacy in other matters was their total abdication of domestic rights. Sons were raised by their mothers and only a few polite words were reserved for daddy. They had their shirts boiled by their mothers; their suits ironed; shoes polished. In fact, they were trained to be helpless in many respects without women.

The three *K*'s ruled Vienna. The woman's place was "*Kinder, Küche, Kirche*" (children, kitchen, church). And although every mother's son grew up to take his place in the man's world, there must have been a secret place in all of their minds that acknowledged the real throne of power in the matriarchy, and resented women for it.

One such resentment was made public and very popular by the time Hitler began his stay in Vienna. Otto Weininger, with his book *Sex and Character,* became an overnight best-selling author by accusing women of being the chaotic forces in the world.[78]

Hitler was also a victim of this duality of feelings toward women—he could hold women up to be objects of virtue, and at the same time believe them to be debased creatures.

Kubizek writes of an incident in which Adolf came into their room on the Stumpergasse while Kubizek was giving a music lesson to a wealthy young girl. Kubizek introduced his roommate to the pupil but Hitler remained silent until the girl had gone, then launched a tirade at Kubizek. Kubizek tells us that "since his unfortunate experience with Stephanie, he was a woman hater. Was our room, already spoiled by that monster, that grand piano, to become the rendezvous for this crew of musical women?" Hitler proceeded to give Kubizek a detailed description of the "senselessness of women studying."[79]

The "affair" with Stephanie, the mysterious, never-spoken-to first love of the young dandy in Linz, is also indicative of Hitler's inferiority complex vis-à-vis women. Stephanie was the perfect object of his adolescent dreams—unapproachable and divine. For a young man with one testicle, who was perhaps afraid of testing his sexual ability, she was the perfect sex object, for if Hitler never spoke to her, he had nothing to fear.

We already know that Kubizek reports that Hitler was "hugely pleased"[80] that women were not admitted to the promenade of his holy Opera House, because they only came to flirt with the officers and could not appreciate the music anyway.

Hanisch, too, noticed Hitler's ambiguity toward women—his respect and, at the same time, disdain. Hitler had "very austere ideas about relations between men and women," Hanisch related.

> But Hitler's high opinion of love and marriage, and his strong condemnation of men's disloyalty, didn't prevent him from having very small regard for women. He used to lecture us about this, saying every woman can be had. All you have to do, he said, is to wear your hat on the back of your head, so your face will be as visible as possible.... He often said it was the woman's fault if a man went astray.... A decent man can never improve a bad woman, but a woman can improve a man. Then he used to relate an experience he had when he was very young, to prove his self-control. During one of his summer vacations from high school in the country, he met a milkmaid who appealed to him, and who liked him, too. Once when she was milking the cow and he was alone with her, she behaved rather foolishly. But Hitler suddenly thought of the eventual consequences and ran away, like the chaste Joseph, knocking over a big pot of fresh milk.[81]

Here are all the elements of the mature Hitler's attitude toward women—he exalts them as the savior of man in marriage, but derides them by saying they all can be had, as if he would even know. We catch an inadvertent glimpse of the sexually terrified young man running in fright from the horrors of a natural sex act.

In the Third Reich, women were considered little more than breeding machines for strong Aryan men. While Hitler rhapsodized publicly on the joys of marriage, in private he was approving of Himmler's stud farms. Hitler hated the idea of female emancipation and branded it another Jewish trick. But he could, at the same time, set aside August 12 as a day honoring motherhood. It was his mother's birthday.

If the stories of sexual perversion concerning Hitler mentioned in Chapter 3 are true, the Oedipal complex may go a long way toward explaining them. Hitler's early attempts at winning love from his father may have resulted in masochism. The only way to gain Alois's love, it seems, was by getting his attention. And the way to get his attention most easily was to irritate him enough to get a whipping. It is interesting in this connection that some of Hitler's most prized possessions in the Munich years were the three riding crops given to him by older women. He carried a crop continually, and had a habit of beating his palm or thigh with it when agitated.

Perhaps it appears facile to credit the incredible sadistic brutality of the Third Reich to the masochistic daydreams of a young, failed painter; but once the painter became a politician, the daydreams could become real-life nightmares.

Had a shaft of psychoanalytical light shone through the façade of Hitler's psyche in his Vienna years, world history might have been considerably different. In the city where psychoanalysis was founded, its need was greatest.

Emperor Franz Joseph and Archduke Franz Ferdinand in the state carriage during a procession around the Ring in 1912.

Turn-of-the-century Vienna, along the Ringstrasse. On the left are the Parliament, Rathaus, University, and Votivkirche; on the right is the Burgtheater. Hitler sent a postcard of this view to his friend Kubizek and later painted the same scene from a postcard.

(Courtesy Bildarchiv d. Oest. National)

The same scene of Vienna photographed more than a generation later with the stamp of the Third Reich, the swastika flag, flapping in front of Parliament. *(Courtesy Historisches Museum der Stadt Wien)*

Hitler's first home in Vienna at Stumpergasse 29 in the Sixth District near the Westbahnhof.
(Photo by author)

A view of Hitler's first lodgings (upper right window) from the court-yard of the Stumpergasse building. One has to lean out the window to get a ray of sunlight.
(Photo by author)

Alser Kirche in Vienna by Hitler. Note the featureless man in the top hat in the left foreground. Little wonder that the Academy complained of too few heads.
(Courtesy Bundesarchiv)

Maria am Gestade by Hitler. The original is a watercolor, 18x27.5 centimeters, the usual size for Hitler watercolors so as to fit into medium-sized frames and sell easily. This was the church to which Hitler led his friend Kubizek the first night Kubizek came to Vienna.
(Courtesy Bundesarchiv)

Anthropogonika, — Urmensch und Raffe im Schrifttume der Alten, ausgewählte raffengeschichtliche Urkunden von J. Lanz-Liebenfels.

(26 Abbildungen.)

Verlag der „Ostara", Robaun bei Wien
Preis 80 H. — 70 Pf.

A sample of the intellectual approach the ex-monk Lanz von Liebenfels employed in his race arguments. From the title page of the October 1906 edition of *Ostara*. This is most likely one of the back issues that Hitler visited Liebenfels in 1909 to acquire.

(Courtesy Bildarchiv)

Unsere Alldeutschen beim alten Schönerer.

(Zeichnung von M. Ju...

A newspaper caricature of Schönerer from 1912 that shows how comically his Pan-German party was viewed by many Viennese. Hitler would later use Schönerer's racial anti-Semitism but avoid the man's fight with the Catholic Church.

(Courtesy Bildarchiv Nationalbibliothek)

Karl Lueger, the mayor of Vienna, shortly before his death in 1910. Hitler would use Lueger's sales-pitch approach to anti-Semitism in the most successfully exploitative manner.

(Courtesy Bildarchiv National)

Gustav Mahler on his
way to the Opera, 1904.
*(Courtesy Bildarchiv
Nationalbibliothek)*

The father of Zionism,
Theodor Herzl, shortly
before his death in 1904.
*(Courtesy Bildarchiv
Nationalbibliothek)*

The satirist Karl Kraus, to whom such men as Schoenberg, Kokoschka, Loos, and Wittgenstein paid intellectual homage. Taken in 1908, shortly after Hitler had come to Vienna.
(Courtesy Bildarchiv d. Oest. Nationalbibliothek)

Arnold Schoenberg, painted by his friend the Expressionist painter Richard Gerstl, not long before Gerstl hanged himself. Undated oil painting.
(Courtesy Historisches Museum der Stadt Wien)

Otto Wagner's design for the Stadtbahn station at Karlsplatz. Drawn in India ink and watercolors, 1889.

(Courtesy Historisches Museum der Stadt Wien)

The Viennese did not know quite what to make of the Secession building during its construction in 1897. The curious flocked around the site all day long, according to the writer Hermann Bahr.

(Courtesy Historisches Museum der Stadt Wien)

Loos's 1910 "eyebrowless" house on the Michaelerplatz (right) and its more highbrow neighbors.

(Photo by author)

The Kiss by Gustav Klimt, 1907.
(Courtesy Oesterreichische Galerie)

Die Windsbraut by Oskar Kokoschka, 1914.
(Courtesy Das Kunstmuseum Basel)

Sigmund Freud with the
ever-present cigar in hand.
*(Courtesy Bildarchiv d
Oest. Nationalbibliothek*

Freud's couch.
*(Courtesy Hans Lobner,
Sigmund Freud Gesellschaft)*

The Männerheim on Melde-
mannstrasse in Vienna's Twentieth District where Hitler lived
for more than three years.
(Photo by author)

"I, Anna Csillag, with my six-
foot-long Lorelei hair." According to Greiner and Hanisch, it
was this advertisement that first
started Hitler thinking about the
power of propaganda. The Anna
Csillag Institut für Haarhygiene
is still to be found in Vienna in
the Hof at Stephanplatz 6.
(Photo by author)

Two advertising posters from 1911, sketched by Hitler. Left: The soap ad is in three colors: the background blue, the table and soap suds white, and the sides of the soap box yellow. Right: More interesting, in the light of the later Hitler, is the Fernolendt shoe polish poster with its red and gold background, black boot, and black-and-white lettering. A red background with black against it would play a significant part in the propaganda of the Third Reich and the high boot would become only too symbolic of that state.

(Courtesy Dr. Müllern-Schönhausen Collection)

Parliament with Rathaus, a painting by Hitler. See signature in lower right-hand corner.

(Courtesy Bundesarchiv)

Hitler's concept of a villa to be built on Vienna's Penzinger-strasse for the architect Florian Müller, drawn in 1911. No such house exists today.
(Courtesy Müllern-Schönhausen Collection)

Michaelskirche and Dreilau-ferhaus. Watercolor by Hitler.
(*Courtesy Bundesarchiv*)

Altes Burgtheater. One of
Hitler's Old Vienna paintings
from his later Vienna years.
(*Courtesy Bundesarchiv*)

Dominkanerkloster (initials in lower left-hand corner). From Hitler's late Vienna period. There is a sentimental charm to the painting despite its crudity of line.

(Courtesy Bundesarchiv)

Ruprechtskirche by Hitler, dated 1912 and sold to the frame dealer, Altenberg.

(Courtesy Frau Senta Altenberg)

St. Rochus Kappelle in Penzing, dated 1912, by Hitler. One of the paintings he sold to Jakob Altenberg and that was expropriated by the Third Reich in 1938.
(Courtesy Frau Senta Altenberg)

Viktor Adler, the father of Austrian socialism, reading a newspaper, circa 1910.
(Courtesy Bildarchiv Nationalbibliothek)

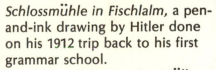

Schlossmühle in Fischlalm, a pen-and-ink drawing by Hitler done on his 1912 trip back to his first grammar school.

(*Courtesy Dr. Müllern-Schönhausen Collection*)

Leon Trotsky spent almost the same years in Vienna as Hitler did. From a picture shortly postdating the Vienna of 1913.

(*Courtesy Bildarchiv d. Oest. Nationalbibliothek*)

Interior of a typical café at the turn of the century. This one was located on Burggasse. The papers ringing the walls on their cane holders were a big draw of the Viennese coffee-houses.
(Courtesy Bildarchiv d. Oest. Nationalbibliothek)

The Cafe Central, at the corner of Herrengasse and Strauchgasse, where men as divergent as Trotsky, Alfred Adler, and Arthur Schnitzler gathered.

(Courtesy Bildarchiv Nationalbibliothek)

Hitler's victorious entry into Vienna, March 14, 1938. The procession travels toward the inner city along the Mariahilferstrasse at the intersection of Neubaugasse.

(Courtesy Bildarchiv Nationalbibliothek)

9

Symptoms of Debility

(1)

HITLER was at loose ends again. Summer was passing into autumn. It was that strange intermezzo time of year when the body begins to shift into high gear, preparing itself for the cold season ahead.

Hitler was now without a partner, having chased away Hanisch. He had no one willing to try to sell his work for a commission. Neumann had finally packed his suitcases and, after trying unsuccessfully to get Hitler to join him, set off for the "promised land"—Germany.[1] Greiner, too, had suddenly disappeared. Hitler's friends would come and go, but he always remained at the Männerheim. In the flux of the world of poverty and young men on the road, Hitler was becoming an institution at the home merely because of his tenure there.

The change of seasons suddenly spurred him into action. Perhaps the certainty of approaching poverty also had something to do with such a drastic decision.

Whatever the reason, it is likely that he read the advertisement in one of the newspapers he perused every morning. It was work, similar to that with which he was accustomed, and he must have believed that there would at least be pleasant working conditions.

The factors that combined are now lost to time, but the legend of what happened still persists. In the fall of 1910, Hitler most likely took a job with a decorative painting and gilding firm that had won a commission to work on some rooms in the Kunsthistorisches Museum.

Hitler's physical size and appearance surely did not help him secure the job, but his ever-growing portfolio of paintings must have convinced his prospective employers that he could at least handle a paint brush and could be trusted with the fine gilt work at the museum.[2]

His white painter's cap and coat must have been something of an improvement over his greasy derby and frock coat. There is no evidence to tell whether Hitler enjoyed his work or not.

The sort of men Hitler worked with on this job becomes apparent in a statement written by one of the *Hofrats* responsible for the administration of the museums. In a memo about the work in progress, this *Hofrat* complained about the men, saying that one worker had actually used a display case as a ladder to reach up to a high spot to paint, and had tipped the case over and thereby ruined an invaluable collection of Peruvian pottery. His *k und k Apostolisch Majestät Obersthofmeisteramt* wished that in future, the workers would take greater care and use ladders instead of showcases.[3]

Hitler probably didn't keep the job very long. Perhaps he stayed with it just long enough to forestall immediate hunger. Such a radical move as getting a job, even though there was a touch of professionalism about it because of the fine gilt work, could not have been much in accord with Hitler's self-image at the time. He was not one to stick to such work, and had he done so, it is likely that some direct evidence of that employment would have been uncovered by now.

Hitler still looked upon himself as an artist, for all of his political tirades. It was still his dream to go to the Academy. This spell of work at the Hofmuseum had more than ever resolved him to pull himself up and out of the lower classes. He was rotting out there at the Männerheim, caught in a rut. Besides, this work had given him a new idea. While working at the museum, Hitler had undoubtedly come into contact with some of the men who were regular employees of the Hofmuseums. Names, at least, of important men at the museums would have been noted by Hitler for some later use. Hitler believed he had an entrée to them, however small. And any little lever he could find in the Viennese system would be seen as potentially valuable.

Later that fall, Hitler returned to the Hofmuseum. This time his wall-painting smock was replaced by his own frock coat and his derby was stuck jauntily back on his head.

Under his arm he carried his portfolio of architectural drawings, the result of the last year of real work, apart from his postcards, posters, and paintings for the frame shops. Using whatever names he had available, he managed to get an appointment to see Professor Ritschel, the director in charge of the care and restoration of paintings. Hitler opened his portfolio in front of the professor for his inspection. He wanted the professor to recommend him for admission to the Academy.

The professor looked over the drawings, not greatly impressed. He noticed that they were done with care and real architectural precision, but his admiration stopped there.[4]

It is not known whether the professor turned down Hitler's request, or whether lethargy once again overcame Hitler, for in any case, no formal petition for entrance was registered by Hitler for the Academy in 1910.

Most likely the professor's reaction had not been sufficiently enthusiastic to convince Hitler of success should he apply again to the Academy. After two previous failures to gain admission, he probably was not very anxious to face the likelihood of another rejection.

Hitler took his portfolio home with him to the Männerheim and brooded over the inequity of the world. Such brooding could not last very long, however. What little money Hitler had earned on his job painting walls was quickly running out. He had to pay his rent again and he had to eat. Hitler had a supply of pictures and nobody to sell them for him. There was no way out but to sell them himself. He had gone the rounds with Hanisch. He knew enough dealers to get started. The memory of the rejections of his Rathaus painting still smarted, but this time Hitler was convinced that if he asked for less money he would have more success.

There was Jakob Altenberg on the Wiedner Hauptstrasse, and there were Landsberger and Morgenstern. Hitler visited them all with his paintings under his arm, and came back to the Männerheim counting his crowns. Suddenly it was all terribly simple—so long as he stuck to formula pictures of the right size, and did not ask for too much money per painting, it looked as if he would have a steady market for his watercolors. The frame dealers and upholstery shops seemed positively hungry for his work.

Some of Hitler's favorite themes were of the churches of Vienna. There was the Karlskirche, the Minoritenkirche, the church of Maria am Gestade which he had so proudly showed Kubizek on the latter's first night in Vienna. Hitler also was fond of painting the Parliament and the Rathaus, despite the trouble he had had with that one initially. There was also the Heiliger Kreuzerhof, the Fisherman's Gate, the Michaelerplatz, the Schottentor, the Old Vienna Naschmarkt, the Hofburg, and other such typical city scenes. Many of these paintings Hitler did in an Old Vienna style, including buildings and signs of another era.[5]

Hitler worked mostly in watercolors, and his stroke is neither strong nor clear in that medium. Much better are his line drawings of buildings which show a firm hand and good eye for detail and design. There is even a certain air about these sketches that gives them a personality—a quaintness almost, that the watercolors totally lack.

It is important to remember how Hitler thought about this work he did for frame and upholstery shops. He had no illusions that this hack work was really art, and he admitted "in a disdainful way that he was only a dilettante and had not yet learned how to paint,"[6] when his fellow lodgers at the Männerheim admired his work.

Many years later, when Hitler was the Führer and his little paintings were selling for 4,000 to 5,000 marks each, he confessed to Heinrich Hoffmann, his photographer, that it was silly for these paintings to fetch so much:

> These things shouldn't cost more than about 150-200 Reichsmarks, even today. It's nonsense to pay out more for them. I didn't really want to become a painter; I only painted these things to make a living and be able to study. For such a picture I never received more than about 12 Reichsmarks. I only painted enough so that I had the necessities of life. I didn't need more than about 80 Reichsmark per month to live. For lunch and dinner I had to figure one Reichsmark. In those years I used to study the night away. My architectural sketches, which I then drew up, were my most prized possessions, the property of my mind, with which I would never have parted as I did those paintings. One shouldn't forget that all my thinking of today, and all my architectural planning, goes back to that time, acquired through those years of night-long work. If I am able today, for example, to draw the plans for a theater with my little finger, it is not the result of some trance. Rather, it is the result of my studies in those years. I am sorry to say that all the best sketches of those years have been lost.[7]

It is evident from this statement how much value Hitler put into his dreams of becoming an architect rather than a painter during the years he was living in the Männerheim.

He finally was able to give full vent to his architectural dreams as Führer, always working very closely with his architects—more so than with his generals—in building the edifices that would symbolize the power of his 1,000-year Reich.

Hitler was greatly enamored of domes and flanking rows of columns. He was an architect of awe; massiveness appealed to him; things that would make people feel small in comparison. An example of this monumental architecture was the planned Kuppelhalle for Berlin which would have had a dome of 825 feet in diameter, a volume sixteen times that of St. Peter's, for a building that would hold 180,000 people.[8]

Hitler also loved to toy with sketches for a magnificent triumphal arch—one that would make Napoleon's in Paris look like a mere tabletop model. His avenues in Berlin would outdo even those of the Champs Elysées. Everything in the Third Reich had to be bigger and better than the world had known before.

When Hitler first saw the new Chancellery completed with its immense dome and long avenues of columns, he was inspired to say: "Good! Good! When the diplomats see that, they will learn to know fear."[9]

Hitler felt great frustration, in these Vienna years of 1907-13, at not being able to achieve his dreams of becoming an architect—though, as Greiner had pointed out to him, it was Hitler's own fault for not taking an evening course to get his *Matura*[10]. Hitler preferred to jeer at those who did not perceive his talents as he saw them and who kept him from becoming a great artist. That was easier than doing something constructive about achieving his ambition. He would gladly admit to being a dilettante in painting, but beneath the skin that realization must have pained him. He admitted it merely to forestall someone else's accusation of the very same thing.

Hitler also pretended to believe there was nothing worthwhile happening in the arts in the degenerate Habsburg Empire. Professors would not know real talent if they saw it.

"More and more," Hitler wrote in *Mein Kampf,*

> clearly I saw at last that the fate of the German nation would no longer be decided here [in Austria], but in the Reich itself. This was true, not only of political questions, but no less for all manifestations of cultural life in general.
>
> Also, in the field of cultural or artistic affairs, the Austrian state showed all symptoms of debility, or at least of unimportance for the

German nation. This was most true in the field of architecture. The new architecture could achieve no special success in Austria, if for no other reason because since the completion of the Ring its tasks, in Vienna at least, had become insignificant.[11]

(2)

One of Hitler's oft-painted typical Old Vienna scenes was the Dreilauferhaus,[12] which had stood at the corner of Herrengasse and Kohlmarkt on the Michaelerplatz. This was one of the old centers of Vienna, made even more important with the construction of the Neue Hofburg and the Michaelertor, through which Franz Joseph often passed on the way in to his palace.

By 1910, The Dreilauferhaus had been torn down, and contests had been held to build on the location a new edifice for the firm of Goldmann and Salatsch, the bottom floors to be office space for these men's clothiers, and the top floors to be apartments.

It was a prime location, and rumors abounded about the dramatic new design of the chosen architect. The Viennese, always ready for a *Hetz,* or scandalous baiting, held their breaths during August of 1910 (at the same time Hitler was having Hanisch sent to jail), while the scaffolding was taken down from the façade of the new building.

Not since the building of the Secession twelve years before had the Viennese had such an opportunity for criticism, for once the façade was revealed to the light of day, horror of horrors, there was hardly any façade at all. Quick as ever to nickname, the Viennese dubbed this austere building the "eyebrowless house" because of its lack of lintel decoration over the windows. It was a spare, clean surface that astounded the Viennese, accustomed to Herculean forms acting as ersatz columns, flowing scrollwork atop massive capitals, and layers and layers of "makeup" on the face of every public building.

This building was an outrage, they felt. The newspapers did not fail to fill their columns with their disapproval:

> Choose a point on the Michaelerplatz from which to observe the new building which has been put up in place of the Dreilauferhaus, and immediately some passerby will latch on to you, repeating out loud what you had been thinking yourself, cursing the revolting edifice to its face, and pass on his way, muttering imprecations. . . . How can anyone have

thought it possible to harmonize this blatantly dissonant modernism with its timeless, historic surroundings?[13]

The public outcry against the building was so great that work was halted on the building. There was talk of pulling it down because its unflinching modernity was an affront to the palatial and historical splendor of the Hofburg with which it shared the square. The building was finally completed, however, but rumor still has it that Franz Joseph never used the Michaelertor again.[14]

Hitler was obviously unaware of this architectural revolution which was causing such a furor in his city. He was so concerned with adoration of the past that the name of the guilty architect, Adolf Loos, though dragged through the newspapers of the time, was unknown to him. Loos was a man whom the architectural historian Nikolaus Pevsner has called "one of the greatest creators in modern architecture."[15] He was also paid tribute by the innovative architect Le Corbusier: "Loos swept clear the path before us. It was a Homeric cleansing: precise, philosophical, logical. He has influenced the architectural destiny of us all."[16]

Loos was one of the foremost promoters of modernism, a father of twentieth-century architecture, and forerunner of the International Movement in architecture.

Yet he was forty before he had his first commission for a building, the Michaeler House. Until that time Loos had made his living by designing interiors of shops and cafés. It was an occupation that he, echoing Hitler's claim of dilettantism in painting, considered only a sideline: "The decoration of apartments has nothing to do with architecture," Loos once responded to a friend who had complimented one of his interior designs. "It has provided me with a living, simply because it is something I know how to do. Just as, in America, I kept the wolf from the door for a time by washing dishes."[17]

At first, Loos had identified himself with the Jugendstil Secessionists, but he had by 1898 made a break with them and their movement. His one contribution to the Secessionists was an article in *Ver Sacrum* of July 1898, entitled *"Die Potemkinische Stadt,"* in which Loos ridiculed the Ringstrasse and its sham façade style: "If I stroll along the Ring, I always have the impression that a modern Potemkin has set himself the task of making someone believe that Vienna is a town inhabited by nothing but *nobili.*"[18]

Potemkin was a favorite count of Catherine the Great of Russia. He erected a cardboard city, á la Hollywood, in the Ukraine, for the visit of the Empress. Speeding by in her train, the Empress Catherine was thus fooled into believing that there was a high level of prosperity in that poor country. In the same way, the small burghers of Vienna, like Hitler, were fooled into believing in the elegance of the capital city, never questioning what deceit lay behind the magnificent renaissance and gothic façades of the Ring.

This was Loos's first and last collaboration with the Secessionists. His design was a direct result of the polemics of the earlier architect Otto Wagner. Wagner had once said that "what is impractical can never be beautiful,"[19] and that was also to be Loos's departure point. Nonetheless, Loos was passionately opposed to the practice of Secession style and of the *Werkstätte* as well, even though Wagner had connections with both.

Loos began to satirize the Jugendstil attempt at total art as overblown and artificial. He felt that their philosophy attempted a tyranny in taste.[20]

While the Secessionists such as Hoffmann and Olbrich were redesigning their customers' flats every two months to keep abreast of the latest styles, Loos worked in a simple, clean style with exposed beams and cozy fireplace corners, gathering fine old Biedermeier furniture from the secondhand stores. He was an enemy of needless ornamentation, and a tireless opponent of what he felt to be the gaudy bad taste of Jugendstil.

Loos was not the first to move away from the excesses of Jugendstil. Klimt and his group had left the Secession in 1905 and tried to become a new avant-garde.[21]

The spark of this more radical revolution in the arts, which left the Secessionists behind and which ultimately led to Expressionism, may well have been lit two years before the clamor about Loos's Michaeler House. In 1908, Klimt's new art group had staged its first show on a vacant lot upon which the Konzerthaus was later built. A prefabricated building was thrown up where, for two years in a row, the new avant-garde of Vienna displayed their work. This show took place the same summer as Franz Joseph's Diamond Jubilee, when Hitler was still on the Stumpergasse, killing bugs.

The show had been both a victory and defeat for the avant-garde, for though the Austrian state had purchased Klimt's *The Kiss,* the show had not been without its detractors and even Klimt had not gone uncriticized in the press.[22]

The attacks on Klimt had been mild, however, when compared to the absolute storm of disgust which had thundered around the head of the new *enfant terrible* of the show, Oskar Kokoschka, and his corner of the exhibition which the press called the "chamber of horrors."[23]

Until the 1908 show, Kokoschka had been a student and employee of the School of Arts and Crafts. From his earliest works, Kokoschka had shown a much more intuitional aspect than Klimt or the Secessionists. His was a fierce, get-to-the-heart-of-the-matter approach. He also had worked for the Wiener Werkstätte, binding books, sketching postcards —for which the Werkstätte was well known—and painting on fans. Those were the sorts of products the Werkstätte turned out, as well as all types of household goods.

Kokoschka was fortunate to be in the 1908 Kunstschau. He had arranged four large tapestry designs on the walls of his room in the exhibition hall and, forgetting that people also had to enter from somewhere, had covered the door with one of these brilliant and primitive designs, thus barring the judges from entry. Klimt had been among the judges who would determine which of the young painters gathered there would exhibit with his group. Kokoschka, "quick to seize the opportunity . . . began to bargain with the judges, standing inside and shouting through the door that he would not let them in until they promised to accept his work unseen."[24]

Klimt, impressed with the brash courage of this young man, had agreed to the bargain, and could only shake his head when he entered Kokoschka's room. Confronted with the younger artist's violent work, such as the poster of the *Pietà* with a blood-red woman and a deathly white representation of Kokoschka himself supported on her knee drawn in primitive angularity, Klimt had only been able to say, "Mad boy. But all the same!"[25]

When the other judges had argued that Kokoschka's presence in the show might ruin the whole venture by turning the conservative Viennese against them, Klimt had replied: "Our duty is to give an artist of outstanding talent the opportunity of expressing himself. Oskar Kokoschka is the greatest talent among the younger generation. Even if we run the risk of sinking our own exhibition, then it will have to sink."[26]

Klimt's worst fears had been fulfilled. The public was happily disgusted with Kokoschka's room. Apart from the tapestry designs and poster, there had been a standing, skull-like head in blue wash with open mouth and straining veins at the neck. It was another self-portrait of the young artist, called *The Warrior*. Every day of the exhibition, there had been found in the figure's mouth "bits of chocolate or whatever; in this way, presumably, the ladies of Vienna expressed their scorn at the work of the 'super-Fauve.'"[27]

Loos, who had come to the 1908 exhibition to heap scorn on the works of Hoffmann, had discovered instead the genius of Kokoschka, and he purchased *The Warrior*. For the rest of his life, Loos became the sponsor and protector of the young man, only twenty-two at the time of the 1908 show.

As a result of the scandal in the press, Kokoschka had lost his post at the School of Arts and Crafts, and Loos began to help him get portrait commissions from his friends and associates such as Karl Kraus, Carl Moll, and Peter Altenberg. These portraits are some of his best early work, bridging the gap between Austrian baroque tendencies and the new world of Expressionism. Kokoschka always maintained a deeply insightful link between painting and subject. It was as if he could see inside his people, into their wounds, frustrations, and mortality.

Kokoschka also took up work at the Cabaret Fledermaus on the Kärtnerstrasse, the brainchild of Hoffmann, and did a recital, dance, and magic lantern show called "The Speckled Egg."[28]

Without help from his friends, the young artist would have had a very hard time of it. As Kokoschka himself wrote: "In Vienna there was no art market to paint for. A few antique dealers, yes, but no art dealers, such as those who today buy up youthful talent like a racehorse and expect it to run like hell until its breath gives out."[29]

Kokoschka could have added to that market some frame dealers and upholsterers from whom another young painter of sorts was earning a living.

As if Kokoschka's performance in the 1908 show had not been enough to alienate him from the Viennese public, the next year he had put on a play, *Mörder, Hoffnung der Frauen* (Murder, Hope of Women), in the outdoor theater of the 1909 Kunstschau. This early forerunner of Expressionist drama was, according to Kokoschka and his biographer Hodin,[30] met by a riot from which Kokoschka was saved by the timely intervention of both Loos and Kraus.[31]

Vienna had become too small for Kokoschka. His scholarship at the

Arts and Crafts School was over, and the director, Alfred Roller, was not a little relieved to be rid of the young man, for the powerful minister of education was complaining to him about this disturbing painter/writer.[32] Even Franz Ferdinand had been compelled to remark on the young painter. The archduke, after seeing some of Kokoschka's work, announced that he should like to break every bone in the artist's body.[33]

Loos sent Kokoschka off to the fresher air of Switzerland in 1909 and again in 1910, during the time that Loos himself was in disfavor with the Viennese public over his Michaeler House. In that same year, 1910, Kokoschka moved to the more intellectually tolerant atmosphere of Berlin.

Kokoschka is the best known internationally of that new wave of Expressionist painters that developed out of the Secessionist movement. Two others are also worth noting.

It was in the year 1908 that the Expressionist painter Richard Gerstl ended what promised to be a fine talent, by hanging himself. He was the eldest of the three painters here examined, and the first to break away from the compelling sway of the Jugendstil artists and Klimt. A close friend of the new, radical composer Arnold Schoenberg, Gerstl had taken that man's wife to his studio in the Liechtensteinstrasse, and when she had wanted to return to her husband, he killed himself.[34]

Gerstl was a Viennese Van Gogh with his use of color and heavy self-expression. Toward the end of his short life—he was twenty-five when he committed suicide—his line was beginning to break down totally to a foreshadowing of abstractionism.

Another major painter of the young Viennese scene had his debut at the 1909 Kunstschau. The four portraits by this young artist at that exhibition, with their obvious borrowing from the Jugendstil phase of Klimt, gave little indication of the later searing Expressionism that Egon Schiele would create.

Such visible display of adoration as copying his style was a natural outgrowth of the power Klimt held over the artistic world of turn-of-the-century Vienna. Schiele, like Kokoschka, had received a benediction from Klimt. As early as 1907, he had sought out Klimt in his studio to look at his paintings. One anecdote has Schiele wanting to trade his drawings with Klimt. Klimt characteristically replied: "Why on earth do you want to swap drawings with me? You draw better than I do."[35]

Klimt put his money where his sentiments were and not only traded pictures with Schiele, but also purchased several more drawings by the artist at a time of financial danger for Schiele. Klimt also recommended Schiele for design commissions to the Wiener Werkstätte and sent him clients to be painted.

By 1910, Schiele had moved into his own genre, creating a poignant world of portraiture that looked deep into his subjects. Emphasizing hands and fingers, Schiele was an artist of line. His own tall, slender figure with long, bony hands became the subject of many self-portraits. Ultimately, his extreme eroticism, taken beyond the bounds of Klimt, ran him afoul of the Viennese press.

One description of an exhibition in 1909 in which Schiele took part complained of the obscenity of the pictures: "Since they [the artists] have at their disposal not merely walls and fences, but canvas and paper, they have understandably seized upon the idea of going through the crisis of puberty before an invited audience."[36]

Sexuality was, for Schiele, "a vital source of inspiration . . . his nude studies . . . have an anatomical, almost gruesome character."[37] In his private life also, Schiele was a very sensual, sexual animal.[38]

His sister, Gerti, was one of his first nude models, until he could afford others. For a time Schiele even earned his living with erotic drawings, often of young girls. It was a course bound for disaster in Vienna.

(3)

If it was not one thing, it was another. First, Hitler didn't know what to do with his paintings. Now he didn't have any paintings to get rid of.

Temptation was very strong at the Männerheim. There were all those newspapers lying around just begging to be read; all those men there providing a captive audience for one's speeches. What was Hitler to do? Without some friend to prod him along when he got lazy, Hitler was lost.

Now Morgenstern on the Liechtensteinstrasse was proclaiming that he had some lawyer who was willing to buy everything Hitler could produce, and suddenly he couldn't produce anything.[39]

Hitler turned the pages of the *Deutsches Volksblatt,* started reading an article about the Jewish conspiracy to corner the world market in cotton, and forgot about such mundane matters as earning a living.

Unfortunately for Hitler, his problems would not disappear when he ignored them. The weekly rent again fell due and Director Kanya was not to be put off like good old Frau Zakreys on the Stumpergasse.

The light of recognition suddenly dawned on Hitler—he was heading for disaster again, just as in the previous winter. His short-term cures were not going to stop this downhill slide into poverty. Hitler played his trump card.

Aunt Johanna had always had a soft spot in her heart for Adolf. In spite of his break with the family in the summer of 1908, she was still there to help him. She had proved her loyalty with the fifty crowns that previous winter, and that sum had enabled him to move to the Männerheim and set up as a small-time painter.

Hitler got out pen and paper again, but not to sketch a picture. He had an easier way out of his difficulties. He probably dashed off a letter to his aunt, outlining his dire need and the attempts he had made, in vain, to be a productive member of society—to earn his way despite all the silly prejudice that seemed to be at work against him in the world. Hitler could be a very persuasive letter writer in his own advocacy.[40]

He sent off the letter and then settled down to some serious work until an answer came. Hitler could work like a slave now, for there was light at the end of the tunnel. He would not always have to paint these boring scenes of Vienna if his letter worked. That little ray of hope acted like a cattle prod and enabled him to keep his head above water that late fall and into the winter of 1910.

On December 1, 1910, old Aunt Johanna, out in Spital bei Weitra, went to her bank and withdrew all her savings.[41] She had lived frugally over the years, often staying with relatives, and saving for that all-important legacy she would leave to prove to the world her worth. The crowns and hellers saved here and there added up to a sizable 3,800 crowns, of which Hitler must have come in for the lion's share, at least 2,000.[42]

Sometime after the first of December, Hitler must have made a hurried trip out to the Waldviertel to Spital to pick up his inheritance, given to him before his aunt's death to avoid the death duties. With the money in his pocket, Hitler must have felt like a millionaire. He had at least two years' grace if he lived simply. Besides that, he could always earn some money on the side with his painting. He was sitting pretty and was determined not to squander his money on nightly theater visits as he had with Gustl.

Back in the Männerheim, he tucked the money away in a safe place in his cubicle, perhaps in his one old suitcase. The mattress was not safe, as it might be checked by the staff. He kept quiet about his good fortune, remembering Hanisch's admonition from the year before to keep his fifty crowns hidden.[43] Herr Kanya might even ask him to move out of the home now that he could afford normal lodgings. That was the last thing in the world Hitler wanted. He had gotten accustomed to the life at the Männerheim, the security and forced companionship. Without trying, Hitler could have all the "friends" he wanted around him. Such an arrangement had all the advantages of friendship with none of the responsibilities.[44]

The inheritance did not change his way of life. He stayed on at the Männerheim and continued to wear the same old stained coat. His hair was still long, and the scraggly beard on his face did not grow any thicker, though he had discovered that with a moustache his unusually wide nostrils were hidden.

Hitler's routine went unchanged. Perhaps he could take in more operas now than before, but nothing like his playboy beginnings on the Stumpergasse. Such conspicuous consumption would be sure to raise suspicions.

The painting now also became easier, as long as he knew he did not have to do it. He tinkered around more with architectural sketches, done solely for his own amusement and not for sale.

Then Josef Greiner showed up again in early 1911. The indomitable Greiner was as full of schemes as ever and brought a breath of fresh air into the stale writing room for Hitler. Greiner immediately tracked down a couple of advertising commissions to keep the wolf away from the door. Greiner's work inspired Hitler to try advertising art again. Now that he understood the theoretical basis—that advertising was a part of the art of propaganda—Hitler found sketching posters almost fun.

In 1911, Hitler turned out several such posters. One advertising poster, for a Firma Fernolendt, shows a pair of black boots against a red background with white letters in the background advertising a fine brand of shoe polish.[45] These colors would later be seen in the Nazi flag. Another poster, equally as crudely drawn, of the same year, is an ad for a washing powder called Neubozon. It is a three-color poster displaying a box of the detergent emptying its contents into a kettle bubbling over with white, frothy soap bubbles.[46]

It seems Hitler was quite taken with soap ads, as it has been reported that the tower of St. Stephans was depicted in another of his posters as it "rises majestically out of a mountain of soap."[47]

There is nothing in any of these ads to hint at Hitler's later propaganda ability. They are poorly drawn posters, with no punch at all in them; no gimmick to sell the product. They were drawn in the early years of advertising when manufacturers with taste still felt that one did not have to advertise a product that was good and essential to life. The ethical questions as to the morality of creating a demand where none would normally exist still fought against the attempted tyranny of advertising. Billboards and television commercials were horrors never dreamed of in turn-of-the-century Vienna.

Greiner kept Hitler hopping with new get-rich-quick schemes. They worked on everything from a tie with a clasp attached to the collar button to keep the tie from loosening,[48] to building model airplanes that they supposedly sold to the top engineers of Vienna.[49]

In the recounting of such tales, Greiner's imagination often runs away from the facts of the matter. Greiner, the heroic schemer, poses now as the great engineer, now as inventor, and later as mentor to the Führer and confidant to such rulers as Mussolini.

Yet there are surprising kernels of truth in his account. Perhaps through Greiner's influence, Hitler landed a job with an architect on the Penzingerstrasse, out near where Lanz von Liebenfels lived.[50]

Under the commission of an architect named Florian Müller, with offices at Penzingerstrasse 115, Hitler completed a sketch for a planned villa. The sketch[51] is an accurate architectural rendering of a villa in the peaked-roof style of the time. The line is sure and firm. There is, however, no evidence that the villa was ever built. How long the connection with Müller lasted is also unknown.[52]

Hitler cooperated with Greiner in these schemes not out of need but out of curiosity. Greiner had the sort of volatile personality that fired people out of their staid routines and made them take chances. If there was anything Hitler needed in the early part of 1911, it was someone like Greiner to spur him—to get the blood pumping again. Hitler was always a potential victim of inertia. He could get stuck in a rut, and relied to a great extent on the energy of people around him to get him started again.[53]

It surely was not a matter of money that sent Hitler to the Theater an der Wien one day that year. Perhaps it was just a desire to test his limits. Perhaps it was that Greiner pushed him into it, and Hitler had still to act the part of the needy artist so that the wily Greiner would not suspect that he had gotten hold of some money. Greiner says that it was a Professor Delug, who supposedly had earlier helped him to get ahead with his own studies and had supposedly helped Hitler with the Müller job, who arranged the singing audition.[54] It should also be remembered that Greiner was, at one time, a lamplighter in "the Cabaret Hoelle in the Theater an der Wien,"[55] and perhaps he still had connections there of one kind or another.

At any rate, no matter how it came about, Hitler showed up one day at the Theater an der Wien to try out for the chorus.[56] The head of the theater, Director Karczag, remembered many years later that the young man was lanky and shabbily dressed:

"Are you a tenor or baritone?" asked Karczag.

"Tenor!"

"Okay, go ahead!"

The young man sang Danilo's opening song, *"Da geh ich zu Maxims'"* from Franz Lehár's *The Merry Widow* so well that Karczag ordered him without more ado to register with the choral director. Barely had he said this than he caught sight of the threadbare, spotted suit the young man was wearing and began to doubt whether he would have the necessary evening attire at his disposal.

"Do you have a dress suit?" he asked the young man.

"Unfortunately no. I can't afford that!" came the answer dejectedly.

"Then I'm sorry, but I can't hire you," said Karczac regretfully. "With us it is required that the chorus take care of their own clothing."[57]

Interesting to note, in relation to this story, is the fact that when he was eight years old, Hitler took singing lessons in Lambach, where the family was then living. Later, he joined the boys' choir of the Benedictine monastery in Lambach.[58] Supposedly, he had had a good little voice in those childhood years, and apparently still had it in Vienna.[59]

Greiner, too, mentions that Hitler sang a tune from *The Merry Widow,* and that it was the clothes that kept him from becoming a member of the chorus.[60] Hitler was slowly learning that, in Vienna, clothes do make the man. He began to see that his looks were working against him in the world. At about this time he finally cut his hair and beard, and purchased a new suit of clothes. Greiner, of course, takes credit for this purchase,[61] but it is more likely that Hitler finally dipped into his precious inheritance to give himself a little self-esteem.

Just eight days after the spring equinox, Hitler's Aunt Johanna died. Upon her death, her affairs were looked into by the family. It is then that Hitler's older half-sister Angela must have learned of Hitler's inheritance. Things were not going well for Angela. She had three children of her own, including little Geli, the future mistress of the Führer. Besides these three was her half-sister Paula for whom she had to care. Her husband, Leo Raubal, never the greatest advocate of Adolf, would no longer say bad things about the young man. He had died on August 10, 1910, while Hanisch was serving his jail term.

Angela was hard pressed to support all these children on her widow's pension, and when she learned about Adolf's good fortune because of Aunt Johanna, she appealed to the guardian of Paul and Adolf, Herr Mayrhofer, for assistance in getting Adolf's orphan's pension to help her out.

All this time Hitler had been collecting the twenty-five crowns monthly under false premises. He had lied to the Linz courts that he was a student at the academy and thus could not support himself.[62]

Josef Mayrhofer advised Angela to see a lawyer, which Angela immediately did, and they brought the problem to the attention of the Linz courts.

One day that spring Hitler must have been very surprised to receive a summons from the court in the Leopoldstadt to report and give evidence of his financial situation. It must have been a nerve-racking time for Hitler because he had failed to register for conscription. The more often his name appeared in official documents, the more precarious his situation would become.

Hitler appeared before the judge in the Leopoldstadt and was ready to comply with anything. The last thing he wanted to do at that time was to make a legal fuss. The record of his statement still exists:

> Adolf Hitler, now living as an artist at 27 Meldemannstrasse, XX. District, has testified as follows in the court of Leopoldstadt: He is able to maintain himself and agrees to the transfer of the full amount of his orphan's pension to his sister, and in addition, inquiries have revealed that Adolf is in possession of considerable sums of money given to him by his Aunt Johanna Pölzl for the purpose of advancing his career as an artist.[63]

Hitler, the loyal brother, turned over his orphan's pension "voluntarily" only after he was forced to by the courts. On May 4, 1911, the Linz court officially transferred the orphan's pension to the fifteen-year-old Paula.[64]

Hitler was now twenty-two and had lived three years in Vienna. He had endured another winter without too much difficulty and spring was shining into the windows of the Männerheim. The trees were in leaf and tulips filled the parks with happy colors. Even Hitler had to admit that life was all right when the sun shone. Poorer now by twenty-five crowns per month, he still had more than enough to make ends meet for a long time.

(4)

While Hitler was auditioning at the Theater an der Wien, trying to get a job in the chorus, Mahler was dying in New York. What had started as a low-level infection of the throat was spreading throughout his weakened body. The streptococci were overcoming his resistance daily.[65]

Mahler sailed for Europe with Alma to be treated by the best bacteriologists in the world. Their first stop was Paris, where he was treated in a sanatorium for a time. Then he traveled home to Vienna, a shriveled skeleton of a man. Flowers filled his room—flowers from his beloved Philharmonic orchestra and even from former enemies at the Hof Opera. The dying man suddenly became a celebrity in the Vienna that had earlier reviled him.

"The death struggle began," his wife Alma later wrote. "The rales lasted for hours. At midnight of May 18 [1911], with a storm of hurricane proportions raging outside, the awful, ghastly rattle suddenly ceased."[66] Mahler was dead.

Earlier in his illness he had requested a simple funeral, to be buried next to his daughter, Maria, in the Grinzing cemetery. There was to be no pomp or speeches, and on his tombstone would be written only "Mahler." "Those who come looking for me will know who I was," he said, "and the others don't have to know."[67]

Vienna went into a mourning that is traditionally reserved for its most famous sons. He would have appreciated it if only half the respect shown Mahler in death had been mustered for him in life. But Vienna has always been noted for the scandalous manner in which it treats its geniuses, only really letting them live after they have died. Even Mozart and Austria's greatest playwright, Franz Grillparzer, suffered from this syndrome.

The newspapers in Vienna were filled with glorious obituaries—the same papers that had besmirched Mahler's name when he was alive; that had laughed at his symphonic forms, and fanned the flames of court intrigue that had ultimately cost him his job at the Hof Opera.

"Gustav Mahler has died in the city where he worked for ten years," read one such obituary. "As the shadow of death closed over him, he began to long for Vienna, the cradle of his flame. For Vienna made him what he was. Here in Vienna, Mahler the composer was honored no less than Mahler the conductor."[68]

That such reporting could be believed by the good citizens of Vienna is amazing. Mahler's symphonies never premiered in Vienna during his lifetime—he was always forced to go abroad for any bit of recognition as a composer. Even in death, Mahler was being cheated of his due. Now it was Vienna that had made him what he was. Mahler was extolled after death only to serve the cause of glorifying Vienna.

That Mahler's achievements were made in spite of, rather than because of, Vienna the popular Viennese press never mentioned.

In other European cities the readers of the daily papers found a different story. In London, for example, one obituary ended by putting the blame for Mahler's early death squarely where it belonged: "Mahler's untimely death is in part an aftereffect of his constant and largely successful struggle against the semi-Oriental atmosphere of Vienna."[69]

Shortly before his death, Mahler had spoken to his wife about the young Schoenberg, who had become something of a protégé of Mahler's. "If I go, he will have nobody left," Mahler complained.[70] Alma promised to do everything in her power to help the composer, as did her stepfather, Moll. Mahler was relieved to know this, for he realized what a difficult road Schoenberg would have to traverse in Vienna. After his death, a Mahler Fund was instituted to help support composers not in favor with the public, and Schoenberg was the recipient of one of these grants.

The Mahler-Arnold Schoenberg relationship had begun as early as 1904 when Arnold Rosé, Mahler's brother-in-law, and his quartet were performing Schoenberg's *Verklärte Nacht*. Mahler listened to the piece, met the composer, and concluded that he had great promise. Since that time, Mahler had been a champion of Schoenberg's music, though not always understanding it himself. As with Klimt and his relations with Kokoschka and Schiele, Mahler believed in championing the younger generation; in passing on the torch.[71]

Schoenberg's extreme atonality, his emancipation of dissonance from any consonant resolution, and his unrelieved Expressionism quickly won him a place in the legion of what the Viennese considered to be weirdos. A Schoenberg concert was an invitation to heckle the artist. Again, in December of 1908, shortly after Hitler's move to the Felberstrasse in his second Viennese winter, a Schoenberg concert at the Bösendorfersaal created the biggest musical scandal to date in Vienna. As it was reported in the daily papers, Hitler was sure to have heard of this radical composer who was "destroying" all that was sacred in the traditional musical idiom:

> The scenes last night between eight and nine o'clock in the Bösendorfersaal were unprecedented in Viennese musical history; there was a downright scandal, during the performance of a composition whose author has already caused a public nuisance with other products of his. But he has never gone so far as he did yesterday. You really would have thought you were in a cats' concert. All the same, the public kept quiet. End of first movement. Then, from the standing room at the back, came shouts of approval. Cue for scandal, which grows like an avalanche, slackens off, picks up again, and finally reaches a fortissimo climax. . . . [Someone in the audience] called out, "Now they are going to play Beethoven, but have the hall ventilated first!"[72]

People hissed and laughed during the rest of the performance. Outraged ladies put their hands to their ears and cried out in pain at the dissonances.

While Schoenberg tried to keep his head up amidst such abuse, he was filled with bitterness at the Viennese and their critics. In a letter to a friend about this incident, he said the critics are "with very few exceptions so incompetent and ignorant that one can judge them only by the degrees of harm they do. Indeed, in that sense, most of them understand their job all right, since they give publicity to an artist who is popular, or put people against one who is unpopular."[73]

The friend to whom Schoenberg was writing was Karl Kraus. Thus the second wave of the Vienna revolution in the arts mirrors the cohesiveness of the first. The first breakaway artists were mainly Impressionistic, Jugendstil innovators. Schnitzler and Hermann Bahr could be taken as exponents of the literary side; Klimt of the painting faction; Mahler in music; Otto Wagner in architecture.

Their counterparts in the second wave, basically an Expressionist movement, were Kraus in literature; Kokoschka, Schiele, and Gerstl in painting; Schoenberg in music; and Loos in architecture. As with the first group, the members of this second group supported and encouraged one another both mentally and materially. Bahr had bought Klimt paintings and had a house designed by Olbrich with a Hoffmann interior, and was also an early proponent of Mahler's musical Secessionist style.

In the second wave of artists, Kraus came to the aid of the new art in the pages of his journal *Die Fackel,* and Loos was one of the first Kokoschka backers, selling his carpets from his living room floor to get the young artist out of the hostile atmosphere of Vienna.

In 1911, shortly after another Schoenberg concert incited a riot to which an ambulance had to be sent,[74] Schoenberg dedicated his basic work in music theory, *Harmonielehre,* to Kraus.

There was also a cross-fertilization between the two movements: Klimt stood up for Kokoschka as did Mahler for Schoenberg, each without fully understanding the art of the younger man. Yet both Klimt and Mahler knew when they saw a spark of genius, and it was this spark they defended in Kokoschka and Schoenberg.

There was a new "Sacred Spring" bursting forth all across Europe by 1911. This was an Expressionistic awakening, revolting against the sway of naturalism and Impressionism. In Paris the Fauves and Picasso were ripping apart color and form; the Blaue Reiter of Marc and Kandinsky were doing the same in Munich. Schoenberg, who was also a credible painter after his friendship with Gerstl, showed some of his work with this group in 1912. Stravinsky would shock the musical world with his *Rite of Spring* in 1913, and the German Expressionists would write their works with heavy personal symbolism, not unlike the works of the Austrian Georg Trakl.

A public polarized more and more from its artists since the time of Beethoven reacted to the new art forms negatively all over Europe, yet nowhere so badly as in Vienna. And nowhere besides Vienna were the new musical forms so scorned and ridiculed. Music is the artistic medium that changes the slowest. Schoenberg learned this in Vienna through his own bitter experience.

Born in 1874, Schoenberg was from a Jewish family which lived in Vienna's Twentieth District, the same district that Hitler called home for more than three years. Schoenberg was, like Wagner, a self-taught musician—for Schoenberg there were few precursors. He had left Vienna at the turn of the century to live in Berlin for a couple of years. He came back to the Austrian capital in 1903 and began shocking the Viennese public immediately with works such as *Verklärte Nacht* and the tone poem *Pelleas und Melisande*. Both of these early works had their occasional dissonances, but nothing that Richard Strauss had not already popularized.

By 1908, however, Schoenberg was positively angering his audiences. His music was the equivalent of a red flag to a bull—not because he was purposely trying to shake the public out of its bourgeois complacency, but because, as he put it, "I am being forced in this direction. . . . I am obeying an inner compulsion which is stronger than any upbringing."[75]

Schoenberg's *Das Buch der hängenden Gärten* and *Gurrelieder* were products of his new inner voice that he was following. The Viennese public followed a different voice, and attacks upon the man and his work grew ever more vindictive.[76]

When Schoenberg in 1911 was given a minor post at the Academy of Music, partly through the intercession of Mahler before he died, there were protests in the Austrian Parliament and a member even challenged the government to justify such an appointment. Schoenberg was eminently qualified as a teacher—witness his two star pupils, Anton von Webern and Alban Berg. During the academic year of 1910-11 he was granted a teaching post in composition outside the official curriculum of the school, but the pay was so small and the atmosphere so hostile that he and his family finally had to leave for the fresher air of Berlin.

Schoenberg was not alone in his escape from Vienna. Kokoschka had already gone to Berlin. Though he would come back for longer and shorter times to Vienna, and have a stormy love affair with Mahler's widow, Alma, his home after 1911 was not Vienna.

Others had left before. Olbrich had left Vienna in 1899 to work under the Grand Duke of Hesse in Darmstadt, and had died untimely in 1908. Mahler was dead after four years of exile from Vienna. Klimt was realizing more and more that the tawdry, personal form of Viennese criticism was too much to put up with. "Away from Vienna," he finally declared after the 1908 Kunstschau, "if I am to exhibit at all."[77]

The desertion of many of the city's brightest lights calls to mind Bahr's prophetic warning of 1900: "The Viennese have never tolerated a great man," he wrote in *Wien,* which had been banned by the Viennese censors. "Neither Beethoven nor . . . Wolf, nor Klimt . . . nor Mahler, not one. . . . What will become of Vienna? Anything at all? Is there any future for the city?"[78]

After 1909, the avant-garde in Vienna was a thing of the past. "No other major exhibitions of avant-garde painting took place in Vienna after 1909; strictly speaking, it is impossible not to regard the period between the closure of the second Kunstschau and the outbreak of the First World War as a culturally barren epoch."[79]

Those who stayed behind suffered the usual calumny. Schiele abandoned the city for a time, but not the country of Austria. He took to living with his model/mistress in small villages around Vienna. But his life-style was too much for rural Austria, just as it was for the capital. After leaving one town because the good townsfolk did not like his corrupting influence, he was later arrested in Neulengbach for seducing a minor. The charge was dismissed, but Schiele was finally convicted on a lesser charge of disseminating indecent drawings. One of the so-called indecent nude drawings, which his young models from the village may have seen on his Van Gogh-like bedroom walls, was burned in front of the artist at the trial. He spent twenty-four days in prison.[80]

Denied paints at first, Schiele painted on the walls in spittle which disappeared as soon as it dried. The last entry of the diary he kept in prison sums up his judgment of the handling of his case: "Inquisition! Middle Ages! Castration! Hypocrisy!"[81]

About the same time, the Vienna Academy of Music decided it would like to get Schoenberg back as a full professor, teaching harmony and counterpoint. His reply most likely speaks for a whole generation of creative artists who were forced to leave Vienna to follow their own inner compulsions. Schoenberg turned down the offer:

> My main reason is: for the present, I could not live in Vienna. I have not gotten over yet the things done to me there, I am not yet reconciled. Perhaps, even, if you should now be as irate with me as I now am with Vienna, perhaps after a while you will think of me less harshly, and

perhaps after some time I shall feel a greater affection for my native city than I do now; perhaps you will then think of me and I shall certainly wish to return. But now I cannot.[82]

(5)

It had been a long time since Hitler had been out of the city. He was beginning to feel like an urban rat, and now that summer was upon the country, his memory flashed back to his childhood summers spent in Spital in the Waldviertel, ancestral region of the Hüttlers, Hiedlers, or Hitlers, as they were variously called. Perhaps it was time for a little trip.

On-again-off-again Greiner had again left the city. Hitler had struck up a new friendship with an inhabitant of the home, a man named Franz.[83] Hitler liked to use diminutives with his friends; thus Franz became Franzl to Hitler. Luckily for Hitler, Franzl didn't suspect that Hitler had an inheritance from Aunt Johanna, so Hitler did not feel it necessary to overplay the pauper role to deceive him.

Hitler borrowed a map of Austria from the library in the Männerheim, took his window seat that no one else ever dared now to take, and settled down to plan a nice little summer trip.

Perhaps Hitler considered asking Franzl to come along, but then he might indeed be put to the complications of at least pretending to pay his own way on the trip by selling paintings and postcards along the way so that Franzl would not learn just how well off he was. Hitler had no intention of saddling himself with such a burden. He wanted a holiday, and the easiest way to do that was to travel alone.

The map was spread out on the table before him; the holy Habsburg Empire with all its subject nationalities accounted for much more land and people than the original Germanic center of the realm. Hitler followed the course of the Danube with his finger to Linz and adjusted the map in the rays of sun coming in the window to be able to read the small letters spelling out Leonding. The village was as small as the letters. The Hitlers had lived in that village near Linz from 1899 to 1905. That would most definitely have to be a stop on his travels.

Then the thought most likely occurred to Hitler that he should do a sort of pilgrimage to his childhood homes. There was Leonding, where he had spent so many happy years; and also up above Salzburg on the German border was his birthplace, Braunau am Inn. Hitler had been only three years old when he left Braunau—perhaps it was time for him to get back in touch with his roots?

It never occurred to Hitler to make a pilgrimage to the Waldviertel where his ancestors came from. He was ashamed of that past—of the illegitimacy of his father, the nagging doubts of his father's real parentage. That was a past he would literally try to bury some day.

Braunau had changed little since Hitler had left. He surely remembered very little of the town, having been so young when the family packed up and moved to Passau and a higher position in the customs service for Alois.

Braunau was a town then of 3,500 inhabitants, and as in most towns that size, existing as an agricultural center, the townspeople liked nothing better than a good bit of gossip.

Adolf's father, Alois, had been there as an assistant inspector in the customs for eighteen years before Adolf's birth, and must have been, through his prolific sexual adventures, a prime topic for the gossip of the townspeople.

Alois was married first at age thirty-six, to a fifty-year-old woman whose only positive traits were her money and the fact that she was the daughter of an inspector in the Imperial Tobacco Monopoly who might be able to further Alois's career.

Alois lived in inns most of the time during his service years, and once married, continued living in the Gasthaus Streif, which allowed him access to a full range of young peasant girls working there as chambermaids and waitresses.[84]

His first wife had become an invalid soon after their marriage, and finally separated from Alois because of his numerous infidelities. Alois continued living with his then current mistress, Franziska Matzelberger ("Fanni"), after the separation, and ultimately she bore him his first child, Alois junior, in 1882. The first wife conveniently died the next year and Alois decided to marry Fanni. It was just in the nick of time, as she was already seven months' pregnant with their second child, Angela.

Alois soon tired of this twenty-year-old woman and brought in from the Waldviertel his young niece, the granddaughter of Johann Nepomuk Hüttler (sometimes Hiedler), who had taken Alois in as a boy. Klara Pölzl, though of peasant stock, had her charms. Fanni was nobody's fool, and sent the young competition packing. Soon, however, Fanni contracted tuberculosis, one of the major diseases of adults at the time. Klara was brought back to minister to the needs of the children—and the physical wants of Alois, twice her age at forty-seven.

Alois Hitler had, since his first marriage, changed quarters, and was now living at the Gasthof Pommer on the top floor. Young Adolf Hitler was to adopt these same living patterns from his father. An inn always cuts one off and sets one apart from a village. One is part of the people and at the same time not a part. Such an abode implied the readiness to be off to bigger and better things at the drop of a hat. The Männerheim must have symbolized such mobility and impermanence to Adolf Hitler as the inns had to his father.

Klara became pregnant with their first child just as the unfortunate Fanni died. She became Alois's common-law wife. Later, through a papal dispensation,[85] the two married. By 1885 they were man and wife and still living at the Gasthof Pommer, just outside the old city walls of Braunau in what is known as the Salzburger Vorstadt. Young Klara continued to call Alois "Uncle" well into their marriage.

The first three years of marriage brought three more children, each of whom died in childhood. By 1888, Klara and Alois had only the two children that Fanni had given him. Then came Adolf.

Another son was always a big event in rural communities—another chance for the name to be carried on. But Adolf was a sickly baby and, as we have already seen, Klara was frightened that she had produced another early candidate for the graveyard. Her hunchbacked younger sister, Johanna, was there at the birth and stayed on to help care for the infant for whom she ever thereafter felt a special bond.

Adolf was protected and cared for with all the love these two women had. He was to be Klara's redemption, her son.[86]

Young Hitler could have heard any of these tales from the old-timers at the local inns, had he but asked. It would have been interesting if he had put up at the Gasthof Pommer, where his father had lived, on his visit to his birthplace. All that remains as evidence of his trip, though, is an oil painting[87] of the Stephanskirche with its baroque cupola sitting stodgily over the banks of the River Inn. Besides this church, there really was not much else of interest in the dull streets, filled with medium-sized houses, for Hitler to paint.

Somewhere along this pilgrimage route, Hitler contracted a stomach ailment that was to plague him on and off for the rest of his life. This ailment might go a long way toward explaining his finicky eating habits. In a letter of July 26, 1911, to his friend Franzl back in Vienna, Hitler elaborated on the illness and his recovery.

> Dear Franzl!
> I am happy to report to you that I am feeling better again and have continued with my travels through my lovely homeland.
> It was surely nothing more serious than a little stomachache, and I'm trying now with a special diet (fruit and vegetables) to cure myself, as the doctors are all idiots. I find it laughable to speak to me of a nervous complaint, when I am one of the healthiest of people.[88]

Interesting to note especially from this letter is Hitler's usual railing against professional men. Professors, he believed, were also all idiots who wore dirty collars and had stale minds. Because he had no specialty himself, he had to refute the ability of those who had. Doctors came in for Hitler's special abuse, perhaps because they had not been able to save his mother. Hitler may well have been thinking of Dr. Bloch when he wrote these lines.

It is also apparent from this letter that some country doctor whom Hitler had consulted about his stomach problems had diagnosed a nervous disorder as the cause. Undoubtedly Hitler's poverty during the 1909-10 winter had played no small part in such a nervous condition; his erratic and less than nutritionally sound eating habits also contributed.

At any rate, bad stomach or no, Hitler continued his travels through his home region, and pushed on to Leonding and perhaps to Linz. An existing oil painting records his visit to the garden house, as their small home in Leonding was called,[89] though no paintings of Linz from this time are known. Perhaps Hitler was afraid of encountering too many questions in Linz, where sister Angela was living. Leonding, scene of so many of Hitler's Karl May-inspired cowboys-and-Indians battles held a fonder spot in his memory.

. . . The family had moved three times after leaving Braunau and before arriving in Leonding. They arrived in the sleepy little village in late 1898 and stayed until 1905 when they moved to Linz, after the death of the father.

Alois had retired in 1895. Near the end of his life, the stern old civil servant was reverting to his peasant ways. He had always pined for a little land to work, so he bought a small property in Leonding—a house and a half acre of land. Next to their land was the local cemetery, and across the way was the village church. Here Alois could keep his bees, meet his cronies in the Gasthaus Stiefler for a quarter-liter of wine now and again, and read the papers. It was a pleasant retirement.

The family had grown to five children by the time the Hitlers moved to Leonding. Klara had given birth to a boy, Edmund, and a girl, Paula, after Adolf. The year they moved to Leonding, little Edmund died of the measles. It was Adolf's first encounter with death, and the villagers remembered years later when the reporters inundated their tiny village for news of the Führer's boyhood that Hitler had been seen, at the time following Edmund's death, sitting on the cemetery walls night after night, gazing up at the stars.[90]

Edmund's death not only deprived Adolf of his beloved little brother, but it also left Adolf the only male child and the one great hope of father Alois. The oldest child, Alois junior, had long ago run off and proven himself a thorough rascal; he had stolen and been caught doing it. The burden of carrying on the Hitler name fell to Adolf. Suddenly Alois, long indifferent to the progress of his third child, began to put fatherly pressure on Adolf to make something of himself.

It had been in the years in Leonding when Hitler went through his radical change, physically and mentally. He went from a successful student to one who barely passed his subjects and continually received poor marks in motivation. He entered the Linz Realschule in 1900, failed the first year, and only barely got through the next three. Finally the school authorities requested that Adolf not come back. One of his teachers later remembered the boy:

> I well remember the gaunt, pale-faced boy who shuttled back and forth between Linz and Leonding. He was definitely gifted, but only in a one-sided way, for he was lacking in self-control, and to say the least, he was regarded as argumentative, willful, arrogant, and bad-tempered, and he was notoriously incapable of submitting to school discipline. Nor was he industrious. If he had been, he would have achieved much better results with his undoubted ability.
>
> He reacted with ill-concealed hostility whenever a teacher reproved him or gave him some advice. At the same time, he demanded the unqualified subservience of his fellow pupils, fancying himself in the role

of a leader, and of course playing many small, harmless pranks, which is not unusual among immature youngsters. He seemed to be infected with the stories of Karl May and the Redskins.[91]

Even as a fifteen-year-old boy, Hitler would continue to lead a gang of Leonding youths younger than he in war games. May's heroic creation of the dauntless cowboy Shatterhand, who ruthlessly exterminated the Indians with his rifle that never ran out of bullets, surely had an influence on Hitler throughout his life.[92]

Hitler did not return to the Linz Realschule in 1904, but instead enrolled in the Steyr Realschule in a nearby town where he boarded during the week.[93]

More important than these school developments was the death of Adolf's father early in 1903. Sitting down to his morning glass of wine at the Gasthaus, Alois suffered a lung hemorrhage and died. Adolf was now free to choose what he wanted to do, no longer pushed by his father to become a civil servant. After Alois's death Hitler simply stopped trying in school, as if he wanted to be dismissed and have done with it.

At home, he was once more the darling of the family. His older half-sister, Angela, married in the fall of 1903, so that there were just he and young, malleable Paula left with mother Klara. Alois's spirit was still invoked, however. Sometimes, while talking, Klara would look over to the windowsill where "Uncle" Alois's pipes were still kept in their rack, as if to ask him for guidance . . .[94]

Hitler probably thought of those pipes as he painted the garden house in Leonding. He had managed to avoid what those pipes stood for. He was on his own and attempting to become something in the arts, in his own desultory way. It felt good to be working in oils again, and suddenly, back at the scene of so many battles between his father and himself over joining the civil service or becoming a painter, Hitler was once again filled with the romantic notion of becoming a famous artist. This ambition came and went in spurts throughout his life. He wrote to his friend Franz:

> In any case, I am working again with brush and palette and have a lot of pleasure from it, if also great difficulty with oil technique.
> Do you know—without any arrogance—I still believe that the world

lost a great deal by my not being able to go to the academy and learn the craft of painting. Or did fate reserve me to some other purpose?

And now dear Franzl—best wishes for your birthday next week and believe me that I wish I could be with you! But at the most, we'll see each other again in fourteen days.

> Until then good wishes from your
> Adolf[95]

Again, in this part of the letter, appear Hitler's characteristic ingratiating techniques, for example, the use of the diminutive form of his friend's name—Franzl. This calls to mind his friend Kubizek whom Hitler called Gustl and always was sure to write to on his name day and birthday. Hitler was always good with name days and birthdays. It saved the work of real friendship.

The letter also reflects Hitler's feeling of frustration as late as the summer of 1911 at being rejected by the Academy. Few have ever fully reckoned with the effect that that profound disappointment had on the rest of Hitler's life.

Even though, as we have seen, Hitler himself later joked about his early painting, calling himself a dilettante and scoffing at the exorbitant prices his paintings fetched after he had become Führer, he must have felt, at the same time, sweet revenge on all those "blockheads" at the Academy.

Hitler was a twenty-two-year-old man/boy with a nervous stomach, a chip on his shoulder, and a perceived injustice against the world.

Like most of the rest of the Viennese, he mistook the violent outburst of Expressionism, unthinkable without Freud's achievement, as a symptom of debility rather than a sign of interior strength. He said so later in *Mein Kampf*.

Anything that did not fit into Hitler's little universe of hate and frustration was obviously decadent, for he perceived himself as the only healthy man in the world. Foolish doctors; stupid academicians.

Hitler's wounds would have still another two years to fester in Vienna.

10

Departure

(1)

ONCE back in the Männerheim in the autumn, Hitler returned to his regimen of painting. There was no pretense to this painting as there had been the previous spring after the windfall inheritance. Over the summer, Hitler must finally have learned the lesson that the future comes even if uninvited. He realized now that season followed season and even a 2,000-crown inheritance would not last forever. Hitler had to defray expenses somehow. He calculated that the orphan's pension he had turned over to Paula, stretched over the two remaining years of eligibility, amounted to over 600 crowns that he had suddenly lost to his little sister. But there had been no choice.

Besides, now that Hitler was his own company, so to speak, he made twice as much on his paintings as when Hanisch had sold them for him.

The mornings were again spent in sketching out the painting from some postcard; then in the early afternoon, after a light lunch, he would daub on the colors and later take the painting out to the dealers.

Through the late fall of 1911 and on into 1912 and 1913, Jakob Altenberg was one of Hitler's most consistent buyers. Gone now were Hitler's scraggly beard and shabby clothing. Though his clothes were not new, he kept them clean and neat, and presented altogether a good appearance when he went on his selling rounds.[1]

Altenberg was in his mid-thirties when he was doing business with Hitler. He was a small man and an elegant dresser. A gold watch chain drooped across his vest and he kept his moustache clipped neatly at his lip.[2] Altenberg would adjust his glasses to look at each new Hitler painting. The dealer would think over the price carefully, though their dealings were usually straightforward and the price varied little. But the appraisal was half the fun, and sometimes, for an especially large painting—the quality varied as little as the price and had little to do with the payment—Altenberg would pay out as much as twelve crowns.[3]

Though Altenberg had only come to Vienna in the late nineteenth century from his native Poland, he had already opened his Wiedner Haupstrasse firm by 1898 and business was improving every day. At his peak, Altenberg would have four frame shops in Vienna, grow a respectable paunch, talk in a smooth and congenial Viennese German, and take five o'clock tea at the fashionable Bristol Hotel.[4]

As the successful Jewish businessman, Altenberg was the perfect example of what Hitler was complaining about in his inflammatory speeches at the home, and what he was reading about in his anti-Semitic pamphlets: the foreign Jew who had come to Vienna and made good; the Jew who had assimilated too well. But according to Altenberg's recollections of young Hitler, the painter never uttered an anti-Semitic remark in his hearing.[5]

Such remarks would have been bad for business.

While Hitler had been enjoying his summer of travel in his old hometowns, the rest of Austria had been hit with a drastic increase in the cost of living, which the Socialists blamed on the government's protectionist agrarian policies. The Socialists lost five seats in the 1911 elections, but had managed to make up for that by beating the Christian Social machine in winning the majority of seats representing Vienna.[6] The Socialists seemed to be filling the void created by Lueger's death.

When spontaneous workers' riots broke out during the summer to protest the rise in the cost of living, the government immediately blamed the Socialists for "arranging"[7] the riots and threatened to meet any further demonstrations with force if necessary.

Whether or not Hitler read of these summer riots, he must have read of the September riots in his morning papers before beginning work.[8]

Workers assembled in droves before the Rathaus to protest the high food prices, and the government kept its word about using force. Police at first were called in to break up the demonstration; when they failed, the infantry and cavalry were brought in with guns and sabers at the ready. The workers continued chanting "We want bread!" "Away with capitalism!" and "Hurrah for the revolution!"[9] in the face of the military. In the ensuing scuffle between military and protestors, scores were injured and at least two killed.

Workers went out into the streets all across the proletarian suburbs in sympathy with these demonstrators. Streetcars were vandalized in a demonstration of utter frustration by the workers; barricades were thrown up across the streets; and the Imperial troops fought street battles with the citizens of Vienna. It looked like 1848 all over again.[10]

For Franz Joseph, almost senile by now, these riots were an ugly reminder of '48, and he was not about to go easy on the workers. A threat to impose martial law to bring peace was published and that succeeded—that along with the arrests of several hundred citizens. Some eighty persons were given stiff prison sentences as a result of the rioting—hundreds of others were confined for shorter periods of time.[11]

Viktor Adler's newspaper, the *Arbeiter Zeitung,* described the troubles as a "demonstration of despair"[12] in an edition that was quickly confiscated by the government.

But arrests and confiscations did not solve the problem of hunger. The Socialist, Adler, was quick to make political capital from the situation by addressing a crowd in Favoriten, telling them that they should not expect a capitalistic state to provide food for its people instead of shielding the agrarian lobby, and that there would be no justice until the class struggle was over.[13]

Hitler followed these events closely from the security of his window seat at the Männerheim. No doubt he broke into an outraged speech once or twice over the iniquity of the Socialists. Or perhaps he had learned his orator's lesson by this time: "Only in the smallest groups did I speak of the things which inwardly moved or attracted me. This speaking in the narrowest circles had many good points: I learned to orate less, but to know people with their opinions and objections that were often so boundlessly primitive."[14]

The violence of the food riots was not confined to the streets. While discussing disturbances on October 5, the Parliament was suddenly interrupted by a commotion in the visitors' gallery. Five shots rang through the chamber before a young man holding a pistol was overcome by the police and bystanders. The shots, none of which found their mark, had been aimed at the minister of justice, Dr. Hochenburger, who was generally held responsible for the violence of the supression of the workers' protests.[15]

This unsuccessful assassination attempt must have only served to inflame Hitler's prejudices. Hochenburger was a ranking member of the pro-Germany groups, and the assailant was accused of being a dupe of the Socialists, whose "hate speeches"[16] had supposedly inspired him to the deed.

Once again, the Marxists, in Hitler's budding cosmology, were the culprits, trying to bring the Germans down. This Jewish conspiracy, as Hitler referred to Marxism, was always the foe of the Germans. What Hitler always failed to understand was that the leaders of the Austrian Socialists were considered too German for hundreds of thousands of Slavs in Habsburg Ruthenia, Poland, and Bohemia who broke away from the Austrian Socialists to form their own brand of nationalistic socialism.

Such disturbances, however, faded into the past as fall drew into the gray closeness of winter and the Viennese sky lowered onto the city, dropping its blanket of snow, cushioning the streets, piling up at the cornices of buildings to threaten the pedestrians below. The yellow glow of artificial lights filtered bravely out of offices in the weak daylight. The hustle and bustle of the city picked up tempo as the season tumbled into the winter gaiety of Christmas. Fir boughs framed the steamy windows of coffeehouses; candy Krampusse glared out of candy shop windows, warning little boys and girls to be good.

Hitler got into the Christmas spirit this year and gave his friend Franzl one of the paintings he had done on his summer tour. It was the painting of the baroque spire of Stephanskirche overlooking the River Inn in Braunau. On the back, Hitler inscribed: "To my dear friend Franzl as a sign of thanks. Vienna, Christmas, 1911, Adolf Hitler."[17]

The new year of 1912 came, and Hitler's inertia remained. He sat at his window seat all day long painting his hackneyed scenes of Vienna. Perhaps he broadened his reading somewhat during this time, but it is doubtful. He had learned to select and read only that which bolstered up his own opinions, so he probably stuck to the daily papers and his dogmatic pamphlets. Perhaps it was in this period that Hitler picked up the *Handbuch der Judenfrage,* a pamphlet written by a Viennese named Theodor Fritsch. This booklet was, as its publisher's blurb described it, "a handy guide to anti-Semitism."[18] It was the kind of tract that Hitler later would love to quote from because it gave his anti-Semitism a pseudointellectual basis, especially when he could quote the great philosophers on the subject—which this pamphlet did for him—to make it seem as though he had culled all these conclusions from personal reading.

This book went through dozens of printings and later became sanctioned reading in schools of the Third Reich.

The year 1912 was an important one for Hitler. According to the Compulsory Service Law of 1889, passed just before Hitler's birth, 1912 was the last year that he could legally register for military service. He should have registered in 1909 when he was twenty. Then he most probably would have done his military service in the spring of 1910.[19]

Hitler was a draft evader during his Vienna period, and it would appear that much of his activity, or inactivity, in these years was caused by that fact. Hitler stayed on in Vienna, afraid to leave before his draft eligibility ran out. In 1912 he was still liable for the draft. Any move would have to wait until he turned twenty-four, in 1913. Then, when crossing the border into Germany and questioned by border guards as to his draft status, he could prove his age and tell them he had long ago fulfilled his military service requirement.[20]

In the spring of 1912, Hitler must have been cruelly reminded of his perilous position while reading through the papers.[21] A new Compulsory Service Law was being hotly debated in Parliament.[22] When passed, it provided for a stiff punishment for draft evaders: a year in prison and a fine of 2,000 crowns for those leaving the Empire without serving their time. One of the new provisions of the law, which it seems Hitler failed to read, was that which extended the age of eligibility for those failing to register in time to age thirty-six.

Hitler must have spent a few sleepless nights over this new law, but in time his anxiety over his military service passed away. Hitler ignored the troublesome issue till he forgot about it.

Again that spring or summer, once the weather got warmer, Hitler felt the urge to travel. The tour of his home region the previous summer had been such a success that he decided to repeat the journey and to take in a village he had neglected on the earlier trip.

From Braunau, the Hitler family had moved, in 1892, to Passau over the border in Germany. They had stayed there for two and a half years, and then moved back to Austria when Alois decided upon an early retirement at age fifty-eight. The tiny village to which the family had first moved after Alois's retirement was Hafeld, about fifty kilometers southwest of Linz.

Hitler was only six when the family moved to Hafeld. They were to stay there for slightly more than two years.

It is interesting that Hitler would later wax nostalgic over this little village of about 100 inhabitants and two dozen houses,[23] for this move had caused an abrupt change in his life. The past year in Passau had been a child's paradise for him. Alois had gotten a promotion to Linz in 1894, but the Hitler family had stayed behind in Passau, for Klara had just given birth to Edmund and the baby could not travel. Young Hitler was thus freed from the tyranny of his father for an entire year, and was free to do whatever he wanted. Klara, normally indulgent to Adolf in any case, now had her hands full with little Edmund and did not even attempt to control Adolf. With his half-siblings Angela and Alois junior off at school, Adolf was king of the castle.

All of this came to an end with the move to Hafeld and back with father Alois who, retired now, had nothing better to do than complain about the children.

At any rate, there must also have been good feelings of home that drew Hitler back to Hafeld in the summer of 1912. The region is beautiful, situated on a high ridge with fruit and nut trees abounding, and a fine view of the Salzkammergut mountains in the distance. Alois had purchased a small farm on a rise of land hidden from the road by an orchard. There were even stables for horses and cows, and a hayloft where the Hitler children played and rolled in the hay. Alois was an ardent beekeeper, and at Hafeld he finally got some hives to tend. Hitler later remembered his father's passion with a touch of humor:

> It was the most normal thing in the world to be stung by bees. My mother would pull out as many as forty-five or fifty stings from the old gentleman when he returned from clearing the hives. He never protected himself in

any way, except by smoking all the time. In other words, it was a good excuse for another cigar![24]

Alois tried to make a success of the farm, but soon learned that he had purchased land that was not much more productive than a paved street in Vienna. The farm continually lost money. The winter winds blew cold off the Dachstein and spring rains bit at Alois's face while he worked the fields. Hafeld was a nice place to visit, but . . .

On May 1, 1895, Hitler, the *Muttersöhnchen* (mother's darling), got his first taste of the outside world when he attended his first day of school at nearby Fischlalm. Young Hitler did well in school in these first years. A teacher from here later remembered the "lively, bright-eyed and intelligent six-year-old who came to school hand in hand with his twelve-year-old sister Angela."[25]

Hitler was at the top of his class at Fischlalm, and also received the highest marks for deportment. In spite of the increasing friction between Adolf and his father, Hitler looked back at this period as a time of flowering:

> Much romping in the open air, the long walk to school, and the companionship of unusually robust boys caused my mother grievous suffering, but this did not prevent me from becoming the opposite of a stay-at-home.[26]

Hitler became a ringleader of a group of boys, and began to break away from his mother's apron strings. Perhaps it was for this reason that he could look back sentimentally to this time even at age twenty-three.

To commemorate his early success in the school there, Hitler painted an oil of the Fischlalm school in the summer of 1912.[27] There had been few successes in his youth after age ten, and high marks at this schoolhouse must have rated a picture. The quality of the painting is among the best that Hitler did during his Vienna years. The line is steady and sure; there is a sentimental air about the building and landscape, a sort of loving simplicity, that makes it an attractive painting. Perhaps there was real feeling behind this picture, and the fact that it was of a building made it easier for Hitler, who by this time could draw buildings in his sleep.

Another painting survives from this trip, that of the *Schlossmühle* in

Fischlalm, with the same quaintness and attention to detail that marks the painting of the schoolhouse.[28] It would appear from these two paintings that Hitler had once again had a happy pilgrimage and could go back to the Männerheim refreshed. He could easily last out until the next spring, now. And then, after that, Germany! Munich was his new dream. The Art Academy there became the new focus of his ambition to lead him through another Viennese winter.

(2)

There would be only two more winters of peace in Europe, ambition or no ambition.

While domestically the economic and political situation was deteriorating, outside the Austrian empire things were even worse. Crisis followed crisis in that generation before World War I, and the Great Powers probed each other's strengths and weaknesses; built great armies and navies; tested each other in Africa, Asia, the Balkans. During this time, Austria sat and watched the approaching crisis like a "hypnotized hen,"[29] unable and unwilling to do anything to help international relations and assuage feelings between the major powers.

Since Aehrenthal's annexation of Bosnia-Herzegovina in 1908, the situation in the Balkans had gone from bad to worse. Increasingly, the new nation of Serbia, with its capital at Belgrade, was becoming the powerhouse of the Balkans. Vienna did nothing to better relations with this strong nation, and Franz Joseph found it increasingly difficult to refuse Chief-of-Staff Conrad von Hötzendorf's saber-rattling pleas.

In 1909 two scandals had broken out in Zagreb. One was a treason trial in which the Habsburg government boggled an attempt to hang conspiracy charges on Croat politicians and Belgrade Serbs. The trial was, from start to finish, a fiasco, and so corrupt that the prisoners had ultimately to be pardoned by the emperor. Another scandal, involving the distinguished Austrian historian Friedjung, resulted in a libel action brought against the historian for articles he had written denouncing certain Serbs and Croats for conspiracy against His Majesty; the change was based on forged information. Friedjung, a trained historian, should have been wiser than to accept, at face value, the information he had received, but the political climate of dislike for the Serbs was so hot in Vienna that it clouded even that honest man's vision. Patriotism, the old war-horse of tired and decadent states, was brought out of mothballs in the final attempt to save the empire.

236 •

Von Hötzendorf's continual urging of a "defensive" war against the Serbs and Italians finally forced Franz Joseph to relieve him of his position in 1911. Aehrenthal died early the next year, and was replaced by Count Berchtold. The old order responsible for the Bosnian annexation had passed, but the policies remained the same. The Austrians practiced ostrich style politics.

But the Balkans would not go away. As Trotsky had written earlier, the Balkans were the "Pandora's box of Europe."[30] With all the Great Powers colliding there, it would be only a matter of time until this powder keg would explode. The fall of 1912 (when Hitler returned from his summer trip to Hafeld) offered the perfect opportunity for the fledgling nations of the Balkans to completely break away from the Ottoman Turks. The Italians had just demonstrated the weakness of Turkey by annexing their Tripolitania without so much as a squawk from Constantinople.

Trotsky had been commissioned by a newspaper in Russia to cover the situation in the Balkans in 1912. On his way to the train station in Vienna in early October of that year, he learned of the outbreak of the First Balkan War. The southern Slavs, Bulgars, Serbs, Montenegrins, and Greeks invaded Turkey and ultimately forced the weak old Ottoman Empire to make a humiliating peace that deprived it of all its European possessions except for the region around Constantinople.

Trotsky was on hand in Belgrade to see the long lines of men from all walks of life, ready to volunteer to go to war. He was shocked, for notable among these men were many of his Socialist friends, men who were supposedly committed to internationalism and ardent enemies of imperialist wars. But here they were in line, volunteering to take up weapons to go out and slaughter the other proletarians who would be fighting on the other side. Watching these men go away to their deaths, Trotsky was filled with a deep sense of tragedy; "a feeling of helplessness before fate . . . and pain for the human locusts carried to their destruction."[31]

Trotsky's years in Vienna had served to pull the wool of civilization over his eyes, and had made him begin to believe in the myth of Western progress and humanity. The horrors and atrocities he witnessed on the Bulgarian side of the war changed his mind about all this:

> The abstract, humanitarian, moralist view of history is barren—I know this very well. But this chaotic mass of material acquisitions, of habits, customs, and prejudices which we call civilization, has hypnotized us all,

giving us the false impression that we have already achieved the main thing. Now comes the war and shows us that we have not even crawled out on our bellies from the barbarous period of history.[32]

Not only was Trotsky shocked by his Socialist friends contributing their bodies to such a barbarous slaughter; he was also afraid that the Slavs would, by pulling mother Russia into the fracas, start a general European war.

Trotsky was not alone in that fear. In Vienna, the voices of war were being heard. Much of the aristocracy was in favor of war in the south, as if to get it over with and perhaps revitalize the realm with patriotic fervor.

Conrad von Hötzendorf had been called back to his office of chief of staff with the outbreak of war in the Balkans and was, as usual, pushing for Austria to launch a defensive war. Franz Joseph was still against Austria's participation in a war in the Balkans—but for all the wrong reasons.

"I don't want war!" he exclaimed that fall. "I've always been unlucky in wars—we'd win, but we'd lose provinces."[33]

Franz Ferdinand was also dead set against Austrian involvement in a Balkan war. Still harking back to the outmoded principle of the Three Emperors' League, he questioned: "Are the emperor of Austria and the tsar to knock each other off the throne to pave the way for revolution?"[34]

Von Hötzendorf had no answer for that question.

Even Wilhelm of Germany, when pressed to join in a general war against the Serbs and Russians during the Balkan crisis, was loath to fight for a "few miserable goat pastures."[35]

Soon enough this first crisis in the Balkans passed with the victory of the Slavs over the Turks. Peace was saved again—for a time. Trotsky, back in Vienna writing of the war, saw the future. As Isaac Deutscher later wrote, "Through the Balkan prism he saw the alignment of the Great Powers as it was to appear in 1914; and he saw it with great clarity, dimmed only by the wishful belief that the French, Austrian, and German Socialists would defend to the end 'the cause of peace against the onslaught of barbarism.'"[36]

Vienna was not much better for Trotsky than the Balkans had been. Once back in the Austrian capital, he was immediately involved in party squabbles. Since his absence in the Balkans he had lost position with the Mensheviks. The split between the rival Bolsheviks and Mensheviks was complete now, and Trotsky's conciliatory gestures between the factions were no longer wanted. He was involved in useless bickering that kept him from his work. He was, more and more, viewed with distrust by both factions of the Communists. Trotsky was too much of an intellectual loner for either faction.

It would be unfair to say that Trotsky was relieved when the Second Balkan War broke out early in 1913. But this war did give him a chance to get away from these petty rivalries in Vienna and cover some hard news.

Since the first victory of the Slavs over the Turks, the victors had fallen out with one another over the spoils. Now a new realignment, pitting Serbia and Greece against Bulgaria, again threatened European peace. Once more the war parties in Austria clamored for war to put an end to Serbia.[37]

This time, Bulgaria was the underdog, and Trotsky's sympathies went out to this country which eventually lost all it had won in the war against Turkey. Once again there were barbarities, foreshadowing those to occur in 1914. And still again, European peace was saved narrowly, more by accident than plan. The belligerents ran out of resources and resolve before the Great Powers had time to rally around an ally.

More important, as a result of the Second Balkan War, when "Serbia had trounced Bulgaria . . . Austria found herself faced with a tough and brash new power, looking for new worlds to conquer, which she had done nothing to placate and everything to infuriate."[38]

The road to Sarajevo had been paved with hate. Most of the world would travel down that road of hate in one more year.

(3)

Time was running out. Hitler must have felt like an enlisted man in the army with time growing short for his duty to be up. Like a soldier, Hitler must have been filled with all sorts of fears that something would happen to spoil his leave-taking.

Comparing Hitler to a soldier in this case is especially appropriate, for it was the military that was giving him these eerie premonitions.

Christmas and New Year came around again, and then it was 1913. That was the year Hitler would turn twenty-four and, he believed, be safe from conscription. He had only to wait until his birthday that April. He just had to sit tight, avoid the attention of the law, and he would be over the border into his promised land.[39]

Hitler maintained the same schedule every day, and gave to his companions at the home the impression of an industrious man: "We all lived pretty thoughtlessly through those days," remembered a new friend of Hitler's from his last months in Vienna. "I believe that Hitler was the only one among us who had a clear vision of his future way."[40]

That way was to Munich and the Academy there where he hoped to study. Just as in his days as the Linz dandy, when he could dream of nothing but living in Vienna, so now Munich filled his thoughts.

Hitler was one of the "in" crowd at the home by this time. He was a solid member of the "intellectuals."[41] Karl Honisch was new to the Männerheim in 1913. He noticed Hitler right away, sitting in his window seat and painting a scene of Old Vienna. Hitler's hair flopped down over his forehead and he was dressed in a worn but clean dark suit. Hitler had taken on the aspect of the grand old man of the home, though there were many older men there. His years of seniority gave him an exalted position with the others.

Honisch, whose name was strangely similar to that of Hitler's earlier companion Hanisch, got along well with Adolf. He looked up to the twenty-three-year-old as someone seasoned, a man experienced in the ways of the world—the world, in this case, being the confines of the Männerheim.[42]

Hitler, in Honisch's eyes, was "industrious and thrifty"[43] and worked from the morning until late afternoon finishing his one picture per day; and then made the rounds of the shops to sell it.

Honisch ingratiated himself with Hitler by fetching him water for his colors and by going across the street to the milk store and buying his milk and special *Iglauer Landbrot* that Hitler was particularly fond of for breakfast.[44]

Honisch's picture of Hitler is much different from the one Hanisch supplied. Gone were the days of Hitler's unmeasured ranting and raving. As Hitler himself said, he had learned how to orate. He was "on the whole, a friendly and charming person, who took an interest in the fate of every companion . . . he was goodhearted and helpful . . . [but] nobody allowed himself to take liberties with Hitler."[45]

Hitler now had become the arbiter of arguments in the home, not the instigator. He had grown so respectable, in fact, that the director of the

Männerheim even sat down and chatted with Hitler sometimes, "an honor seldom granted to an inmate."[46]

There was a strong sense of social order in the Männerheim, perhaps even stronger than outside, for the home was such a controlled world that there was little room for a real misfit. Hitler's time at the Männerheim—three years an occupant—accorded him a respected position in that barracks-room environment. He responded well to this newfound respect, and returned it in kind. He was seen more than once "with a hat in his hands"[47] to start collections for other inhabitants who did not have enough money to stay on at the Männerheim. Thrust by dint of his tenure into a position of respect, Hitler wanted, in the best bourgeois manner, to live up to it.

Hitler had other friends besides Honisch at this time. There was Herr Schön, an out-of-work farm manager. He was seven years Hitler's senior, and he and Hitler carried on lively conversations about farming and the techniques involved.

There was also Herr Redlich, an unemployed academician, with his "short blond beard and teacher's face."[48] We cannot be certain if Redlich was the same educated man from the Hanisch days whom the other inhabitants called the Professor and who one day cornered Hitler on a question of Schopenhauer. Perhaps not, as Hitler and Redlich were quite chummy by 1913, carrying on "intellectual" conversations in which Hitler tried out his pamphlet philosophies.

There were plenty of less skilled men around with whom Hitler rubbed shoulders, many from those nether regions of the Dual Monarchy that Hitler so reviled. Unskilled workers such as Leib Jaroslawski from Russia, Max Fischer and Otto Rezer out of Hungary proved to be good sounding boards for Hitler's readings and theories. Simon Robinsohn, the one-eyed keymaker who had lent Hitler money in Adolf's early months at the Männerheim, was still around, though it is doubtful that Hitler put the touch on him anymore. There were also other craftsmen among the Männerheim tenants, such as the book-binder Michael Josifoff, from Russia.[49]

The regulars at the home came and went, and still Hitler stayed on. His newfound easy, noblesse-oblige manner could only be broken down at special times. The men would be sitting around the writing room addressing envelopes, playing chess, binding books, or painting, and someone would bring up some topic for discussion. Hitler was no longer easily aroused; he kept his head down and continued to dab splotches of color onto his paper. The conversation would go along nicely for a time, with the usual bantering give-and-take between intimates, until the key words "Reds" or "Jesuits"[50] were uttered. Honisch could then see the light shine in Hitler's eyes as he continued, very deliberately, to paint. He might utter a word or two to elucidate the argument for his friends. Nothing too dogmatic or dramatic, however—at this early point.

If the conversation continued, then Hitler would finally get to his feet, as in the old days, paint brush or pencil flailing in his hand and "lightning in his eyes,"[51] and go into his tirade about the Socialists ruining the country and the Jesuits poisoning the minds of the children, "not avoiding vulgarisms, in a very impetuous way."[52] He would toss back his head to emphasize a point, and continually brush at the forelock hanging down. Slowly, he would calm down from the speech, which often his audience barely understood, look around at the faces of the men in the room and then sit back resignedly to his painting "as if to say: a pity for every word wasted on you, you won't ever understand."[53]

The twenty-one-year-old Honisch went back to his work, a little shocked at the display and not quite sure what had been said, but impressed nonetheless.

Hitler had few pleasures in these months. He was saving up for Munich and working diligently at painting. He still attended the Opera, but not so regularly and only in the standing section. After working all day in the writing room with his comrades, Hitler was socially isolated. He was never seen in the local pub with the other men, and it was quite an occasion for him to smoke a cigarette. The day after a performance at the Opera, the men in the writing room knew to expect a morning-long critique of the singing.[54]

Hitler did allow himself one vice—his craving for sweets. Getting to Germany should not be so all-consuming an ambition as to ruin every one of life's pleasures, after all. Hitler chose a strange place to give vent to the passion, back in his old neighborhood near the Westbahnhof.

The Café Kubata was a middle-class coffeehouse by Viennese standards. There were the omnipresent marble-topped tables and bentwood Thonet chairs, but the newspaper selection could boast nothing like the 300 journals and papers in assorted languages hanging in their bamboo racks from the musty walls of the Café Central.[55] It could boast none of the literati and none of the intellectuals of that famous institution; nor was there a revolutionary colony like the Central's. But Hitler liked the pastries at the Kubata, of which the owner, Maria Wohlrab, never failed to give him an oversized portion.

There is a mystery about the Café Kubata. It opened in December 1912, that is, three years after Hitler left the Westbahnhof district. The coffeehouse, located at Schweglerstrasse 25, could not have been an earlier haunt of Hitler's, though he did frequent plenty of coffeehouses in the district in 1907-9 where he read the papers and munched on pastries. What was the draw of this coffeehouse, that would bring him halfway across Vienna to eat a pastry that could be had in hundreds of other coffeehouses closer to the Männerheim, thereby saving him the walk or tram fare?

A partial answer to this may be found in the person of Marie Rinke, who worked in the Café Kubata. This was the same Fräulein Marie from the Felberstrasse days whom Hitler sometimes met in the streets near his house.

These three years later, Marie was a waitress in the Café Kubata and, from its opening, Hitler was one of the regulars. What further connection existed between the two, whether romantic or platonic, is unknown. Perhaps Marie was Hitler's Vienna Stephanie.

Maria Wohlrab, the owner, liked Hitler, but she unexplainably had the devil of a time pronouncing his name. She ended up by simply calling him "Dolferl,"[56] a nickname that seems infinitely harder to pronounce than Hitler. Hitler was, according to her, always "well dressed"[57] and often came to the café in the company of a pal named Wetti or Pepi,[58] some friend from the Männerheim whom Hitler would drag across Vienna when he came calling on Fräulein Marie.

Hitler got extra portions of pastry for good reason. He knew the right people to befriend and managed to ingratiate himself with Wohlrab early on by fetching her a bag of sugar or coffee when she needed it from the grocery store at the corner of the Märzstrasse and the Gürtel.

But, according to Wohlrab, Hitler was no mere sycophant. He once stayed away from the coffeehouse for several days because he'd heard Frau Wohlrab upbraiding her kitchen help in a most acrimonious manner.[59]

Usually, however, things were less traumatic at the Café Kubata, and Hitler took his normal corner seat, wolfed down his pastry and read the newspapers. He was a much quieter and more responsible customer than Maria Wohlrab was accustomed to. He was biding his time, waiting for the clock to run out on his Vienna sojourn.

(4)

The clock was running out for all of Vienna, that "proving ground for world destruction."[60] Hitler later claimed he saw the sand filtering out of Vienna's hourglass at the time. In *Mein Kampf* he always refers to the old empire's death as inevitable. The days of this inevitability were flying by like the calendar sheets blowing away in a trite movie version of the passage of time.

The thirteenth year of the new century. Unlucky thirteen. It began auspiciously enough with a rash of suicides. There were the three young men who poisoned themselves in a café on the Neulerchenfelderstrasse because of "erotic motives. . . . In spite of their youth, all three had enjoyed zealously acquaintainces with young girls who were just as precocious as they."[61]

Another suicide in a Prater café was the result of a man losing his notary job. He shot himself in the chest in front of the other customers who were quietly sipping their morning coffee. A nineteen-year-old also shot himself because he had lost all his money gambling in Monte Carlo.[62]

"Suicide was a way of life in Vienna." Such a joke could easily have been coined by the black-humored Viennese for whom, in the words of Karl Kraus, the situation may be desperate, but never serious. Suicide was a romantic escape from the problems of life—an operetta view of life and death. Suicide was as viable a choice in times of stress as choosing between political parties in an election. Central Europe has always maintained one of the world's highest suicide rates. Perhaps it is the *Föhn* which blows steady, warm, and unnerving off the Alps; perhaps the gray winters. Perhaps the gray outlook.

Suicide had claimed the lives of great and small alike in Vienna. In 1889, the year of Hitler's birth, Crown Prince Rudolf shot himself at Mayerling. The poet Adalbert Stifter died in 1868, two days after slashing his throat with a razor to avoid dying of cancer of the liver. In 1906 the writer Ferdinand von Saar shot himself. The playwright Ferdinand Raimund had shot himself in 1836 after a dog bit him and he had convinced himself it was rabid.

The father of statistical thermodynamics, Ludwig Boltzmann, took his life in 1906. The writer Otto Weininger shot himself in 1903. The architect Eduard van der Nüll hanged himself after the emperor's careless remark criticizing part of the design of the Opera House. As we have already seen, this suicide prompted Franz Joseph's safe public formula for the next fifty years: *"Es war sehr schön, es hat mir sehr gefreut."*[63]

Poets, painters, musicians, physicists—no one was immune to the lure of suicide. The Expressionist painter Richard Gerstl hanged himself in 1908; the poet Georg Trakl died in 1914 of a drug overdose. Three brothers of the philosopher Ludwig Wittgenstein took their own lives; the brother of Gustav Mahler, himself a promising musician, killed himself. The daughter of Arthur Schnitzler died of blood poisoning after slashing her wrists. The son of Hofmannsthal would shoot himself in the family home at Rodaun a decade after Hitler left Vienna. The psychologist Wilhelm Stickel, who had, in 1910, written a monograph on suicide for the Psychoanalytical Society, later killed himself. The writer Stefan Zweig and his wife, halfway around the world in South America, after fleeing from Nazi Europe, took their lives rather than try to accommodate to a new and terrifying world.

Even the military was not free from suicide, as we shall see presently in the case of Alfred Redl. Earlier in the previous century, the general Baron Franz von Uchatius, who now has a street named after him in Vienna, as have several of the other suicides mentioned here, killed himself after the barrel of a cannon that he had developed split upon test-firing.

There were also those who tried or often contemplated suicide: the painter Alfred Kubin tried to shoot himself on the grave of his mother in 1896; the composer Alban Berg tried to kill himself after an unsuccessful love affair; Hugo Wolf tried to do himself in while suffering from syphilis. Ludwig Wittgenstein more than once reported suicidal feelings. Any death that was somewhat dubious in circumstances would begin gossip of suicide.

Just as Vienna had earlier given Freud the background for his sexual theories of neurosis, so would this preoccupation with death later spur him on to his theory of the death instinct.

Emile Durkheim had diagnosed the condition in 1897 in his work on suicide. Suicide was not an individual action, but a reflection of a society's mood and temperament:

> At any given moment, the moral constitution of society established the contingent of voluntary deaths. There is, therefore, for each people a collective force of a definite amount of energy, impelling man to self-

destruction. The victim's acts, which at first seem to express only his personal temperament, are really the supplement and prolongation of a social condition which they express externally.[64]

If the suicide rate in Vienna was any indication of the moral force of the community, then the innards of the empire were already dead, just as Hitler complained.

The spirit of the time can be gleaned from its newspapers. The foreign news was not good. Front pages were taken up with the Second Balkan War and the fears of an extended European war. Franz Joseph was jolted into action by this concern and wrote a letter to the minister president of Romania, asking him to stop the conflict between his nation and Bulgaria before things got out of hand in the Balkans.[65]

Elsewhere in the papers, it was prophesied that "the world should be happy if peace can be had without the help of a magician."[66]

In London, reports had it that the peace conference set up to handle the settlements of the First Balkan War was breaking down due to the impatience of the Turkish delegates.[67]

It seemed that the peace movement, one of whose mainstays was the Viennese Bertha von Suttner, was always one step behind the war movement.[68]

The weather had turned cold in January 1913, with fresh snowfall on Sunday, the twelfth. The Wienerwald was blanketed white in the "first snow-Sunday"[69] of the year. There were five to eight centimeters of snow, and the temperature was down to minus two degrees centigrade. The skies were low and gray, and as the week progressed, the thermometer dropped several degrees further and the landscape around Vienna became a "picture out of deep winter."[70]

There were ice floes in the Danube. The sidewalks became treacherous obstacle courses with the buildup of black ice. Several accidents were reported because caretakers had not taken care to sand the sidewalks in front of their buildings.

With a cold winter ahead of them, the Viennese were also afflicted by another increase in the price of crude oil. The price had gone up 800 percent in just five years.[71]

Things looked rather bleak that second week of January, 1913. Today, with the benefit that hindsight affords, the situation seems even bleaker than it could have then.

But the Viennese were not crying. It was *Fasching,* the traditional ball season. Whatever the fates bring, the Viennese get out their finery in January and February and go on a merry round of waltzes. The situation may be desperate, but never serious . . .

There was the Ball for Disabled Veterans, sponsored by Franz Ferdinand, and the Fleet Club Ball, both at the Musikverein; the Opera Ball, with the highest of high society; the Businessmen's Ball at the Sophiensälle. There was even a Washerwomen's Ball, attended, in the best Schnitzler tradition, by more than one aristocratic dandy in hopes of a casual fling with a sweet young thing. The fine balls were held in magnificent halls under crystal chandeliers; string orchestras played familiar Strauss waltzes; champagne sparkled in cut-glass from Lobmeyers under the soft, yellow candlelight. The women were dressed to the nines in "evening gowns embroidered with gold and pearls . . . pearl strings adorned hair and throats . . . necklines plunged on evening gowns made of the finest tulle and crepe de chine."[72]

Other entertainments abounded to keep the minds of the Viennese off the world situation. There were the Burgtheater, Hof Opera, Volkstheater, and Volksoper. Mozart, Verdi, and Wagner operas played the second week of January, and Pablo Casals was due in February. The Philharmonic was playing music from Berlioz, and the Russian Ballet was in town on the fifteenth and sixteenth performing *Petrouchka*.[73]

For women who wanted a special makeup application, an ad in the newspaper offered to paint their lips a "rosy red"[74] for only two crowns, fifty hellers—almost what Hitler paid for a week's lodging at the Männerheim.

For the more literary and scientific minded, there were also readings and lectures. Rainer Maria Rilke was in town reading his poetry at the Neue Wiener Bühne. Dr. Paul Kammerer was lecturing at the Urania on "Breeding and Race."[75]

Vienna, teetering on the abyss, was alive with frivolity and culture. There was something for everyone in Vienna that January.

Perhaps no one in the world has ever looked less the sort of person interested in balls and ballet than the burly, thick-moustached, darkly intense young man with slanting Oriental eyes who disembarked from the Cracow train at Vienna's North Train Station that mid-January. That Viennese winter of 1913 certainly held no fears for this young man, already too familiar with the severities of a Siberian winter.

He carried his suitcase in his right hand; his left, shorter arm hung at his side.

Joseph Dzugashvili, alias Koba, son of a Georgian serf, looked like a man with a mission, and indeed he was. He had been sent by the great Vladimir Ulyanov, alias Lenin, to Vienna to gather information on the nationalities question and to write an article on it. Vienna, capital of 50 million comprising twelve nationalities, was the perfect place for such a research.

This was a big chance for the thirty-four-year-old who was only, unbeknown to him, weeks away from his final arrest and Siberian exile.

This man would also be better known to the world by another name. Just before coming to Vienna, Koba had changed his alias once again, signing one of his newspaper articles with the name he would bear for the next four decades: Stalin, Russian for man of steel.[76]

The Austrian Empire was a haven for Russian revolutionaries. Lenin was living in safety in Habsburg Cracow. In Vienna, besides Trotsky, there were Nikolai Bukharin, the future leader of the Communist International, and Alexander Troyanowsky, future Soviet ambassador to the United States, among other lesser-known Russians.

Tito, then known as Josip Broz, was working in nearby Wiener Neustadt that same winter. Three years younger than Hitler, Broz demonstrated few traits of the Communist leader he would become. In 1913 he was still too busy trying to crawl up from his peasant background into the middle class to give any thought to socialism. Impressed by the dazzling cars at the Daimler factory where he worked, Broz set about becoming a dandy. He took fencing and dancing lessons to this end. His frequent trips to Vienna reconfirmed his bourgeois goals of the time, though he hadn't even enough money to visit the cheapest of coffeehouses that Hitler frequented. He left Vienna in the summer of 1913 to serve his military duty—unlike Hitler, who left at about the same time to avoid his.[77]

Stalin was therefore not friendless when he came to Vienna. He was a new light in the Bolshevik constellation; a member of the Central Committee and a favorite of Lenin's, as well as the recent editor of St. Petersburg's *Pravda,* a newspaper that was in direct competition with Trotsky's Vienna-based paper of the same name. The crude, rough-speaking Georgian bear that Stalin was, moved in with the Troyanowskys at Schönbrunnerschlossstrasse 30 for the month he was working on the article on the nationalities problem.

Russia with its 200 nationalities provided as much a problem for organization as did the Habsburg Empire. There are indications that Lenin sent Stalin to Vienna for other reasons, too. Lenin handed over control of the Petersburg *Pravda* to another man, and most likely wanted Stalin out of the way for the time being to ease any hard feelings.

During his stay in Vienna, Stalin met Trotsky briefly. Trotsky was on his way to the Balkans to cover the second war and was visiting a former colleague before departure. It was cold outside, and they were seated around a samovar talking, "when suddenly, without knocking at the door, there entered from another room a man of middle height, with a swarthy grayish face, showing the marks of smallpox. The stranger, as if surprised by Trotsky's presence, stopped a moment at the door and gave a guttural growl, which might have been taken for a greeting. Then, with an empty glass in his hand, he went to the samovar, filled the glass with tea, and went out without saying a word."[78]

Trotsky's friend had to tell him who the stranger was; that this Dzugashvili was an important young man in the Central Committee of the Bolsheviks, and seemed to be gaining influence with Lenin. When Trotsky heard that he was also editor of the Petersburg *Pravda* for a time, his hair stood on end with anger. He never forgave the Bolsheviks for appropriating the name of his paper—and it was theirs that survived.

To Trotsky, there was little appealing about this young Russian from the Caucasus. For him, the man represented the log cabin, brutish aspect of Russia that he felt had to be changed for any revolution to be successful there.

Years later, Trotsky would remember Stalin's "dim but not commonplace appearance . . . [and] morose concentration" that he read on his face at this first meeting. There was a fixed hostility in Stalin's "yellow" eyes that made Trotsky uneasy.[79]

There was no love lost for Trotsky on Stalin's part, either. He had seen the intellectual before and had written of him in derogatory fashion in his paper. To Stalin, Trotsky was a "noisy champion with fake muscles" and his "beautiful uselessness"[80] enraged the young terrorist out of the Caucasus.

Twenty-seven years later, Stalin's hate had not dimmed. One of his agents tracked down Trotsky in Mexico and killed him with a pickaxe.

Though Stalin spoke only halting German, he was able to get on with his research with the help of Bukharin and with translations of the Austrian Socialists' works. Men such as Otto Bauer and Karl Renner had already written on the nationalities question. Indeed, for Austria as for the Austrian Socialists, it was the question of national autonomy that was killing them. Rivalries between the nationalities in the empire resulted in a weakening of the Socialists when, as we have seen, the Czech, Polish, and Ruthenian Socialists began to resent the German-ness of the Vienna Socialists, and to form their own organization to help workers of their own class. This was, of course, in direct contradiction to the supposed internationalism that socialism promoted.

Bauer and Renner in their writings had not resolved this problem for the Austrian Socialists, and may have only increased its danger with their concept of national-cultural autonomy for the minorities.

Stalin's subsequent work, which he later labeled "rubbish"[81] in an interview with one correspondent, was titled "Marxism and the National Question." For Stalin, as his thoughts developed in this article, the party was without nationality—the old Marxist phrase "Workers of the world unite!" still had validity for him. Stalin questioned the reality of such a thing as the nation and implied that in a true social democracy such cultural and ethnic differences would wither away.[82] By no means should all the nationalities be catered to, but rather they should be lifted to a higher level of culture by a strong central party.

Such a solution to the nationalities question was not unlike Franz Ferdinand's concept for the Balkans: unification with Vienna that would ultimately give all the Balkans a shared culture. It was such a concept, and the danger it posed to the cause of Pan-Slavism and the Serbs in their fight for control of the Balkans, that would cost the archduke his life the next year.[83]

That Stalin should come to Vienna to study the nationalities problem only serves to point up the enormous problem facing the Austrian Socialists. Viktor Adler was assailed from all sides—from the rightists, such as Hitler, as being the head of a Jewish conspiracy, and from the other leftists as being too German in approach.

The Russian revolutionaries such as Trotsky and Stalin—it was one time they agreed—found these Austrian Socialists too soft on all questions. As a political force, they could have stepped firmly into the vacuum left by Lueger's death, if they had been organized. But battles inside the party weakened them.

Shortly before Stalin's departure from Vienna in mid-February, the Socialists showed signs of beginning to pull together. Franz Schuhmeier, a Socialist deputy, was shot down in the same train station from which Stalin would be leaving a few days later. Schuhmeier had been a man of the people, from Ottakring, and much loved by all Socialists. He had led the fight for universal manhood suffrage and for schools free from clerical influence. His assassin was the brother of an important member of the Christian Social party.

This death rallied the Socialists as nothing else could. More than a quarter of a million people marched in Schuhmeier's funeral procession—more even than for Lueger.[84]

But as Trotsky had witnessed in the Balkan Wars, such Socialist solidarity could not be counted on in times of national alarm. When the test would come in the summer of 1914, Austrian Socialists would once again prove loyal to their empire rather than to the other proletariat of the world.

(4)

Hitler's twenty-fourth birthday, on April 20, 1913, had come and gone. May had opened the world to green-gold softness and fecundity. Hitler was preparing for his departure.

It was strange to realize that more than three years of living could be packed into one small suitcase. Hitler's little cubicle was quickly cleaned of any of his traces. He took down his Schönerer slogans from over his bed. No longer would he have to feed on these mere words. He would soon feast on the reality of living in Germany.

Clothing was never a burden for Hitler, with his one good suit and a couple of changes of linen. The paints were stuffed into the suitcase along with perhaps a copy or two of the recent editions of *Ostara* for reading along the way.

It was not a sad leave-taking for Hitler. He had been planning it for a long time. A "longing rose stronger and stronger in me," he described later, "to go at last whither since childhood secret desires and secret love had drawn me."[85]

The paints had been packed just in case he had to continue for a time in Munich to make his living as he had done in Vienna. His plans were a bit confused—he wanted to enter the Munich Art Academy and also to become an architect: "I hoped some day to make a name for myself as an architect and thus, on the large or small scale that fate would allot me, to dedicate my sincere services to the nation."[86]

Hitler would later remember with what relief he left the moribund Habsburg Empire to enter the German realm where "common blood gains peace and tranquility."[87]

These were represented as fine and noble reasons on paper in 1924. The truth was that Hitler was on the run from the army.

The army was at once the bulwark of the empire and a joke. Its very presence in the far-flung parts of the empire helped to give the realm a degree of stability, but it was no real army in the modern sense of the word. It held a record of disaster in every major war from 1740 on.[88] While armies in the rest of the world were literally losing their color, by assuming olive, gray, or khaki for their camouflage potential, the Austrian Army was still the most smartly and brightly dressed army in Europe. Tunics of blue or green over sparkling white trousers lent a look of dash to the *"k und k"* army that its performance lacked in the field. Its generals were considered in many quarters to be better band directors than field tacticians.

In many ways, the army was the glue that held the motley empire together. In its multi-national makeup, it managed to transcend nationalities and give its full loyalty to the emperor. It was the yellow flag with the black eagle that symbolized any security the realm felt.

Officers were accepted at court, and, like members of the aristocracy, used the familiar *du* with one another. The code of honor extended in the Austrian army long past its obsolescence in other services. Into the twentieth century, an officer's challenge to duel had to be obliged. Schnitzler had lost his commission by ridiculing this practice in his 1900 story, *"Leutnant Gustl,"* but the practice continued until 1911.

The army had its critics, but it was still the most loved institution in the empire. Even university students, faced with serving their country, both hated and loved the military. Intellectuals would flock to the colors at the onset of World War I.

The army, though a worthless military machine because of inept command by the archdukes and a dearth of professionalism in its officers, was still the center of the empire. More so than the bureaucracy or the Church, the army, with its ultimate field marshal, Franz

Joseph, *was* the Austro-Hungarian Empire. As long as it stood, the empire would stand. When it crumbled, even the most optimistic loyalist could not fail to see that the end was near.

There had been scandals before. The empire had been shocked by the case of a young officer who had been sent to prison for twenty years for killing a fellow officer. Having failed in his ambition to become a staff officer and escape provincial Linz—Hitler had felt comparable disappointment as an eighteen-year-old—this young officer had sought revenge. It took the bizarre form of sending so-called aphrodisiac pills to ten of his comrades, anonymously. Far from promoting lust, the pills contained a deadly dose of cyanide. One of the ten took the pill and died. It took seven months to track down the disillusioned officer and sentence him. Meanwhile, the newspapers had a field day uncovering adultery and other vices among the officers concerned.[89]

There had also been the usual cases of officers falling deeply into debt and taking the honorable way out—which meant a bullet in the brain.

But not even the calloused Viennese were prepared for the shock of the Redl case. A letter containing 6,000 crowns and a list of names—probably of spies—was discovered in the spring of 1913 at the General Post Office. Austrian security left it there as bait to capture whoever came to pick it up. Weeks passed and no one came.

It was Sunday, May 24. In the Männerheim out in Brigittenau, Hitler was all packed and ready to leave for Germany that very day.

At the General Post Office on that day, the letter was finally picked up. The agents watching the place had, however, been caught off guard. They missed the man, but managed to get the number of his taxi. Later, after finding the taxi and getting a description of the man, they managed to track him down to the Hotel Klomser. After describing the man to the desk clerk, the detectives were amazed to learn that the man fit the description of Colonel Alfred Redl, commander of the Eighth Army in Prague and former head of the counterespionage service. That such a man would himself be guilty of espionage was unthinkable, but when confronted, the colonel panicked and tried to escape.

Redl willingly confessed to being involved in espionage. It seemed that he had a particularly expensive lieutenant to maintain. Redl, a homosexual, had been discovered by a Russian secret agent, blackmailed because of his homosexuality, and had been in the pay of the

Russians for the previous seven years. The Russians had at first given Redl some names of Russian agents in Austria in order to establish his position with the Austrians.

As a Russian "mole" on Conrad von Hötzendorf's staff, Redl was later able to supply the Russians with Austrian military secrets, including Plan Three, which was the Austrian contingency plan for a surprise attack on Serbia. Redl also gave the Russians information on the Austrian spy system in Russia and information about his army's plans for the defense of Galicia. The consequence of this leak was disastrous for Austria. Fifteen months before the outbreak of World War I, the Austrians had to revise their plans for Serbia and Galicia without any information coming in from spies inside Russia.

In the early hours of May 25, the colonel, upon von Hötzendorf's order, was left alone in his hotel room with a loaded pistol. He took the "honorable" way out.

The Viennese, when the news hit the streets that Monday, seemed to thoroughly enjoy the scandal. They had had nothing like this since Mayerling. The rot, it was now apparent, had spread to the army. There was very little left for the optimists to grab onto.

Hitler probably heard nothing about the scandal until settled in Munich later in the week. He left Vienna the same day that Redl was discovered, and he was well on his way to Germany by the time the news broke. When he did finally hear of Redl, the news merely confirmed his own judgment of the dying empire.

The twenty-fourth was a busy day for Hitler. First there was a visit to the Café Kubata to say good-bye to Maria and Marie. His friend Pepi or Wetti was again in attendance and took Maria Wohlrab aside. "Dolferl has a difficult day today," he told her. "He's traveling to Germany and if he gets through successfully, he's a lucky man."[90]

Hitler walked over to Wohlrab after eating his last pastry at her establishment, and shook her hand. "I don't think," he said, "that I'll ever be able to come back to Austria. But if I do, I'll be sure to visit you!"[91] That Hitler did not think he would be able to come back to Austria after fleeing from the draft is made obvious by this farewell.[92]

There is no record of his farewell to the mysterious Fräulein Marie.

Back at the Männerheim, Hitler and another companion he had found who wanted to travel to Germany took their leave. Honisch remembered that his friends were sorry to see Hitler depart. There were most likely a few words of advice from the intellectual Herr Redlich: "Neither a borrower nor a lender be," or something along those lines. Hitler's small battered suitcase was in his hand, and he set off on foot with his anonymous companion.

"We lost a good comrade with him,"[93] Honisch remembered. Hitler's departure left a hole in the "intellectual" society of the Männerheim for a while.

As he left the outskirts of the city, Hitler's thoughts must have been not unlike those he had when writing *Mein Kampf* eleven years later:

> Vienna was and remained for me the hardest, though most thorough, school of my life. I had set foot in this town while still half a boy and I left it a man, grown quiet and grave. In it I obtained the foundations for a philosophy in general and a political view in particular which later I needed to supplement only in detail, but which never left me. . . . I do not know what my attitude toward the Jews, social democracy, or rather Marxism as a whole, the social question, etc. would be today if at such an early time the pressure of destiny—and my own study—had not built up a basic stock of personal opinions within me.[94]

After traveling a short distance on foot, mulling over his life in Vienna, Hitler and his friend must have resorted to public transport, for two days later Hitler was in Munich. He registered with the police as living at Schleissheimerstrasse 34. His profession now had enlarged— he was both "painter and writer."[95]

He had arrived in his promised land.

Epilogue

(1)

HITLER rode in the back of the black, six-wheeled Mercedes as it sped through Braunau am Inn, the little town of his birth. Flowers hung gaily from balconies, and it seemed that the whole town was out in force to greet his motorcade. The jitters he had felt ever since ordering the invasion[1] were slowly being replaced by a pleasant flush of victory.

As the car traveled past the hundreds of thousands[2] of Austrians lining the motorway during the four-hour drive to Linz, that feeling of victory multiplied accordingly. It was the long-awaited homecoming of the prodigal Austrian son.

Gone now were Hitler's fears about outright annexation of little Austria into the greater German Reich.[3] To hell with world opinion. Hitler would show the world what he could do.

The date was March 12, 1938, almost a quarter of a century to the day from the time Hitler had left Vienna to discover his fortunes in Germany.

Fortunes there had been. Hitler had taken part in World War I, winning the Iron Cross. As with so many other dissatisfied, directionless youths, the war had given Hitler a meaning and focus for his life. After the war and the unsuccessful Communist uprising, Hitler's rightist theories that he had hatched at the Männerheim became a way of life for him. By 1919 he had stumbled into the German Workers party, and by October of that year had given his first public speech at the Hofbräuhauskeller, marking the beginning of his political career. Long gone were his prewar artistic dreams. In 1920 Hitler had risen to the top of the party and changed its name to the National Socialist German Workers party. Somehow, the raving, bearded artist from the Männerheim had become more believable to audiences after the horrors of World War I and the humiliating peace treaty that ended that carnage. Hitler's blend of hate, fiery oratory, and promises to the little man had mesmerized an entire population. His unsuccessful *putsch* in November 1923 and his term in Landsberg prison made him into a minor martyr. The depression and a widespread sense of national dishonor thrust him into power in 1933. The failed artist who had learned his political lessons in the political vacuum of turn-of-the-century Vienna filled just such a political vacuum in Germany.

But despite all his blustering threats and temper tantrums, Hitler had yet to show the world his muscle. For him, it was most fitting that such a demonstration should come in Austria, scene of his early defeats.

It had been a great sadistic pleasure the month before to confer with the Austrian chancellor, Schuschnigg, at Berchtesgaden. To Hitler, Schuschnigg, with his attempted praise of the view out the study window of the Berghof,[4] seemed the epitome of the Austrian intellectual/bureaucrat.[5] He was the same kind of man who, with his meaningless pleasantries, his artificial good manners, had barred Hitler's way at every turn in Vienna: from entering the Art Academy and from becoming an architect. These were the kind of men whom Hitler's father had looked up to all his life.

And here was "Herr Schuschnigg"[6] coming to Hitler, trying to save his puny land from what Hitler believed was its destiny.

"The whole history of Austria," Hitler had shouted at the Austrian chancellor, "is just one uninterrupted act of high treason. That was so in the past, and it is no better today. This historical paradox must now reach its long-overdue end. And I can tell you here and now, Herr Schuschnigg, that I am absolutely determined to make an end of all this. The German Reich is one of the Great Powers, and nobody will raise his voice if it settles its border problems."[7]

Schuschnigg had sat and listened to Hitler at first with a degree of composure, but as Hitler worked himself into one of his colossal rages, the Austrian chancellor began to feel the cold sweat of fright on his back.

Hitler had acted the part of the offended neighbor state to the hilt. He accused the Austrians of building defense works on their borders with Germany.

"Listen!" Hitler had threatened that February 12. "You don't really think that you can move a single stone in Austria without my hearing about it the very next day, do you? You don't seriously believe that you can stop me or even delay me for half an hour, do you? . . . Who knows—perhaps you will find me in Vienna one morning like a spring storm. . . . Afterwards, the army, my SA, and the Austrian Legion would move in, and nobody could stop their revenge—not even I. Do you want to make another Spain of Austria?"[8]

Hitler continued his tirade and warned that Schuschnigg had better comply with his as yet unspecified demands, or else. "Think it over, Herr Schuschnigg, think it over well. I can only wait until this afternoon. If I tell you that, you will do well to take my words literally. I don't believe in bluffing. All my past is proof of that."[9]

When Schuschnigg asked Hitler what conditions he proposed, it became apparent that the Führer had not planned that far ahead. "We can discuss the details this afternoon."[10] With that, he dismissed the Austrian chancellor.

The men lunched together before resuming their talks. It was a festive time for Hitler, as he built castles in the air for the German Reich. He bragged of skyscrapers higher than any in America— buildings that existed nowhere but in his mind.[11]

After lunch, Hitler kept Schuschnigg waiting two hours while he drew up his list of demands with his advisors. The list proved to be a death knell for Austria. Schuschnigg was to agree to an economic union with Germany, the lifting of the ban on the Austrian National Socialists, an amnesty for National Socialist prisoners, and the appointment of National Socialists like Seyss-Inquart to such vital posts as minister of security and of the interior.

At first Schuschnigg refused, saying he could not sign such a document. Under the Austrian constitution he had no such powers. Then Hitler called in General Keitel to bluff the Austrian. Finally, later that same day, under duress, Schuschnigg signed the agreement.

Once safely back in Vienna, however, Schuschnigg had decided to call a plebiscite for March 13 to decide whether Austria wanted to remain independent or to form a union with Germany. The Austrian chancellor was sure that such a vote would show the world that Austria did not want Hitler.

Hitler learned of the planned plebiscite immediately. He was as sure as Schuschnigg of the results. He could not let the plebiscite take place. He had been double-crossed again by a Viennese. He would not let it happen another time.

"Operation Otto," the annexation of Austria, was put into effect. Hitler's forces would march into Austria on March 12, one day before the plebiscite.

There was one great fear lingering in Hitler's mind. What would Mussolini say to this venture played out so close to his borders? It was only late on the night of March 11 that Hitler got the go-ahead from Il Duce. Hitler replied in stammering gratitude, like a little boy grateful for a new football, that he would "never, never, never, no matter what happens,"[12] forget the Italian's help.

That same day, Goering had issued the ultimatum demanding Schuschnigg's resignation. Nazis all over Austria were called out. They crowded into the halls of the Chancellery and occupied offices in Vienna. The Austrian chancellor complied with the German's wishes, but the president of the republic, Miklas, surprised everyone by sticking to his guns and refusing to appoint the Nazi Seyss-Inquart as the new chancellor. A phony telegram was arranged between Goering and Seyss-Inquart the night of the eleventh, asking for Germany's help to "prevent bloodshed"[13] in Austria's troubled times. Miklas finally gave in and appointed Seyss-Inquart, but by then it was too late to stop the German invasion.

That very night, Heinrich Himmler had arrived in Vienna to secure control of the secret police. Once the German SS forces were flown in, the inevitable arrests followed, Schuschnigg being among the first to be shipped off to Dachau. The arrests in Vienna alone were to total 76,000.[14]

Hitler had plenty of time, on his way to Linz, to gloat over the way things had worked out. His motorcycle escort sped alongside his Mercedes and as he occasionally looked out to the darkened streets, he noticed with satisfaction that his orders had been carried out: windows all along the route were closed and lighted.

Linz provided a joyous homecoming for Hitler. He spoke from the balcony of the town hall to a huge, flag-waving crowd below:

> If Providence once called me forth from this town to be the leader of the Reich, it must, in so doing, have given me a commission, and the commission could only be to restore the dear homeland to the German Reich. I have believed in this commission. I have lived and fought for it, and I believe I have now fulfilled it. You are all witnesses and sureties of that. I know not on what day you will be summoned. I hope it will not be far distant . . .[15]

Hitler gave the cheering masses below the stiff-armed salute which they returned with cheers. Refrains of *Deutschland über Alles* broke out in the crowd and lasted deep into the night. Finally even Hitler had had enough of the jubilation. He could not sleep in his hotel room at the Hotel Weinzinger because of the noise outside. He finally had to send a message for the crowds to be quiet.

The next day was Sunday, March 13, the day of the planned plebiscite. Hitler made the short trip out to Leonding to the cemetery to place wreaths on his parents' graves. When he came back to the hotel there was his old friend Kubizek, now balding and a petty bureaucrat, town clerk at Efferding. The two talked together for an hour and Hitler once again, in the companionship of his old friend, flew into architectural daydreams of how he would transform Linz into one of the great cities of the Reich.

Nearby, in the Landstrasse, the old family doctor, Dr. Bloch, must have sat trembling, wondering if he would share the fate of other Austrian Jews.[16]

Hitler stayed on in Linz for one more night before making the final conquest. He put off the return to Vienna as a child puts off the sweetest and crunchiest part of a candy bar. Besides, Hitler wanted to wait for Himmler's assurance that everything was secured in Vienna. Hitler wanted no scenes spoiling his final victory over the city that had witnessed his earlier humiliation.

(2)

In Vienna, all was in readiness for the Führer. Himmler had seen to his work with brutal efficiency, eliminating any "dangerous" elements of the population. Small bands of Austrian National Socialists were seeing to the rest.

By Sunday the thirteenth, the Viennese were waiting expectantly for Hitler's arrival. Stuka dive-bombers buzzed over the spire of St. Stephans, now draped in the blood-red Nazi flag with the black swastika in the middle.[17] Gangs of young toughs, wearing the swastika armband, roamed the streets, tearing down the Austrian flag wherever they found it, and substituting their own. Windows of Jewish businesses all over the city were painted with the scarlet letters: *J. V.: "Jude, verrecke!"* ("Croak, Jew!").[18]

The city was gathering into a hysteria, ready to unleash a storm of ugly hate and sadistic violence. The "Oriental element that Hitler had introduced into German anti-Semitism"[19] was preparing to bare itself coldbloodedly to the world.

The special degree of hate Hitler still held for Vienna would soon be obvious to all. This city would now pay for the crimes it had done to him.

Hitler was aided in his vendetta by resentment against a huge influx of eastern European Jews who had flooded into Vienna after World War I. The Viennese had become even more virulent against all Jews, the newcomers and the previous inhabitants.

The "red danger" of the Communists had also increased the appeal of strong nationalistic parties such as Hitler's, and the Heimwehr, set up to combat the Communists, had provided a ready-made militia for Hitler. The depression had been the final straw in Vienna as in Germany.

Austria, shrunk to a fraction of its imperial size after its losses in World War I, was desperate for new remedies. Cut from empire to rump state, the Austrians still had dreams of recovering their previous glorious Reich.

Vienna was a different city from the one in which Hitler had lived as a down-and-out painter on the Meldemannstrasse. The cultural renaissance had largely and all but literally died with the war. The bitter postwar year of 1918 had witnessed the deaths of artists and politicians alike. Klimt, Schiele, Otto Wagner, and Kolo Moser had all died that year. Viktor Adler also passed away on November 11, 1918, the day before his long-awaited republic was declared.

The war had changed the world and the optimistic way man looked at it. Freud had been proved right—the instincts have primacy over culture. The dark, hidden side of man emerged into the world during the war; the carnage poisoned the minds of an entire generation.

What World War I had not spoiled, and the depression further tainted, Hitler was sure to destroy. The annexation of Austria sent Viennese Jews hurrying to the corners of the earth—those who were lucky enough to escape. Freud, old and dying of cancer of the palate, emigrated to England as did the writer Stefan Zweig. Schoenberg landed in America and Wittgenstein took a chair at Cambridge. Alma Mahler-Werfel and her husband Franz Werfel would have to make an odyssey all across Europe before finding safety in the New World.

Others, like the painter Moll and the Socialist Renner, would be "carried along by the euphoria of union"[20] and be among the crowds cheering Hitler into their city.

Hitler had said in Linz, when Seyss-Inquart had handed him the law passed by the provisional Austrian government declaring, "Austria is a province of the German Reich,"[21] that a "good political action saves blood."[22] Tears ran down Hitler's cheeks as he held the proclamation.

But in Vienna no blood was spared. The German Army was accompanied by SS and "40,000 policemen plus the Death's Head Formation of Upper Bavaria as a second wave."[23]

The Austrian Legion, those who had migrated to Bavaria when the Nazis had been banned in Austria, came back to town with a vengeance, falling on opponents and so-called racial enemies alike. Homes and businesses were expropriated at will.

> With bare hands, university professors were compelled to scrub the streets. Devout, white-bearded Jews were dragged out and forced by howling youths to do knee bends and shout "Heil Hitler" in chorus. Innocent persons were caught en masse in the streets like rabbits and dragged off to sweep out the latrines of the SA barracks. All the morbidly filthy hate fantasies orgiastically conceived in the course of many nights were released in broad daylight.[24]

Worse was yet to come. Austrians would fill the concentration camp of Dachau, which the Austrian Legion had built during their exile.[25]

(3)

Hitler had learned his Vienna lessons well. He had schooled himself on Lueger and Schönerer and come up with a blend of the worst of both of them. He carried around his rejections from the Academy like a chip on his shoulder—an accusation against the world. From the years of close contact with all types of men in the Männerheim, Hitler had learned the fine art of manipulation. And somewhere back there in the recesses of his brain, there was still the long-cherished dream of becoming an architect. Now that he was Führer, he was the supreme architect of the German nation in all spheres.

He must have started out in fine spirits on Monday, March 14, 1938. But the fine spirits were soon dampened on the road to Vienna. Almost 70 percent of the armored vehicles and cars broke down on the road to the capital,[26] and Hitler was caught in the middle of the breakdown. All he could do was bluster and fume at General Jodl to get his damn machinery out of the way. It was a good thing for the Germans that the Austrians had not put up any resistance, for the Germans would have been easy targets.

It was afternoon before Hitler reached the outskirts of Vienna, and he must have had the feeling that something was going wrong with his triumphant homecoming, for "he was not in the best of tempers."[27]

His Mercedes and motorcycle escort entered Vienna from the direction of Schönbrunn Palace. Hitler probably looked to the right as they passed by the summer house of the Habsburgs in front of which he had spent so many afternoons at his stone table and bench under the shade of the chestnut trees.

The crowds which had been waiting all day for him buoyed his spirits somewhat as he traveled down the Mariahilferstrasse where he had himself watched the old emperor in his carriage thirty years before.

Hitler stood in his open Mercedes flinging out the Nazi salute amidst the tolling of bells and wild cheering at this "reunion . . . which mocked all description."[28] There were tears of joy on the faces of loyal Germans of Vienna who welcomed Hitler's arrival as their salvation. He brought with him the long-awaited union of the Germans, thus finishing the work which Bismarck had started. The cheers of "One people, one reich, one leader," repeated over and over like a litany, whether directed at Hitler or not, were the honest outpourings of the Viennese citizens' hearts. Their days of third-class statehood were at an end.

Or so they thought.

It was a momentous occasion for Hitler when his cavalcade streamed into the Heldenplatz in front of the Hofburg, which he had so often told

Kubizek would be a prime spot for mass meetings. Hitler went to the balcony overlooking the square. The crowds spread out in front of him like a mass of ants. Banners, red against the March sky, fluttered in the breeze. Stillness crept over the crowd unwillingly. Hushes rippled in a wave backward from the Hofburg; the ripples spread out in concentric rings. Hitler stepped to the microphone. It was the moment he had been waiting for.

He looked again at the crowd and began to announce his life's "greatest report of a mission accomplished."[29] "As Führer and Chancellor of the German Nation," he began, "I hereupon report to history the entrance of my homeland into the German Reich."[30]

The crowds cheered on cue, just as they had seen in the newsreels of the obedient crowds at the Nuremberg rallies.

Hitler went on, unable to control an I-told-you-so impulse of revenge. "I have proved by my life that I am more competent than the dwarfs, my predecessors, who brought this country to destruction."[31]

It was a victory, clearly, but there was a hollowness to it. Hitler felt his glorious homecoming somehow slipping from his hands. The master of crowd psychology, who could sense the mood of a crowd as he spoke and gear his speeches accordingly, Hitler could not have failed to miss something in the cheering going on wildly beneath him. The lingering doubt must have been there: what were all these Viennese cheering for, Hitler, or the Anschluss which would take Austria out of the political anonymity into which it had slipped in 1918?[32]

Hitler stayed at the sumptuous Hotel Imperial, a place he would likely have been begging in front of thirty years earlier. Outside, the Ring was lit up as night drew in. The black Russian crows out of Leningrad were still in the city, waiting for the late Russian thaw to begin their migrations homeward. The birds strutted along under budding lime trees, poking a superior, almost disdainful beak at the wet earth now and again like tramps searching for cigarette butts.

Hitler's foul humor increased as the time in Vienna ticked away. A festive banquet was held in his honor that night. At one point, "Neubacher, the Burgomeister of Vienna, was asked by another guest how wide the Danube was at a certain point in the city. Neubacher said he did not know, whereas Hitler immediately supplied the correct answer. But the burgomeister's ignorance had dispelled the Führer's high spirits and . . . he remained in a bad mood for the rest of the night."[33]

Vienna was doing it again to Hitler. He loved to show off his knowledge of unrelated facts and figures. He had a mind for such insignificant details. That the burgomeister of Vienna should not know the width of the Danube was unforgivable. And what is more, he probably did not care. It was in one ear and out the other.

Hitler's mind must have wandered over such subjects as he picked at the rest of his meal. Vienna, the city of façades, could never be trusted. They cheer you to your face and plot to overthrow you at the same time. Here he was, the Führer of the German Reich, wasting his words on deaf ears. Hitler was still too rough for these Viennese with their slick manners. He was still the overeager provincial to them. He was quite all right for a national hero, but no one you would care to have to dinner. He might slurp his soup. As if knowledge of the width of the Danube was bad form; just not done in polite circles.

The next day Eva Braun and her mother flew to Vienna,[34] unexpected by Hitler. She surprised him at the hotel and he bawled her out for her foolishness in traveling without a guard. His anger was probably compounded by the fact that he had no desire for his mistress to see him in a time of weakness. And Vienna was weakening him.

There was something in the Viennese air inimical to Hitler; something that stunned and depressed him. There was a feeling, the same he had had in his years at the Männerheim, of being excluded from the life of the metropolis.

By the afternoon of Tuesday the fifteenth, Hitler and Eva were on a plane headed back to Germany.

The prodigal son's victorious return to the city of his first defeats lasted only twenty-four hours.

A month later, another plebiscite was called in Austria and Germany to decide on the Anschluss. Not surprisingly, if one knows Nazi voting and tallying techniques, 99.75 percent of the Austrians and 99.08 percent of the Germans voted for the Anschluss.[35]

It was like Bosnia-Herzegovina all over again.

Hitler had told Burgomeister Neubacher, in a public speech, that he should "be assured that this city [Vienna] is in my eyes a pearl. I will bring it into that setting which is worthy of it and I will entrust it to the care of the entire German nation."[36]

Whatever "setting" the Viennese expected from Hitler and the Anschluss, they all too soon learned the facts of the matter. Vienna was to be relegated to the status of a second-rate German city. Culturally, it would come nowhere near the status accorded Berlin or Munich in the Reich. If Hitler's plans had been carried out, even Linz would have superseded Vienna in the Reich.

Hitler could not shake his Viennese connection. "No hero, leader, or dictator of the first half of this century was ever so marked and molded by a modern city as was Hitler."[37] Vienna had chased him out before: denied his artistic talents; laughed at his antisocialist ideas; and with its multinational feet, tramped on his feelings of German nationalism. Suddenly, twenty-five years later, the tables were turned. Hitler had come back the hero to tell the Viennese what was right and wrong.

But there had been no pleasure in Vienna's capitulation. For him it was as if a whore had given herself to him. How does one find satisfaction with such a woman when all the time one knows she is holding something back?

It had been a hollow victory. Hitler ran from the city again, just as he had in 1913. For all of Hitler's talk of fate and his links to divine Providence, he had no way to make Vienna really care about him.

Hitler would later say to a leader of the Hitler Youth that "Vienna was so detestable it should never have been admitted to the Union of Greater Germany."[38]

No amount of victory or defeat in war could make Hitler forget Vienna. He took his hate for the city, just as he took his dreams of becoming an architect, to the grave with him. In the last days of his life, when Hitler himself, in true Viennese fashion, was preparing to commit suicide, he and Goebbels were talking of Vienna and Hitler readily agreed when Goebbels declared: "It would have been much better if Vienna had resisted and we could have shot the whole place to hell."[39]

Rejected by Vienna in his youth—as had been Freud, Mahler, and Schoenberg, among others, in their prime—for Hitler there would never be anything but a pyrrhic victory in that city. His "hardest . . . most thorough school"[40] might finally have given him a diploma—but it was in the wrong discipline. He had taken Vienna's political limelight, but he still longed for the artistic recognition the city would never offer.

Notes

References here are given in a shortened form. The last name of the author is used to identify books or articles to be found in the Bibliography. When the author has more than one entry in the Bibliography, his or her name is given in addition to a key word of the title. Thus, for example, Alma Mahler-Werfel's *And the Bridge Is Love* is differentiated from her *Gustav Mahler: Memories and Letters* by the key words *Bridge* and *Memories*. "Smith" refers to Bradley Smith's book unless otherwise noted. The abbreviation HA refers to the Hauptarchiv der NSDAP; HA materials are listed by file and reel number. Personal interviews are listed by name and the circumstances surrounding the interview described.

Prologue

1. This was a characteristic pose for Hitler, as seen in his many portraits. Some psychoanalysts claim this was an unconscious defense of his genitals, the result of his monorchism. See especially Waite, p. 150ff.
2. Toland, p. 30.

3. There is some indication that in the fall of 1905, after dropping out of *Realschule,* Hitler studied under a Professor Gröber in Munich, as mentioned, among other places, in Payne, p. 44.
4. Toland, p. 21.
5. Kubizek, p. 104.
6. Ibid., p. 103.
7. Ibid., p. 104.
8. Ibid., p. 106.
9. Ibid., p. 102.
10. Payne, p. 42. Jetzinger (p. 148), however, pokes several holes in this assertion and generally believes the idea of the lung complaint to be a later invention of Hitler to account for his school failure.
11. Smith (pp. 70ff. passim) examines this abrupt personality and physical change of the young Hitler at age eleven and comes up with two possible explanations for it. One is that the death of his brother Edmund in 1899 affected him greatly and sent him into a funk about man's mortality. Coupled with this could have been renewed pressure from his father Alois for his one remaining son to carry on the Hitler name with some aplomb. (Alois junior had by this time proven himself a wastrel in his father's eyes, had left home, and could not take any pressure off half-brother Adolf.) Also, as Waite mentions (p. 146ff.), Hitler's monorchism, as is usual in boys at age eleven, could have created a personality change as he came into puberty. Another possible explanation of Hitler's abrupt change at age eleven could have been physical in nature, the result of the epidemic encephalitis Hitler contracted, perhaps from some mild childhood disease that damaged the midbrain and went into remission, to appear later as Parkinson's disease. Hitler may have caught the measles that his brother Edmund died of, and it is a fact that for the last three years of his life Hitler did suffer from something very like Parkinson's disease, though other observers claim it was the drugs he was taking at the time. If the encephalitis theory is correct, it would go a long way also toward explaining Hitler's "magical" eyes as a pupillary abnormality due to Parkinson's disease. Waite attributes these eyes largely as a secondary psychological manifestation of monorchids in general, who tend to fix on breasts and eyes as a "testicle substitute."
12. Jenks, pp. 38-39.
13. Kubizek, p. 145.

14. Idem.
15. Copy of *Meldezettel* on file at Bundespolizeidirektion Wien.
16. Kubizek, p. 144.
17. See Henry Wickham Steed's *Through Thirty Years, 1892-1922: A Personal Narrative* for other such interesting observations of Vienna and the European scene in these years.
18. George Steiner, in the *New Yorker,* July 23, 1973. This quotation was taken from a review of the book *Wittgenstein's Vienna* where the critic Steiner went on to say that "from the 1890s until its enthusiastic swoon into Hitler's arms in 1938, Vienna was the foremost generator of our current sensibility."
19. Crankshaw, p. 332.

1. Beginnings

1. Hitler, *Mein Kampf,* p. 19.
2. Maser, pp. 39-41.
3. Copies of these sketches are in the possession of Professor Dr. August Priesack in Munich. Though his source for the sketches, and for the rest of his extensive Hitler collection, cannot be divulged, there is little doubt as to the authenticity of these sketches. Dr. Priesack most graciously allowed me to view his collection of unpublished Hitler sketches and paintings. He will be publishing his own book of Hitler paintings and photos shortly and some of his discoveries should prove to be a mild sensation, adding new light to areas of Hitler's life long hidden in the shadows. The four sketches from the 1907 entrance exam are entitled *"Des Beschauers Erlebnis auf einen Spaziergang"* ("The Observer's Experience on an Outing"). They are dated from September 1907 and have the same style that later Hitler drawings in the same genre would have. Hitler was always much better with pen and ink or pencil than he was with watercolors and oil.
4. Hitler, *Mein Kampf,* p. 20.
5. Quoted in Maser, p. 356, n. 5.
6. To be fair to Hitler, at least one other of the applicants who failed that year went on to become a professor at the same Academy (Maser, p. 40). Toland also points out (p. 25) that Marc Chagall was rejected by the St. Petersburg Academy. Though this is not to suggest that Hitler's talent was misunderstood genius. Few draw-

ings exist from these early years, but those that do remain show a somewhat unskilled hand at work on paintings, primarily architectural in nature, and in the style of Rudolph von Alt, an Austrian master. The complaint from the examiners about "few heads" points to Hitler's perpetual weakness in painting the human form. He was always more comfortable with inanimate objects. But the rejection from the Academy did not mean, per se, that Hitler was without talent.

7. Maser, p. 40.
8. In special circumstances, for example when the applicant displayed exceptional talent, this requirement was waived.
9. Hitler, *Mein Kampf,* p. 20.
10. Toland, p. 25.
11. Kubizek, p. 114
12. Idem.
13. Kubizek, p. 114-15.
14. Maser, p. 44-46; Picker, p. 149.
15. Kubizek, p. 117.
16. Ibid., p. 115.
17. This episode in Hitler's life has been the subject of many pages of research in many books. It is still uncertain whether Hitler did arrive home before his mother's death in December or not. Jetzinger (pp. 175-79), in his well-researched but perhaps biased book, attempts to prove that Hitler was not present at the death of his mother. Kubizek (pp. 120-26), on the other hand, paints a picture of a loving son taking care of his dying mother. The family doctor, Dr. Bloch, in a 1941 article for the American *Colliers'* magazine, also has Hitler at home caring for his mother before the death. In Toland, pp. 26-27 and 927-28, Hitler is home well before his mother's death. Toland uses relatively new information, including the deciphering of Dr. Bloch's casebook which proves Hitler was consulting the doctor in Linz on October 22. I have chosen to follow Toland's interpretation of the affair, though it is possible that Hitler did not arrive until after the death and stayed on that fall at the Stumpergasse as Kubizek inadvertently disclosed on p. 166: "Adolf told me that during the past winter [1907] when he was still alone in Vienna he had often been to warmed public rooms in order to save fuel." Whether this is just sloppy chronicling on Kubizek's part, or actually a slip of the tongue, is not known. Hitler

could well have kept his flat in close proximity to the Westbahnhof so that he could travel back and forth between Vienna and Linz to see how his mother was doing.

18. Toland, p. 928

19. Quoted in Toland, p. 26.

20. Toland, p. 26.

21. For a good discussion of Mahler's life see *Mahler,* by Kurt Blaukopf, to which the following account is primarily indebted. Also see *Gustav Mahler in Wien,* edited by Pierre Boulez and others; *Gustav Mahler, The Wunderhorn Years,* by Donald Mitchell; and two books of reminiscences by Mahler's wife, Alma, *Gustav Mahler—Memories and Letters* and *And the Bridge Is Love.*

22. During these years, Mahler's sister, Justine, was his helpmate, traveling and living with him. She was a combination housekeeper and emotional mate, an arrangement that had for Mahler all the material advantages of marriage with none of the psychological drawbacks of such a union. All Mahler's spare emotion and energy were needed for his compositions, not for the rigors of marriage.

23. Blaukopf, p. 131. The next year Mildenburg, through no intervention on Mahler's part, was brought to Vienna. By this time, however, their affair had cooled considerably. The two remained friends, and in 1909 Mildenburg married the Viennese writer Hermann Bahr.

24. Blaukopf, p. 136.

25. Wagner was undeniably a favorite with the Viennese. During Hitler's stay in Vienna, Wagner operas were performed on at least 426 evenings (Fest, p. 769). Hitler once reckoned that he saw *Tristan* between thirty and forty times in that same period (Cameron and Stevens, *Secret Conversations,* p. 270).

26. Eventually Mahler succeeded. He convinced the Viennese that perhaps the Opera was really a place to hear great music; that the lights should be turned down to enhance the performance instead of glaring brightly so that the upper crust could see and be seen even during the singing.

He even stood up to the emperor himself, refusing to reinstate one of Franz Joseph's favorite, though over-the-hill, singers.

Mahler's schedule in the early years of the twentieth century was a clockwork of perfection. Up early, he would work at the flat in the mornings, working over the musical sketches he created as a summertime composer. Then by ten he would be at the Opera, managing the affairs of that prestigious house. Promptly at one in the afternoon, after having first called home to make sure the soup would be on the table punctually, Mahler would storm into the flat, wash his hands, and sit down to a light meal. More than once he had to argue with his cooks not to force the heavy delicacies of *Leberknödel* soup on his sensitive digestive apparatus. He would nap for a short time after lunch, and then spend the afternoon in a brisk walk around the Ring or in the park of the nearby Belvedere. After five o'clock tea, it was back to the Opera, either to conduct the night's performance or to watch over at least two acts to make sure everything was in order.

Mahler's pleasures were simple and unchanging. He occasionally enjoyed a good cigar with a glass of Spätenbrau beer, but disliked overindulgence. When he really wanted release he would treat himself to a couple of glasses of Chianti, Moselle, or Asti Spumanti which were sufficient to loosen his tongue and start him on a string of anecdotes which *he* always found terribly amusing.

27. Mitchell, p. 431.
28. Alma Mahler led one of the more illustrious lives of turn-of-the-century Viennese women. Naturally limited by the conservative times and the male-dominated society, the usual role for the strong and creative woman was as a power behind the throne. In this role Alma was supremely successful. Married to Mahler when she was twenty-two, she went on to a whole succession of famous marriages and liaisons after his death in 1910. Among her lovers was the painter Oskar Kokoschka. Other husbands included the architect Walter Gropius and the writer Franz Werfel.
29. Mahler-Werfel, *Bridge,* pp. 12-13.
30. Toland, p. 27.
31. Ibid., p. 26.
32. Kubizek, pp. 124-25; Paula Hitler's Counterintelligence Corps interview, quoted in Toland, p. 928; and Bloch's story in *Collier's* magazine.
33. Kubizek, p. 126.
34. Bloch, *Collier's*; also his interview in HA, File 17, Reel 1, "Adolf Hitler in Urfahr."
35. Idem.

36. Toland, p. 28.

37. The monetary affairs of the young Hitler have been another subject of great interest to biographers, who have tried to ascertain whether Hitler's first year in Vienna was one of such great want as he later claimed in *Mein Kampf*. Jetzinger (p. 188) investigated the subject at length and concluded that Hitler had a monthly income of 83 crowns, incorporating the orphan's pension of 25 crowns per month and both inheritances from mother and father. Other biographers, for example Maser (pp. 42-43), suggest that this figure could have been appreciably higher and of a fixed sort rather than a constant depletion of the capital as Jetzinger maintains. Toland (p. 29) adds a new bit of evidence which suggests that Hitler's inheritance from his mother might have been given to his sister and that he may actually have had very little with which to start out. I take the middle course, subscribed to by Smith (pp. 111-12), which affords Hitler a comfortable life-style for at least the first year, with his orphan's pension and his father's patrimony. Using Jetzinger's estimate of 83 crowns a month, Hitler could have led a very pleasant life, for "at that time a lawyer's salary, after one year's practice in court, was 70 crowns per month, that of a teacher during the first five years of his career, 66 crowns. A post office official earned 60 crowns, while an assistant teacher in a Vienna secondary school before 1914 received a monthly salary of 82 crowns. Benito Mussolini, who in 1909 lived in Trentino (then Austrian territory) and was both editor of *L'Avenire del Lavatore* and secretary to the Chamber of Labor, received a combined salary of 120 crowns" (Maser, p. 43).

38. That Mayrhofer, the guardian, granted an equal share of the orphan's pension to Hitler indicates he thought the youth was attending the Academy. Cf. Smith, p. 113.

39. Maser, p. 44. Cf. also the account of the Vienna Gestapo of 1941, Smith, p. 113.

40. Ibid., pp. 44-45.

41. Ibid., p. 45. An interesting note about this correspondence is that the photocopied letter in Maser's possession and the copy of the letter Hitler sent Frau Motlach, the one in the Gestapo file, are both dated 1909 instead of 1908, though different months are used in each. Also, Frau Hanisch mentions Hitler's age at the time as

being nineteen, whereas in early 1908 he was still only eighteen. This would suggest that perhaps the Roller letter was actually written in 1909, but that Frau Hanisch mentions Hitler's mother's death which occurred in December of 1907.

42. Kubizek, p. 140.
43. Idem.
44. Kubizek, pp. 140-41.
45. Blaukopf, p. 205.
46. Idem.
47. Kubizek, p. 140. Hitler was later to say, in 1939 when remeeting Kubizek, "In that hour it began!" (idem).
48. Blaukopf, pp. 180-85.
49. The Mahler clique in Vienna included such people as Peter Altenberg, Hermann Bahr, Hugo von Hofmannsthal, Arthur Schnitzler, Stefan Zweig, Sigmund Freud, and Gustav Klimt (Blaukopf, pp. 219-20).
50. Ibid., p. 218.
51. Idem.
52. Blaukopf, p. 219.
53. Mahler-Werfel, *Memories,* pp. 89-90.
54. Boulez et al., p. 187.
55. Kubizek, p. 143.
56. Ibid., p. 145.
57. Hitler, the tour guide now, most likely forgot to add in his enthusiastic description of the Opera that its architect, Eduard van der Null, committed suicide because of criticism leveled against his design of the house, criticism that even the Emperor Franz Joseph inadvertently assented to by saying in public that the steps were too low. Van der Null killed himself shortly after hearing the emperor's remarks. Franz Joseph never again gave true criticism in public after that but always kept to the safe formula, *"Es war sehr schön. Es hat mir sehr gefreut."* ("It was very nice. I liked it very much.")
58. Kubizek, p. 145.
59. Ibid., p. 149.
60. Ibid., p. 153.
61. Ibid., p. 157.
62. Ibid., 154. Also see Jetzinger, p. 195.
63. Kubizek, p. 157.
64. Idem.
65. Kubizek, pp. 157-58.

2. Portrait of the Artist

1. Kubizek, p. 155.
2. Ibid., p. 185.
3. Jetzinger, p. 198.
4. Kubizek, p. 186.
5. Idem.
6. Idem.
7. Kubizek, p. 188.
8. Ibid., p. 192.
9. Ibid., p. 187.
10. Ibid., p. 188.
11. Idem.
12. Kubizek, p. 189.
13. Kubizek (p. 187) relates that he and Hitler rarely saw the end of any performance because of the *Sperrsechserl* they would have to pay the concierge upon coming home after the doors were locked. Also, to avoid paying cloakroom fees, they usually went without hat or coat to the theater and opera.
14. Idem.
15. Kubizek, p. 191.
16. Idem.
17. Idem.
18. Kubizek, p. 154.
19. Idem.
20. Idem.
21. Kubizek, p. 178.
22. Ibid., p. 182. Cf. also Jetzinger, p. 196.
23. Kubizek, p. 192.
24. Ibid., p. 195.
25. Ibid., p. 192.
26. Idem. This story of Kubizek's should be read with care. Hindsight always accords more meaning to remembered incidents than they may have had at the time. Kubizek's memory at this point is probably affected by after-the-fact knowledge that Stravinsky and Bartok were doing about the same thing as he says Hitler was doing, at the same time. What is important here is that Hitler should have attempted such an ambitious venture at age nineteen, not that it was as innovative as Kubizek paints it.
27. Kubizek, p. 196.

28. Ibid., p. 198.
29. Hitler was terribly fond of allusions to a wolf or wolves. See Waite, pp. 27ff., for a psychological discussion of his "lone wolf" syndrome. Hitler's first name, Adolf, derives from the German Athalwolf, or noble wolf. His dogs were invariably wolfhounds; he was often fondly referred to as Wolferl by the ladies who mothered him. He had a home called the Wolfschanze, and more than one servant or colleague of the Führer's bore the name Wolf.
30. Kubizek, p. 202.
31. Ibid., p. 153.
32. Picker, p. 111, n. 3.
33. Quoted in Toland, p. 31.
34. Roller stayed on at the Opera after Mahler's departure, until 1909. According to a story by Mahler's wife (Mahler-Werfel, *Bridge,* p. 33), Roller may have inadvertently started the wheels in motion that eventually made Mahler resign his post at the Hof Opera. Roller decided that he wanted to write and stage a ballet and Mahler gave his approval. But when Roller called for rehearsals at the same time as the ballet master, and most of the dancers showed up for Roller's and not the ballet master's, the battle was joined. The ballet master went straight to the emperor, and Montenuovo and Mahler had their first falling out when Mahler sided with Roller.
35. Quoted in Vergo, p. 23. Vergo's is altogether an excellent book on the art movements of pre-World War I Vienna. Another valuable book which covers much the same ground is Nicolas Powell's *The Sacred Spring.*
36. Vergo, p. 31.
37. Quoted in Vergo, p. 34.
38. Ibid., p. 39.
39. Mahler-Werfel, *Bridge,* p. 12.
40. Quoted in Comini, *Klimt,* p. 25.
41. For twenty years Klimt summered with his mistress's family, the Flöges, at the fashionable resort of Attersee. A powerfully built man, Klimt loved rowing, and his favorite dress in the summer was a flowing gown, designed by himself and sewn at Emilie's shop, which afforded him ultimate freedom of movement. The carefully attired Viennese with their stiff collars and straw hats taking the summer air in the Austrian lake district must have stumbled all

over themselves seeing Klimt and Emilie decked out in their flowing robes. A story is told also, demonstrating Klimt's boyish prankishness. When visiting Emilie in her fashionable dress shop, the Casa Picola on the Mariahilferstrasse, it was Klimt's playful habit to construct little paper hats and then drop them out the windows onto the heads of the customers at the café below. The interior of the Flöge shop was done by the Werkstätte with Kolo Moser collages. Klimt himself often designed dresses and material for Emilie and her sister.

42. Vergo, p. 57.
43. Quoted in ibid., p. 60.
44. At this same time in Munich, Franz von Stuck was being hailed as the "painter prince" (cf. Comini, *Klimt,* p. 4) for paintings which were similarly erotic. Klimt even borrowed from Stuck stylistically in his earlier periods. Stuck was a favorite painter for Hitler later in the Führer's life (see Waite, pp. 64-69). Stuck's sensuality was even more pronounced than Klimt's: pythons wrapped around and through naked women's thighs were a major motif of this painter. Hitler may even, as suggested by Waite, have assumed the appearance of a character out of a Stuck painting, *Die Wilde Jagd,* which was painted in the year of Hitler's birth. The lock of hair and moustache and gaudy Wagnerian dramatism are all there in this early painting.
45. Vergo, p. 61. The university paintings were displayed in 1907 but it is doubtful that Hitler saw them then. They were destroyed in 1945 when Hitler's retreating SS set fire to the castle where they had been removed for safekeeping.
46. Quoted in Powell, p. 131.
47. Kubizek, p. 86.
48. Ibid., pp. 86-95.
49. Ibid., p. 95.
50. Hitler, *Mein Kampf,* p. 20.
51. Kubizek, p. 182.
52. Ibid., p. 164.
53. Idem.
54. Ibid., p. 180.
55. Ibid., p. 164.
56. Idem.
57. Quoted in Vergo, p. 162.

58. Quoted in Vergo, p. 90.
59. Powell, p. 47.
60. Kubizek, p. 165.
61. Ibid., p. 166.
62. Idem.
63. Kubizek, p. 168.
64. Ibid., p. 163.
65. Ibid., p. 174.
66. Idem.
67. Idem.
68. Kubizek, p. 171.
69. Idem.
70. Kubizek, p. 172.
71. Quoted in Vergo, p. 91.
72. By 1907, Wagner's special school for architecture was so popular with Austrian architecture students that 200 students from abroad had to be denied admittance (Vergo, p. 114).
73. Vergo (pp. 90-118) provides a good, short discussion on Wagner. See also Geretsegger and Peintner's book on Wagner, and *Moderne Architektur* by Wagner himself.
74. Geretsegger and Peintner, p. 183.
75. Vergo, p. 114.
76. The life-style Hitler led in Vienna in the first few months was one that shut out reality and cut him off from outside influences. What is harmless frivolity in a youth can be disastrous in a grown man. It was Hitler's ultimate failure to progress and mature beyond his youth that was deadly for the world, not that as a youngster he lived in a dream world. Up to this early part of the Vienna period, Hitler was a normal, though somewhat eccentric adolescent. He did not act retarded nor were his actions especially horrendous; it is only historical hindsight that fits all the trends of a person's life to the final product. Hitler's close working comrade, Albert Speer, related in his memoirs that he felt Hitler's development to have stopped in about 1910.
77. Maser, p. 67.
78. Thomas Mann, *Gesammelte Werke,* vol. 12, pp. 775ff.
79. Maser, p. 65.
80. Picker, p. 167.

3. The Sink of Iniquity

1. Blaukopf, p. 136.
2. Kubizek, p. 235.
3. Ibid., pp. 235-36, from which the following account is taken.
4. Ibid., p. 235.
5. Zweig, p. 68.
6. Idem.
7. Schnitzler, *Youth in Vienna*, p. 124.
8. See especially *Das Tagebuch ein halbwüchsigen Mädchen*. This is the actual diary of one such "good" middle-class girl, Gretl, who is raised to be the typical bourgeois wife and mother, but who knows absolutely nothing about her own sexuality as she approaches puberty. It is the story of her awakening to the mysteries of sex, kept even more mysterious by parental consent.
9. Zweig, p. 74.
10. See especially Otto Friedländer, *Letzter Glanz der Märchenstadt*, pp. 150-72, for a fine discussion of women in turn-of-the-century Vienna and the place of sexuality in their life.
11. Quoted in Waite, p. 51.
12. Zweig, p. 81.
13. Ibid., pp. 75-76.
14. Ibid., p. 83. According to a 1912 study, quoted in Maser (p. 197), 75 percent of the Vienna medical students had their first intercourse with prostitutes; 17 percent with domestic servants and waitresses; and only 4 percent with middle-class girls who could be potential wives.
15. Jenks, p. 123.
16. Idem.
17. Jenks, p. 124.
18. Ibid., p. 125. Some more informed Viennese of the time, such as Karl Kraus, did see the hypocrisy inherent in such laws and championed the cause of prostitutes. But in general, the public voice condemned the social blight of prostitution, which that very public made a necessity in a time of bourgeois marriages of convenience.
19. Zweig, p. 85.
20. Ibid., p. 87.

21. Ibid., p. 83.
22. Ibid., p. 87.
23. Salten, p. 116. The best account of sexuality in the lower classes of Vienna is the classic *The Memoirs of Josephine Mutzenbacher* by Felix Salten, which originally appeared in 1895. It is the true story of Josephine, or Pepi as she was called, who was born in Ottakring in 1849 and became one of the most famous courtesans in Vienna in the 1880s and '90s. Retired to a ranch in Carinthia, she summoned Salten, author of *Bambi,* to write her memoirs. The result was much more than pornography. With humor and humanity, Salten relates Pepi's adventures which started at age five with the current *Bettgeher.* By age seven, Pepi had developed what she considered sex appeal, attracting neighborhood boys and men alike. By her teens she was well trained in the ways of love, even with her father. She first became one of the legion of street hookers in Vienna, but soon graduated to much higher positions as the mistress of important industrialists—a true tale of rags to riches.
24. Friedländer, p. 159.
25. Marek, p. 295-97.
26. See *Herzl* by Amos Elon.
27. Pauli, p. 18.
28. Johnston, p. 42.
29. Zweig, p. 88.
30. Idem.
31. Idem.
32. At the extreme end of this weird glorification of sexual battle scars, it is reported that no officer could be elected to an elite Swedish military club without furnishing proof of having once had syphilis. In the early years of the 1900s in Germany, most men had had gonorrhea and at least 20 percent, syphilis (Tannenbaum, p. 184).
33. Quoted in Murstein, p. 258. For a biographical account of this pioneer of perversion, see *Reigning Passions* by Kathryn Perutz, London, 1978.
34. Johnston, p. 234.
35. Marek, p. 323.
36. Fest, p. 21.
37. Kubizek, pp. 60-72.

38. Ibid., pp. 63-64.
39. Jetzinger, p. 232. Jetzinger was the one to finally track down the mysterious Stephanie.
40. Kubizek, p. 228.
41. Ibid., p. 228.
42. Ibid., p. 235.
43. Ibid., p. 233.
44. Idem.
45. Kubizek, p. 238.
46. Ibid., p. 239.
47. Kubizek (p. 234) tells a humorous story of walking down the Mariahilferstrasse one day without friend Adolf along to cramp his style. But Hitler's propaganda slogans worked in absentia, for when a "pretty . . . flighty" thing gave him an inviting wave, he could only remember the "flame of life" and the fear of extinguishing it forever with such a rash act as love.
48. Kubizek, p. 173.
49. Ibid., p. 239.
50. Ibid., p. 226.
51. Ibid., p. 227.
52. Ibid., p. 229.
53. Ibid., p. 229-30.
54. Ibid., p. 237. For a later companion's corroboration of this apparent normal or nonexistent sexuality, see Greiner, p. 99.
55. Kubizek, pp. 146-47.
56. Idem.
57. Idem.
58. Kubizek, pp. 236-37.
59. Idem.
60. Idem. Greiner (p. 98) tells a similar tale that occurred in a vegetarian restaurant on the Spiegelgasse. Again Hitler was the worldly one, recognizing the homosexual for what he was.
61. Greiner (pp. 54-67) tells one such story of Hitler's love for an Aryan beauty named Gretl who was posing for Greiner for a lingerie ad. Hitler took such a shine to the girl that at one point he tried to rape her when she refused his advances. She later married a Jew, according to this account, and Hitler had to be stopped by private detectives from taking a whip to the couple at Karlskirche. Following this unhappy love affair, Hitler supposedly buried his

sorrows in the arms of prostitutes on Taborstrasse, part of the Jewish ghetto, where he caught some venereal disease which destroyed his interest in women altogether. Greiner's love of drama creates a fine story here, but it is anyone's guess as to its authenticity. It does fit in with the persistent rumors of Hitler catching a disease from a Jewish whore in Vienna which later accounted for much of his anti-Semitism. Cf. Maser, p. 195, and Bullock, p. 16. Wasserman tests carried out in 1940, however, discount the possibility that Hitler suffered from syphilis (Maser, p. 196), but it is still possible that he did contract some minor disease. *Mein Kampf* is indeed filled with references to syphilis as the destroyer of the West and to prostitution in Vienna. It is not improbable that there could have been something specific behind this mania on Hitler's part, though it is doubtful if the story told by Greiner is it.

62. Kubizek, p. 235.
63. Ibid., p. 236.
64. Ibid., p. 234.
65. Hitler, *Mein Kampf,* p. 59.
66. Idem.
67. Idem.
68. How tempting to have Hitler and Freud meet on the Ring after the Wedekind play; Freud unaware of the down-at-heel student and Hitler casting a wary look at the middle-class doctor, inwardly fuming at the ever-present cigar with which Freud was polluting the night air!
69. An Oxford doctor in 1905, for example, said of woman and sex: "Nine out of ten women are indifferent to or actively dislike it; the tenth, who enjoys it, will always be a harlot." Quoted in Tannenbaum, p. 184.
70. Freud, *Collected Papers,* IV, p. 210.
71. Cf. Marek, pp. 307-13, and Johnston, pp. 221-37, for good, short discussions of the Vienna medical tradition. That tradition included such men as the famous surgeon and friend of Brahms, Billroth; Rokitansky with his ground-breaking work in pathological anatomy; Joseph Skoda, the developer of percussion and osculation in the diagnosis of chest ailments; Semmelweis, who died insane and friendless before knowing that his great contribution of antisepsis had been recognized by the world; Hebra and

his pioneering work in dermatology; Brücke, under whom Freud studied, a renaissance man who added art and phonetics to his excellent work in physiology; and Meynert and his valuable work on the anatomy of the brain.

72. As late as the 1870s, lunatics were still imprisoned in the Fools' Tower behind the General Hospital. Insanity was more a crime than a sickness, and if judged a sickness at all, it was thought most likely to be the result of some illness like meningitis. Freud's researches were therefore controversial in the extreme and alienated him from the Viennese medical community.

73. Freud later generalized from hysteria to neuroses as a whole. For purposes of this discussion the terms can be taken as synonymous.

74. Marek, p. 315.

75. In an interview Freud once summed up his schizoid feelings for Vienna: "Like you, I love Austria and Vienna, although unlike you, I know its abysses." Quoted in Marek, p. 317. Life was proceeding apace by 1908 for the bourgeois Freud. He worked his usual twelve-hour day; walked twice daily around the Ring; smoked twenty cigars each day which he always purchased at the same little tobacco shop near the Michaelerkirche across from the Neue Burg; collected archaeological pieces; traveled in the summers to the Alps, Italy, and Greece; had the barber come each morning to clip his beard and trim his hair; and kept up a steady stream of correspondence with colleagues all over the world.

76. Quoted in Murstein, p. 290. There is a good discussion of Freud's own sexuality in the same book, pp. 288-97.

77. Quoted in Ibid., p. 291.

78. Kraus, *Werke,* III, p. 351.

79. From a 1900 letter to Freud's friend Fliess (Marek, p. 313).

80. Reich, pp. 12-17. Wilhelm Reich was a Galician Jew who studied under Freud in Vienna after World War I.

81. For studies of Hitler's sexuality, see especially Langer, *The Mind of Adolf Hitler* and Waite, *The Psychopathic God.* The Langer book is the result of a secret wartime report on Hitler's mental state, including his sexual perversion.

82. Waite, p. 233.

83. Idem.

84. Bullock, p. 16.

85. Waite, p. 233. Supposedly Hitler was once blackmailed by a man who had gotten hold of such a sketch done of Hitler's niece Geli Raubal in a pose that normal models would never have assumed.

86. Jetzinger, pp. 215-16. Indeed, Jetzinger points out, how would such a monkish youth as Kubizek portrays Hitler as being even know of the Spittelberg red-light district?

87. Waite, p. 235.

88. Maser, p. 196. Since this was recorded in 1952, well after Hitler's death, there seems no reason for the doctor in question not to tell the truth.

89. Though discounted by such biographers as Toland and Maser. Evidence also exists to discount the perversion stories. There is Hitler's doctor's evidence that Hitler surely had sexual intercourse with Eva Braun (see Maser pp. 204-5). There is Eva's own diary which contains one mention of her and Hitler's sex life: "March 1935. . . . He needs me only for certain purposes. . . . It can't be otherwise. . . . When he says he loves me, he only means it at that moment" (idem.). These "certain purposes" could, however, be interpreted quite broadly.

90. Langer, p. 134.

91. Waite, p. 238, quoted from OSS reports. This information comes from Otto Strasser and is probably not the most reliable. One wonders why Geli Raubal would ever confide in Strasser. But according to Langer (p. 134), there were also other, unnamed informants who corroborate these stories of perversion.

92. Waite, p. 239. Cf. Maser, p. 198. Other women who had relationships of one sort or another with Hitler, including the actress and director Leni Riefensthal and the actress Mady Rahl, have remained silent on their connection with Hitler (Maser, pp. 204, 382).

93. Waite, p. 241, from OSS interviews in 1943 with Mueller's director, A. Zeissler.

94. Idem.

95. The Soviet medical authorities who examined the burned corpse which was "presumably" that of Hitler, found no left testicle "either in the scrotum, or on the spermatic cord inside the inguinal canal, or in the small pelvis (Bezymenski, pp. 67, 77).

96. Maser, p. 205.

97. Ibid., pp. 198-200.

98. Roehm once said of Hitler: "He thinks about the peasant girls. When they stand in the fields and bend down at their work so that you can see their behinds, that's what he likes, especially when they've got big round ones. That's Hitler's sex life. What a man" (quoted in Langer, p. 93). Eva Braun also supports the theory of the passive Hitler wanting to be dominated by the big female. Talking of a new love of Hitler's, probably that for Unity Mitford, she wrote: "She's called Valkyerie and looks like one, legs and all. But that's the kind of measurements he likes. If it's true, irritation will soon whittle her down" (Maser, pp. 205, 383).
99. Langer, p. 182.
100. Kubizek, p. 228.
101. Kubizek, letter to Jetzinger, May 6, 1949, quoted in Waite, p. 241.

4. Political Awakening

1. Kubizek, p. 107. According to this account, Hitler was a "pale, thin youth."
2. Kubizek, pp. 241-43, for the following account.
3. Kubizek, p. 165.
4. Ibid., p. 242.
5. Ibid., p. 243.
6. Hitler, *Mein Kampf*, p. 77.
7. Kubizek, p. 246.
8. Idem.
9. Idem.
10. Kubizek, p. 246. Other researchers, such as Jetzinger, have refuted this scene from Kubizek, saying that there is no record of such a demonstration in the newspapers of 1908. Indeed, in a later edition of Kubizek's book, the mention of the beer price increase is deleted. It is possible Kubizek was referring to the riots in the fall of 1911 when he and Hitler were no longer together. I include this account because it is indicative, in spirit, of the changes Hitler was going through even in the time he knew Kubizek, and for the simple fact that absence of evidence is not evidence of absence. Hitler himself mentions a similar scene in *Mein Kampf*, p. 41: "I gazed at the endless columns of a mass demonstration of the Viennese workers that took place one day as they marched four abreast! For nearly two hours I stood there watching with bated breath the gigantic

human dragon slowly winding by. In oppressed anxiety, I finally left the place." But far from feeling sympathy for the poor in this account, Hitler only confirmed his opinion of the "pestilential whore" (ibid., p. 38) that socialism was for him.

11. Kubizek, p. 159.
12. May, pp. 38-39; Janik and Toulmin, p. 49.
13. Crankshaw, p. 24.
14. Quoted in Marek, pp. 346-47.
15. Payne, p. 29.
16. Kubizek, p. 175.
17. Crankshaw, p. 368.
18. Ibid., p. 370.
19. The fat was in the fire when Sophie took a post as lady-in-waiting to a noble family in Bohemia, whose eldest daughter it appeared Franz Ferdinand was courting. But a lost watch that contained a picture of Sophie instead of the daughter tipped off the enraged mother to the duplicity and forced Franz Ferdinand's hand.
20. Court procedure and aristocratic behavior were bulwarks of the realm. There were two layers to good society: the *Hochadel,* or upper nobility, and the *Briefadel,* or lesser nobility. Never the twain should meet. They had their own societies and responsibilities. The higher nobility consisted of eighty families who were related to the royal family and who held aristocratic titles. So intermarried were these families that they were in reality one large family. The familiar *du* was used among members of this class and they used pet names for each other and for members of the imperial family, like characters out of an English Restoration comedy. Perhaps the only one not to play this game was Franz Joseph himself, who was addressed as "Your Majesty" even by his own children. Everything was *"kaiserlich-königlich,"* or imperial-royal, this or that. A later writer, Robert Musil, derided this *"k und k"* aspect of Viennese life by dubbing the era and land Kakania, or shitland, in baby talk.
21. Quoted in Johnston, p. 40.
22. Jetzinger, p. 195.
23. Hitler, *Mein Kampf,* p. 39.
24. Ibid., p. 38.
25. Ibid., p. 123.
26. Kubizek, p. 161.
27. Ibid., p. 162.

28. Idem.
29. Kubizek, pp. 248-49.
30. Ibid., p. 160.
31. Ibid., p. 245.
32. Ibid., p. 244.
33. Idem.
34. Kubizek, p. 206.
35. Ibid., p. 208.
36. Ibid., p. 213.
37. Ibid., p. 213-16. Jetzinger (pp. 208-9) is doubtful about this incident as well, contending that Kubizek would not have been called
    up for military service until the next year. But Kubizek remained
    adamant about this in interviews with Jetzinger and it is possible
    that the incident refers to his registering for the draft, which all
    youths were obliged to do at age twenty.
38. Kubizek, p. 217.
39. Ibid., p. 219.
40. Ibid., pp. 224-25.
41. Smith, p. 119.
42. Kubizek, p. 177.
43. Idem.
44. Kubizek, pp. 249-50.
45. Ibid., pp. 150-51.
46. Idem. That this was a symptom of slovenliness on Hitler's part is
    made apparent by Jetzinger's researches, especially p. 189, where
    he points out that a good middle-class *Gasthaus* of the time sold a
    monthly subscription for a lunch of meat, vegetables, and dessert
    for only 25 crowns. This was an amount Hitler could easily have
    afforded at the time. His Spartan diet was pure unimaginative
    laziness on his part rather than a sign of destitution.
47. Kubizek, p. 160.
48. Ibid., p. 150.
49. Ibid., p. 159.
50. These *Festzug* floats were a forerunner of those used in American
    football parades such as that at the Rose Bowl in California on
    New Year's Day.
51. *The Kiss,* perhaps one of the most symbolically and visually erotic
    paintings of all time, was a final announcement of Klimt's façade-
    as-content style, and a bridge between the perpetual Austrian

penchant for baroque and the modern movement. In this picture two people are represented in embrace, cloaked by flowing robes such as Klimt and Emilie wore. The robes are organic, part of the bodies they cover. In the foreground is a plethora of vivid color dots representing a flower-covered grass carpet. The man is seen in profile, the woman full-faced; head cupped by his hand, she is kneeling as he bends to her neck and cheek in a kiss. Here clearly is a couple in ecstatic embrace, prelude to coitus. Yet though the couple are fully clothed, to escape censor by the critics, on the robes is a seemingly meaningless decoration that tells the story perhaps even better than with representative genitalia. On the man's robe the decoration is made up of rectangles standing on end. The woman's robe has corresponding decorations in ovals and curves. In a city where Freud was looking for a phallic symbol in every tall building, the iconography of the robe ornament was obvious. In an amazing turnabout, the important "position which *The Kiss* occupied in Klimt's oeuvre was, for once, recognized at the time of the exhibition" (Vergo, p. 183) and the picture was purchased by the Austrian state—one of the highest honors it ever gave Klimt.

52. Kubizek, p. 259.
53. Ibid., p. 260.
54. Idem.
55. Kubizek, p. 259.
56. Ibid., pp. 125-27.
57. Ibid., pp. 125-26.
58. Ibid., pp. 256-57.
59. Quoted in Crankshaw, p. 347.
60. Quoted in Marek, p. 389.
61. Pauli, p. 102.
62. Toland, p. 38.
63. Paula Hitler, 1946 interview, quoted in Toland, p. 38.
64. Idem.
65. Though cited as a fair certainty in this context, the Panholzer connection has, in fact, never been conclusively proven other than from the Picker and Maser evidence. There is still the nagging question of why Hitler, a painter, would want to study under Panholzer, a sculptor.
66. Copies of these as yet unpublished drawings are in the possession of Dr. Priesack in Munich.

67. Heiden, p. 53.
68. Kubizek, p. 160.
69. Ibid., p. 245.
70. Idem.
71. Copy of *Meldezettel* on file at the Bundespolizeidirektion of Vienna.

5. The Student

1. Hitler, *Mein Kampf*, p. 41.
2. Kubizek, p. 150.
3. Jetzinger points out (p. 206) that Hitler's and Kubizek's friendship must not have been very strong or that perhaps Kubizek was happy to be rid of Hitler, for Kubizek could very easily have tracked down Hitler through the Zentralmeldeamt, the registration office on the Berggasse near Freud's house.
4. Kubizek, p. 163.
5. Ibid., p. 173.
6. Hitler, *Mein Kampf*, p. 34.
7. Kubizek, p. 182.
8. Ibid., p. 183.
9. May's influence on Hitler continued into later life so that one observer, Karl Alexander von Müller, as quoted in Fest, p. 135, remembered him as a May character: "I could see him . . . lay aside his riding whip, velour hat, and trench coat, finally unbuckling his cartridge belt with revolver attached and likewise hanging it on the clothes hook. It all looked very odd, reminiscent of Karl May's American Indian novels."
10. Kubizek, p. 182.
11. Hitler, *Mein Kampf*, p. 40.
12. Jetzinger (pp. 216-17, 237), in interviews later with Kubizek, pinned down that chronicler to only two books that he could definitely remember Hitler having read in the four-month period they were together in Vienna. One was a book on early German and Norse myths and the other an archeological work with ancient symbols of old cultures. The latter book is where Hitler first saw the swastika. Jetzinger claims also that Hitler was educated mostly on the pamphlets that flourished in the day. See also *Mein Kampf*, p. 56, where Hitler himself speaks of buying anti-

Semitic pamphlets. Also, Wilfried Daim, author of *Der Mann, der Hitler die Ideen Gab,* in a private interview with this author in Vienna added his opinion to Jetzinger's. Daim concludes that Hitler was educated almost solely by pamphlets and Wild West writer Karl May. Greiner, though he lists many titles that Hitler supposedly read, also mentions the pamphlets that Hitler read when he knew him (p. 89). In a revealing doctoral dissertation by Eleonore Kandl, "Hitler's Oesterreichbild" (Vienna, 1963), the author points out that (p. 60) there was a lending library just next door to Hitler on the Stumpergasse, but it was not known if Hitler used this library. As to Kubizek's assertion that Hitler was a steady user of the National Library, Kandl reports that reading cards have existed only since 1945 and that it was fairly improbable that a youth like Hitler, with no school affiliation, would have been given borrower's rights in 1908. From all the talk of Hitler's immense reading during this early period in Vienna, there is therefore evidence for only the two books that Kubizek mentioned. These, with some illustrated books on the Franco-Prussian War of 1870-71, from which he "became more and more excited about war, or for that matter with soldiering" (quoted in Payne, p. 26), plus May and Liebenfels appear to make up his "copious reading" by the time he was twenty.

13. Hitler, *Mein Kampf,* p. 35.
14. Kubizek, p. 184.
15. A. von Ende, "Literary Vienna," *Bookman,* vol. 138 (October 1913), p. 151.
16. Kubizek, p. 162.
17. Idem.
18. The Vienna coffeehouse is a unique institution, started at the end of the last Turkish siege in the seventeenth century. The vast stores of coffee found abandoned by the defeated Turks began a tradition that has lasted for 300 years. The coffeehouse is a large and well-furnished establishment where customers are always at home. The purchase of a small cup of coffee ensures the customer a full day or evening of comfort, the original houses being so spacious that no one ever needed to be turned away. Over the years tradition grew around the coffeehouses: magazines and newspapers from all over the world were supplied the customers; billiard tables, chess sets, and cards were available as were writing

materials and, in the better coffeehouses, standard reference books. Messages could be left for clients; mail could be addressed to one's coffeehouse—in short, these establishments became a second home for many Viennese whose real homes were small and noisy. Writers and students began to use the coffeehouses to work in, finding the atmosphere better there than at home where there might be crying children. Knowledgeable head waiters at certain coffeehouses could direct visitors to various tables, depending on their taste for discussion. A large part of Vienna's intellectual life began to be carried on in the coffeehouses, and by the turn of the century they had become an artistic-intellectual tradition, with each artistic group having its own favorite haunt where the new ideas would, like modern programmed learning, be instantly tested and spun out, debated and derided until a yea or nay be given them.

19. Hitler, *Mein Kampf,* p. 19.
20. Ibid., p. 57.
21. Damon, "Austrian Antisemitism," *The Nation,* June 14, 1900, p. 453.
22. Ibid., p. 454.
23. Idem.
24. Damon, p. 455.
25. Ibid., p. 454.
26. Even the powerful Rothschilds were not exempt from the anti-Semitic laws. The representative of that great trading and banking family in Vienna was not allowed to own his own house. He got around this restriction by renting all the rooms in the hotel where he lived as a permanent guest.
27. Goldhammer, p. 9.
28. Ibid., p. 10.
29. Ibid., pp. 39-40.
30. Jenks, p. 127.
31. Ibid., pp. 127-28.
32. Ibid., p. 45.
33. Ibid., p. 141.
34. As a member of a German-nationalist fraternity at the university, where he studied law, Herzl's name was affixed to a manifesto which proclaimed that a Jew was "from the day of his birth, without honor and void of all the more refined emotions. . . . He is

ethically subhuman . . . and any association with him has to be avoided" (quoted in Schnitzler, *Youth in Vienna,* p. 128). Bahr was also a member of this fraternity. Herzl was later bounced from the fraternity when they belatedly discovered he was a Jew.

35. The editor of the *Neue Freie Presse,* Moritz Benedikt, was born a Jew and later baptized a Christian. He refused any mention of Zionism in his paper.

36. Hitler mentions in *Mein Kampf,* pp. 54-55, that he read this paper in Vienna. It is also probable that Hitler was familiar with the *Alldeutsches Tagblatt,* whose editorial offices were just down the street from him on Stumpergasse (see Kandl, pp. 62-63). He must have read the display-case copies once in a while, but he probably "enjoyed most" (Jenks, p. 141) the *Deutsches Volksblatt,* because it concentrated primarily on anti-Semitic themes.

37. The following account is taken from the testimony of Marie Fellinger, born Rinke, HA File 17.

38. Idem.

39. Idem.

40. Kubizek, p. 189.

41. Perhaps the best example that has existed in the second half of the twentieth century for the cult power of a man such as Wagner is the Beatles. They were more than mere musicians and composers, they were a way of life for their fans. They produced radical changes in the lives of the people who felt they understood the group. There was a terrific sense of feeling "inside" once one was initiated into their life-style and musical puns. A feeling of superiority and ultimate importance went with the purchase of their albums. A ticket to one of their concerts was a prized possession; a glimpse of them in real life was a cherished memento. They were a measuring stick by which one judged others: Were they or were they not fans of the Beatles? Imagine then the drawing power of this pop group in a man with a more trained intellect who actually propounded his philosophy outside of his music. That was Wagner.

42. Rauschnig, *Gespräche,* pp. 215ff.

43. Idem.

44. Idem.

45. Kubizek, p. 79.

46. Hitler, *Mein Kampf,* p. 52.
47. Kubizek, pp. 249-51.
48. Ibid., p. 250.
49. Ibid., p. 251.
50. Hitler, *Mein Kampf,* p. 54.
51. Quoted in Fest, p. 36.
52. Much has been written about the possibility of Hitler's grand-father on his father's side having been Jewish. The story goes that Hans Frank, once governor general of Poland, was called in by Hitler in the late 1930s to investigate the rumor that his father, Alois, had been the illegitimate child of Maria Anna Schickl-gruber and the nineteen-year-old son of the Jewish family Fran-kenberger in Graz for whom she was working. Payments were supposedly delivered for the first years of Alois's life, even after Maria Anna married Georg Hitler and was living in the Waldvier-tel. An unpublished doctoral dissertation on file at the Vienna Institut für Zeitgeschichte sheds interesting light on this old story. The work is entitled *Das Ende des Zweiten Weltkrieges und die Besatzungszeit im Raum vom Zwettl und in Niederösterreich* and was written by Karl Merinsky in 1966. In this dissertation the author pays special attention to the troop encampment in the Waldviertel and the practice range that all but used the small town of Döllersheim for target practice once Hitler had taken over Austria. Hitler's questionable grandmother was born in the little town of Strones nearby and was buried in the churchyard of Döllersheim. The dreary rural drama of the illegitimate birth of Alois; the illegal changing of the registry thirty years later to make it seem Alois was a born Hitler and not a legalized one; the doubts of Jewish heritage in Hitler's mind—all these things were played out in and around Döllersheim. By the time the German army got through practicing with their big guns, the village of Döllersheim, having been evacuated for that very purpose, was destroyed, including the grave of Maria Anna Schicklgruber. The area is still an army troop installation. Merinsky, after patient researching, was unable to trace the Frankenberger connection any further. But he does suggest—and this is the most important point of the Jewish-grandfather story—that whether or not Hitler was of Jewish origin is in itself unimportant. The important thing is that

Hitler doubted his own heritage and through this doubt may have been driven to the extremes of anti-Semitism to prove to the world his "pure Aryan" background.

53. In *Mein Kampf*, p. 56, is a description of the beginnings of Hitler's anti-Semitism: "I now began to try to relieve my doubts by books. For a few hellers I bought the first anti-Semitic pamphlets of my life." Of interest here is Hitler's equating such pamphlets as *Ostara* with books.

54. See Wilfried Daim's *Der Mann, der Hitler die Ideen Gab* for a full discussion of Lanz.

55. Quoted in Fest, p. 36.

56. Idem.

57. Idem.

58. Quoted in Smith, pp. 124-25.

59. Idem.

60. As reported in Daim.

61. In *Mein Kampf* (p. 81), Hitler uses this very argument: "By rejecting the authority of the individual and replacing it by the numbers of some momentary mob, the parliamentary principle of majority rule sins against the basic aristocratic principle of Nature." Democracy and humanitarianism, these Social Darwinists argued, were soft and unnatural in the state of nature. The strongest survived in nature; so should it be in society. The destiny of nations is determined on biological grounds, and only by the rigors of selection, involving breeding and extermination, can faulty lines of evolution be eradicated and the strength of the nation and of mankind be preserved and advanced. As early as the mid-nineteenth century, the French aristocrat Gobineau became the spokesman for aristocratic conservatism by arguing that the downfall of nations could be traced to promiscuous racial interbreeding and the infiltration of bad blood into the upper classes from the lower classes. In Austria another early race philosopher, Ludwig Glumpowicz, a Polish Jew who had converted to Protestantism, wrote *Der Rassenkampf*, arguing that every state originated in a struggle between a conquering and a conquered race and that the social system as we know it is only a holdover from these two races. Yet another Habsburg legacy who was influential in this respect was Christian von Ehrenfels, a professor of philosophy in Prague. Displaying that traditional

Austrian professional polyphony, Ehrenfels was many men in one. He was a composer who studied counterpoint under Bruckner and revered Wagner to such a degree that he walked from Vienna to Bayreuth for the premier of *Parsifal*. He studied philosophy under Brentano, the same man under whom the founder of Phenomonology, Husserl, studied. Ehrenfels wrote plays and essays and lectured equally well on physics as he did on Wagner. He was the father of Gestalt psychology and, indeed, coined the word *Gestalt* to designate an integrating principle or form. And he was also a student of eugenics, advocating polygamy as a cure for racial degeneration which he felt had been caused by industrialization. He believed that the most virile men should practice polygamy with robust women, and he proposed the establishment of homes where these women could rear their children.

62. The book basically compared the Greek, Roman, Teuton, and Jewish civilizations. Through the use of erudite scholarship, Chamberlain attempted to prove that the Greeks had created art and philosophy; the Romans, the state and law; the Teutons, the hope and possibility of freedom; while the lowly Jews had been a negative influence on civilization ever since their betrayal of Jesus, practicing both usury and exploitation.

63. What Chamberlain neglected to mention was that Jews took to moneylending because it was the only profession from which, for a long period of time, they had not been barred. Christians were kept from practicing the profession because of biblical prohibition, but society needed the economic stimulus that such institutions as banks could give it. Chamberlain also neglected to say that of the high interest rates Jewish moneylenders traditionally charged, by far the greater portion went into royal coffers as a form of indirect taxation.

64. Opinions vary on this question. Some reporters, for example Greiner and Ravenscroft (see note 84 below), say that Hitler did consume Chamberlain's writings ravenously and even covered the margins with his notes. Others, for example Smith (p. 126), argue that it is far more likely that Hitler picked up his ideas almost solely from the pamphlets he could find for a few hellers.

65. Hitler may also have run across Ehrenfels's name in the papers that year, for two days before Christmas of 1908 the bearded old

professor spoke before Freud's Psychoanalytic Society to espouse polygamy for the health of society and to save it from the mongols that he was convinced would doom superior individuals to extinction. Later in the year, Hitler may have also read Glumpowicz's name in the newspaper. The professor and his invalided wife committed double suicide so that he might forestall the agonies of death he faced with cancer of the tongue.

66. Hitler, *Mein Kampf*, p. 56.
67. Ibid., p. 57.
68. Idem.
69. Hitler, *Mein Kampf*, p. 65.
70. Ibid., p. 273.
71. Quoted in Bullock, p. 16.
72. As discussed in Chapter 3, there has been much speculation as to the sexual origin of Hitler's anti-Semitism. The extreme erotic images he uses in *Mein Kampf* evidence that cause. Reports contradict each other as to Hitler's degree of anti-Semitic feeling during his Vienna years. Kubizek (p. 79) states that "when I met Adolf Hitler [1905], his anti-Semitism was already pronounced." Greiner (pp. 75-77) adds his vote to the picture of an anti-Semitic Adolf as early as the Vienna years. He believed that Hitler's Jew-hatred had some "erotic" (p. 89) ground to it. A closer associate, however, of 1910, who had every reason to want to besmirch Hitler's name when he wrote about the man in the 1930s, thought Hitler "didn't care much about anti-Semitism . . . [and] doesn't agree with many of the insanities [of the Third Reich] but is a prisoner of his circle" (Hanisch, p. 272). One should also look at the case of the Jewish doctor in Linz. Dr. Bloch could have been held responsible in Hitler's eyes for the death of his mother. Waite (p. 188) suggests that Bloch may have been tied up in Hitler's Oedipal complex: the doctor undressed Hitler's ailing mother and examined her breasts, as Hitler himself, if he had been attracted to mother Klara as many psychohistorians believe, wanted to do. There could then have been transferred hate from Hitler's dead father to this new "father," who in a way transgressed against Klara, and then father-hatred transferred to Bloch the Jew, ergo Jew-hatred. Yet Bloch, miraculously, was saved after the Anschluss, one of the few Jews in Austria to escape the brutally thorough hands of the Nazis. The

year after Klara's death, Hitler sent the doctor a hand-painted postcard at the Christmas season. Another contributing factor to Hitler's growing anti-Semitism was undoubtedly his feeling of rejection after being twice denied admission to the Academy. Supposedly four out of the seven professors on the board who rejected him were Jews, and Hitler wrote later in a letter to the Academy that "for this the Jews would pay!" (quoted in Waite, p. 190). However accurate this report is, Hitler easily could have used his rejection as a reason to hate; he could have seen the Jews, who were very prominent in the arts and business (though not the visual arts), as his oppressors.

73. Hitler, *Mein Kampf,* p. 118.

74. David Irving, in his *Hitler's War,* deals with this question in depth, and from his evidence it would appear that the extermination of the Jews was carried out more as economic policy than as racial policy, and that Himmler was the man primarily responsible for it; see pp. 12-16, 325-32, 391-93, 503-5, 509-10, and 575-76. For evidence that Hitler was unaware of the policy of liquidation until the midwar years see pp. 601-2, 630-32, 645, 660, and 717-19.

75. One wonders whether Hitler, the first example of the truly modern man, chewed up by the machine of Vienna and spit out as so much waste, could have accommodated any such strong passion as hate. Fromm (pp. 411-85), among others, builds a strong case for Hitler's basic lack of any true emotion. At core, Hitler may have been devoid of feeling—in essence a true necrophiliac whose one love was destruction. For a man who could not love—as his whole life proved—it is also questionable whether he could truly hate. Seen in this light, Hitler's entire life was just one extended con game in which he adopted masks to cover his own emptiness. As such, he is also the perfect example of the Viennese façade.

76. Quoted in Payne, p. 591.

77. Hitler, *Mein Kampf,* p. 34.

78. Ibid., p. 30.

79. The material world of the nineteenth century had created a new god—Science. Such creeds as Scientism and the even more rational Positivism held that science would wrest all cosmological mysteries from the churches and that science itself would then take on the Temple of the Microscope aspect. All mankind's problems would be solved through the knowledge of natural and

social processes. But as the Industrial Revolution progressed and the inconsistencies of technological civilization became all too apparent to everyone, faith was lost in such rational systems. The working-class ghettos, child labor, the breakdown of the family—these and other negative results of industrial progress went a long way toward killing faith in Science and beginning a new foundation for mystery.

80. The Wittgensteins are a fascinating study in Viennese culture themselves. Father Karl was a millionaire industrialist somewhat on the same level as a Krupp or a Skoda in central Europe. He fathered nine children, eight of whom reached adulthood. Three of the sons committed suicide. Karl was a great patron of the arts and a lover of music. Brahms, Mahler, and Pablo Casals were no strangers to the Wittgenstein home. Ludwig was the youngest son of this remarkable man. His older brother Paul, even after losing his right arm, went on to become a successful concert pianist. Ravel wrote his famous *Concerto for the Left Hand* for brother Paul. One of the sisters was a fairly competent painter, an ardent fan of Klimt's, and she talked her father into putting up much of the money for the new Secession building. Another daughter became a close friend of Sigmund Freud. Ludwig grew up around all these influences, himself a friend both of Kraus and the architect Adolf Loos, and was a representative of turn-of-the-century Vienna though his *Tractatus* did not appear until 1919.

81. *Deutsch-Österreichische Literaturgeschichte,* Vienna, 1918, p. 1935.

82. List, after suffering from near blindness for a year, suddenly felt he had found a new reservoir of intuition because of his lack of sight. It is interesting, too, that Hitler had a period of blindness as a result of gassing in World War I.

83. List's "von," like Liebenfel's, was unearned, an affectation the courts eventually made him give up.

84. See Ravenscroft, *Spear of Destiny.* This book is one of the most authoritative on the subject of occultism in the Third Reich, yet its major premises are as yet unprovable in a historical sense. The blood brotherhood that Ravenscroft writes about is difficult to track down. A doctoral dissertation by Inge Kunz, *"Herrenmenschentum, Neugermanen und Okkultismus,"* Vienna, 1961, looks closely at List, his life and works. No mention is made in this

dissertation of the 1909 episode. Another book on the same subject, though with less of the Vienna angle, is *Occult Reich,* by J. H. Brennan (London, 1974). Also see *The Occult and the Third Reich* by Jean and Michel Angebert, New York, 1974. The problem with all these books, still, is that of proof. The hard evidence for Hitler's own mystical powers is difficult to assemble, though the Third Reich did some amazing things along these lines, all factually verifiable.

85. Kunz, p. 4.
86. Ibid., p. 11.
87. Waite, p. 92.
88. The swastika long had been a popular symbol for many of the Pan-German groups. In 1907, Lanz von Liebenfels raised the swastika flag over his castle in Niederoesterreich. Schönerer, the Pan-German politician, had used the swastika on his publications as early as 1899. According to German mythology, the swastika was the fire whisk, the symbol of the vital force that had spun the primal substance into the creation of the universe. In ancient Indo-European symbolism, the swastika is the wheel of life: the symbol of the gonads or the Chakra of the highest spiritual organ, depending on whose interpretation you are reading. It was a universal symbol, used by groups reaching from the Eskimos in Greenland to Southeast Asia to the Plains Indians of North America. When Hitler adopted the swastika as the symbol for the Nazis, he either through inadvertance or conscious deliberation reversed the direction of the arms. Magicians would say that this reversal also reversed the intent of the symbol, from the white magic of the wheel of life to the black magic of Nazi destruction.
89. Waite, p. 97.
90. See Ravenscroft for this account.
91. Coincidences abound in the history of the Nazis. Dietrich Eckart, a later crony of Hitler's in the early Munich years and a strong influence on the future Führer, was also a subscriber to Liebenfel's *Ostara.* His life follows surprisingly along the lines of Hitler's. An unsuccessful playwright as a youth, he resorted to sleeping on park benches when his money ran out. Living in flophouses in better times, Eckart also blamed the Jews for his problems and failures. A known morphine addict and heavy beer drinker, Eckart derived some sort of inspiration from all these experiences

to become a halfway respected journalist-playwright by the time
Hitler met him. Eckart was an early member of the Thule Society
which met at the swank Vier Jahreszeiten Hotel in Munich. This
group was outwardly just one more fringe Pan-German club
promoting German mythology, spreading anti-Semitism and
encouraging the formation of a greater German Reich. But at
heart, the Thule Society was a magical society just as the Freemasons originally were. Thule is the name of one of the early lost
continents, like Lemuria and Atlantis, in which occult buffs
believe. Thule was special for race-conscious Aryans, though, as
the home of the "Old Ones," the great race of early Germans of
whom List wrote. Whether or not the club ever acted on its
mystical premises or used them only as some silly and meaningless initiation gibberish is not known. But other members of the
club are known—Rudolf Hess, Alfred Rosenberg, and Adolf
Hitler were among later members.

92. See Greiner, pp. 86-93, for Hitler's occult leanings (to be read with
    caution, however).
93. Idem.
94. Jetzinger, pp. 219-20.
95. The following account comes from Hitler's own account in *Mein
    Kampf,* pp. 39ff. But there are voices to the contrary. Jetzinger
    (pp. 131-33) pokes many holes into this story, first by the use of
    Hitler's own words in a letter he later sent to his draft board: "I
    was a young, inexperienced man," Hitler wrote of 1908/09,
    "without any financial support and too proud to accept it from no
    matter whom." There is no mention in this account of working. If
    Hitler had worked, he would surely have told his draft board in
    order to put himself in a better light to their eyes. In another letter,
    quoted by Payne (p. 582), Hitler lies so much about how much he
    worked that one suspects anything he might have to say on the
    subject: "I was not yet eighteen when I worked as an unskilled
    laborer on construction sites, and in the course of two years I
    performed most of the tasks of a day laborer." In *Mein Kampf,*
    pp. 39ff., he worked only two weeks as a construction laborer.
    Also, as Jetzinger points out, if Hitler had worked, he would have
    risked losing his orphan's pension. Smith also questions Hitler's
    work experience (p. 123), surmising that Hitler's attitude toward
    the lower classes and his physical frailty would have stopped him

from taking on such demeaning and demanding work. Olden (pp. 32ff.), however, takes the story at face value and even describes Hitler as a navvy, a mere bricklayer's assistant, bringing bricks and mortar to the journeymen. Greiner supplies a somewhat garbled account of the same story Hitler gives us, except that in his account Hitler was a sort of foreman and one day the men threw him off the scaffolding into a lime pit for his antisocialist ravings (pp. 42-45).

96. Hitler, *Mein Kampf,* p. 39.
97. Kubizek (p. 247) mentions Hitler's "fear of becoming a proletarian" even in 1908.
98. Hitler, *Mein Kampf,* p. 39.
99. Ibid., p. 40.
100. Idem.
101. Orwell, pp. 26-27.
102. Copy of *Meldezettel* on file at Vienna Bundespolizeidirektion.
103. Orwell, p. 144.
104. Ibid., p. 194.
105. Copy of *Meldezettel,* Vienna Bundespolizeidirektion.
106. Hitler, *Mein Kampf,* p. 106.
107. Ibid., p. 107.
108. Ibid., p. 106.

6. Down and Out

1. The following account is taken from Hanisch, pp. 239ff., Smith, pp. 128-30, and Toland, pp. 40-41.
2. Toland, p. 41.
3. *Statistisches Jahrbuch 1909,* pp. 836, 838.
4. A generation later, the "showers" at Belsen and Dachau would work with equal efficiency, but with a much different intent.
5. Hanisch, p. 239.
6. Idem.
7. Hanisch later supplied information about Hitler's 1910 period in Vienna to Heiden. He also wrote an article himself which was published in the United States by *The New Republic* in April 1939. By that time, however, Hanisch was already dead, having been arrested in 1936 by the Gestapo and dying of "pneumonia" not long thereafter. Hanisch, after Hitler had gained power, faked

many Hitler "originals" and sold them in Vienna. Though his character is questionable, his stories about Hitler in general are taken as the truth by most historians. They do ring true of Hitler's character and do not always show Hitler, who by the time this account was written was far from a bosom friend, in a bad light. As with all of the amateur-writer old cronies of Hitler, Hanisch should be read with caution. I have cited those bits of information that are corroborated by other witnesses or that at least do not appear to be wildly false and sensational.

8. Hanisch, p. 240.
9. Idem.
10. Idem.
11. Hanisch, p. 239.
12. Greiner, p. 16.
13. Smith, p. 127.
14. Greiner, p. 111.
15. Heiden, p. 55, is the source of the Simon Denk Gasse address. This is a questionable address as no police record exists from this lodging, though in many situations no record was kept of illegal rentals. Also, the address is far removed from the usual Hitler haunts in the Mariahilf and Westbahnhof area, though this does not totally negate its possibility.
16. Smith, p. 127.
17. Jenks, p. 38.
18. Johnston, pp. 65-66.
19. Jenks, pp. 36-39. About 7 percent of Viennese houses had bathrooms, according to this account.
20. Ibid., pp. 36-38.
21. Ibid., p. 32.
22. Klaeger, pp. 146-55.
23. Ibid., p. 3.
24. Toland, p. 40.
25. Kubizek, p. 163.
26. Hanisch, p. 240.
27. Idem.
28. Greiner, p. 28.
29. Idem.
30. Greiner, pp. 22ff.
31. Idem.

32. Idem.
33. Hanisch, p. 240.
34. Idem.
35. Idem.
36. Idem.
37. Idem.
38. Jenks, pp. 26-28; Honisch, statement HA, File 17, Reel 1; Greiner, pp. 10-11.
39. Jenks, p. 27.
40. Copy of *Meldezettel* on file at Vienna Bundespolizeidirektion.
41. Hanisch, p. 241.
42. Idem.
43. Payne, p. 85; cf. Greiner, p. 40.
44. Hanisch, p. 241.
45. Toland, p. 44.
46. Ibid., p. 43.
47. Idem.
48. Hanisch, p. 241.
49. Greiner, p. 30.
50. Hanisch, p. 298. Note that in the transcript Hitler says that he only knew the man as Walter Fritz, then goes on in the next sentence to call him Hanisch, not Fritz.
51. Smith, p. 135.
52. Personal interview with Frau Senta Altenberg, the daughter-in-law of Jakob Altenberg, in Vienna, March 1979.
53. Hanisch, p. 272.
54. Personal letter to author from Leopold Landsberger, son of Joseph, February 14, 1979. According to this letter, the Landsbergers were also Jewish and started as gilders in 1833, going into the frame business about the turn of the century. Leopold has no personal remembrances of Hitler, though he confirms that "there is no doubt that my father had bought Hitler's watercolors, usually depicting landmarks of Vienna, but he was not aware of it at the time. . . . After Hitler had taken over in Austria . . . there were one or more letters to the editor, to the effect that the writer had picked up from the Kunsthandlung Landsberger a watercolor done and signed by Hitler."
55. Hanisch, p. 272.
56. Idem.

57. Idem.
58. Hitler statement, HA, File 2, Reel 36; Hanisch, p. 299.
59. Hanisch, p. 242.
60. Idem.
61. Idem; Greiner, pp. 20-21.
62. Hanisch, p. 241.
63. Kubizek, p. 160.
64. Hanisch, p. 271.
65. Ibid., p. 272.
66. Ibid., p. 242.
67. Smith, p. 137.
68. Hanisch, p. 298.
69. Greiner, p. 18.
70. Hanisch, p. 297.
71. Hanisch statement, HA, File 17, Reel 1.
72. Smith, p. 144.
73. Hanisch, p. 298.
74. Ibid., p. 241.
75. Ibid., p. 297.
76. Ibid., p. 242.
77. Greiner, p. 23.

7. The Granite Foundation

1. Hanisch, p. 241.
2. Hitler, *Mein Kampf,* p. 121.
3. Hanisch, p. 241.
4. Jenks, p. 41.
5. Kolo Moser's father was a concierge at this same time at the Theresianum Gymnasium. Kolo grew up at the school and used all the crafts facilities of the school in his own development, becoming something of a king of arts and crafts in Vienna.
6. A journalist visiting Vienna in 1900 noted Lueger's radical swing to anti-Semitism thus: "Some years ago Lueger, not then in office, said 'Only a rascal or a fool can become an anti-Semite.' He himself belongs to the first class. His really notable talents he has employed in the service of every party that would forward his personal ambition" (Damon, p. 454).

7. See Jenks, pp. 44ff., for a good, short discussion of Lueger and his development.
8. Ibid., p. 49.
9. Idem.
10. Quoted in Jenks, p. 50.
11. Quoted in Marek, p. 352.
12. Lueger built a municipal gas works which replaced that of a private English company which had given the city a fine sepia hue every night, but provided only enough illumination, as the Viennese joked, to see the dark. He was also largely responsible for setting out a green belt around the city, known as the Vienna Woods, and saving it from land speculators. Lueger also had a water pipeline built from the Rax mountains to the city and enlarged and electrified the tram system, with Otto Wagner building the city railway. The Central Cemetery was expanded and beautified during his term in office and provision was also made for cheap burials. He built schools and old-age homes, increased hospital space, started city housing and employment agencies, enlarged parks. A public beach was built on an inlet of the Danube; large flower pots were installed around the city's street lights. There were relief agencies for the poor and school lunch programs for impoverished children. Lueger's new municipal socialism took care of the little man from birth until death, and it was all done without substantially increasing the taxes on that little man.
13. Johnston, p. 66.
14. Idem.
15. The following scene is from Hanisch, p. 242.
16. Quoted in Johnston, p. 383.
17. Ibid., p. 384.
18. Hitler had gotten drunk after the completion of his fourth year in Realschule and had shown his contempt for the whole system of education by tearing up his certificate and using it as toilet paper. The next day, however, awakening with a hangover, he remembered that he had nothing to show his mother. Visiting the director of the school and about to tell a lie about the certificate so as to obtain a duplicate, he was presented with the evidence by the enraged director. A farmer had found the torn and soiled certificate in the road and had returned the pieces to the school. The

director gave Hitler such a talking to that the now terribly frightened child became so embarrassed about the incident that he vowed he "would never drink again" (Hitler, *Secret Conversations*, p. 202).

19. Hanisch, p. 242. Cf. Hitler's dreams of being a new Rienzi, Kubizek, p. 140.
20. Hanisch, p. 242.
21. Idem.
22. Greiner, p. 81.
23. Hitler, *Mein Kampf*, pp. 124-25.
24. Jenks, p. 109.
25. See Jenks, pp. 73-112, for a fine short discussion of Schönerer and Pan-Germanism. Schönerer was not from one of the old families of Austria, though he would have liked people to believe him so. His grandfather had been an immigrant to Vienna and worked as a caretaker and house painter, an occupation that Hitler was to have some experience with in Vienna. Schönerer's father had been trained in engineering and had risen out of obscurity through work on the Semmering railway line. He had earned an honorary title, the "von" was added to the name, and when young Georg came along he had every opportunity for advancement in the lesser nobility. Born in Vienna, Georg traveled widely as a young man and at twenty-seven, settled down as a squire on his own estate in the Waldviertel of Niederoesterreich not far from Zwettl. He worked with his peasants for land improvement and was sent to the Reichsrat from his district in 1873.
26. Never had the maxim that politics make strange bedfellows been more appropriate. Still in these early years of political life, Schönerer was a hard-fighting and fair-fighting reformer, pleading for progressive income tax, broad-based elections, and a balanced budget. There was little hint of his later virulent anti-Semitism. He was already something of a German nationalist, adopting the sentiment that had been in the air of Europe since the Napoleonic Wars had forced cooperation between the German principalities. He was also an admirer of Bismarck, who himself had strangely enough not been greatly enamored of the German nationalism movement. Bismarck had distrusted all "isms" as he would have distrusted a cretin with a gun.
27. Bahr, *Selbstbildnis*, p. 143.

28. Quoted in Jenks, p. 84.
29. Idem.
30. Jenks, p. 91.
31. The *Neues Wiener Tagblatt* was run by Moritz Szeps, father of Bertha Szeps-Zuckerkandl, at whose home Mahler had met Alma Schindler and whose salon was visited by men such as Gustav Klimt.
32. Quoted in Jenks, p. 96.
33. This was the year of the Badeni language ordinances. Schönerer played out his part in the Reichsrat circus with such élan that, as Mark Twain reported, at one point he grabbed the president's bell and rang it with abandon. He later stretched the limits of debate to a well-placed right hook to the nose of one of the Czech ministers. See Jenks, p. 101.
34. In the Realschule in Linz in 1903-4, Hitler was taught religion by Father Schwarz, a short, fat, and ugly man who constantly kept a snot-stained handkerchief in the folds of his robe. Hitler delighted one day in retrieving the dropped handkerchief and presenting it to the priest, held at arm's length in disgust (Hitler, *Secret Conversations,* p. 198). He also confessed "sin of the flesh outside marriage," writing it on the blackboard to shock the old priest (ibid., p. 199). Confirmed in the church at fifteen, Hitler sulked through the ceremony and gave no thanks for gifts he received. He could wait only for the moment he reached his village of Leonding again to join his village friends and play Indians (quoted in Payne, pp. 37-38). All in all, Hitler formed a detestation of all religion in his early years. He found it absurd and something that should be left for old women and priests.
35. Quoted in Jenks, p. 108.
36. Hanisch, p. 271.
37. Idem.
38. Hanisch, pp. 271-72.
39. Greiner, pp. 30-34.
40. Adapted from Hanisch, p. 272.
41. Ibid., p. 297.
42. The Café Central was also the meeting place of the Jung Wien writers as well as of Alfred Adler's psychology group.
43. Johnston, p. 101.
44. The name Trotsky first appeared on forged papers that he used for

his second escape from Siberia. It was the name of his warden in Siberia.

45. For information on Trotsky during his Vienna period, see Deutscher, *Prophet,* pp. 183-210, and Trotsky, *Mein Leben,* pp. 199-209.

46. Quoted in Deutscher, *Prophet,* p. 183.

47. Trotsky, p. 208.

48. Deutscher, *Prophet,* pp. 191ff.

49. The voice of moderation, the Vienna *Pravda* was not well received by the Bolshevik faction of the Russian Communists. Trotsky and his paper were forever in financial arrears and publication was erratic. But by the spring of 1910, it looked as if the rift between the Mensheviks and Bolsheviks had been repaired and Lenin's faction agreed to assist the paper financially.

50. Deutscher, *Prophet,* p. 184.

51. Alfred Adler, the only one of Freud's group to become a member of the Social Democrats, was also a habitué of the Café Central and became a friend of Trotsky's. In fact, this friendship inspired Adler to make one of the first syntheses of Freud and Marx. A year to the day before the funeral of Lueger, Adler had declared that Marx and Freud were brothers in philosophy by recognizing the primacy of instinct.

52. Trotsky, p. 204.

53. Idem.

54. Jenks, p. 165.

55. Trotsky (p. 199) describes how as early as 1902, when passing through Vienna on his first exile, he had come up against the Viennese love of tradition that confined Austrian socialism to a moderate, evolutionary course. Searching out the building of the *Arbeiter Zeitung,* Adler's paper, he was impatiently told by a man there that it was Sunday and he could not expect to bother a good Viennese on Sunday.

56. Trotsky, pp. 199-200.

57. Quoted in Deutscher, p. 190.

58. Ibid., p. 186.

59. Trotsky, p. 200.

60. Trotsky's one criticism of Adler concerned the man's oratorical abilities. Like Hitler, Trotsky was deeply concerned with the power of the spoken word. He himself was a powerful orator who could

ride the emotional undulations of an audience like a good jockey handling a horse. He spoke like one in a trance, leaving behind carefully prepared notes to merge emotionally with the audience (see Howe, p. 18). Adler, for all his strengths as a speaker, could not control his voice. Trotsky felt Adler wasted his voice, growing hoarse and coughing by the end of a speech (see Deutscher, p. 187). Interesting also is the connection that Trotsky formed with Adler's son Fritz. Albert Einstein had gone to school with this young man in Zurich, where they had both studied physics in 1899. Young Adler, Einstein, Trotsky, and Stalin were all born in 1879—ten years before Hitler.

61. During his university years, Viktor Adler also became a fast friend of Mahler. The musician often came to the Adler villa in Döbling and played the piano—a piano that Viktor bought specially for him—to a group of friends who started a Wagner club in 1878. Strongly affected by Wagner, as were Hitler and a whole generation of German youth, Adler was influenced by Wagner's ideas ever after. Indeed, Mahler and Adler both pursued Wagner-inspired courses in their own lives, but by different paths. Inherent in both is Wagner's refutation of mechanistic society; his attempt to regain lost innocence through the very self-consciousness that had caused the losing of innocence; the preaching of the oneness of all experience. Mahler and Adler basically were always trying to live the role of poet-priest that Wagner first described—Mahler with his art, and Adler with his political involvement that often utilized Wagnerian dramatics in demonstrations. For a stimulating discussion of the Wagner-Mahler-Adler connection, see McGrath, *Dionysian Art and Populist Politics in Austria*.

62. Quoted in Jenks, p. 172.

63. Ibid., p. 171.

64. Adler was not on hand to enjoy the fruits of his triumph. On May 1 he was sitting in Cell 32 of the Landesgericht prison in Vienna, serving a four-month term for political crimes. This was the same jail where Schönerer served his four-month sentence two years previously for tearing apart the offices of the *Neues Wiener Tagblatt*.

65. Quoted in Jenks, p. 172.

66. Hitler, *Mein Kampf*, p. 38.

67. Ibid., p. 119.

68. Idem.
69. Quoted in Marek, p. 503.
70. Hitler, *Mein Kampf*, p. 119.
71. Ibid., pp. 120-21.
72. Ibid., p. 122.
73. Idem.
74. Idem.
75. See Whiteside, *Austrian National Socialism Before 1918,* and Carsten, *Faschismus in Oesterreich,* for good discussions of the Austrian roots of the Nazi movement, especially for this early form of National Socialism forming in Bohemia to which Hitler never paid credit.
76. Hitler, *Mein Kampf*, p. 65.
77. Ibid., p. 41.
78. Ibid., p. 42-43.
79. Ibid., p. 43.
80. Ibid., p. 45.
81. Ibid., p. 43.
82. Ibid., p. 30.
83. Smith, p. 137.

8. Super Egos

1. Payne, pp. 26-27.
2. Hanisch, p. 241.
3. As commander of the German forces in World War II, Hitler was to show the same lack of foresight about a Russian winter.
4. Greiner later wrote his dubious memoirs of Hitler in a much criticized book, *Das Ende des Hitler-Mythos.* Some historians discount Greiner in toto as an impersonator who had heard of Hanisch's stories about the young Hitler, noticed there was a coincidence of his own name and that of one of Hanisch's "characters," and wrote completely phony stories of Hitler and himself. Still other biographers take Greiner at face value. I try to steer a middle course suggested by Wilfried Daim in a personal conversation in Vienna: Greiner can be trusted—with caution. Daim, who interviewed Greiner personally, felt he was the Greiner Hanisch mentions in his Hitler articles, and that he did know Hitler sometime in the Vienna period. Because of Greiner's confused time line

—he says he met Hitler first in the Männerheim in 1907, when Hitler was still living on Stumpergasse in his first months in Vienna —and his fantastic claims in the book, it would appear that Greiner is not to be completely believed. But like Kubizek and Hanisch, many of his stories can be corroborated by other witnesses and fit into the general pattern of Hitler's life at the time. I place the time of the Hitler-Greiner relationship in the summer and fall of 1910, and again in the spring of 1911, as according to Greiner, pp. 108-10. I disregard Greiner's claim that he knew Hitler as early as 1907, but rather use his own later claim that he had "returned to Vienna in 1910" and fallen in with Hitler again. That Hanisch knew of Greiner and Greiner knew of Hanisch in their respective stories points to the 1910 relationship. Unfortunately, I could track down no *Meldezettel* for Greiner, which could help to put an end to this mystery.

5. Hanisch, p. 241.
6. Idem.
7. The summer solstice was later to be a feast day for the elite SS.
8. Smith, p. 138; Hanisch, p. 241.
9. Hanisch, p. 241.
10. Idem.
11. Greiner, p. 31.
12. Ibid., p. 23.
13. Ibid., p. 24.
14. Ibid., p. 29.
15. Ibid., p. 39. See Hanisch, p. 241, for a similar story.
16. Greiner, p. 39.
17. Following account adapted from Hanisch, p. 241, and Greiner, pp. 40ff.
18. Hanisch, p. 241. The Csillag firm is still in business in Vienna and this advertisement can be seen in the front window of the shop, copied out of an old newspaper.
19. Greiner, p. 41.
20. Ibid., p. 40.
21. Ibid., pp. 40-41.
22. Hanisch, p. 241.
23. Greiner, p. 42.
24. Hanisch, p. 271; Greiner, p. 70.
25. Hanisch, p. 271.

26. Mahler-Werfel, *Bridge,* p. 43.
27. Idem.
28. Mahler-Werfel, pp. 51ff.
29. Idem.
30. Idem.
31. Mahler-Werfel, p. 52.
32. Idem.
33. Mahler-Werfel, p. 53.
34. Idem.
35. Mahler-Werfel, p. 52.
36. Ibid., p. 53.
37. Hanisch, p. 298.
38. Idem. Klimt had earlier won the hearts of the Viennese by painting the same scene.
39. Idem.
40. Idem.
41. Greiner, p. 110.
42. HA, File 20, Reel 2; File 36. Frau Pichler was later to make a good living from these two paintings during the hard times of the 1930s. She charged admission to see the paintings done by the Führer and then she won favor with Hitler's regime by returning the paintings to him in 1938. She wrote in a letter to Hitler that she was only sorry she could not do likewise with the *Gloriette* which she had also once owned, because it was "inconveniently" in the hands of a Jewish owner (File 20, Reel 2).
43. HA, File 29, Reel 2.
44. Hanisch, p. 299.
45. Idem; HA, File 40, Reel 2.
46. Hitler was paying more in the Männerheim, twelve crowns per month, than he had at Frau Zakreys's where the rent was ten crowns. Somehow he never thought of leaving the home, however, once he was on his feet again. There must have been something reassuring about barracks life for Hitler, the loner, content with the anonymous companionship that forced communal living produces.
47. HA, File 1741, Reel 82.
48. Hanisch, p. 299.
49. HA, File 1741, Reel 86.
50. Idem.

51. Hanisch, p. 299; HA, File 40, Reel 2.
52. Hanisch, p. 299.
53. Ibid., p. 300.
54. Jones, p. 87.
55. Freud was forever to blame his ailing stomach on a barbecue prepared by the philosopher William James while he was in America. See, for example, Johnston, p. 222.
56. Jones, pp. 87ff.
57. Ibid., p. 88.
58. Blaukopf, p. 7.
59. Jones, p. 88.
60. Quoted in Blaukopf, p. 10.
61. For an interesting account of this historic meeting between Freud and Mahler, see Kuehn, "Encounter at Leyden."
62. Jones, p. 89.
63. Quoted in Blaukopf, p. 11.
64. Mahler-Werfel, *Bridge,* p. 53.
65. Kuehn, pp. 357-58.
66. Quoted in Blaukopf, p. 11.
67. Ibid., pp. 12-13.
68. Idem.
69. See especially Waite, *The Psycopathic God,* and Langer, *Mind of Adolf Hitler.*
70. Waite, p. 143.
71. Friends of Alois later testified that he was awfully rough—"*saugrob*" (Waite, p. 140).
72. Bezymensky, pp. 67, 77.
73. Waite, p. 163; Langer also presents a similar theory.
74. Hitler, *Mein Kampf,* pp. 142-44.
75. Perhaps it was even the sadomasochistic style of lovemaking in which the older Adolf indulged.
76. In *Mein Kampf,* on the same page (213) are two such references: the "Goddess of Suffering took me in her arms," and "Dame Care" was given Hitler for a new mother after his died.
77. Hitler, *Mein Kampf,* p. 56.
78. Something of a poetic prodigy, Weininger expanded his doctoral dissertation into the book published in 1903 that took Vienna and much of Europe by storm. He turned, as some critics say, disappointed Oedipal feelings and Jewish self-hatred into a philosophi-

cal system. Stealing or borrowing from Freud's as yet unpublished work on bisexuality—a patient of Freud's was also a close friend of Weininger's—the young scholar developed mathematical formulas for character, depending on how much of each sexual quotient the person had. For Weininger, there was no such thing as pure male or pure female. These were only abstract concepts. In reality, all people are combinations of both principles, Weininger contended. The male principle stands, he said, for creativity and rationalism; the female principle, for fecundity and chaos. Citing sources from Plato to Kant. Weininger went on to show how various proportions of sexuality in individuals create character. All the positive achievements in human history, Weininger argued, are due to the masculine principle: art, religion, literature, the state. The Aryan race is the embodiment of the masculine principle—echoing the word of Houston Stewart Chamberlain, whom Weininger idolized—while the Jews are the embodiment of the feminine principle, responsible for all the negative tendencies in history. The same year as the publication of *Sex and Character,* Weininger, himself a Jew, grew despondent, took a room in the house where Beethoven had died, and shot himself through the chest one fine autumn day. Weininger's strange, overripe intellectuality and his suicide are two common features of turn-of-the-century Vienna, a culture that was in many ways itself overripe and self-destructive.

79. Kubizek, p. 152.
80. Ibid., p. 186.
81. Hanisch, p. 297.

9. Symptoms of Debility

1. Hanisch, p. 272.
2. This surmise is the result both of oral legend at the Kunsthistorisches Museum in Vienna and of research in the Austrian Staats Archiv. Two stories circulate at the museum: one was passed down from the director of the museum in 1938, Dr. Dworzak; the other comes from a Dr. Eichler who was director of the Antiken Sammlung in 1938. After the Anschluss, Hitler was given a tour of the museum by both Dworzak and Eichler. According to the story from Dworzak, related to me by Dr. Kügler, director of the Museum Library, Hitler noticed at one point that a small cameo

called the Aspasios Gemme, which had been in the museum before the First World War and was taken by the Italians in 1921 as part of the war reparations, was no longer there. Dworzak asked the Führer how he could know this, and Hitler replied that he had worked in the museum. Eichler's story, related to me by the current director of the Antiken Sammlung, Dr. Oberleitner, is that Hitler supposedly worked in Room 9 of that collection. While leading Hitler through the antique collection in 1938, Eichler noticed that Hitler stood for a long time in silence in Room 9, looking around as if in fond remembrance, but he said nothing to Eichler. Both of these stories are supported by evidence in the Staats Archiv that reports renovations in the Antiken Sammlung during the period Hitler lived in Vienna. Unfortunately, however, the two stories point to different rooms. In the time Hitler was in Vienna, the Aspasios Gemme was kept in Room 14 of the Antiken Sammlung, according to a contemporary guidebook to the museum, while Room 9 housed the terra-cotta collection of Greek funereal vases. To complicate matters further, renovations were done in two different periods by two separate firms: Rooms 7 to 13 of the museum were renovated in 1907-8 (see OME, Akten 50/B/4, 1908, Staats Archiv) while Room 14 was done in the fall of 1910 (OME, Akten 50/B/1, 1910, Staats Archiv). It would have been possible for Hitler to have worked there at either time. The first period coincides with the "missing months" during which Hitler either stayed on in Vienna after being rejected for the first time from the Academy or returned to Linz to care for his dying mother. There are no witnesses from this time to allow us to be certain one way or another where Hitler was, and this early period fits Hitler's own story in *Mein Kampf* and various autobiographical letters he penned, claiming that he was forced to take on construction work from the moment he arrived in Vienna. The 1910 date seems more probable, for it coincides with Hitler's period of want, which 1907-8 was not. In 1907 Hitler was still too much of a dandy to soil his hands with work. That both stories mention the Antiken Sammlung, which was housed in the Hochparterre at the time, seems to corroborate Hitler's having worked there. Rooms 9 and 14 were not far from each other, and while working mainly in the one—say Room 14 in 1910 where the Aspasios Gemme was kept— it is conceivable that Hitler could easily have visited the other during rest periods. Hitler loved to cite trivia to shock experts with his knowledge of detail. The story of the Aspasios Gemme rings very true of Hitler in this regard also.

3. OME, Akten 50/B/8, 1909, Austrian Staats Archiv.
4. Statement by Professor Leidenroth, HA, File 1741, Reel 86.
5. HA, File 36, Reel 2.
6. Honisch statement, HA, File 17, Reel 1.
7. HA, File 36, Reel 2.
8. Maser, p. 67. Maser offers an interesting discussion of Hitler as artist, pp. 39-69.
9. Quoted in Waite, p. 166.
10. Greiner, pp. 26-27.
11. Hitler, *Mein Kampf,* p. 123.
12. HA, File 36, Reel 2.
13. *"Das Haus gegenüber der Burg," Neue Freie Presse,* December 4, 1910.
14. Powell, p. 87.
15. Quoted in Powell, p. 83.
16. Quoted in Vergo, p. 161.
17. Ibid., p. 165. Loos was born in Moravia, that remarkable section of Bohemia which produced Freud, Mahler, and Kafka as well as other Central European intellectuals. He was the son of a sculptor and stonecutter, and attended the Polytechnic School in Dresden. After this training, Loos set off for adventure in the New World and lived and worked in America from 1893 to 1896. He supported himself by an odd assortment of jobs, including stints as a music critic and as a dishwasher. He lived the down-and-out life that Hitler later experienced in Vienna, but for Loos it was a positive experience. He later remembered that "in the lowest quarters of New York you can for ten cents in a mass dormitory, sleep more cleanly and agreeably than in an inn in an Austrian village" (quoted in Münz and Künstler, p. 18). Loos came to Vienna in 1896, a year before Mahler and the advent of the Secession, and took work in the architectural firm of the husband of the Viennese feminist Rosa Mayreder, who was also the librettist for Hugo Wolf's opera *Der Corregidor.* A polemicist as well as an architect, Loos continued his newspaper writing back in Vienna, writing essays for the *Neue Freie Presse* on everything from architecture to how to dress and

eat. He became friends with Karl Kraus, Peter Altenberg, and the groups that met at the Café Central.

18. Quoted in Vergo, p. 162.
19. Quoted in Münz and Künstler, p. 14.
20. Loos criticized, for example, Josef Hoffmann as having "nothing in common with the style of our time" (ibid., p. 17). For the architect Olbrich, Loos reserved particular scorn, describing in one of his articles a shop window that had a display of cutlery "for people who can eat, after the English fashion, and after designs by Olbrich for people who cannot eat" (Loos, *Sämmtliche Schriften,* vol. 1, p. 289).
21. There were, in fact, two separate movements underway in Vienna just after the turn of the century. "The situation in Vienna was such that there had been the beginnings of a successful revolution by the moderns. The most important names in the various fields were Josef Hoffmann, Gustav Klimt, Hermann Bahr and Gustav Mahler. . . . It was in general a decorative tendency . . . increasingly emotional and antiintellectual. The first revolution was succeeded by a second, more radical one, with Adolf Loos, Karl Kraus, and Arnold Schoenberg at its head, and, later, Kokoschka also" (Hodin, p. 64).
22. One reviewer, from the *Neues Wiener Tagblatt,* referring to Klimt's portrait of Adele Bloch-Bauer which was shown that year, could not resist the delightful pun that there was *"mehr Blech als Bloch"* (more *Blech* than Bloch) in the painting (quoted in Vergo, p. 181). *Blech* is slang for rubbish. Klimt's lovely *Danaë* had also drawn blasts from the same critic who described the woman pictured as "rolled up like a bundle of old washing . . . she permits us to admire her thigh and half her bosom" (ibid., p. 187).
23. Hevesi, p. 313.
24. Hodin, p. 65.
25. Quoted in Hodin, p. 65.
26. Quoted in Vergo, p. 200.
27. Kokoschka, p. 21. Also displayed at this show were the drawings that "OK," as Kokoschka signed his name, had made for a children's fairytale book that he had also written and which was published by the Wiener Werkstätte that year. This book and the posters of his "chamber of horrors" were some of the earliest

examples of Expressionist painting. "OK" had gone far beyond the manipulation of the façade that Klimt had mastered. He had gone to the root of the conscious world as Freud had done. And like Freud, dreams played an important part in his work. The book of fairytales was entitled *Die Träumenden Knaben* (The Dreaming Boys), and the tapestry cartoons were called *Die Traumtragenden* (The Dream Bearers). Kokoschka would later write that "consciousness is the source of all things and ideas. It is a sea with visions as its only horizon" (quoted in Vergo, p. 193).

28. Hodin, p. 62.
29. Kokoschka, p. 25.
30. Ibid., pp. 28-31.
31. Vergo examines this statement (pp. 248-49) and says that he found no mention of such a scandal in the Viennese papers of the day, but rather that the public "greeted this drama, meant no doubt as a piece of fun, with sympathetic good humor."
32. Kokoschka, p. 31.
33. Vergo, p. 199.
34. Powell, p. 165.
35. Karpfen, pp. 85-86.
36. *Neue Freie Presse,* December 1, 1909.
37. Vergo, p. 214.
38. Comini, in her *Egon Schiele,* pp. 5-6, hypothesizes that one factor in Schiele's "lifelong obsession with sexuality was that his childhood years had been overshadowed by the recurrent illness and advancing syphilitic insanity of his father, Adolf Schiele. . . . Almost as though in retaliation for the venereal origin of the disease that had shadowed his family, the boy threw himself into a stormy adolescence of sexual exploration and activity. He learned not only the secrets of his own body, but also those of [his sister] Gerti's. When he was sixteen and she twelve, they repeated their parents' honeymoon trip to Trieste, spending the night in a hotel."
39. In the next three years, Firma S. Morgenstern at Liechtensteinstrasse 4, a frame shop which specialized in Biedermeier frames, was to buy many of Hitler's works. Among them were: *Heiligen Kreuzer Hof, Rotenturmtor, Fischer Tor, Michaelerplatz, Dreilauferhaus,* and *Hofburg mit alten Durchlass 1890* (HA, File 36, Reel 2). Morgenstern also put Hitler in touch with a lawyer named Josef Feingold, who had his offices in the Third District at Beatrix-

gasse 6. Feingold, who was according to the Nazi report, *"schein-bar nicht arisch, aber durchaus seriös wirkend, Kriegsteilnehmer* (apparently not Aryan, but gives the impression of reliability, war veteran), supported many young artists between 1910 and 1913. Hitler was one of those whom the lawyer helped by purchasing his pictures regularly. Feingold gave away many of these pictures to friends (HA, File 28, Reel 2).

40. Especially interesting in this regard is the letter Hitler sent his draft board in January 1914 to explain why he had not registered for the draft earlier, quoted in Jetzinger, pp. 262-64: "With regard to my failure to report for military service in the autumn of 1909, I must say that this was for me an endlessly bitter time. I was then a young man without experience, receiving no financial assistance from anyone, and too proud to accept financial assistance from others, let alone beg for it. Without support, compelled to depend on my own efforts, I earned only a few crowns and often only a few hellers for my labors, and this was often insufficient to pay for a night's lodging. For two long years I had no other mistress than sorrow and need, no other companion than eternally unsatisfied hunger. I never knew the beautiful word *youth.* Even today, five years later, I am constantly reminded of those experiences, and the reminders take the form of frost blisters on my fingers, hands, and feet. And yet I cannot remember those days without a certain pleasure, now that these vexations have been surmounted. In spite of great want, amid often dubious surroundings, I nevertheless kept my name clean, had a blameless record with the law, and possessed a clear conscience—except for that one constantly remembered fact that I failed to register for military service. This is the one thing which I feel responsible for. It would seem that a moderate fine would be ample penance, and of course I would pay the fine willingly." This letter is interesting in that it is one of the first times Hitler wrote about himself, and already he has the whining quality that fills the pages of *Mein Kampf.* He is the poor, wronged little man, tossed by the winds of fate. He tries and tries—his failure is not his fault. It is a letter filled with half-truths and simperings. His clean record with the law is dubious at best—he lied to the police about Hanisch and should have been tried then and convicted of perjury. He was supported during his Vienna years by the orphan's pension, until his sister Angela learned of his inheritance that the letter to Aunt

Johanna was to secure for him. Doubtless that letter followed just such lines as the one quoted above to his draft board.

41. Jetzinger, pp. 231-32.

42. Ibid., pp. 226, 232.

43. Hanisch, p. 240.

44. Hitler always ran out on friendships when they became too close—witness Kubizek and Hanisch. This would hold true later in life for close associates, both male and female. Hitler would remember name days and birthdays and special anniversaries so as to endear himself to people, but he avoided any of the intimacies and hard times of friendship. He was a classic taker in any relationship. Whenever he was put into a position of having to give emotionally, he ran away. He had nothing to give.

45. Müllern-Schönhausen, p. 106. The latter's book, *Die Lösung des Rätsels Adolf Hitler,* is, as Toland says (p. 930), "a confusing hodgepodge of fact and fantasy." But as with the other sources for Hitler's early years, there are kernels of truth in it. Those kernels lie, I feel, in Müllern-Schönhausen's collection of paintings and Hitler memorabilia. Kept in a bank vault in Vienna, the collection comes from Hans Bleyer-Härtl, an Austrian Nazi, lawyer, and sometimes writer. He defended the Dollfuss murderers and after the Anschluss became rapidly disenchanted with the Nazis—but not with Hitler, it would seem, for he managed to scrape together quite a collection of the Führer's paintings and sketches at a time when their market value was extremely high. The book aside, I feel that a large part of the collection is genuine and so I will also later quote Müllern-Schönhausen for other paintings and letters. He is not without his detractors, of course. In the past, the validity of his collection has been called into question primarily because of the offbeat and slightly sensational nature of his book. Although one must also be cautious about parts of the collection, I feel that the book is insufficient reason to denigrate the collection.

46. Müllern-Schönhausen, p. 105.

47. Fest, p. 48.

48. Greiner, p. 113.

49. Ibid., pp. 101-5. This is one case of Greiner's imagination literally flying away with its own invention.

50. In one of his fits of largesse, Greiner (pp. 35-36) admits to having influence with a professor at the Vienna Art Academy, Professor Delug, who admired his work and wanted to further his career.

Supposedly, this same Delug arranged a job for Hitler with an architect or builder (Greiner, p. 42). A look at the archives of the Vienna Academy shows that there was a Delug attached to the Academy in those years. He was an architect. Whether or not he had contact with Hitler could not be proven conclusively. Also, according to a sketch included in Müllern-Schönhausen, p. 107, Hitler in 1911 drew a sketch for a house *"im Auftrag des Baumeisters Florian Müller."* Whether Greiner is referring to this incident or another is not certain, but I put the two together as fitting chronologically.

51. Müllern-Schönhausen, p. 107.

52. Greiner, pp. 42-45, tells a story not unlike Hitler's own in *Mein Kampf* about young Adolf's difficulties with the other workers. Hitler's antiunion and antisocialist talk with the more hardy of the workingmen supposedly resulted one day in Hitler being thrown from the scaffolding of a building project, a lime pit breaking his fall. This incident understandably ended Hitler's work with the architect after only a couple of weeks on the job. Whether this Greiner reference is to the Florian Müller job or is pure fantasy is undetermined.

53. Hitler was not devoid of energy himself, but the energy created in others, especially as seen in his huge Nuremberg rallies and in his speeches, was ultimately fed back to Hitler by the enthused, sometimes near-orgiastic audiences. Also, the kind of men with whom Hitler later associated, including petty criminals, deviants, and misfits, were rough approximations of his comrades in the Männerheim. Bormann, Himmler, Roehm, Goebbels, Goering, Hess—all were characters of whom one could have found close approximations in the Vienna Männerheim.

54. Greiner, pp. 70-71.

55. Hanisch, p. 241.

56. If taken alone, Greiner's account should probably be looked on as one more instance of his overactive imagination. But there is a corroborating witness to this story. Rosa Albach-Retty, the Viennese actress, in her memoirs, recounts the same story. It is not only similar, but the same in almost every detail, save Delug's involvement. The story she tells was related to her by Wilhelm Karczag, director of the Theater an der Wien before World War I; he was the man who auditioned Hitler for a part in the chorus.

57. Albach-Retty, p. 238.

58. HA, File 17, Reel 1.
59. Hitler also attended school at this monastery for two years and thought, for a time, of joining the monks and becoming one day, perhaps, an abbot. This was several years before his antichurch sentiments came to the fore. In several places in this monastery at Lambach, for example, over the ornamental doorway, is carved the swastika. These swastikas existed even when Hitler was a young boy attending school there. They were probably meant as a punning coat of arms for an early abbot of the monastery named Hagen. That abbot probably thought it would be good fun to have his own cross, the *"Hagenkreuz"*—very similar in pronunciation to the German for swastika, *Hakenkreuz.* See Payne, pp. 20-21.
60. Greiner, p. 71.
61. Ibid., p. 112.
62. Jetzinger, p. 229.
63. Quoted in Payne, p. 89; cf. Jetzinger, pp. 226-29.
64. Idem.
65. Mahler-Werfel, *Bridge,* pp. 58-66. Ironic in this regard is that the operetta, a piece of which Hitler sang at his audition, Franz Lehár's *The Merry Widow,* was a favorite of Alma and Gustav Mahler. They were, however, both too highbrow to buy the sheet music for it, and forgetting one of the tunes, they grew desperate to find a way to learn it. They went to a music store with a plan—Mahler would keep the owner busy with questions about how his own compositions were selling while Alma looked up and memorized the forgotten passage (ibid., p. 32).
66. Ibid., p. 66.
67. Ibid., p. 63.
68. *Illustrierte Wiener Extrablatt,* May 19, 1911.
69. Quoted in Mitchell, p. 414.
70. Mahler-Werfel, *Memories,* p. 182.
71. The relationship between Mahler and Schoenberg had also been helped by the fact that Mahler's wife had studied under the same man, Zemlinsky, with whom Schoenberg studied. In fact, Schoenberg married Zemlinsky's sister. Although the Mahler-Schoenberg friendship was not without its stormy passages, Mahler was always there when the younger composer needed him. One such occasion came early in 1907 when the Rosé Quartet was again performing a

Schoenberg piece, the D Minor String Quartet. A virtual riot broke out at this performance. "To many people, the work seemed impossible, and they left the hall while it was being played; one particularly witty person left by the emergency exit. At the end, moreover, people could be heard hissing. Mahler was seated among them, and, immediately up in arms at this artistic injustice, he set upon one of the dissatisfied customers, telling him, with his wonderfully emotional involvement, "It's not for you to hiss!' The stranger, who would have been meek as a lamb in front of his own concierge, was full of pride when faced by a spiritual monarch, and replied, 'I hiss at your symphonies, too!' This scene was held very much against Mahler" (Reich, *Schoenberg,* pp. 20-21). Obviously, sponsorship of such a rebellious artist as Schoenberg did little to improve Mahler's position at the Hof Opera.

72. Reich, *Schoenberg,* p. 35.

73. Quoted in ibid., p. 37.

74. Johnston, p. 139.

75. Reich, *Schoenberg,* p. 49.

76. Even members of the more radical, modern musical community deserted Schoenberg. Richard Strauss, who with *Salome* and *Elektra* pushed chromaticism to new discordancies, soon backed off from Schoenberg's extreme stance. Strauss was designated by Mahler as one of the arbiters of Schoenberg's support; the German composer would later write Alma Mahler that "only a psychiatrist can help poor Schoenberg now. . . . He would do better to shovel snow than scribble on music paper" (quoted in Reich, *Schoenberg,* p. 16). Upon hearing this judgment, Schoenberg made a pithy reply to the comfortable composer: "He [Strauss] is no longer of the slightest artistic interest to me, and whatever I may have learned from him, I am thankful to say I misunderstood" (ibid., p. 17).

77. Quoted in Vergo, p. 205.

78. Ibid., p. 16.

79. Ibid., p. 202.

80. Schiele kept a diary in prison (see Comini, *Schiele in Prison*). The April 17, 1912, entry describes his luxurious surroundings: "Dust, spiderwebs, cough-spit, crumbling plaster of this room . . . where the bunk touches the wall the stains are thickest and the limey whitewash has been rubbed off. As though polished, the bricks are

like blood smears, all smooth and with a dark, fatty shine. I know now what a dungeon is."

81. Quoted in Powell, p. 150.
82. Quoted in Reich, *Schoenberg,* p. 61.
83. According to a letter, see Müllern-Schönhausen, pp. 195-97.
84. Payne, p. 10.
85. Klara was the daughter of Johann Nepomuk's second daughter. Alois being the legally adopted son of Johann Nepomuk and possibly the illegitimate son of Johann's brother Georg, the relationship between Klara and Alois was complicated. They were legally uncle and niece and perhaps also second cousins by birth.
86. See Smith for the best account of Hitler's childhood.
87. Müllern-Schönhausen, pp. 91-92.
88. Ibid., p. 91.
90. Payne, p. 23.
91. Professor Eduard Hümmer's character sketch of young Hitler for the 1924 Munich Putsch trial is quoted in Jetzinger, pp. 105-6. See also Kandl for an excellent discussion of teachers' and fellow students' opinions of the young Hitler.
92. The first months in office, Chancellor Hitler read through the entire works of May, nearly seventy volumes (Fest, p. 446). In World War II, Hitler often confused the Russians for characters out of a May novel and called them the Redskins (Payne, p. 28). Tradition also has it that Hitler once advised his generals on the Russian front to carry May as a sort of tactician's field book.
93. That same year, the future philosopher Ludwig Wittgenstein would enter the Linz Realschule that Hitler had been forced to leave (Janik and Toulmin, p. 174).
94. Smith, p. 29.
95. Müllern-Schönhausen, pp. 195-97.

10. Departure

1. Altenberg statement, HA, File 1741, Reel 86.
2. Description according to interview with Altenberg's daughter-in-law, Senta Altenberg, in Vienna.
3. HA, File 1741, Reel 86, and File 36, Reel 2.
4. Altenberg interview.
5. HA, File 1741, Reel 86. Cf. Greiner, p. 77, in which Greiner states

that Hitler was always very polite to his Jewish customers and then laughed behind their backs.

6. Jenks, p. 188.
7. Idem.
8. These riots occurred at about the same time that Einstein was visiting Vienna, trying to secure a chair at Prague University.
9. May, p. 142.
10. This may have been the mass demonstration Kubizek referred to (p. 246) as happening in 1908.
11. Jenks, p. 188.
12. May, p. 142.
13. Jenks, p. 188.
14. Hitler, *Mein Kampf,* p. 68.
15. The young assailant, Nikolaus Njegusch, was a cabinetmaker's assistant who, at his trial, later said he had been driven to the crime by the minister himself. Adler had been giving a speech in the Parliament the day of the shooting, and the would-be assassin had seen Hochenburger "laughing and joking during Adler's recital of the woes of the common people" (Jenks, p. 189). Njegusch drew a seven-year jail term and died in prison. He was a foreshadowing of the violence and frustration that had been penned up too long in the lower classes and would soon come spilling out in proletarian revolutions. The old order had received the hemlock. A calling to account was promised by this attempted assassination.
16. Jenks, p. 189.
17. Müllern-Schönhausen, p. 92. Franzl is a mystery person in Hitler's life. In no later accounts or remembrances is such a person mentioned, nor surprisingly did Franzl publish any remembrances, after Hitler became famous, to capitalize on the old friendship. But that the friendship lasted as long as any Hitler had during the Vienna period is attested to by the letter written the summer before and by the Christmas gift.
18. Waite, p. 97. The author of this tract included a whole series of anti-Semitic quotes from men from Erasmus to Voltaire to Wagner, to prove that the Jews were conspiring with the Freemasons to seize world power. This was the familiar old argument of the "Jewish peril," dressed up in respectable intellectual clothes; it claimed that the press was controlled by the Jews and that the arts were also under their power. The Jews were responsible for

"degenerate atonal music," and Freud and company were trying to "destroy the German soul . . . the destroyers of the German family" (Waite, p. 98).

19. See Jetzinger, pp. 248-64, for a thorough discussion of Hitler's military situation in Austria.

20. Ibid., p. 251.

21. Hitler mixed so little in real life in these Vienna years that it is almost sure he received the news of that world only via the morning papers. Hitler later carried this ostrichlike behavior with him into his political career. Up to his last days in the Berlin bunker, he refused to see the destruction that was happening all around him in Berlin. Earlier in the war he would drive along in his staff car with the blinds pulled securely down, blocking off any intrusion of the facts on his dream world. The Männerheim was good practice for such a life.

22. Jetzinger, p. 250.

23. Payne, p. 17.

24. Hitler, *Secret Conversations,* p. 567.

25. Quoted in Payne, p. 18.

26. Hitler, *Mein Kampf,* p. 3.

27. Müllern-Schönhausen, p. 96.

28. Ibid., p. 104.

29. Crankshaw, p. 389.

30. Quoted in Deutscher, *Prophet,* p. 202.

31. Idem.

32. Idem.

33. Quoted in Barea, p. 355.

34. Quoted in Pauli, p. 263.

35. Quoted in Crankshaw, p. 384.

36. Deutscher, *Prophet,* p. 205.

37. One of the aristocracy later complained that "if Count Berchtold had been a man, he would have intervened in the war between Serbia and Bulgaria even at the risk of war with Russia" (quoted in Barea, p. 356).

38. Crankshaw, p. 393.

39. There is another possible account of Hitler's activities for the period of November 1912 to April 1913. According to Hitler's sister-in-law, the wife of half-brother Alois junior, Hitler paid a visit to England during that period. See Payne, pp. 93-97, from the

account written by Bridget Hitler, *My Brother-in-Law Adolf.* This account, which could be true, has Hitler using the ticket sent to Angela to visit the temporarily successful Alois in Liverpool. Alois was the opposite of Hitler in his outgoing manner and endless schemes—in fact, he sounds more like a Greiner or Hanisch than a Hitler. While visiting his brother in Liverpool, Hitler supposedly resumed his old sleeping habits: up at noon and loafing around the house under foot all day. He roamed the streets of Liverpool, making friends with some of the German colony, but typically for Hitler, steering clear of the locals. It was the same as his existence in Vienna. He visited London once, according to this account, and was impressed mainly with the Tower Bridge. It is interesting to note that Hitler took with him to his death his prejudice in favor of the English—of their strength and resourcefulness. Perhaps this was only part of the old Continental respect for the British Empire and their frequent mimicry of the English; perhaps it was truly founded on personal experience. Bridget began to worry that she would have a perpetual free-loading guest on her hands and also wrote that Adolf was using his dead brother Edmund's birth certificate to evade the draft. This information lends some credibility to an otherwise flimsy account that has Hitler back in Vienna in time for his twenty-fourth birthday. Several things contradict this story, however. The testimonies of Karl Honisch and Maria Wohlrab (HA, File 17, Reel 1) contradict Bridget's tale. As will be seen, both these people separately reported knowing Hitler in the late 1912 and early 1913 period. This was the time of the reported visit to England. There is also the fact of Hitler's draft status. There is no reason, after having all but hidden himself in Vienna for all these years, that he would risk a trip to Liverpool, crossing and recrossing the frontier and risking arrest by officials there for draft evasion. He may have been, as Bridget reported, traveling under Edmund's documents. This also may account for Hitler's *Meldezettel* showing no break in residency at the Männerheim. The trip to England cannot definitely be ruled out, but I find it very, very unlikely.

40. Honisch statement, HA, File 17, Reel 1.
41. Idem.
42. Idem.
43. Idem.

44. Idem. Hitler's peculiar eating habits have often been commented upon. Later in his life, the Führer had another favorite bread, *Oldenburgerisch Roggen Brot,* that was the first thing that went into the suitcase whenever he traveled. It reportedly reminded him of the bread he had eaten as a youth in Vienna (see Picker, p. 466).

45. Honisch statement, HA, File 17, Reel 1. It should never be forgotten that the source of much Hitler information we now have is from Gestapo interviews such as this Honisch statement. It would seem, at first thought, that such reports as filed in the Haupt Archiv of the NSDAP could not fail to be biased. A person would have had to be a fool to besmirch Hitler's name to his own henchmen. Yet the Nazis were the original objective journalists—purely by accident. Because of their obsessive thoroughness, they gathered helpful and harmful information alike. For example, they recorded all the information of Hitler's poor school record and filed it neatly away instead of destroying it. It should also not be forgotten that the Gestapo acted quite independently of Hitler and even tried to gather evidence that could be negative to him with which they might strengthen their own position.

46. Honisch statement, HA, File 17, Reel 1.

47. Idem.

48. Idem.

49. Siegert, *"Judenmord—Warum?"* p. 41.

50. Honisch statement, HA, File 17, Reel 1.

51. Idem.

52. Idem.

53. Idem.

54. Idem. Hitler surely knew of the famous Viennese tenor, Leo Slezak, whose daughter, Gertl, he later met through Goebbels. She was a Hitler favorite until he learned of a Jewish grandmother in the family (see Picker, p. 288).

55. Schweiger, *"Wiener Kaffeehaus,"* p. 19.

56. Wohlrab statement, HA, File 17, Reel 1.

57. Idem.

58. Idem.

59. Idem.

60. Kraus, *Die Fackel,* No. 400 (summer 1914), p. 2.

61. *Wiener Zeitung,* Jan. 1, 1913, p. 21.

62. *Neue Freie Presse,* Jan. 14, 1913.

63. Johnston, p. 176. For a good discussion of the Viennese attitude to death and suicide, see ibid., pp. 165-80, and also Janik and Toulmin, pp. 64-65.
64. Durkheim, p. 299.
65. *Wiener Zeitung,* Jan. 13, 1913, p. 1.
66. *Neue Freie Presse,* morning paper, Jan. 15, 1913, p. 6.
67. *Wiener Zeitung,* Jan. 13, 1913, p. 1.
68. One of the shining lights of the international peace movement that was so strong just before the outbreak of World War I was the Viennese Bertha von Suttner. In her writings, such as *Lay Down Your Arms,* and her speeches, she did as much for the cause of peace as any person of her time. A personal friend and one-time secretary of Alfred Nobel, she was largely responsible for convincing that inventive man to leave a prize for peace among the other endowments he was planning. She received the Nobel Peace Prize in 1905, the fifth recipient, and died only one week before the shooting in Sarajevo that would make all her life's work in vain. An aristocrat, born Kinsky, she alienated her class by her "outlandish" work. Her husband led in founding the Union for Defense Against Anti-Semitism, whose members included the famous surgeon Billroth and the operetta king Johann Strauss. Greiner (p. 81) reports that Hitler joined this society to see what the enemy was up to. In her life and works, Bertha von Suttner represents the best in Viennese involvement in all spheres of life: a friend to writers such as Schnitzler, and to politicians, business magnates, and rulers.
69. *Wiener Zeitung,* Jan. 13, 1913, p. 9.
70. *Neue Freie Presse,* Jan. 14, 1913, p. 9.
71. Idem.
72. Idem.
73. Idem.
74. Idem.
75. Idem. Although not properly a part of the story of turn-of-the-century Vienna, Rilke, as was Kafka, was a Habsburg legacy from Prague. One wonders if Rilke looked up his old friend and lover, Lou Andreas-Salomé, while in Vienna that January. She had come in October of 1912 to study under Freud, and would stay until the spring of 1913. Andreas-Salomé was one of those fascinating women who could only have existed in the days before feminism, for much of her fame rests, as does Alma Mahler-Werfel's, on the

men she knew and loved. A confidante of Nietzche's and lover of Rilke and later close friend to Freud, Andreas-Salomé was also a writer and pioneering psychoanalyst. See her own memoirs, *Lebensrückblick,* and Peter's *My Sister, My Spouse* for more information on this complex woman. Kammerer, who was giving the lecture on "Breeding and Race" (did Hitler go to such a talk that was grist for his mill?) was also one of the more fascinating inmates of turn-of-the-century Vienna. A natural scientist who had laboratories out in the Prater, Kammerer carried out experiments at that time to prove the Lamarckian theory of inherited characteristics. See Arthur Koestler's engrossing book, *The Strange Case of the Midwife Toad,* for a full account of this man. He later committed suicide when his findings were called into question. In 1912, a year after Gustav Mahler's death, Kammerer fell under the spell of Alma Mahler and hired her as his assistant. Her job, ironically, was to tend to the praying mantises at his institute. Alma finally tired of the gnomelike scientist's advances and confronted Kammerer's wife with her husband's attempted infidelity. Kammerer had threatened to shoot himself on Mahler's grave if Alma did not accede to his advances.

76. The Russians had a penchant for changing their names. Partly it was for protection in their undercover work, partly to heighten the drama of their lives. Trotsky is not remembered by his real name, Bronstein, but by his assumed name used to escape from Siberia. Stalin most definitely would never have gotten beyond the Caucasus with a name like Dzugashvili. He might have remained a petty terrorist in the oil fields of Baku if he had not taken on the simple, six-letter alias by which the world would know him. Hitler also might have stayed on indefinitely at the Männerheim had not his father, years before, made the trip to the village of Döllersheim, there to legally assume the name Hitler. (There were too many strikes against Alois already, with his big feet, barrel chest, and modest stature, to prosper with a name such as Schiklgruber.) Young Dzugashvili was no stranger to Vienna in 1913. According to police records from a *Meldezettel* on file at the Bundespolizeidirektion of Vienna, he had registered once before, on September 20, 1903. At that time he was living in the Ninth District at Frankgasse 6. He listed his age falsely as thirty; and reported honestly that he was married, but that his beautiful young wife was in his home-

town of Gori. He was working as a servant for a Herr Zakieff, supposedly. He left Vienna just three days after Christmas that same year. The purpose of this first Vienna trip has remained a mystery. The two Vienna trips were to be the longest trips abroad that Stalin would make in his entire life.

77. See Auty, *Tito,* for a good account of the Wiener Neustadt time.
78. Deutscher, *Prophet,* p. 209.
79. Idem.
80. Deutscher, *Prophet,* p. 210.
81. Smith, *Young Stalin,* p. 276.
82. Tucker, pp. 152-57. Cf. the article "Marxism and the National Question" by Stalin to see how he went about handling the question of nationalism versus Communism.
83. Though there are signs of borrowing in the article, and it is probable that Lenin edited the manuscript, still this paper proved Stalin as a potential Communist theorist besides being the man of action. The Vienna trip, however, also throws some doubt on Stalin's activities in these years. A letter written during his Vienna stay, "his one and only letter from abroad to Russia during his first thirty-three years" (Smith, *Young Stalin,* pp. 286-87), raises suspicions of Stalin being a double agent. For a fascinating discussion of the possibility of Stalin working for the Okhrana, the tsarist police, see *Young Stalin,* pp. 272-90, and Hingley, pp. 33-39. These works conclude that one cannot be really sure whether Stalin, the exploiter par excellence, was a double agent or not. His Vienna interlude is never highlighted in any of the official biographies, which only serves to increase the mystery surrounding his visit.
84. Johnston, p. 101; Barea, p. 344.
85. Hitler, *Mein Kampf,* p. 124.
86. Idem.
87. Idem.
88. Johnston, p. 50.
89. Marek, p. 410.
90. HA, File 17, Reel 1. Hitler's friend's words to Maria Wohlrab must refer to Hitler's fears of the border crossing and the possibility that he might be apprehended there as a draft evader.
91. Idem.
92. Another indication of this premeditated draft evasion was the "destination unknown" which is written on the *Meldezettel* after he

had left the Männerheim (HA, File 17, Reel 1). Hitler knew he was heading for Munich, but did not want the police to be able to track him.

93. Honisch statement, HA, File 17, Reel 1.
94. Hitler, *Mein Kampf,* p. 125.
95. Copy of *Meldezettel,* HA, File 17, Reel 1.

Epilogue

1. Fest, p. 546.
2. Ibid., p. 548.
3. Idem.
4. Schuschnigg, pp. 19-32.
5. Payne, p. 301.
6. Schuschnigg, pp. 19-32. Hitler refused to call Chancellor Schuschnigg by his title during the interview for psychological reasons.
7. Idem.
8. Idem.
9. Idem.
10. Idem.
11. Idem.
12. Quoted in Fest, pp. 547-48.
13. Idem.
14. Bullock, p. 380.
15. Hitler, *My New Order,* p. 467.
16. Bloch, however, must have received special treatment, for he went untouched through the Hitler years.
17. Jenks, p. 218.
18. Payne, p. 308.
19. Fest, p. 549.
20. Idem.
21. Bullock, p. 380.
22. Idem.
23. Fest, p. 549.
24. Zweig, pp. 405-6.
25. Carsten, p. 241.
26. Bullock, p. 381.
27. Idem.
28. Quoted in Fest, p. 549.

29. Idem.
30. Idem.
31. Rauschning, *Revolution,* p. 3.
32. Fest, p. 549.
33. Maser, p. 57.
34. Infield, p. 199.
35. Payne, p. 311.
36. Hitler, *Speeches,* p. 1457.
37. Jenks, p. 219.
38. Quoted in Payne, p. 310; said to Baldur von Schirach, leader of the Hitler Youth.
39. Idem.
40. Hitler, *Mein Kampf,* p. 125.

Bibliography

Albach-Retty, Rosa. *So kurz sind hundert Jahre*. Munich, 1978.

Andreas-Salomé, Lou. *Lebensrückblick*. Frankfurt am Main, 1968.

Auty, Phyllis. *Tito*. London, 1970.

Baedeker, Karl. *Wien 1908-09*. Vienna, 1908.

Bahr, Hermann. *Selbstbildnis*. Berlin, 1923.

Barea, Ilsa. *Vienna*. New York, 1966.

Bezymenski, Lev. *The Death of Adolf Hitler: Unknown Documents from Soviet Archives*. New York and London, 1968.

Blaukopf, Kurt. *Mahler*. London, 1969.

Bloch, Dr. Eduard. "My Patient Hitler," *Collier's*, Mar. 15, 22, 1941.

Boulez, Pierre, et al. *Gustav Mahler in Wien*. Zurich, 1976.

Brennan, J. H. *Occult Reich*. London, 1974.

Bullock, Alan. *Hitler: A Study in Tyranny*. New York, 1953.

Cameron and Stevens. *Secret Conversations*. New York, 1964.

Carsten, F. L. *Faschismus in Oesterreich*. Munich, 1978.

Comini, Alessandra. *Egon Schiele*. New York, 1976.

———. *Gustav Klimt*. New York, 1975.

———. *Schiele's Prison Diaries*. New York, 1977.

Crankshaw, Edward. *The Fall of the House of Habsburg*. New York, 1963.

Daim, Wilfried. *Der Mann, der Hitler die Ideen gab*. Vienna, 1958.

Damon, L.T. "Austrian Antisemitism." *The Nation,* vol. 70 (June 14, 1900), pp. 453-55.

Deutscher, Isaac. *The Prophet Armed: Trotsky, 1879-1921.* Oxford, 1969.

————. *Stalin: A Political Biography.* Oxford, 1967.

Durkheim, Emile. *Suicide: A Study in Sociology.* New York, 1951.

Elon, Amos. *Herzl.* New York, 1975.

Ende, A. von. "Literary Vienna," *The Bookman,* vol. 38 (October 1913), pp. 141-55.

Fest, Joachim C. *Hitler.* New York, 1975.

Field, Frank. *The Last Days of Mankind—Karl Kraus and His Vienna.* Toronto, 1967.

Franz Joseph. *The Incredible Friendship.* Edited by Jean de Bourgoing. New York, 1966.

Freud, Sigmund. *Collected Papers.* London, 1959.

Friedländer, Otto. *Letzter Glanz der Märchenstadt.* Vienna, 1969.

Fromm, Erich. *The Anatomy of Human Destructiveness.* New York, 1973.

Geretsegger, Heinz, and Marx Peintner. *Otto Wagner, 1841-1918: The Expanding City.* London, 1970.

Goldhammer, Leo. *Die Juden Wiens.* Vienna and Leipzig, 1927.

Greiner, Josef. *Das Ende des Hitler-Mythos.* Vienna, 1947.

Hanisch, Reinhold. "I Was Hitler's Buddy," *The New Republic,* Apr. 5, 12, 19, 1939, pp. 239-300.

Haslip, Joan. *The Lonely Empress.* London, 1965.

Haupt Archiv der NSDAP, microfilms on file at the Hoover Institution, Stanford University, Stanford, California.

Heiden, Konrad. *Der Fuehrer.* Boston, 1944.

Heston, Leonard and Renate. *The Medical Casebook of Adolf Hitler.* London, 1979; New York, 1980.

Hevesi, L. *Altkunst—Neukunst.* Vienna, 1909.

Hingley, Ronald. *Joseph Stalin: Man and Legend.* London, 1974.

Hitler, Adolf. *Aquarelle.* Munich, 1935.

————. *Hitler's Secret Book.* New York, 1961.

————. *Mein Kampf.* Boston, 1942.

————. *My New Order.* New York, 1941.

————. *Secret Conversations.* New York, 1953.

————. *The Speeches of Adolf Hitler.* Oxford, 1942.

Hodin, J. P. *Oskar Kokoschka: The Artist and His Time.* London, 1966.

Infield, Glenn B. *Eva and Adolf.* New York, 1974.

―――. *Hitler's Secret Life.* New York, 1979; London, 1980.

Irving, David. *Hitler's War.* New York, 1977.

Janik, Allan, and Stephen Toulmin. *Wittgenstein's Vienna.* New York, 1973.

Jenks, William A. *Vienna and the Young Hitler.* New York, 1976.

Jetzinger, Franz. *Hitler's Jugend—Phantasien, Lügen—und die Wahrheit.* Vienna, 1956.

Johnston, William M. *The Austrian Mind.* Berkeley, 1972.

Jones, Ernest. *The Life and Works of Sigmund Freud.* Vol. 2. London, 1953-57.

Kandl, Eleonore. *Hitler's Oesterreichbild.* Doctoral dissertation catalogued at Vienna Nationalbibliothek, 1963.

Karpfen, Fritz, ed. *Das Egon Schiele Buch.* Vienna and Leipzig, 1921.

Kempf, Beatrix. *Woman for Peace: The Life of Bertha von Suttner.* Park Ridge, N.J., 1973.

Klaeger, Emil. *Durch die Wiener Quartier des Elends und Verbrechens.* Vienna, 1908.

Kokoschka, Oskar. *My Life.* New York, 1974.

Krafft-Ebing, Richard von. *Psychopathia Sexualis.* Stuttgart, 1907; New York, 1965.

Kraus, Karl. *Werke.* 14 vols. Munich, 1952-66.

Kubizek, August. *The Young Hitler I Knew.* Boston, 1955.

Kuehn, John L. "Encounter at Leyden: Gustav Mahler Consults Sigmund Freud." *Psychoanalytic Review,* 52 (1965), pp. 345-65.

Kunz, Inge. *Herrenmenschentum, Neugermanen und Okkultismus: Eine soziologische Bearbeitung der Schriften von Guido List.* Doctoral dissertation catalogued at the University of Vienna Library, 1961.

La Grange, Henri-Louis. *Mahler.* Garden City, N.Y., 1973.

Langer, Walter C. *The Mind of Adolf Hitler: The Secret Wartime Report.* New York, 1972.

Levine, Isaac Don. *Stalin's Great Secret.* New York, 1956.

Liptzin, Sol. *Arthur Schnitzler.* New York, 1932.

List, Guido. *Gesammelte Werke.* Vienna, 1913.

Loos, Adolf. *Sämmtliche Schriften.* Vol. 1. Vienna and Munich, 1962.

Lutzow, F. "Austria at the End of the Century." *Nineteenth Century,* vol. 46 (December 1899), pp. 1008-19.

Lux, J. A. *Otto Wagner.* Munich, 1914.

————. "A Vienna Workmen's Home," *International Studio,* December 1903, pp. 150-53.

Mahler-Werfel, Alma. *And the Bridge Is Love.* New York, 1958.

————. *Gustav Mahler: Memories and Letters.* New York, 1956.

Malcolm, Norman, and Georg Henrik von Wright. *Ludwig Wittgenstein: A Memoir.* Oxford, 1958.

Mann, Thomas. "Bruder Hitler." *Gesammelte Werke.* Vol. 12. Munich, 1953.

Marek, George R. *The Eagles Die.* New York, 1974.

Maser, Werner. *Adolf Hitler: Legend, Myth and Reality.* New York, 1971.

Masur, Gerhard. *Prophets of Yesterday.* New York, 1961.

May, Arthur J. *Vienna in the Age of Franz Joseph.* Norman, Okla., 1966.

McGrath, William J. *Dionysian Art and Populist Politics.* New Haven, 1974.

McGuigan, Doroth Gies. *The Habsburgs.* New York, 1966.

Mitchell, Donald. *Gustav Mahler: The Wunderhorn Years.* London, 1975.

Müllern-Schönhausen, Dr. Johannes von. *Die Lösung des Rätsels Adolf Hitler.* Vienna, 1959.

Münz, L., and G. Künstler. *Adolf Loos.* London, 1966.

Murstein, Bernard I. *Love, Sex and Marriage Throughout the Ages.* New York, 1974.

Nebehay, Christian. *Gustav Klimt Dokumentation.* Vienna, 1969.

Olden, Rudolf. *Hitler.* New York, 1936.

Orwell, George. *Down and Out in Paris and London.* London, 1948; New York, 1972.

Paget, W. "Vanishing Vienna." *Living Age.* Vol. 246 (Sept. 23, 1905).

Pauli, Hertha. *The Secret of Sarajevo.* London, 1966.

Payne, Robert. *The Life and Death of Adolf Hitler.* New York, 1973.

Peters, H. F. *My Sister, My Spouse.* New York, 1962.

Picker, Dr. Henry. *Hitler's Tischgespräche im Führerhauptquartier.* Stuttgart, 1976.

Powell, Nicolas. *The Sacred Spring.* New York, 1974.

Rauschning, Hermann. *Gespräche mit Hitler.* Zurich, 1940.

————. *The Revolution of Nihilism.* New York, 1939.

Ravenscroft, Trevor. *Spear of Destiny.* New York, 1973.

Rector, Frank. *The Nazi Extermination of Homosexuals.* New York, 1981.

Reich, Wilhelm. *The Mass Psychology of Fascism.* Middlesex, 1975.

Reich, Willi. *Schoenberg: A Critical Biography.* New York, 1971.

Sacher-Masoch, Leopold von. *Venus im Pelz.* Dresden, 1901.

Salten, Felix. *The Memoirs of Josephine Mutzenbacher.* Hollywood, 1967.

Schnitzler, Arthur. *My Youth in Vienna.* New York, 1970.

Schuschnigg, Kurt von. *Austrian Requiem.* New York, 1946.

Schweiger, Werner J. "Wiener Kaffeehaus," *Austria Today.* Vol. 5 (spring 1979), pp. 16-19.

Siegert, Michael. "Judenmord—Warum?" *Profil.* No. 9 (Feb. 27, 1979), pp. 41-44.

Smith, Bradley F. *Adolf Hitler: His Family, Childhood, and Youth.* Stanford, Calif., 1967.

Smith, Edward Ellis. *The Young Stalin.* New York, 1967.

Smith, Irving. *Trotsky.* Englewood Cliffs, N.J., 1973.

Stalin, I. V. *Marxismus und nationale Frage.* Vienna, 1945.

Steed, Henry Wickham. *Through Thirty Years, 1892-1922.* London, 1924.

"Tagebuch eines halbwüchsigen Mädchens, Das." Leipzig, 1919.

Tannenbaum, Edward R. *1900: The Generation Before the Great War.* New York, 1976.

Toland, John. *Adolf Hitler.* New York, 1976.

Trotsky, Leon. *Mein Leben.* Berlin, 1961.

Tuchman, Barbara W. *The Guns of August.* New York, 1962.

————. *The Proud Tower.* New York, 1967.

Tucker, Robert C. *Stalin as Revolutionary: 1879-1929.* New York, 1973.

Vergo, Peter. *Art in Vienna 1899-1918.* London, 1975.

Wachsmuth, Guenther. *The Life and Work of Rudolf Steiner.* New York, 1955.

Wagner, Otto. *Moderne Architektur.* Vienna, 1896.

Waite, Robert G. L. *The Psychopathic God, Adolf Hitler.* New York, 1977.

Whiteside, Andrew. *Austrian National Socialism Before 1918.* The Hague, 1962.

Zuckerkandl, Bertha. *Oesterreich intim, Erinnerungen 1892-1942.* Frankfurt, 1970.

Zweig, Stefan. *The World of Yesterday.* New York, 1943.

Index

Index

Freud, Martin, 90
Freud, Sigmund, 9, 16, 43, 70-75, 111,
 123, 165, 167, 183, 189-93, 245,
 263, 267, 276, 285, 310, 318, 328,
 331
Friedjung, Professor, 236
Fritz, Walter. *See* Hanisch, Reinhold
Frühlingserwachen, 58

Gasthaus Marhold, 177
Gasthaus Stiefler, 226
Gasthof Pommer, 224
German Workers' Party of Bohemia,
 172, 312
Gerstl, Richard, 9, 209, 219, 245
Gestalt, 119, 297
Glascow School, 40
Glechheit, 168
Gloriette, 91
Glumpowicz, Ludwig, 296, 298
Gobineau, 296
Goebbels, Joseph, 267, 323, 330
Goering, Hermann, 260, 323
"Golden Dawn," 123
Greece, 236-39
Greiner, Josef, 176, 184, 199, 212,
 312-13
Grillparzer, Franz, 216
Gropius, Walter, 181, 182
Gurdjieff, 123
Gurrelieder, 220

Habsburg Empire, 6-7, 10, 83-90, 203,
 248, 252-53
Habsburgs, 7, 83-90, 93
Hafeld, 234
Handbuch der Judenfrage, 233, 327
Handele, 116, 126
Hanisch, Magdalena, 22-25, 275-76
Hanisch, Reinhold, 135, 140, 141-43,
 146, 148, 149, 153, 162-63, 174,
 183-89, 303-4
Hansen, Theophil von, 11
Hemingway, Ernest, 123
Hermanskogel, 93
Herzl, Theodor, 10, 64, 111, 112-13,
 163, 293
Hess, Rudolf, 302, 323
Hesse, Grand Duke of, 220
Himmler, Heinrich, 125, 198, 260, 261,
 323

Hitler, Adolf,
 addresses, 6, 104, 129, 130, 133, 136-
 37, 145, 304
 ancestry, 222, 295, 326
 Anschluss, 257-61, 263-67
 anti-Semitism, 69-70, 95, 109, 115-21,
 295, 298-99
 as architect, 45-49, 52-55, 202-3, 213,
 322-23
 as artistic personality, 53-54, 227-28
 as clochard, 128-30, 136-37, 141-43
 autopsy by Russians, 194
 concept of women, 61, 196-97, 315
 diet, 146-47, 224-25, 307, 330
 draft evasion, 93, 103, 233-34, 240,
 321
 early childhood, 193, 222-24, 225-28,
 234-36
 finances, 13, 21, 94-96, 127, 128-29,
 148, 149, 177, 211, 215, 229, 275,
 277, 289
 first visit to Vienna in 1906, 3-4
 formal education, 2, 13, 14, 226, 227,
 235
 illness and death of mother, 14, 15,
 20-21, 272
 illnesses, 5, 224-25, 270
 learns the use of propaganda, 157-58,
 177, 178-80
 love of music, 35-36, 38, 213-14
 monarchism, 77
 occult connections, 124-26, 302
 painting, 145, 146, 147, 201-3, 235-36,
 240-41, 271, 320-21
 physical description, 1-2, 79, 126,
 134, 148
 political development, 81-83, 91-92,
 103, 127-28, 164, 169-74, 287-88
 psychoanalysis of, 193-98
 readings, 37-38, 166-67, 291-92
 rejections from Fine Arts Academy,
 11-12, 33-34, 54, 102-3, 201
 return to Vienna in 1938, 263-67
 sexuality, 58-59, 65-69, 75-78, 283-84,
 286, 287, 298-99
 trip to England, possible, 328-29
 vindictiveness, 186-88
 Wagner, Richard and, 114-15, 180
 work, 127, 200-201, 302-3, 316-18
Hitler, Alois, 3, 193, 198, 223-24, 225-
 26, 227, 234, 299, 326